To Laura
, Hope you en~~~~~   ~ng this
incredible journey with me!

Ray x

LIFE
WITHOUT
A TIE

LIFE
WITHOUT
A TIE

by Ray Martin
2022

WIGMORE
HOUSE

LIFE WITHOUT A TIE
© 2022 by Ray Martin. All rights reserved.

CATALOGUING INFORMATION
ISBN: 978-1-7396177-0-7
CREDITS
Editors: Victoria Villaseñor & Nicci Robinson
Production Design: Global Wordsmiths
Cover Design: Patrick Fogarty
Photo credit: Madan Gurung, on our way to Everest Base Camp, May 2010

Acknowledgements

Without the kind support of the following people, this book wouldn't be the same and probably wouldn't exist. I am sincerely grateful to all of you. Thank you to:

Sophie McGovern, for your guidance and encouragement in the early stages of my journey, which helped build my confidence.

Simon Powell, for listening to me read my work and guiding my thinking for the cover.

Caitlin Verney, for your patience and feedback as I read many of the chapters in my first draft.

Amanda Hayman and Graeme Healey, for creating a welcoming space in your home in the later stages, giving me loads of encouragement, celebrating small wins along the way, and letting me read my second drafts to you.

Nousheh Hodgson, Anna Magee, Tony Barton, Aaron Quinn, Kieran Rea, Fla Geyser, Reuben Lowe, Elizabeth Taylor, Claire Trigger, Tessa Odoni, Dani Brooks, Poyee Dorrian, and Laura Jelly for reading and reviewing the manuscript ahead of the launch.

Steve Chamberlain and Jane Duncan Rogers, for generously sharing your knowledge and experience of book publishing, reviewing the manuscript, and giving me and my team your feedback.

Bernie Woods, for your personal friendship, encouragement, support, and ideas throughout my writer's journey.

Jacob Florijn, for encouraging me to start my writer's journey, connecting me with my editing team, your generosity in hosting events for all of us in your home, and for being a sparring partner and a joyful, vocal cheerleader for years.

Patrick Fogarty, for creating the amazing cover.

Bernadette Russell, for kindly writing the foreword.

Last but not least, I want to acknowledge my editing team, Nicci Robinson and Victoria Villaseñor. You believed in me and encouraged me to tell my story, gave me loads of support when I began the long journey, and encouraged me to keep going when I lost faith in myself. You enhanced my work with your skilful and creative input to make sure this book turned out to be the best it could be. You guided and educated me along the way to understand the world of book publishing and have been tireless and energetic companions on my journey!

Contact the author:
Via LinkedIn: Ray Martin
www.thedailyexplorer.com
Email: ray@lifewithoutatie.com

Foreword
by Bernadette Russell

Hello. My name is Bernadette Russell. I'm an artist, author, storyteller, and tree planter.

A few months ago, I met Ray online when I was delivering a talk about hope, connected to my most recent book How To Be Hopeful. The call was hosted by a wonderful organisation we are both associated with called The Happy Start Up School. I'd accepted the invitation because I was intrigued and honoured to be asked to speak in what I assumed to be a business context. My life and work seem a long way away from the world of commerce and entrepreneurs. I wasn't sure whether I was a good fit or that the people on the call would be interested in what I had to say. I doubted that I'd have much to offer them in the way of practical wisdom.

However, like Ray, I'm always interested in what turns up in my life, the opportunities that present themselves, especially the surprising stuff, and I always try to ask the question "What can I learn from this?" Yes, I was curious. The event turned out to be fun and energising. People asked interesting questions, and we had inspiring conversations about many things, including the importance of kindness and self-compassion and the power of stories. Afterwards, Ray asked me if I would write a foreword to his book. Again, I was surprised, pleased, and intrigued. He told me his story, and it captured me.

I'm from a theatre background, so I'm a trained storyteller, but also, as all human beings are, I am a storyteller by nature. Stories have the power to change hearts and minds, to transform lives, and to creative positive, lasting change in the world. Statistics, studies, and surveys can help and support, but nothing beats stories. As the wonderful poet and novelist Ben Okri says, "Stories can conquer fear, you know. They can make the heart bigger."

What I was captured by was Ray's courage and willingness to tell his story and to dare to live greatly, to set out with his few possessions to see what the world had to offer and teach him, and to see what he had to offer and teach in return.

This book is, in many ways, a classic hero's journey story, with all the ingredients of those epic sagas from so many different cultures around the world containing trials, allies, adversaries, friends, foes, obstacles, triumphs, love, loss, treasure, and hard-won wisdoms. These kind of stories and myths have always resonated throughout history and culture, serving to inspire and dare us to gather the courage to set out on our own hero's journey too.

By contrast, at almost the same time, like Ray, I also set out to find answers from a place of despair. I didn't travel all over the world. I pretty much stayed in my own neighbourhood, but I entered the world with an open heart as Ray did, connecting with strangers, and embracing opportunity and experience as it came to me. I offer that only to reinforce Ray's message that we each must follow our own path without comparing our experiences with others. Wisdom can just as easily be found in your own back garden as on a tropical beach (although tropical beaches are very nice of course!)

This story makes it clear that your journey is your journey, your calling is your calling, and we each can live, as Mary Oliver so beautifully wrote, our "one wild and precious life" as best we can according to our circumstances. We live in challenging times, when uncertainty has become part of our everyday landscape, but this book reminds us of the positive side of uncertainty; it reminds us that the future—our futures, as they are as yet unwritten—could be wonderful.

Perhaps in such times, the most important thing for us to be asking ourselves is: what is our calling? In a world full of troubles, what can we each offer as a gift to the world? Ray set out to find his calling, but as in all great heroes' journeys, he also understood the utmost importance of the return. Our adventures, self-discovery, and travels are essential, but the return is too, along with the gift that we bring back to our friends, family, and communities when we do come home. What Ray has brought back to the village with his book is a generous sharing of stories, insight, and wisdom, and a gentle and compassionate offer to dare to do what he has done, like the beautifully illustrated fool in the Rider Waite Smith tarot deck who steps towards the sunshine beyond the cliff edge, perhaps knowing that a fall is exactly what they need, trusting the net will catch them, or that the ground will be soft underfoot.

This book is a cry to free yourself from self-imposed expectation; to re-define success and wealth on your own terms; and to take charge of your story and decide where it is you would like to go next. Your adventure could be like mine, in your own neighbourhood or, like Ray's, it may be on the other side of the world. Your questions and answers will of course be your own. Your calling will be different, and the gift you bring back to the village uniquely yours.

So, enjoy reading this book, as I did. Then pack your knapsack and stride into the world to see what you can find. See you when you get back, and I look forward to hearing what you have learned!

Bernadette Russell

www.bernadetterussell.com
Twitter @betterussell
Instagram @bernadetterussell

Dedicated to Jelly Blount,
who tragically lost her life to cancer.
Your light shines on.

Introduction
The Journey Ahead

IN INDIA DURING THE 1930s, A YOUNG BOY HAD BECOME OBSESSED WITH eating a lot of sugar. His mother was very upset about it, but no matter how hard she tried to break his habit, he continued to satisfy his sweet tooth. Totally frustrated, she decided to take her son to see Mahatma Gandhi, who was the boy's idol.

Being many miles away, she had to walk for hours in the scorching sun to reach Gandhi's ashram. There, she recounted her difficult journey and shared with Gandhi her unpleasant situation.

"Bapu, my son eats too much sugar. It's not good for his health. Would you please advise him to stop eating it?"

Gandhi listened to the woman carefully and thought for a while. "Please come back after two weeks, and I will talk to your son."

Confused, the woman took her boy by the hand and left. She made the long journey home and two weeks later, they returned as Gandhi requested.

When they arrived, Gandhi looked directly at the boy and said, "Boy, you should stop eating sugar. It's not good for your health."

The boy nodded and promised he would stop immediately. The boy's mother was puzzled. She turned to Gandhi. "Bapu, why didn't you tell him that two weeks ago when I brought him here to see you?"

Gandhi smiled. "Mother, two weeks ago I was not qualified to advise the boy because I was eating a lot of sugar myself. Now I have stopped."

Twenty years ago, you might have considered me unqualified to write the book you are about to read. At that time, my main goal in life was being a successful and admired businessman. And back then, you might have labelled me as such. I was married to a wonderful woman, and we were blessed with a high income and a comfortable, affluent lifestyle. Together, we created a profitable and highly regarded leadership development, coaching, and training business.

The constant challenges of running and expanding the company kept me growing too. It brought out the best in me. Public recognition of this came in 2002 when *The Daily Telegraph*, a leading UK newspaper, selected me to receive their business leadership award, acknowledging my work as an exemplary CEO. It was a dream come true. Consequently, people admired me, and some asked me for guidance about life, happiness, and success. They thought of me as someone who had life handled, although the reality was quite different. They had no idea just how fragile my persona was. That isn't surprising, because I kept some parts of myself well hidden from everybody, including those closest to me.

Despite this public recognition, I struggled to feel worthy of it. In the first chapter of my story, I'll take you briefly back to that period. There, it becomes clear that behind my confident outward appearance, my appetite for taking risks in life, and for really stretching myself had been slowly shrinking, and it gave rise to a feeling of shame. In my early forties, I'd settled into a comfort zone. I felt increasingly lousy, unattractive, and looked older than my years. I was dissatisfied with myself. Back then, I avoided making big changes because they seemed too risky. I was worried I might lose the money, status, and privileges that life had given me.

I had firmly established a reputation as someone who could set and achieve ambitious goals and financial targets. No one pushed harder than me to make their business grow, no matter what the obstacles, how much energy it took, or what pain had to be suffered. Despite that, I rarely felt truly happy. My friends would sometimes say, "Why don't you take a break?" I'd think, I haven't got time. I'm too busy achieving my goals, and I'd dismiss the suggestion immediately. True happiness remained elusive and always promised to arrive sometime in the future, after the next achievement. I found it hard to fully appreciate and enjoy what I already had.

The fear of being exposed threatened me, so I directed my energy into obsessively maintaining my successful image, no matter what. It was too dangerous to acknowledge the raw facts within my reality. Most of the time, I pretended that none of it was going on. Most of us are pretty good at deceiving ourselves, not to mention others.

I hoped things would somehow change without me having to reveal my dilemma or do anything radical. Bit by bit, my happiness eroded. I guess you could say I wasn't living life true to myself, something many people ultimately regret when their life comes to an end. I was trapped and couldn't see a way out.

And then my life came crashing down. It became impossible for me to avoid making big changes. In the space of just three months, my illusory, secure, and successful life had been completely dismantled, and it took my marriage, company, home, and father with it. I was devastated. I believed that happiness would never be mine again.

My self-esteem crashed too. How would my family, friends, and colleagues, not to mention clients who'd heard about the crumbling of my life, judge me? It called my character into question and could potentially contradict their positive assumptions about me. My inevitable exposure as a fake, a fraud, and a liar was bound to come out. It was only a matter of time. The gap between my reality and my well-groomed public image felt like a mask, a deception.

Living in that gap gave me an increasingly negative outlook that *had* to be addressed. It became my priority. It was as if my life depended on it. I wanted to reconnect with my fundamental values and move forward. As time passed, and I reflected on what had happened, many questions came to my awareness. How much of my life had really been consciously and responsibly authored by me? How often had I let other people make decisions for me? How had I been complicit in creating those unwanted conditions? I pondered those questions deeply for days. In hindsight, it was obvious that much of my time had been spent meeting everyone else's needs at the expense of my own.

I realised this had to change. My mindset and way of life had served me very well up to this point, in the sense that I was successful, but it was no longer right for me. My thinking went into overdrive. I tried to figure out how to escape the life I'd unconsciously built—driven by materialism, status, and achievement—that held me captive. There had to be a way to untie myself from it.

The vision of how to do it, or what the alternative might look like, eluded me for months. In my depressed and diminished state, it seemed impossible to creatively reinvent my life. But then, a stroke of luck. I found the story about Gandhi and the boy eating sugar, and it led me to an epiphany. He asked the boy to stop eating sugar only after he'd *experienced* giving up

3

sugar himself. He had lived through the struggle directly to learn what he needed to know about the impact of such a decision. He understood he had no authority over the boy by virtue of his job; he was not a nutritionist or a doctor. He was simply someone the boy trusted because he was an honest, transparent, and down-to-earth man. For Gandhi to tell the boy to stop eating sugar, there had to be complete integrity. Perhaps that's why he always used to say, "Let your life be your message."

I thought long and hard about how to apply the wisdom in Gandhi's actions. What might living true to myself mean in day-to-day life? What would be the best way to rebuild the foundations of my happiness in a joyful and sustainable way? When these life changing events first unfolded, I'd just wanted to get through it in one piece and restore my own happiness. I hadn't thought at all about the impact I might have on other people if I made fundamental changes in my own life. But as time passed, my viewpoint subtly changed.

I decided to focus totally on myself for the first time in years and really get to know myself properly once again, with the faith that the insights and wisdom I needed would come. Gandhi had always said that if you want anything to change, you must first *be* the change you want to see in the world. If you're a leader of any kind, it's considered essential to "walk your own talk." In my hour of need, life gave me an opportunity to apply this principle in a profoundly personal way. Via my inner voice of wisdom, or intuition, the universe guided me to leave my existing life for a while, become a traveller, and go on a journey. The purpose was simply to follow my heart and discover what living life true to myself meant. The critical task was to redesign and shape my life in a way that felt authentic and exciting without any concern for how that might appear to anyone else. As you can imagine, that wasn't an easy thing to put into motion. We're conditioned to worry about our reputation and image, sometimes above all else. But what is the cost of that?

As I contemplated and accepted this guidance, my inner voice continually spoke to me, and the message was clear. I had to free myself from the powerful yet largely unseen influence of the "silent collective" for a while. I had to step out of my usual setting completely to look at life with fresh eyes. After much procrastination, the moment came when it felt right to quit being a businessman and leave the UK to start my journey. While my rational mind argued for maintaining the status quo, my gut feeling told me something profound would come from taking a step into the unknown, and I trusted that feeling. It was scary, exhilarating, and necessary.

Taking the first steps
With some careful planning, I re-engineered my life financially to get my living expenses down to the lowest level possible for a couple of years. By existing on a very modest daily budget and sacrificing some of life's luxuries, my resources took me an awfully long way without me having to worry about how to cover my basic needs. Once I'd made a viable financial plan, I stopped taking on work and put my business activities on indefinite hold.

The Universe played a major part in how my journey began. An encounter in Australia unexpectedly led to me performing live on stage as a comedic actor. That spark really lit the fuse and led to my decision to sell my house in London. I subsequently sold or gave away many of my possessions until there was virtually nothing left. Taking those steps felt a bit scary but extremely liberating. It set up the conditions for a perfect experiment.

I detached myself from everything that had defined me, which gave me the freedom to move in any direction without many of the needs typically associated with identity, status, privilege, or material benefits. I was now in a great position to road test the popular theory that happiness is not to be found in any of these things and to know absolutely if it was true or not. At forty-five years of age, I probably became one of the oldest backpackers out there.

When I left, I guessed that it would take me about six months to figure things out and return to England to start my "real" life again. By the time you reach the end of my story, you'll see just how wrong my estimate was! I didn't return for over fourteen years. Moment by moment and day by day, life magically unfolded in front of me in ways I could never have imagined before my departure. I was pulled apart, put back together, and learned lesson after lesson. To keep myself psychologically safe throughout, I defined ten guiding principles. There was plenty of laughter, some heartache, and above all, many chances to improve myself.

My improvised journey traversed four different continents and twenty-eight countries, including China, New Zealand, Tibet, and Nepal. From the beginning, as if by universal decree, people showed up for conversations that signposted turning points at just the right moments. Each one of them brought a unique gift and significantly influenced my direction, decisions, and beliefs about life. Some of those amazing people inspired me to run marathons, write my story, walk in the Himalayas, hike the Grand Canyon, and traverse the Nullarbor Plain in Australia.

You'll also read about my journey into mindfulness, which began with a ten-day silent meditation retreat in a Buddhist monastery. Without the pressure of a job or any obligations, I expanded my consciousness through attending retreats, self-development workshops, and reading hundreds of books, all of which gave me valuable opportunities to reflect on my past. In turn, I'll invite you to reflect on your experiences as you take this journey with me.

Throughout this book, I'll share the raw truth about my personal quest to find true love and how it took me from London to California, the Caribbean, and beyond. I'll tell you about some of the key relationships and friendships I encountered, as well as what they taught me. I made connections with wonderful people all over the world, and many have remained friends ever since. Whenever it was time for me to learn something, the right teachers came forward. They enabled me to produce a blog, learn languages, make films, teach English, and learn how to meditate. Collectively, they all contributed to a permanent change in my outlook on the world.

My entire fourteen-year journey happened without me having a plan of any kind or a home in the conventional sense. What began as a temporary, nomadic experiment morphed into my permanent way of life. By responding to events and encounters in a more intuitive, courageous, open-hearted, and conscious way, abundant opportunities for personal growth came to me. I inevitably embraced many of these and unintentionally became what is commonly referred to these days as a global nomad.

My setup today still comprises my laptop and a bag of stuff weighing twenty-two kilos. Life has helped me learn how to live productively and happily with very few material possessions. There's no certainty about what's coming next. That concept would have been hard for me to entertain as the successful business leader I used to be. Today, I'm deeply aware that my life is entirely of my own creation, and I've realised it always was. I've established a strong foundation of self-love, self-acceptance, and a deep sense of gratitude for the life that flows through my veins. Every moment feels precious. Life is simple and uncomplicated. My health is much improved, and my levels of anxiety and stress are much lower than they were. It's an amazing feeling.

Through reading this story, you'll understand how I removed my ties, how I tested my ability to live modestly, how I learned to trust life and know with certainty that I can be happy, no matter what. That doesn't mean my life is devoid of sadness or suffering. It means if and when those experiences come, I have a strong foundation of happiness and contentment, so I've no need to be fearful of those feelings. On my path, I learned how to apply kindness and compassion to myself, and I know with absolute certainty that comparisons with others are no longer necessary.

I guess you could say I was lucky to have had the opportunity to experiment with life in this way. On my travels, I met many people who told me they were searching for answers to life's big questions in the same way I was. We shared our stories and talked for hours. Some of them even asked me if I planned to write a book about my journey and the lessons I learned. Initially, my response was always no. Who wants to read about someone finding themselves? But more and more people asked me the same question. After a couple of years, it dawned on me that the experimental way of living I'd chosen seemed to inspire quite a few people. They are the reason this book exists.

When I began to write it, it occurred to me that I was in a unique position to tell you this story. There probably aren't many people who've experienced a long and unpredictable journey like the one you'll read about, who've also had a long and successful career in the corporate business world. I hope my story might enable you to reimagine life in a way that is meaningful to you. If you find even one useful or inspirational idea, I'll have fulfilled my purpose in writing it.

Becoming an Experientialist

In the last decade or so, I've observed a huge and growing interest in alternative models of living. People want lives that are less restrictive. They are less motivated by the acquisition of material wealth than their predecessors. In his book *Stuffocation*, James Wallman highlights this growing trend. He concludes that individuals now invest more of their time, energy, and resources into having experiences as opposed to owning possessions, and he shows how that stance has really transformed their lives. People are moving away from values based on materialism towards values based on what he calls experientialism. This shift has been slowly gaining momentum and will eventually affect all of us. Wallman confirms something that I know deep in my bones: you can be content in life without much stuff. After fourteen years of living with practically none, becoming an experientialist has been a welcome change for me.

When my journey began, becoming an expert in the subject of alternative lifestyles was never my goal. If you met me today, you'd find an ordinary person, engaged with life, who has been on a long journey of exploration to find the path that felt right. It worked for me to follow my heart. It was hard to do at first, yet my ability to do just that continues to improve with each day, month, and year. Many of the insights I've had and the wisdom I've gleaned are now woven into my work as a coach and mentor.

If you ask me, "Have you found the perfect life, or does such a thing exist?" you may be disappointed to hear that my answer is no. Life is an ongoing journey and my experimentation and exploration continues. I'm committed to becoming the best version of myself that I can be, someone I'm proud of, who I can genuinely love and accept fully with all of my flaws. I may never get there, but how wonderful is it to try? How incredible is it to be open and curious and find that you're living in a more conscious, enlightened state?

Your journey and your story are different to mine and everyone else's on this planet. Maybe some of the questions I ask throughout the book will help you reflect and grow, make you start to question things so you can begin, or add to, your own journey. If you resonate with anything in the pages that follow and feel like you want to start your own exploration, I'm here for you. Know that you have my heartfelt encouragement and support to experiment with your life in a way that works for you. I hope you enjoy the journey ahead and that yours is enriched as you travel it with me.

"To accept the challenge of the unknown is courage. The fears are there, but if you go on accepting the challenge again and again, slowly, slowly those fears disappear. The joy that the unknown brings, the great ecstasy that starts happening with the unknown, makes you strong enough, gives you a certain integrity, makes your intelligence sharp. You start feeling that life is not just a boredom. Life is an adventure. Slowly, slowly fears disappear and you go on seeking and searching for new adventures. Courage is risking the known for the unknown, the familiar for the unfamiliar, the comfortable for the uncomfortable arduous pilgrimage to some unknown destination. One never knows whether one will be able to make it or not. It is gambling, but only the gamblers know what life is."

Osho, *Courage: The Joy of Living Dangerously*

Chapter One
Loosening the Ropes

"When one door of happiness closes, another opens, but often we look so long at the closed door that we do not see the one that has been opened for us."

Helen Keller

COME WITH ME ON A LITTLE JOURNEY INTO MY PAST. IT'S SATURDAY, MAY 28, 2011. I'd like you to imagine a small, quiet, and picturesque green village on the southern shores of Lake Constance in Switzerland. The morning sky is bright blue with one or two scattered clouds, the sun is shining, and you can hear the wonderful melody of birds singing. There are a handful of houses scattered here and there on the hillside rolling down to the lake.

My ex-wife Charlotte lives there with her husband and two children. We've arranged to meet at her home. I've flown all the way from Thailand, and my German girlfriend, Sylvia, is with me. It's five and a half years since my departure from the UK and the beginning of my life without a tie.

I've carefully orchestrated my arrival at Charlotte's house to coincide with the arrival of a large cardboard box, delivered by courier from the UK. The box has been lying in storage in England for seven years since our divorce in 2004, and it contains something that ties us to our shared past. Now the moment has come when that tie is finally going to be cut.

Like most people who get divorced, Charlotte and I had to come to an agreement about how to split our money and our stuff. According to the law firm Seddons, the average cost of divorce in Britain is around £70,000. Between £17,000 and £30,000 of that goes towards paying lawyers' fees. The rest is lost in paying off debts and sharing assets. We've all heard horror stories about couples where conflict erupted, leading to acrimony. Judith Woods, a journalist in *The Times*, reported one such story a few years ago:

"Giles and Ann-Marie Harvey Kavanagh, a pair of highly

paid lawyers who'd been married for ten years, entered into a bitterly contested, five-year long divorce battle, over wealth and the custody of their children. The pair managed to squander £1.7m in various legal costs. Even after the sale of their £3.2m Surrey home, they only had £90,000 left to share between them. The judge presiding over their case said, "You have succeeded in wrecking the ship of your marriage, as well as the lifeboats, and have driven full tilt onto the rocks."

Fortunately, it was the complete opposite in our case. As odd as it might sound, our friendship was as strong as ever when we reached our financial agreement, despite the fact we were going our separate ways. There had been a wonderful sense of grace, generosity, and ease on both sides. What could have been a tough and sticky conversation was straightforward. Despite that, there was one item that neither of us had wanted to deal with at that time. We didn't have the stomach for it. We felt too emotionally raw. I'm referring to our huge collection of photographs amassed from the twelve years we'd shared together. There were thousands of personal snapshots and hundreds of professional images captured in the daily life of our consulting business. How should we divide those?

As we awkwardly tried to figure out what to do with them, a flash of inspiration hit me. What if we postponed going through these pictures for at least five years? I reasoned that delaying this time-consuming ritual would probably save us both a lot of unnecessary heartache. By waiting a few years, healing could take place. Then we'd be able to meet as two wholesome, happy, and satisfied individuals distanced from our memories as a couple. If my theory was correct, we might even re-visit these pictures in a spirit of joy and celebration, validating what an amazing time we'd shared as we perused them together for the last time. We might also reminisce a little, while deciding who got to keep which of the pictures. Charlotte accepted my proposal and into storage they went.

In hindsight, this turned out to be a brilliant decision and reminds us that in moments like these, trusting your instinct is often the right thing to do. The day of reckoning had now arrived. Neither Charlotte or I had envisaged Sylvia being there, yet I was immensely happy that she came to join us and share this historic moment.

LIFE WITHOUT A TIE

Inside Charlotte's house, we opened the box and tipped out the contents over her coffee table. As we poured over hundreds of pictures, the three of us laughed, drank, and talked intimately for a few hours. We recalled stories about the events where some of the photos had been captured. Charlotte's two delightful young children seemed to enjoy the cordial atmosphere as they played nearby. You'd have been hard-pressed to imagine a happier scene. It felt like a loving way to write a full-stop at the end of the sentence that described my former life with Charlotte. And it brought me two unexpected blessings.

First, my relatively new relationship with Sylvia was enhanced as she heard these stories from my ex-wife about my past. They helped her understand and appreciate me. Second, Charlotte was relieved to see that I was in a stable and loving relationship. We'd stayed in touch since our divorce and in those early years, she'd been troubled that I might not meet anyone to share a heartfelt connection with, as we had. It had weighed heavy on her heart. At long last, she could let go of her concern and be happy for me, which made me happy too.

As I left Switzerland with my share of our photographs, a deep sense of satisfaction filled me. It was evident that my relationship with Charlotte had transformed during the seven years we'd been apart. By listening to my heart and paying attention to my instincts, the Universe had helped me steer the right course through the stormy waters of a massive and complex transition. I'd shifted from being the rejected partner in our marriage to a close, trusted friend, and vice versa. Our twenty-year friendship was still intact, and neither of us had suffered any lasting damage. When we divorced, the potential loss of our friendship was the thing that had worried me the most. Yet, it was clear our friendship was as good, if not better, now than when we were married. After that weekend, it felt okay to forgive myself for my part in a marriage which ultimately didn't work out.

The thing is, from a personal growth perspective, the fact that it *didn't* work out was perhaps the best thing that could have happened. When viewed through that lens, you could say our divorce gave me a way out of the trap my life had become. Allow me to briefly take you further back in time to the early nineties, when this story really begins.

People who study earthquakes constantly observe tremors that register on their seismographs. These can appear weeks or even months before an event and indicate that a big shift or movement is going to happen.

Let me pinpoint for you the exact moment I became aware of the first of several tremors that would change my life. It signalled a coming shift of huge proportions. I'll explain how those tremors, which I largely ignored, started an unlikely chain of events, and how I eventually gave up my financially secure and desirable life to start again from scratch.

A Vision of Freedom

Charlotte and I met in 1990. We both worked in an innovative marketing and training organisation called The Programmes Group. We became friends and spoke to each other occasionally at company social events. She was a talented and capable trainer, whilst my expertise was in business generation and contract sales. Our jobs were demanding, and we travelled frequently, so for quite a while, we rarely ran into each other at the office.

In 1992, we were both offered new jobs within the group, in a start-up consulting company called Merchants, based in Knightsbridge, London. Without reference to each other, we both accepted and moved to London. As we were friends, we got on well. We were both single and shortly after the move, we became a couple.

In my early thirties, my burning ambition was to become a successful, wealthy, and widely respected businessman. To my way of thinking, this was the most effective and guaranteed route to prosperity, financial independence, and freedom. Charlotte knew that and wholeheartedly supported my vision.

I constantly read stories about people who started businesses, and my head was always full of ideas about making money. My job at Merchants was to sell services that helped clients grow their businesses, and years of experience had enabled me to become pretty good at that. Running my own venture had always appealed to me, and I had the energy for it. I believed that with the right team and a great proposition, there was an excellent chance of making it work.

The major hurdle was not having any capital, which left me heavily dependent on collecting my salary every month. The relatively high cost of living in London made it almost impossible to create any surplus income. All the research I'd done hadn't revealed a single example of a person who'd created significant wealth whilst being an employee for someone else. I was caught in a vicious circle, and a leap of faith was needed to break it.

LIFE WITHOUT A TIE

At thirty-four years of age, it seemed like the perfect time to make that leap. So just after my birthday, I made a bold and courageous promise to myself to abstain from being an employee for the rest of my life (a promise I have kept to this day). It was an empowering decision because it created urgency. With virtually no savings, I challenged myself to figure out how to start a business that would meet all of my material needs and enable me to generate wealth. It felt like a tough and scary choice to make, yet with Charlotte's support it seemed achievable and worth the risk.

My first step was to inform the owner of the company I worked for that I was quitting. He not only understood what I was doing and why, but he also had no issue with me declaring it. In fact, he was genuinely supportive. When it came to making money, he had plenty of experience, and he'd often shared it with people who worked for him. He'd encouraged us to be more entrepreneurial and think beyond the confines of a job. To be provocative, he sometimes referred to employees as "wage slaves," knowing it would get a reaction. Over time, it certainly had the desired effect on me, and I left the perceived safety net of organisational life to do my own thing.

Leaving my job might sound easy but I can assure you, it was anything but. The culture that existed in this unique organisation was compelling. The management team were radically supportive of my personal development, and they advocated and encouraged open, honest communication at all times. This may be more common now, but in the early nineties, it was highly unusual. It attracted an outstanding group of talented, energised people with a shared vision to change the world. We created a powerful, collective alignment as well as a sense of meaning and purpose in our work. There were frequent, enlivening social events in our community. Working there felt more like belonging to a loving family or spiritual tribe of brave warriors than being a typical job. With a huge interest in self-awareness and personal growth, this fed me enormously and felt amazing.

My twelve years in this group had strengthened my character and opened my heart. Quitting meant unplugging myself from this incredible support structure and saying goodbye to many of my best friends. Yet the pull of wanting to find my own way and build my own power and autonomy was stronger. Charlotte was ready to leap too. Trusting our instincts, we resigned and departed for pastures new.

Perhaps we should have put more thought into our exit. With limited funds and without a clear idea about what business to start, my brother kindly offered refuge in his London house for three months. That gave us time and a bit of breathing space to figure out what to do next. The following year was a struggle and harder than I'd imagined. Much to my annoyance and frustration, my lack of entrepreneurial experience made it difficult for me to assess which business opportunities had the best chance of success. To pay our bills, I took on short term consulting assignments which made it even harder to focus on the dream.

Whilst my struggle continued, Charlotte tried a few different things for herself to see where they might lead. She enjoyed training and developing others in leadership and management skills, something she had a passion and a special talent for. After a couple of years, she'd gained enough experience from piecemeal project work to know she really wanted to make a go of it. She had a vision to launch her own consulting, coaching, and training company. Having both previously worked in a business in the same field, we had just enough confidence to know we could make it work, and with Charlotte delivering our service, we were confident we could achieve excellent results for clients.

Every business needs to generate customers, and that was at the centre of my expertise. Charlotte (who was now my fiancée) needed a strong marketing and sales plan that would really enable her business to work and reach a decent level of profitability. Wanting to create wealth and gain our independence, we decided to team up and work together. That put us in control of our lives and would create freedom for us later on. Back then, my expectation was that within a couple of years, the business would be solid enough for me to exit and pursue my own dreams, although it was never entirely clear to me what they were.

In January 1997, we launched our new company, First Place Consulting, and worked hard to ensure it succeeded. Before the launch, we reckoned that the toughest part of our challenge would be securing new clients. That can be difficult for any new business, yet we found it was relatively easy as we were so passionate and enthusiastic about what we were doing. We saw how we could create a powerful advantage over our competitors, and we could see how to deliver a better service. With this insight, we quickly became quite adept at persuading clients to choose us as their business partner.

Once the clients started coming, we discovered that the toughest part of our challenge was recruiting great people and transferring our passion and enthusiasm to everyone in our team so that we could build an organisation with a great reputation and solid character. We all had to walk our own talk, not just Charlotte and me. That provided the evidence our clients would need in order to really believe in us and keep choosing us in the long term. Building, nurturing, and sustaining our tribe became our obsession.

We both knew it was possible to engender a set of values within our team. We did everything we could to inspire everyone to live by these values and make them a tangible part of our company culture. We'd seen this work powerfully at The Programmes Group, and it gave us the belief that we could replicate it. We committed ourselves to our vision and looked to confirm the realisation of it in two ways. First, by building a company we felt truly proud of, no matter how profitable it was. That would validate our success energetically. Second, by entering the League Table of Top 100 UK Consultancy Firms within three years, which would validate our success financially. It was the combination of these two that would be the best outcome.

Two and a half years later, in 1999, after much hard work, First Place Consulting was included in the Top 100 UK league table for the first time. We were ranked in 97th place. Not only were we financially sustainable, which was a relief, we'd established our "Heart and Soul Management" manifesto, which contained a core set of eight actionable principles. These were the blueprint for building an exceptional performance culture in our team and had also been widely adopted by our clients. I felt overjoyed that we'd attracted talented people who wanted to come with us on our journey and who were inspired by these principles. It felt so satisfying for both of us to have realised this from a standing start and with no investment capital. We were in bliss!

During those early years, I grew into the CEO role of our rapidly expanding company. Yes, it was extremely challenging, but somehow my desire to gain mastery in the position was bigger than my fear of what might go wrong. Of course, there were private moments of doubt when I felt out of my depth. Some meetings and conversations I held with senior executives were terrifying. I hid this from my team because I felt it was my duty to set an example and be the strong one that everybody could rely on. I believed it wouldn't work to show any weakness back then.

Sometimes, the pessimist in me wondered if we'd simply been lucky.

I worried about how we were going to sustain our growth. My anxiety invalidated much of the success we achieved and enjoyed. Other times, I fretted that it would be many years before I'd be able to hand over the entire venture to Charlotte and be free to pursue my own path. Those thoughts made me feel trapped. But those moments were fleeting and always passed because I was constantly distracted by the never-ending flow of day-to-day operational issues that needed my attention.

The Tremors of Change

A peak moment in my personal growth came in 2002, five years after our launch. The prestigious *Daily Telegraph* Business Leader of the Year Award was up for grabs, and a few of my colleagues nominated me for consideration. Much to my surprise and delight, the judges selected me as the recipient. It was a great honour, and I felt my efforts had been officially recognised.

The judges told me they were particularly impressed with the purposeful culture and vision in our organisation, and how they could see that everyone in the company lived and breathed it too. This was music to my ears, and confirmation that our vision for First Place had been fulfilled. The business was established, highly regarded and profitable, and that ensured a great life for Charlotte, myself, and our growing team.

Strangely, as well as being a peak moment, winning the award also felt like a kind of ending, or at the very least, a turning point. Five years of my life had been totally dedicated to pushing with Charlotte to reach the top of a huge mountain. For a brief moment, we paused to enjoy the experience of mastering that challenge. It was a chance to reflect on and celebrate all the hard work that Charlotte, our team, and I had done together. Clearly, the decision to quit being an employee and create my independence had paid off handsomely. In fact, far more had come to me than I'd hoped for.

In that moment of pause, the first tremors of change I alluded to earlier started to register. It's hard to describe the feeling, because it was a strange, unfamiliar, and uncomfortable sense speaking from a deeper place in myself. Looking back, I believe my voice of inner wisdom was telling me that my part in this venture was complete. But it made no sense to my logical mind to be thinking that. With the award in my hand, a great team, and a bright future in front of me, it was impossible to acknowledge the existence of this voice to myself, let alone anyone else.

LIFE WITHOUT A TIE

Success in business, and the recognition it brings, can be very seductive. It was certainly true in my case. Yet if you'd looked closely at my life, you would have seen that success had come at a high price. Our focus on growing the company had been so narrow that investment in the quality of our personal relationship had taken a back seat for some time, and it was beginning to show. On the surface, our shared life was very comfortable, and we knew our routines well. A permanent state of busyness provided the perfect excuse to avoid real and necessary communication between us.

When we did find time, personal conversations between Charlotte and me about the quality of our relationship sometimes became strained and difficult. In our marriage, I wasn't truly happy, and we both had needs that weren't being met. For me, it was like having a toothache but being terrified of visiting the dentist. It was the lesser of the two evils to grin and bear it. Making money rather than being happy had become my focus.

Despite the pain this reality brought, I dismissed my feelings and found ways to avoid acting on them. If Charlotte pressed the issue, I became frightened because I didn't know how to clarify or articulate my needs in a kind or compassionate way. Looking back, it was quite overwhelming for me to feel so emotionally vulnerable. To protect myself, I'd be extremely self-righteous and defensive. It made me impossible to talk to, and you could have rightly described me as close-minded and aggressive. It wasn't a consciously chosen response on my part; it felt more like an automatic, uncontrollable knee-jerk reaction. The result was tense, unresolved arguments followed by short periods of silence in which my real intention was to punish Charlotte rather than make things better. I'm ashamed to admit just how destructive and damaging this behaviour was to our personal relationship. If our clients and staff could have witnessed me at those times, they would have been quite shocked.

This situation was never resolved. We rarely made love and related more like brother and sister than husband and wife. We suffered the pain of a miscarriage when our first attempt to start a family in early 2003 went awry. In the aftermath, it became obvious that Charlotte's picture of how our shared life should look was quite different to mine. Our visions of the future, as well as our needs, were seriously diverging, putting even more strain on our marriage. As time passed, the thought of engaging in a conversation to try and address this gave me knots in my stomach and induced a sense of panic you might associate with being told to adopt the brace position when landing in an aircraft. So I stuck my head in the proverbial sand and experienced my anguish in secret.

My spirit slowly suffocated. My biggest reason for leaving the safe and secure world of employment had been to find a way out of the system. I was searching for a way of living that had much greater freedom and in which I could build my financial resources. Working far less hours and enjoying more life experiences would be truly possible if and when this dream was realised. The circumstances in place around me meant this wasn't likely to happen for years, if ever, as long as my life remained on the same trajectory. I felt helpless and dejected.

My health was suffering as a result. Seriously overweight and unfit, old age was knocking on my door prematurely. In a photograph taken with my dad in 2001, we looked more like brothers than father and son, and that disturbed me. Despite my success in public, my anxiety about my appearance left me feeling unattractive and because of that, I saw myself as a dismal failure. It's what Robert Holden, author of *Success Intelligence* refers to as "Fraud Guilt." Feeling like a fake stopped me from being able to enjoy the success we had worked so hard for.

People say that when you find yourself in a situation like this, you have a choice to make. You either take personal responsibility for what's happening and create the changes that are necessary for your well-being, or you deny responsibility, take no action, and adopt a wait-and-see approach. In the latter case, it usually means that other people will eventually decide for you when things become too unbearable for them. The second route is often easier—some say it's the coward's route—and the risk of going that way can result in catastrophic, uncontrollable consequences.

I believe there is a third way, although I wasn't paying much attention to it at the time. Based on personal experience, it looks to me as if we all create the circumstances in our lives that yield the greatest opportunity for our personal growth. We may not recognise them as such, or choose to respond when they arise, yet they materialise all the same. It's as if the Universe has your back and no matter how badly things are going wrong, how tough or upsetting events get, they are ultimately happening in your best interests and will result in changes that are good for your well-being.

Despite my belief in this phenomenon, my lack of courage meant I chose to do nothing and adopt a wait-and-see approach. This created a subtle feeling of tension and led to a small, yet measurable, increase of those seismic tremors registering on my personal graph. And with it came a ton of uncertainty and a growing awareness that an earthquake could occur at any moment.

In August 2003, I was tired and worn out, partly from working hard and partly from suppressing the truth about our marriage. An opportunity to attend a spiritual health retreat in Portugal materialised out of the blue. It seemed like a great opportunity for me to take a time-out and enjoy two much-needed weeks that might help me recover some clarity and lost energy.

It was an idea I'd discovered a few years earlier, when I read a book called *Manhood* by Steve Biddulph. He writes about the multiple challenges men face in the modern world. He suggests that, at the age of forty, men should consider taking a sabbatical from their life to create space to reflect on what's happened and how they want to adapt going forward. It had really appealed to me, and I promised myself that one day, I would take the opportunity. That time had come, and I hoped the retreat would give me enough distance from my everyday life to see things more clearly.

A couple of days before I left for Portugal, my father suddenly became very ill with a heart condition and was taken to the intensive care unit at Harefield Hospital. Now there were two massive problems to worry about. I spoke to the doctor who was looking after my dad. He advised me to go ahead and attend my retreat as there was no point in me hanging around the hospital. If my dad's condition deteriorated, he assured me that he'd notify me immediately. Knowing my dad was in safe hands, I decided to go.

Ten days into the retreat, Charlotte called me with an urgent update from the doctor. He feared the worst and urged me to come home as quickly as possible. She'd arranged my flight and drove to Luton Airport to meet me. After I landed and entered the terminal building, I saw her waiting a few feet away. She smiled, walked towards me, and gently touched my forearm. That moment will remain etched in my memory forever. It was another tremor, the strongest of them all. In that moment, it was crystal clear to me that an earthquake was coming. It was the moment this journey you're reading about actually began although it took a while longer for me to realise it.

It was the faintest of touches, yet it sent a shockwave through my body like I'd never felt before, similar to the kind of powerful jolt you get when you accidentally touch a live electric socket. My whole body recoiled for a split second. My intuition sensed that something was seriously wrong, though there was no evidence to support the feeling. It preoccupied me for days afterwards, even with my attention firmly on my dad, who was fighting for his life.

Fortunately, within a couple of weeks, his condition had stabilised and improved. That weird, shock-inducing touch back at the airport was still haunting me. I invited Charlotte to talk so I could explore what was going on with her. In response to my gentle questioning, she seemed quite evasive in her answers, which troubled me further.

Eventually, in one of several conversations in our kitchen where I kept on digging, I couldn't bear it any longer.

"I know something's wrong, and I've asked you a hundred different ways to tell me what it is. I'm going insane. I want an honest answer, and we're not going to leave this room until I get one."

My ultimatum hit home. She revealed she'd met someone she felt strongly about. She reluctantly and tearfully let me know she wanted to leave our marriage and resign from her role in the company. As you can imagine, this was devastating. At first, I couldn't believe it. There was no way it could be true. It had to be a joke, right? When Charlotte confirmed it wasn't, it shocked me to my core. It felt like I'd been stabbed in the stomach.

My emotional stability and my self-image disintegrated rapidly. As unbelievable as it might seem, my main concern was about how to present this devastating and unflattering news to the outside world. How could I explain this to everyone who knew us? I was overpowered by guilt and shame, and the risk that my family and friends would judge me as someone who failed to meet the basic requirements of being a loving and kind husband was huge.

A few days later, I called a meeting for everyone in our company and faced the painful and potentially humiliating task of informing them. I had to admit publicly that, despite Charlotte and me sharing a vision for our business, our personal needs were different, and we were separating. I suspect they'd already sensed that something wasn't quite right, but now it was being confirmed officially. Fortunately, they were understanding and showed great empathy towards us both. My fear of being condemned never materialised.

LIFE WITHOUT A TIE

Feeling angry that our great company, which we'd painstakingly and lovingly created together, was in danger of going into demise, I initially blamed Charlotte for being the person who had pulled the plug on our dream. After a while and much reflection, it wasn't possible for me to really maintain that point of view. During those ten days in Portugal, I'd examined the heavy feelings I'd been suppressing and saw that something needed to shift. Somehow, that time alone had inadvertently prepared me for huge changes, though this development wasn't exactly what I'd expected.

In hindsight, as is usually the case with most of our major crises in life, Charlotte's decision to leave was arguably one of the best things that could have happened to me in terms of its impact on my experience of aliveness and creativity. The loss of my marriage was a massive blow, and it mortified me, yet true happiness had eluded me for some time. Maybe the Universe really did have my back and was acting on my behalf.

Christmas 2003 was bleak. Despite my desperate attempts to persuade her to stay, Charlotte was clear that there was no way back for her. She moved out of our home, which left me to sit in pain and misery in a quiet, empty house and cry. Having to admit that I'd totally bombed in my role as a husband gutted me, especially as I'd exceeded all expectations in my role as Charlotte's business partner.

My father was still in hospital and, bit by bit, was losing his battle to live. He passed away in early January 2004. He never knew about my separation from Charlotte. My decision to shield him came from a belief that it would support his recovery, as he most likely would've stressed about it if he'd known. When he sometimes enquired why she didn't come to visit him in the hospital, my repertoire of plausible excuses was well stocked. Maintaining this pretence tore me up inside. At a time when I most wanted and needed my wife's emotional support, she simply wasn't there.

Despite our personal separation, we still had to meet at our office in Chiswick every day to work together and run our business. This gave rise to a strange, almost surreal existence. We planned and agreed on an exit date for Charlotte, which put some light at the end of this dark, peculiar tunnel. Doing that also gave me a line to cross, after which there might be some relief from the constant feelings of grief and sadness that had taken up almost permanent residence in my body.

23

In business, we'd been a brilliant double act. The odds of finding someone who would be as perfect to work with were about a million to one. The idea of working without her felt as unimaginable as Lennon without McCartney, Ben without Jerry, or Batman without Robin. During the final few months, my energy for running our business simply vanished. Admitting the truth about that meant I had to let our wonderful team of people go. The systematic dismantling of First Place, my pride and joy, was the first major ripple effect of our parting.

At the end of March 2004, the door of our now-empty office was closed for the last time. Still living true to our values, Charlotte and I wanted to find jobs for all of our team members who needed one, much to the delight of one or two of our competitors who were aware of the quality training they'd received from us. We made sure that all our client obligations had been fulfilled and every loose end was attended to. The company documents were boxed up and shipped to my house for storage. On paper, the company was still alive and operating, but there was no office, no team, no work and, last but not least, no intention on my part to generate any beyond this point.

The Decree Absolute
The second and most significant ripple effect of my parting with Charlotte came a month later when our legal divorce was granted by the court. Like most things we'd done together, we faced that moment as a team. We stood outside the courthouse, both holding our divorce certificates, and acknowledged each other fully, with kindness and compassion for the pain we'd both suffered. That was a beautiful lesson for me in knowing what unconditional love means in practice.

I returned to my empty house; nothing looked or felt the same as it had done only six or seven months earlier. I comforted myself with a cup of strong tea at the kitchen table, whilst reflecting on the loss of everything that identified and defined me. A few of my deepest beliefs about life no longer seemed true. The illusion that marriage was supposed to last forever was smashed. It made me question everything that was important to me.

Hampered by the lack of energy or drive, my inner voice spoke to me throughout that period. The message it gave me was loud and clear.

"It's time to get out of this life you've created. You're done with it. It's time for something new."

LIFE WITHOUT A TIE

I had no idea what that meant or what it might look like. Trying to get a picture was intensely frustrating, like trying to complete a jigsaw puzzle without being able to see the illustration on the box lid. Elisabeth Kübler-Ross famously depicted five stages of grief in her book *On Death and Dying*, published in 1969. These stages represent the normal range of feelings people experienced when they deal with change in their lives or in the workplace. She observed that all change involved loss at some level. The five stages help people understand their reactions to change. They are denial, anger, bargaining, depression, and finally, acceptance. Bizarrely, reading about this reassured me. In the space of just a few months, I'd grappled with the first three and could see there was further to go. It changed my perspective and made life feel less emotionally turbulent.

In the meantime, the logistical impact of these changes was coming home to roost. The high levels of expenditure that underpinned my affluent lifestyle had to be met. They were the same as they'd always been when Charlotte was there. Only now, there was only me to pay for it all. With no money coming in from the company, it was going to be a huge struggle to fund everything. The thought of facing that didn't appeal to me at all.

I sat in front of my laptop looking at the spreadsheet with the cash-flow projections for household and personal expenditure and a feeling of tightness built up inside me. If nothing changed in the financial picture, my cash would run out in a matter of months and a deficit would start to accumulate. It seemed deeply unfair, and I felt agitated and resentful to be in this situation.

The fearless part of me simply acknowledged this as the end of a chapter. These facts were simply pointing me towards the exit. The anxious and frightened part of me wanted to blame Charlotte for this dilemma. It was her fault that I had such an expensive lifestyle, which required a huge income to be sustainable. In good faith, I'd gone along with it to make her happy. Now it was the cause of my suffering. To give you an idea of how I felt, imagine you're an actor in a play, cast in a supporting role alongside a superstar lead. The script and the set have been constructed to showcase their star talent. The props have been carefully selected to enhance their character. You're both in the middle of a scene when suddenly, without warning, they walk off stage and out of the theatre, never to be seen again. You're alone on stage with no-one to interact with. Members of the audience are sitting with their mouths wide open, aghast at the silent, motionless set. That's more or less how it felt for me after the divorce.

But as time went by, it dawned on me how little ownership I'd taken in a lot of the joint decisions we'd made. It'd been more convenient and easier for me to abdicate responsibility to Charlotte. When asked, I'd say, "If you're happy with that choice, then it's fine for me too, so go ahead." It required too much effort for me to really think about each decision and its implications. Charlotte took control of our domestic budget while I focused my attention on making sure we always had enough money coming in from the business. Consequently, I'd paid little attention to what we'd spent on our home. Nor had I seen ways we might have reduced our level of consumption. It hadn't been part of my thinking at all.

The consistent and predictable flow of money coming from First Place had now stopped. Without any serious changes, the only way to make the amount of money I required was by doing more of what we'd been doing before. Of course, this was impossible without Charlotte and our team. It was a catch-22 situation that left me feeling totally alone, up shit creek without a paddle.

Throughout 2004, I was unable to find a way out of this predicament. It was painful to be so stuck without any vision for the future. Some financial tinkering enabled me to liquidate a reasonable amount of cash that was tied up in an investment, so that I could cover my household expenses for a few months.

But nothing anesthetised my pain or created any clarity. A month-long visit to a close friend of mine in the United States, which I'd hoped would help, was fruitless. To add insult to injury, a romantic weekend on Long Island with a hot date turned out to be an unmitigated disaster. It was definitely not the time for starting a new relationship.

Back in London with my tail between my legs, my therapist assured me that, in spiritual terms at least, everything was as it should be. The year culminated in me having painful throat surgery just before Christmas in order to rectify a terrible snoring problem. It seemed I'd been lucky enough to have been married to the only woman in England who wasn't troubled by my nocturnal racket. Given it could severely impact my chances of holding down any sort of relationship with a future girlfriend, it seemed worth the risk and hassle of an operation.

It was a big relief to see that year out. Between my father's death in January and the painful throat surgery in December, there was nothing to cheer about and plenty of dark days. Many of the features that gave form to my life and my identity had been removed or obliterated. It felt like someone had fired an Exocet missile into the centre of my life and left me standing in the middle of a huge, hundred-foot-wide bomb crater, paralysed with grief and fear.

Unravelling

In her book, *The Gifts of Imperfection: Let Go of Who You Think You're Supposed to Be and Embrace Who You Are,* Brené Brown says, "People may call what happens at midlife 'a crisis,' but it's not. It's an unravelling—a time when you feel a desperate pull to live the life you want to live, not the one you're 'supposed' to live. The unravelling is a time when you are challenged by the universe to let go of who you think you are supposed to be and to embrace who you are. Midlife is certainly one of the great unravelling journeys, but there are others that happen to us over the course of our lives: marriage, divorce, becoming a parent, recovery, moving, an empty nest, retiring, experiencing loss or trauma, working in a soul-sucking job. The universe is not short on wake-up calls. We're just quick to hit the snooze button."

Despite the unravelling in my life, the new year felt like a turning point. As 2005 got underway, my throat was healing nicely. The fear and grief that had been such a dominant feature of my experience in 2004 was giving way to a growing feeling of gratefulness and optimism. I still hadn't resolved what I would do with my life going forward, and the question continued to trouble me. Then out of nowhere, a sudden flash of inspiration came.

Around the first anniversary of my father's death, he was strongly present in my thoughts. He was seventy-three years old when he passed away. Without understanding why, my attention and curiosity were drawn to this fact. I felt an urge to determine precisely how many days he'd been alive. I grabbed my calculator and pressed the buttons. His life, at least physically, had lasted 26,902 days in total. There was a pen and some blank paper on my desk, so I grabbed a piece and wrote that number on it. I stared at it for a couple of minutes.

In that moment, 26,902 days seemed like a short amount of time. It made me wonder if it was typical for men in general. How long might my lifespan be, measured in days? How many days did I have left? On the

27

internet, I found data sources that statistically validated the average age of death of UK men, which turned out to be eighty years (29,200 days). It's similar for most developed countries. The data is constantly tracked by the government and pension fund managers, who keep a close eye on this for obvious reasons.

By subtracting my already lived days from the statistical average and removing a couple of years from the end, when I might be too old, immobile, inactive, etcetera, to live a life of quality, my estimate was that I had about 12,500 active days left. In total. That assumed I maintained my present level of health and fitness. You'd be correct in thinking that this was a best-case scenario. An unexpected, premature death would obviously reduce that number.

Some people consider this a taboo subject. Thinking about the end of your life in this way may make you uncomfortable. You may feel scared or even depressed. Yet it was a catalytic and empowering moment as it helped me appreciate and value the finite nature of time itself. It changed my thinking. My unanswered, rhetorical question switched from "What should I do with the rest of my life?" to "What experiences are most important to me in the next 12,500 days?" This new question generated quite different answers.

If you were to ask yourself the same question, what answers might arise for you?

Facing the inevitability of my own death, acknowledging it and accepting it, has been one of the best ways of directing myself to live life fully. An amazing, freeing perspective came from acknowledging my mortality. Very subtly, my thinking started to shift. When sitting quietly to contemplate this new question, things such as career or work didn't appear anywhere in the answers that came to me. Neither did accumulating more material goods or a specific amount of money. Also absent was achieving notoriety or fame. Materialistic aims, driven by my ego, no longer felt worthwhile.

Instead, my attention was drawn toward my feelings, which could only produce blurry images whenever I tried to rationalise them. However, they told me something, like a kind of code that didn't make complete sense mentally but did instinctively. Some basic themes were emerging, at least. How could I use the loss of status and the crash of my self-esteem to grow into the adult I wanted to be in the world? How would I ever experience true love? How would I find and create my home, the place where I truly belonged? What was my life's work, my calling? Where and how could I be of greatest service? When would I see many of the amazing places I'd always dreamed of? Was there something waiting for me out there that I hadn't even imagined? These embryonic questions were like tiny little thought seeds which needed to be watered before they would blossom into tangible realities. Have you ever asked questions like these of yourself?

There was one major unresolved issue. I was still tied to my existing life, emotionally, mentally, and financially, with running costs too high for me to justify. Although it was hard to see exactly how to change the status quo, knowing and accepting my position expanded my sense of optimism. I chose to sit with my questions for a while and ferment them. The super-coach Tony Robbins says that if you look closely at the word "question," you'll see it can be broken down into "(What is the) Quest I (am) On?"

I kept asking myself, "Am I going to be a businessman for the rest of my life?" It made me think of the actor, David Schwimmer, who played Ross in the *Friends* TV sitcom. He played this character for a decade, and when the show ended, he found it incredibly difficult to be convincing in any other role he took on as he and his character had become one.

Being the same version of myself for my entire life didn't appeal to me. With only one life, I wanted to experience as many different roles, characters, and cultures as possible. Even though things had worked out well for me in business, the path I had chosen up to now—the one that my peers, colleagues, family, and society had expected me to follow and approved of—no longer felt like it was for me. There was nothing left to prove in that arena. I'd done it to the best of my ability and passed the test. My perspective on the alternatives was widening.

Many years ago, a former mentor gave me a piece of sage advice for situations when you're searching for something and are constantly frustrated that you cannot find it, no matter what you try or how much effort you make. "When you are unable to figure out how to help yourself, find someone else to help for a while. Take your attention off yourself and give it one hundred percent to them. Then wait and see what happens. An insight will come, followed by a breakthrough." Left with virtually no other option, his approach sounded like it might be worth a try.

Chapter Two
Becoming Untied

IN EARLY 2005, MY SEARCH FOR SOMEONE TO HELP WAS WELL UNDERWAY. OUT of the blue, an email arrived from a dear friend, Elizabeth Taylor. She lives in Sydney, Australia and had been diagnosed with breast cancer. She and her husband Matt had been close friends of mine for many years. We'd shared a house together in England when we were in our twenties. Years later, they'd moved to Australia, where their son Pete was born. I'd met him about five years earlier during a Christmas holiday visit.

Elizabeth told me about her illness. She needed to undergo intensive chemo treatment which was going to cause disruption to their daily lives. She and Matt both had full-time jobs and, with a young son to look after, she agreed that my temporary support would take some of the pressure away and give them an extra pair of hands at a difficult time. My offer to stay with them for three weeks was promptly accepted. It was April 2005 when I flew to Sydney.

It was a source of great pleasure for me to accompany Elizabeth during her visits to the hospital. It meant Matt could take care of the household and look after Pete whilst still doing his full-time job. After the full course of treatments and surgery, Elizabeth eventually made a full recovery. Her presence and friendship are sources of happiness and gratitude to this day. Being there for Elizabeth and her family gave me a much-needed break from worrying about my own future. In fact, I hardly had time to think about it. The cycle of negative thoughts that had been dominating my attention and playing with my emotions for several months disappeared, as did the incessant mental noise that came with it. My world was a much calmer place upon my departure from their home.

It turned out the advice given to me by a mentor had been a godsend. There were five small but crucial words in his wise guidance: "wait and see what happens." Annoyingly, he gave no indication as to *how long* one has to wait. Whilst I was in Sydney, nothing magical or unexpected happened to me. Cynically, I let go of any hope that it might, and the expectation soon evaporated. Perhaps my mentor was just trying to make me feel more optimistic when he said that to me. Maybe it didn't work every time.

Despite my cynicism, that unexpected, magical something was in fact already brewing. As I left Sydney, I had no idea that I was hurtling towards an event that would alter the course of my entire life. And it was an event that simply wouldn't have been *possible* had my trip to Sydney not materialised. It started to unfold a couple of days later, when the second leg of my month-long visit to Australia took me fifteen hundred miles north of Sydney to see my friend Julie Parker, who is a native of Cairns, a small, coastal city in tropical Queensland.

Our paths had crossed some years before in London when she lived and worked there. Despite the fact we hadn't seen each other in person for a few years, she was a reliable and trusted friend who'd really been there for me the year before. She generously gave me her time, attention, and support during numerous phone calls as the full impact of my divorce and my father's death kicked in. She was a great listener and had let me pour my heart out, which had helped calm me down. Her presence gave me a feeling of being understood, accepted, and comforted, which I was deeply grateful for. In those conversations, I noticed that she didn't judge my failings or force her opinions on me. In direct contrast to many of my local friends, her way of being had an authentic and present feel to it, and I was curious to find out what made her behave like that.

The opportunity to see her for ten days before returning to England was as exciting as winning the lottery. Julie had wisdom about life. It was easy to listen to her and consider any advice she gave me. We didn't always agree about what would the best thing for me to do, but I didn't mind that. She asked insightful and provocative questions which sometimes made me feel uncomfortable, yet they always enabled me to think more deeply and gain new insight. I felt fortunate she was there.

One evening after listening to me talk about my lack of vision, she made a suggestion: "Why don't you put those questions to one side, take some time off, and go backpacking for a while. Go and explore what the world has to offer and see where life leads you."

"Julie, why would I want to *waste my life* backpacking aimlessly around the world? You can't make any money doing that. It's a totally ludicrous idea."

In light of what I've done since, that memory still makes me cringe. At the time though, her suggestion scared me and triggered some fear and defensiveness. Perhaps I wasn't as ready to let go of my life as a London businessman as I'd thought. Her suggestion was duly filed in the back of my mind, marked "No further action required."

The type of adventurous, independent travelling that Julie was talking about was so far outside of my reality that it struck me as completely inconceivable. Yet, I understood *why* she'd advised me to think about it. Listening to stories about her own journey through life, I discovered that she'd quit her lucrative corporate job to spend four years backpacking around Asia. It had been a life-changing decision for her. She lived in India for a big chunk of that time and had even met the Dalai Lama. Her colourful stories of events during that period mesmerised and fascinated me.

Out of Order
After a couple of days, Julie invited me to go to the Rondo Theatre one evening to see a play. "It's Mum's birthday, and we're getting tickets for the show on Thursday. Would you like to join us?"

Live theatre performances are usually a source of great entertainment, so I happily accepted. The play was called *Life After George*. When the day came, we jumped in the car, drove across town to the theatre and took our seats. Unusually, the three-hundred-seat Rondo Theatre was set up in the round, so instead of the stage facing the audience head on, it projected out in a kind of T-shape like a wide catwalk about fifteen feet into the audience, with seats placed in a huge U-shape around the stage, at the front, and to the sides. The actors were surrounded by the audience, giving a cosy, more intimate feeling for both viewers and performers.

During the interval, I read the actors' biographies in the programme. As I did so, an advertisement caught my attention. On the last page, in a small box in the corner, the theatre company was inviting people to come forward and audition for the next production. They had purchased the rights to perform a very well-known British comedy farce called *Out of Order*. Seeing it triggered my ironic sense of humour and without thinking, I immediately turned to Julie and her mum, pointed at the ad, and said, "Look! *Out of Order* is a play from the UK. They should ask me to be in that; I have the perfect English accent." Intended as a joke, I hadn't expected a response.

"That's such a great idea, Ray," Julie had said. "You'd really bring some authenticity to the production. The director is a personal friend of mine, and I'm sure he'd be thrilled to meet you. Why don't you go to the audition?"

For a split second, I indulged myself and excitedly imagined the possibility of me landing a part in the play. What an amazing opportunity it could be for me. Then reality kicked in. My thoughts made a rapid U-turn as the pessimistic voice in my head decided to have its say. *You'll never get through the audition. Don't be ridiculous. You haven't got any talent or experience. And even by the slim chance that you manage to fool them, they'll find out you've no talent as soon as rehearsals begin. It's way too dangerous. Don't you dare go."*

"Have you gone mad? Why on Earth would they ask me? I've no training at all as an actor, no experience, and all the people auditioning will be way better than me. Plus, they'll really want these parts. There's no way I'm good enough to get picked."

Julie frowned but said nothing.

"You know, back in England there are five clients waiting for me to go home, all wanting my help. The money I'll earn is essential to cover my huge living costs there. I just can't afford to turn it down."

Julie gently nodded. "Ray, I see what you mean. What you say makes sense. In that case, it probably isn't worth trying for a part. Why not just attend the audition purely for fun? At least you could say you did something interesting while you were on holiday."

That sounded like a far more palatable idea, and it appealed to the explorer in me. There was nothing to lose and everything to gain from attending. The experience might even be fun and exciting!

"Yeah, you're right, Julie. Let's do it!"

The audition happened a couple of days later. Before it began, I filled in a two-page application form, giving the casting director my personal details and information about my acting experience. There was no point in lying or stretching the truth since there was virtually no chance of me being chosen. So, in answer to the question, "What acting experience have you had?" I wrote, "None since leaving school." In the business world, people are used to sometimes overstating their résumés, so it felt good to be honest and not maintain any pretence. Basically, I gave myself total permission to be awful!

LIFE WITHOUT A TIE

Having to perform in front of other people didn't really bother me that much. Years of experience speaking to large audiences at business conferences gave me confidence that I'd be okay. As I entered the theatre, I felt relaxed. My expectation was that the casting director wouldn't regard me as a credible contender, and that made it easy for me to decide I'd just throw myself fully into it and do whatever I was asked to. By going all-in, my satisfaction was guaranteed, no matter the outcome. My main aim was simply to enjoy it.

Having said that, I have to admit that the possibility of making a memorable impression on the director, Wayne Rees, excited me. Maybe he'd see the true potential in me. Maybe he'd invite me to take on a major role. He had no idea that I was booked on a flight to London three days later, and it seemed like a really bad idea to make him aware of that. I decided to omit this information to ensure he gave me a fair, unbiased chance. I didn't want to be ruled out solely because of geography.

The story told in *Out of Order* centres around a lecherous Member of Parliament during an action-packed overnight stay at the Westminster Hotel in London, where he secretly meets the young woman he's having an affair with. It's a comedy, lots of things go wrong and he has to turn to his Parliamentary Private Secretary, George Pigden, to sort out ensuing calamities and restore order. If you're old enough to remember the *Carry On* movies, you'd know the type of bawdy innuendo, gags, and outrageous antics to expect.

Around forty people showed up for the auditions. Once they were underway, Wayne Rees organised us into groups to read characters from different scenes in the script. For the next hour or so, we switched around as Wayne observed and made notes. He briefly described each character to us and watched to see how we'd play that person. His instructions were minimal, so I relied on my intuition and experience and trusted that. The whole thing was a lot of fun and felt like charades in a big party game. By the time it was over, I had the feeling that I wasn't as bad as I'd imagined. In fact, by my own assessment, I compared favourably with many of the actors who'd shown up.

It was a tantalizing paradox. On the one hand, the prospect of acting on stage was terrifying because I didn't believe I'd be any good, meaning it was pointless to even want it. On the other hand, the prospect of doing something extraordinary and completely out of character felt intensely exciting. The tension between my vulnerability and my desire was like a rubber band being fully stretched to breaking point. Have you ever found yourself in a similar situation? If you have, you'll know what I'm talking about.

When the audition was over, Wayne called us together.

"Thanks for coming. You can all go now, except Ray Martin. Ray, would you mind staying behind for a couple of minutes?"

I didn't know why he'd singled me out. It triggered a feeling of nervousness. Maybe there was something amiss on my application form. Maybe he wanted to let me know that there was no chance of getting a place. Perhaps he'd been impressed with me. It was impossible to tell.

Wayne walked across the stage and sat down next to me. "Thanks for coming, Ray. I was impressed with you tonight and wanted to check out your situation before I sit down and think about who to cast."

As you can imagine, it was a massive relief to hear him say that. In an instant, the tension between my vulnerability and my desire was released.

"So, what is your situation exactly? Are you living here? Would you be able to handle a three-month schedule of rehearsals with the team?"

I tried hard to answer each question calmly. My imperative was to maintain the illusion that I was living in Cairns for fear he'd have to exclude me otherwise. It was a made-up story, but there seemed little point in changing it now. He seemed pretty close to offering me a part, and I didn't want to give him any excuse to change his mind. Wayne knew it would be my first role, so I didn't expect him to trust me playing one of the main characters. Surely, it would have to be a bit-part character with only one or two lines. You know the type. A waiter who enters during one scene and says, "Here's your tea, sir," and promptly exits, never to be seen again. But my speculation about it didn't really matter. My work obligations in England were calling me back, which meant that accepting any part would be impossible. Nevertheless, I still wanted to know that I'd been good enough to be offered a part. Then I could feel good about myself, even though I'd have to turn it down.

Wayne told me he'd make his casting decisions in about a week. He was unaware that would be after my arrival back in England. "If you decide you'd like me to be in the play, just call me on this number." I pointed to my Australian cell number on my application form. Even though it was probably the last time I'd see him, it had been a memorable experience, and I'd appreciated having the chance. I jumped in my car and raced back to Julie's house to tell her what had happened.

I knew instinctively that Wayne was interested in me taking part. Maybe he *might* consider me to play one of the two main characters. Richard Willey was a fairly strait-laced, upper-class Englishman. Maybe Wayne might be comfortable with me taking on that role. The character of George Pigden was more demanding. He was Richard's rather effeminate and idiotic private secretary and at the centre of all the comedic activity.

It was fairly obvious that whoever was selected to play George Pigden needed to be versatile. George appeared in almost every scene and had over four hundred lines of dialogue. He also needed the strength to move a dead body. On top of that, the actor needed the comedic timing to deliver a number of clever one-liners and the charm to seduce two women in different scenes, involving a passionate kiss with each. With my lack of acting experience, I believed it was highly unlikely that Wayne would consider me for either of these roles, especially the latter.

Julie sensed my excitement as we talked about the audition and the conversation with Wayne. We contrived a plan in case Wayne wanted to cast me, despite the fact I'd be back in England when he made his decision. If and when he called, Julie agreed to do two things. First, she'd tell Wayne that I'd had some sort of family emergency and had flown back to London for a couple of days. Second, and most importantly, Julie would find out which part Wayne was offering. It may sound arrogant to you when I say this, but it would be impossible for me to justify spending three more months in Cairns for a small, insignificant walk-on part. The pressure on me to pay my bills at home was too great and could force me into debt. It was an unreasonable wish on my part, but I let Julie, and the Universe, know that I'd only return if Wayne invited me to play either of the two main characters. Whilst neither of us believed this would happen, we still prepared for that scenario.

Three days later, my flight touched down at Heathrow Airport. Within a couple of hours of arriving home, the phone rang. It was Julie. My future was hanging in the balance and couldn't be settled until we'd received the expected call from Wayne Rees. "Did Wayne call? What happened? What did he say? Which part is it? Tell me, Julie, for god's sake. Tell me!" The energy and intensity of my questions was like a kid's on Christmas Day.

"Are you sitting down?"

I was. "Wayne wants you to be in the play…in the role of George Pigden!"

For a few moments, my tongue was motionless in my wide-open mouth. The unthinkable had happened. With no acting experience, Wayne Rees offered me the leading role in an acclaimed British play. Accepting it would mean appearing on stage, every night, in front of a live audience and delivering a solid, professional performance. Suddenly, my life felt like an episode of *Faking It*, with me in the middle of a surreal fantasy. It was unbelievable. After I'd calmed down from the shock, Julie said that Wayne was expecting a response from me the following day.

Before accepting, there were two obstacles I had to overcome: gaining acceptance from five clients to a further postponement of work and convincing myself I could actually carry it off. Regarding the latter, I decided to get some advice. Luckily, I knew two people who might give me their opinion about it. One was my sister-in-law, Kitty, who is a professional actress. The other was a woman called Annie. We'd met in London a few weeks before my departure for Sydney, and she was an experienced stage performer. If they thought it was possible for me to handle the demands of the character and make it through the rehearsal schedule without any formal training or experience, that would tick one of the two boxes I needed before saying yes and taking this challenge on. Both gave me the thumbs up.

The next challenge was to enrol the support of those five clients, all of whom had been patiently waiting for me to return from Australia. It didn't feel right to notify them my plans had suddenly changed, and they would have to wait another three months. My dad taught me that it's vital to keep your promises and be true to your word, and doing that had always served me well. For my own integrity, I needed to explain in an open and honest way exactly what happened in Australia, and I hoped they would respond positively. That meant going back into the feeling of vulnerability I'd experienced at the audition. I felt truly inspired to return to Australia and take on the role of George. It had happened so suddenly; there was a sense of divine intervention about it, as if the Universe wanted me to do it. It dawned on me that this was the outcome that had been predicted by my mentor when he told me to find someone else to help for a while and wait for something magical to happen. At the same time, my self-judge dutifully reminded me that I shouldn't get carried away on a whim, that earning a living was vitally important, and that taking part in a play was a huge and expensive waste of precious time. I felt under massive pressure to say no to Wayne.

I sat in the turmoil of that dilemma and let it wash over me. To counter my self-judge, my self-coach voice now spoke to me loud and clear and told me I had to go back to Australia, no matter what. If every one of those five clients gave me their blessing, I would take that as a sign it was okay for me to go. Their consent would give me a powerful, objective confirmation from the Universe that this was meant to be happening.

In my thirties, I'd learned the value of positive confirmation signals during my training as an aircraft pilot. Every aircraft has a navigation instrument called a VOR, which is a kind of direction-finding device. It's circular and has a moving pointer which shows which direction to fly in. Pilots use them to navigate from one point to another. The instrument in the cockpit connects with grounded radio beacons, of which there are hundreds located around cities, airports, and airfields. Importantly, each beacon has a unique radio frequency so it can be identified. If you fly from London to Brighton, you tune your VOR to the frequency of the Brighton beacon, and the needle points toward it. Then, you simply fly the aircraft in the direction indicated until you arrive there. Obviously, it's vital you select the right frequency, otherwise you might be flying towards the wrong beacon. Once you've selected the beacon, you must confirm it's the right one by pressing a button which triggers an audible Morse code signal. The five-second beeping sound you hear in response is unique to that beacon and gives you a *positive confirmation* you're heading the right way.

One phone call at a time, I told each client the story of the audition and reassured them that honouring my commitment to them was my number one priority. I was transparent with them about how excited I was to be offered this once in a lifetime opportunity and asked them if they objected to me returning to Australia, as it would impact them. With my heart wide open, I was able to convey what it meant for me to go. Most of them were aware of my personal circumstances, and I was deeply moved by the way they understood and empathised with my needs at that difficult time.

They all gave me their thumbs up. I had my confirmation. My thoughts drifted back to that evening at the Rondo Theatre in Cairns. It had all seemed so ludicrous just a few days ago. Although I still had doubts, I felt ready and committed now. Both obstacles had been overcome.

There was just one final hoop to jump through before I purchased my ticket—an imminent telephone conversation with Wayne Rees. When he made that call the following day, I thanked him for the invitation to play George. "Wayne, you know I have virtually zero experience. This may turn out badly. Are you completely sure you want me? When the run starts, you'll have two or three hundred people coming to the theatre every night, paying for their tickets, and expecting to see a great performance. That's a lot of pressure and stress for you. Do you really want to take such a big risk on me in the lead role?" There was silence for a few, agonisingly long seconds whilst he considered my questions.

"I understand you, Ray," he said calmly. "Back here, we're all in agreement; we think you're the perfect person to play George Pigden. We know you don't have much experience, but we believe you can do it. We'll support you all the way to make sure you're well-rehearsed for the role."

Hearing him say that was an enormous relief. Without hesitation, I accepted the role and was on a plane back to Australia two days later. There was something magical and unexpected about the whole thing. There was no way on Earth I could've planned for it. The statistical odds that such an opportunity would present itself seemed as improbable as winning the lottery. It was exactly what I needed when I needed it.

For the first time since the collapse of my former life, I was unconcerned about my future. Life was just so exciting in that moment. The theatre in Australia wasn't offering me any money to take part. Despite that and the financial pressures, my wise and instinctive self knew this was the right path to take and doing so would guarantee no regrets for me years later.

I Wasn't Alone on Stage
My understanding of regrets had been updated significantly the previous year by an Australian nurse called Bronnie Ware, whose best-selling book is aptly called, *The Top Five Regrets of The Dying*. She worked in a hospice and talked with thousands of people in the last days and weeks of their lives. She asked them all the same question: "What do you most regret about your life?" After several years of listening to their responses, she confirmed that no matter who they were, whether they had been a CEO or a janitor, famous or not, everyone more or less said the same five things, in order of importance. They all wished they had:

LIFE WITHOUT A TIE

1. Lived their life true to themselves
2. Not worked so hard
3. Stayed in touch with close friends (who drifted out of their lives)
4. Expressed their feelings more
5. Allowed themselves to be happier

Reflecting on this list, you could summarise Ware's viewpoint as "Don't waste your time living someone else's life." That sentiment was echoed by the late Steve Jobs, founder of Apple Inc., in a famous commencement speech he made to graduates at Stanford in 2005. Most people experience one or more of these regrets because their life choices are based on the dreams, visions, and goals of other people and do not fully address their own deepest, heartfelt needs.

In that context, my decision to take part in the play took on much greater meaning and significance. It wasn't simply a choice to do something challenging or pleasurable, even though it was obviously both. More than that, saying yes to Wayne Rees meant a mindset reorientation in making major decisions. It meant following my heart and inner wisdom. I started to remake the commitment to living life true to myself. My concern about not having enough money in the future, which might have stopped me before, was acknowledged and put to one side for a while.

In Australia, my transformation into the character of George Pigden began. Two months of rehearsals and the monumental task of memorising my lines consumed around two hours every day. My character had a notably different personality than me. We were probably about the same age, but that's where the commonality ended. Wayne Rees skilfully directed me to get to grips with the type of man George was—how he moved, what his voice sounded like and how he related to the other characters in the story. On stage, I had to lose myself and become George completely and authentically.

During rehearsals, Wayne directed me to make adjustments here and there, until he was happy that my portrayal of George was exactly as he wanted it. We practiced every scene many times. In two particular scenes, George has to initiate some passionate kissing with his boss's wife and Nurse Foster, who bizarrely looked a lot like my ex-wife. They were challenging, and fun, and on the edge of my comfort zone.

After two months, my transformation into George was complete, ready for our opening night and the first performance in front of a public audience. Despite one or two hiccups, it went extremely well. I remember how amazing it felt when we had the curtain call at the end and received resounding applause from the audience. Because George was the central character in the story, I had the privilege of being the final person to return on stage whilst the audience were clapping. Most nights, I could hear the volume and intensity of their clapping go up as I came out of the wings. I felt appreciated, even adored. It was obvious they loved the play. The icing on the cake came in the form of several complimentary reviews of the play in the local newspapers.

Out of Order ran for two weeks. Taking part was so empowering and about a million miles away from the low moments I'd experienced in the time leading up to it. For three wonderful months, the Universe gave me an opportunity to experience being someone else—a totally different person to the one I usually thought of as me. The shift I'm describing wasn't just something I felt whilst being George on stage. The changes of routine to my daily life had changed my thinking and perspective. For three months, I'd had no targets to reach, proposals to write, meetings to attend, problems to solve, or clients to discuss business issues with. Instead, I'd rehearsed lines, chatted with actors, dressed up in strange clothes, wore make-up, and talked in a funny voice.

The Four Ties
When the play run came to an end, it was time to return to London. It was a moment I dreaded. It meant the end of this wonderful, new reality and the resumption of me playing a different character. Only this time, it wasn't going to be in a fictitious story. It occurred to me that the character of Ray, who I'd faithfully played every day for the last forty-four years without question, was as much of a construction as George Pigden had been. The only difference was that my persona hadn't been consciously and explicitly authored by me.

True, I did have a say in some of the fine-toothed detail that defined me and the story of my 'real life.' But fundamentally, my character was largely the consequence of conditioning by everyone around me and the environments I was raised in. This was the most powerful insight that came from being George. This was the precise moment that the advice given by my mentor (help someone else and see what happens) made complete sense. It was the breakthrough that I'd hoped and prayed for when I sat through months of stuckness back in England a few months earlier.

Once again, the daily episode of the drama that was my life was set to resume. With a fresh perspective, I realised I wouldn't just be the actor but the scriptwriter, voice coach, editor, and director too. Seeing it that way gave me the power to change any aspect of my character. There was no plausible reason why it was necessary or desirable for me to remain typecast in the role of businessman, which I'd put myself in for the last ten years. Maybe I could kill that character off. That would free me to cast myself in a completely different story with a new setting, script, and different secondary characters. The possibilities were infinite and knowing that was mind-blowing.

It may sound simple to say this. Yet only three months earlier, I was tied to playing or defining myself in that way. Before the trip to Australia, I'd had no choice. That was who I thought I was, and I'd never consciously considered being someone different. I found others who talked to me about similar experiences they'd had. Some recalled having similar insights when they reflected on what happened. After listening to them, it struck me that people described being tied to their identity in four different ways:

1. Partner or spouse
2. Career
3. House/home
4. Community (family and friends)

For some, it seemed unthinkable that they could let go of or change any one of these. It's not that surprising. During my upbringing, my parents, teachers, people on television, and other influential members of society had constantly voiced their opinions about these things. They'd led me to believe that success in life came from having a lucrative career with lofty status, marrying the right person and starting a family, buying a lovely house (which then has to be filled and constantly refilled with stuff), and establishing a powerful set of friends.

There'd been no way to question these at the time. I'd unquestionably accepted their beliefs and bought into this story, which was a very popular one in that era. I'd inadvertently created a life for myself that was virtually impossible to escape from or even radically modify.

Just pause for a moment here and reflect on this for yourself. Who do you see yourself as? Who is the character that you commonly refer to as "me?" What story have you been sold regarding the "ideal" life? What are the ties that bind you to your life and character? What are you putting off because it wouldn't be consistent with the story you've acted out so far?

In my coaching work, I meet people who are presented with opportunities to define themselves differently. They usually come to see me in a state of turmoil. These four primary ties tend to be the source of their unravelling. For example, one client was offered a new job in a different city, paying substantially less money but offering him far more meaningful work. He told me, "I can't really accept; my partner would never agree to it." Our partner or spouse is the first tie that influences our decisions when such opportunities for change arise.

I've heard similar stories regarding the second tie of our career. "I have to keep building my résumé. It would never work for me to take a big chunk of time off—how would I explain the gap it would create in my CV?"

Some people make huge sacrifices to accept jobs that are located miles away from where they live. Consequently, they only get to see their partner and kids at the weekend and are isolated from their friends. They convince themselves their new job is much better for their CV. In the name of career progress, they 'tough' out the resulting period of suffering. This levies a huge toll on their energy and happiness.

The third tie, which people of my generation often mention, is the house. Or more specifically, the mortgage debt that needs to be serviced to live in the house. Although many younger people who are at the early stages of their career are not affected as much by this, some have similar ties to debt. In his book, *Choose Yourself*, James Altucher highlights the massive growth in student loans taken on to help people gain a degree or similar qualification so they're viable in the job market. His description of this debt is apt: "A leash which society uses to bind you to a life in which your main objective is the repayment and servicing of those debts."

Being tied by a mortgage applied to me. Servicing that debt required a substantial amount of money every month. Living in West London, the cost of the mortgage, plus all of the sundry taxes and household expenditures that went with it were way in excess of what it was actually worth to me. Living in that house had affected me emotionally too. Being there was a constant reminder that my dreams of raising a family and happily growing old with my wife were not possible. I felt trapped in a downward spiral of self-pity.

The fourth tie, our community of family and friends, didn't create as much inertia as my tie to the house. Having been independent and free spirited most of my life, being distant from old friends and making new friends was something I was used to. My family and close friends were fully aware that I wanted to shake everything up after all that had happened. I sensed they'd be supportive, no matter what choices I made. They were conditioned to rarely seeing or hearing from me. After several years of being single-minded and totally focused on my work and career, my family only expected me to show up for a social visit once in a while. I've met people whilst travelling who have strong and close ties with their families. They told me they felt a sense of isolation and disharmony when these connections weren't nurtured on a regular basis.

The list of things that keep us tied or stuck in our lives can be extended beyond these four alone, depending on your circumstances. They're there for a good reason. They provide stability for our personality in the same way that the guy ropes attached to the four corners of a tent keep it securely tied down. If *one* of those ropes comes undone, the tent starts flapping a little, and it's fairly easy to rectify. Two ropes become untied, and the tent is more unstable. If three ropes come undone at the same time, it's highly unstable. And if all four ropes are untied, simultaneously, the tent collapses. You have no tent at all!

Imagine how you'd feel if you untied yourself from your partner, home, career, and your family and friends all at the same time. That will give you a sense of what I faced when I returned from Australia and contemplated a radical shift in a completely new direction. My acting debut had been a wild, liberating, and life-changing experience. It seemed impossible to justify returning to the life I had. Yes, it was a comfortable life with lots of privileges. But I felt so uninspired. Being in that play had reminded me that powerful growth experiences and going into the unknown and feeling inspired by my own daily life was more valuable to me than maintaining my accustomed level of material comfort.

All my senses were telling me that this would be a fantastic exit point from the only way of life I'd known. If there was a way to re-engineer my finances so I could survive for a while on a much smaller income, then I'd have the freedom to try something radically different. I certainly didn't want to fall victim to the regrets that Bronnie Ware identified through her conversations with people who were dying.

On my return to London, I explored the option of renting my house out. I spoke to a few friends who were private landlords to understand what that involved. I could see the benefits and disadvantages and opted to sell the property. By moving to a smaller home, my living costs would fall dramatically, and I'd need substantially less income each month. That would alleviate the need to work full-time. Being self-employed meant I'd have more flexibility around work, and it was feasible I could generate the money I needed by working significantly fewer hours. The net result would be more time and freedom to explore other interests. At last, I had a plan that felt inspiring.

Becoming a Minimalist
Selling the house wasn't a decision I took lightly. Living there had given me some much-needed stability after the divorce in the same way that a heavy anchor keeps a boat secure in the harbour during a storm. After the play and the realisations that followed, I was ready to let it go. There was something more energetically powerful in letting go completely than by making what felt like a temporary arrangement. My inner voice had kept whispering to me quietly that being debt free was going to be important in my future, and I paid attention to this. By selling, none of my energy would be tied up in worrying about debt, property management, or dealing with the needs of a rental agent and tenants.

Throughout 2005, one year after the divorce, I was beginning to notice subtle changes in myself. One of these was a reorientation in my decision-making, away from *thinking* and more towards *feeling*. It had started with my decision to be in the play, which was directed by my heart. That was followed by my decision to sell the house. These were really empowering steps. I saw how disconnected I'd become from my inner voice of wisdom and inspiration. It had gone quiet amidst the noise and business of making money and living the good life. Taking those steps helped me hear it again, as if someone had found the volume control and turned it back up. I felt more and more connected to my inner wisdom and had more energy.

This internal reorientation, in which I paid more attention to my feelings, started to have a profound effect as more insights were finding their way into my conscious thoughts. It helped me remember my perspectives on life as a young boy, which had influenced my outlook back then, but which I'd long since forgotten. For example, I remembered when I was twelve or thirteen years old, I'd talk to my mates at school about my contempt for the widely accepted concept of a career. As a naive young boy, this had seemed like an appalling idea. The terrible deal that people made, which resulted in them being forced to work for most of their lives in exchange for a bit of status and a guaranteed pension, was horrifying.

I grew up in the sixties. Back then, the period of time left for most retirees when their career ended was relatively short. Many of them never actually did any of the things they spent their whole working life imagining they would do. They died a few short years after they stopped working and were unfulfilled. What's the point of working for years and years to save enough money to start really living and then dying so soon that you never enjoyed it? That didn't make any sense to my young mind. I constantly searched for someone who could help me understand this paradigm, but no one ever gave me a satisfactory explanation.

That influenced me to dream of life as a grown-up in a different way. I wanted to defy the convention and be different. It was perhaps simplistic logic, but I'd tell my friends at school that I was going to work twice as hard and earn twice as much money as normal people do in the first half of my adult life, until, say, the age of forty or forty-five. That would give me enough money to get through the second half of my life without having to work. By achieving this goal, I would be able to save half my life for playing and enjoying instead of working. I had no clue as to how I'd do that, but it didn't stop me wanting it.

In all the years that had passed since, I'd forgotten those conversations. It both amazed and scared me in equal amounts when I started to remember how creatively I saw the world when I was too young to know better. I could clearly see how much my limiting beliefs restricted my choices as an adult. Have you ever felt this way? What beliefs did you hold as a child that you've long since forgotten? How did you imagine the life of an adult would feel long before it actually materialised?

Tapping back into my younger mindset shifted my thinking. I wanted to continue the adventure and live a different daily life to the one I was familiar with. Rather than move to a smaller home in London immediately, I decided to put that on hold for a while, perhaps six months. No more of the usual plans, goals, and targets. I wanted to step into the unknown and explore a new way of living. The suggestion that Julie had made to go travelling for a while now didn't seem as ridiculous to me as it had done back then. Perhaps I could take a one-way journey for a while and trust that life would lead me in the right direction and keep me out of harm's way. Being an open, curious explorer would be my new daily life.

As things became clear, it dawned on me that eliminating any unnecessary consumption and drastically reducing my living costs was essential. Although it seemed like a big stretch, it might make it possible for me to take a long enough break from the world of business to have a major reset. First, the house had to be sold. Then I'd have a new problem to deal with. What should I do with all the stuff accumulated in it? Should it all go into a storage unit?

To answer that question, I contacted friends who'd lived abroad as expats and asked them about their experiences. To cut a long story short, over ninety-five percent of them said more or less the same thing: "We wish we'd decided to get rid of it rather than store it. We spent a lot more on storage than we imagined and when we returned, we didn't really want most of the stuff that was there. We hardly missed any of it."

According to Madeleine Somerville in *The Guardian*, the personal storage industry in the USA was virtually non-existent a generation or two ago. It now rakes in $22 billion each year, and it's not because we're short on space. In 1950, the average size of a home there was 983 square feet. Now, they have ballooned and almost tripled in size to an average of 2,480 square feet. And it's not because of our growing families, which, in the Western world, are steadily shrinking from an average of 3.37 people in 1950 to just 2.6 today. It's all because of our *stuff*. We're drowning in furniture, clothing, children's toys, games, kitchen gadgets, and trinkets that don't do anything but take up space. They look pretty for a season or two before being replaced by other, newer things—equally pretty and equally useless.

Somerville concludes that if you have more stuff than you do space to easily store it, your life will be spent as a slave to your possessions. Our addiction to consumption is a vicious one, and it's having a markedly negative impact on virtually every aspect of our lives. We shop because we're bored, anxious, depressed, or angry. We make the mistake of buying material goods and thinking they're treats which will fill the hole, soothe

LIFE WITHOUT A TIE

the wound, and make us feel better. The problem is, they're not treats. They're responsibilities, and what we own very quickly begins to own us.

At a rough guess, storing the stuff in my house would cost a couple of thousand pounds a year. Had I chosen that option, I would have spent a small fortune. Luckily, my voice of inner wisdom kept saying, "Simplify." I'd come to this point of view in part from books I'd read about minimalist living and as a result of clearing the stuff from my dad's house after he passed away. I saw the colossal number of things he'd hoarded in the belief that they might "come in handy" one day. It took my brother and me a whole day to put the entire contents of his desk, cupboards, drawers, and garden shed into dozens of large plastic refuse sacks, which we then took to the municipal dump. Who is likely to have to deal with the stuff you'll leave when your time is up?

Clearly, we all have the tendency to acquire way more stuff than we need. Minimalist living, as a concept, seemed to be a perfect antidote to excessive consumption and global warming. A vision started to emerge in my mind. I decided to simplify everything and take just a few essential items with me on my journey. When I imagined letting go, it felt liberating and confirmed this was the right way to go.

I now had to sell or give away my stuff to people who really wanted or needed it. I made a list of every item in the house and circulated it via email to family and friends, with pictures, descriptions, and suggested prices. A few of them took things from the list and whatever they didn't want, I sold on eBay. I gave away the few small items that were left. I boxed up my personal effects, a few books, mementos, and some items of clothing, and took them to my mum's house for storage in her attic.

I'd cleared my stuff in readiness to go travelling. Through doing it, I accidentally and unexpectedly discovered how good it felt to reduce my personal footprint in the world. It had raised my awareness about consumption, and I saw for the first time how much waste I'd created in the massive number of things I'd acquired. Tragically, a lot of hard work and money had been squandered on those things, which, for the most part, had only brought temporary or incremental pleasure.

By the end of October 2005, the house was sold and all my stuff had gone. It took me about three months to deconstruct my entire life. Just in case my choice to be a traveller turned out to be a disaster, I stored my laptop, car, and much cherished Triumph motorcycle for safekeeping in London. They would be useful if I made an early U-turn back to my familiar life.

My property agent eventually came to collect my keys to the house. I made one final, emotional tour of my silent, empty home as I left. Breathing in and out slowly, I walked through every room, picturing as many happy events as I could recall throughout my time there, as well as a few that were not so happy. I felt an overwhelming sense of gratitude to the Universe, or higher power, if you prefer, for my time there. Like all things in life, it had come to an end.

On November 12, 2005, I headed to Heathrow Airport ready for an adventure, with one bag containing about twenty-two kilos of stuff, my passport, and credit cards.

"The most important kind of freedom is to be what you really are. You trade in your reality for a role. You trade in your sense for an act. You give up your ability to feel, and in exchange, put on a mask. There can't be any large-scale revolution until there's a personal revolution, on an individual level. It's got to happen inside first."

Jim Morrison

Chapter Three
From Business Leader to Backpacker

LOGISTICALLY, I WAS PREPARED FOR THE EXPECTED AND DRAMATIC CHANGE in lifestyle after leaving my large West London house to live out of a backpack in Thailand. However, it quickly became obvious that I wasn't well prepared at all, mentally or emotionally. When my eleven-hour flight from Heathrow landed at Don Muang Airport in Bangkok, I was reluctant to leave my warm, cosy aircraft seat. You know those times, like when you're all snugly and tucked up in bed at the weekend? You don't really want to get up, even though your best friend is coming round for lunch. You know there's tons to do, but you stay in bed as long as you can before you finally surrender and drag yourself out?

I stepped out of the air-conditioned aircraft and had to accept I was no longer in London. I was no longer living in a spotless and pristine house serviced by a Brazilian cleaning lady twice a week, with a managed garden and no end of conveniences close at hand to make my life easy. My former character had been written out of my script, and there was no new character to replace him yet. One part of me didn't want to let go of the privileged life I'd enjoyed as Ray the Businessman. I was like a sugar addict who'd decided to stop eating chocolate but had hidden three Snickers in a kitchen cupboard in preparation for a future moment of weakness. Whilst it felt good to be living in a more minimalist way, I'd be lying if I didn't confess that the thought of staying in a grubby Thai backpacker hostel made my gut ache.

As I walked down the steps to disembark, the sauna-like temperature and humidity of Asia hit me full-on. Within two minutes, I was sweating as my body tried to adjust to the hot, sticky, and unfamiliar Thai climate. Coming from London in mid-November, it was like I'd arrived on a different planet. Inside the noisy, chaotic, and dilapidated terminal building, I headed to my connecting flight whilst the voice inside my head frantically squawked, *What have you done? What the hell have you done? Are you sure this was a good idea?*

Despite all that, another part of me felt curious and excited about this radical change. I'd never been a backpacker before, so I was totally unfamiliar with the world of hostels. My fear about how bad they might be was based entirely on a scene from *The Beach*, a nineties film starring a young Leonardo DiCaprio. He meets a shady character in Bangkok who reveals the whereabouts of a secret island to him. The hostel where they met had a dark, filthy, dilapidated dormitory containing about twenty rickety, steel-framed bunkbeds with heavily stained mattresses covered in torn, grubby sheets. They were occupied by a few sweaty, smelly, semi-drunk, semi-stoned hippies with dreadlocks and tattoos, sleeping or rolling joints while a rusty, three-bladed metal fan slowly whirred away on the ceiling overhead. The dorm had two cold showers and only one toilet, which didn't flush and looked like it was last cleaned in 1972. It doubled up as home to a colony of cockroaches.

The image of that crappy hostel imprinted on my brain made me feel squeamish. My former life seemed like a million miles away. In that life, most people are trading up from low budget towards more comfort and luxury as they get older, and stay in nicer, more expensive hotels. I felt like I was driving the wrong way down a one-way street. But although I may have been travelling in contraflow to the majority, I was excitedly going backwards towards an experience I'd completely missed during my youth.

Unlike most of my friends at the time, I never went to university and never experienced taking a gap year. That's when it's perfectly normal to travel budget and camp, or sleep in hostel dorm beds for a couple of pounds a night. Life had gifted me an opportunity to collect a missing piece of personal experience from the jigsaw puzzle of my own history. *This* was my gap year, happening right now, unfolding in front of me. I actually felt grateful to be doing it as an older, wiser, and more experienced person.

On the other hand, at my age and with no experience as a solo traveller, I was the proverbial fish out of water. The majority of backpackers were in their mid-twenties. How was I going to get along with them? What would be required from me as I transitioned into my new life as a budget traveller? To ponder these questions and avoid the risk of freaking myself out, I planned to spend my first four days renting a brand new, private, luxury pool villa in a small village called Lamai on the tiny island of Koh Samui. Even though it was more expensive than a hostel and I'd exceed my planned daily budget, it gave me an opportunity to gently get used to

LIFE WITHOUT A TIE

being in Asia without having to suffer too many shocks to my system.

Annie

My transfer flight from Bangkok to Koh Samui took an hour. I arrived in Lamai to be welcomed by my new girlfriend, Annie, who was waiting at the villa for me. It was great to see her, and I felt thrilled about the days ahead. Let me briefly take you back about six months to the moment we met. It was at a business networking event above a pub in Clerkenwell, London. When we were introduced, I thought she was gorgeous. She was an actress and was relaxed, fit, and suntanned. It was a year after my divorce, and I'd begun to feel like I could handle a relationship again. I commented on how well she looked and asked how come she was so tanned.

"I've just come back from a wonderful, extended vacation in Thailand. I loved it so much, I've decided to move out of my flat in London and go and live there for a while."

Despite having known her less than ten minutes, I was disappointed as it seemed to rule out any possibility of us hooking up. When Annie described what daily life in Thailand was like, what she'd said made sense. She enjoyed the relaxed, carefree feeling she'd experienced there. It sounded amazing, yet I didn't think this lifestyle was an option for me. I was also evaluating my own future and believed that my life would remain rooted in London. No matter, there was definitely a lovely connection in my exchange with Annie, and I wanted to get to know her better, despite the fact she'd planned to leave. Instinctively, the timing of our meeting seemed important. Maybe the Universe had her cross my path for a reason? I had no idea why.

A couple of days later, we met again. We went to the cinema to see a movie called *Sideways*. Ironically, it's a comedy drama about a heavily depressed, divorced guy who's desperate to get a book published! He constantly laments what he hasn't achieved in life and eventually meets a woman who is willing to accept him for who he is. It's a touching story. Seeing the film with Annie made it easier to talk honestly with her about my own divorce. We had a long and humorous conversation about it. Being with her felt effortless, natural, and engaging. Perhaps it was because we both assumed there was no way we could end up in a relationship. Whatever the reason, it felt great.

We met a few more times as she prepared for her departure. I'm not sure what you would call our encounter, perhaps a wonderful fling. We were grateful for the intimacy we'd experienced in those precious few weeks. Surprisingly, it was actually me who left England first. As explained in chapter two, I'd made arrangements to stay with the Taylor family in Sydney before I'd met Annie. She gave me a good reason to change my mind, but my desire to go to Australia was strong and soon, it was time for me to go. Annie would depart for Thailand while I was away, so we said goodbye, knowing it would be for good. We didn't expect to see each other again.

About four months later, when I returned to London after my triumphant performance in *Out of Order*, my mindset was more expanded than the one I'd left with. The experience of being George Pigden blew my mind, and my vision of what was possible had irrevocably changed. I was ready to consider a way of living that was totally different from the one I was familiar with, one much closer to the one Annie had described. It surprised me to discover that Annie hadn't left for her new life yet.

Her departure had been delayed due to complications with the plumbing in her apartment. She couldn't rent the place out until that was fixed, and it had taken ages. Her misfortune meant we could spend another evening together. Had the Universe somehow intended this to happen so that we'd meet again? She'd often been in my thoughts while I was in Australia, and I liked her immensely. Perhaps the Universe was giving me the chance to express these feelings to her. Over dinner, she announced she was almost ready to go. I felt an urge to open up and lay my cards on the table. Even though she'd soon be gone, I wanted to explore the possibility of a joint future. But I held back and avoided the conversation.

I did that for a good reason. A few weeks after we met, I'd gently ventured into this territory with Annie, and she made it crystal clear she wanted to leave the UK with no baggage or complications. Despite feeling disappointed, that made complete sense when I looked at it from her perspective, and I had no issue accepting it. As far as I was aware, nothing had changed for her since then, which made it seem pointless to take the risk of suggesting it again. I kept my feelings to myself and dodged the possibility of being rejected.

One week later, she hosted her farewell party, which gave me the opportunity to finally say goodbye. I was sad we were going in different directions and wanted to get it over and done with. After an hour or so, I said goodbye and decided to leave. Unexpectedly, as I had one foot out the door, Annie asked if she could see my video recording of *Out of Order*. She was an actress and wanted to see how my debut had turned out and offer me feedback. To avoid the feeling of loss, I'd gone into a state of withdrawal but reluctantly agreed. I returned the next day to her apartment. She watched the play and then, much to my surprise, she opened up and laid her cards on the table for me.

"I've changed my mind about you, Ray. While you were in Australia, I kept thinking how good it would be if we were more involved, but I don't feel that I know you well enough to travel together. That's making it difficult for me to ask if you'd like to join me and come to Thailand."

Join her? Her courageous and welcome admission was an unexpected, life-changing moment. It instantly opened up a new possibility, a fork in the road. For the first time, I considered becoming a traveller, just as Julie had suggested. Annie's offer was from the heart, and it reached right into mine. She planned to spend the next year or so in Thailand and complete her trip in Australia the following Christmas. Then she'd either return to England or invent a new plan for herself.

The more I imagined it, the more appealing it seemed. It would be the perfect transition out of my life in London. It would help me become a new version of myself and reboot my journey. It was a defining moment. Responding to her openhearted stance and throwing caution to the wind, I made a bold suggestion. "Why don't you move in with me while my house is being sold? It'll probably take a few weeks, which is more than enough time for us to get to know how we feel about each other. If we don't get on well, we'll find out soon enough."

You might think this was a risky decision. But I'd witnessed Nic Meredith, a close friend of mine in a similar situation a year before, and it worked out perfectly well for him. He'd been my companion on a road trip in California and Arizona three years earlier. We'd visited a small town called Sedona to connect with an old friend called Paul, who'd lived there for over a decade. Paul knew loads of local people and introduced us to a few of them. Nic was in an open, expanded state of mind and relished the opportunity to engage with new people in Paul's community. One of them, a sassy female journalist and TV presenter, made a particularly strong impression on him, and they connected instantly. To cut a very long story short, less than a year later, they were married, and he moved to the USA for good. Witnessing that chain of events had deeply enriched my own sense of optimism and belief in the power of universal guidance. I figured this would help us explore the reality of what a shared life might be like. It was a kind of trial period that I hoped would satisfy the need on both sides for more certainty. Of course, there was a risk that even if we got on well in the house, we might not survive as a couple on the road, but I was willing to take that risk.

People say that travelling with a partner 24/7 for long periods is enough to test even the best relationships, but neither of us knew that from personal experience. The downside seemed small and the upside massive. In my assessment, the best-case scenario could be true love, happy-ever-after. The worst-case scenario was that we would separate somewhere down the road, hopefully as good friends, dust ourselves off emotionally and continue independently with our own journeys. I was definitely up for it.

Annie accepted my proposal and moved in. She arrived at my house with her backpack and yoga mat, and our trial period began. Most days, she did her own thing while I dealt with matters related to my business and the impending sale of the house. In the evenings, we'd talk, research, and create our future life together. We studied the Lonely Planet guidebook and perused websites provided by other travellers. Our shared purpose made the intensive familiarisation period flow pretty well.

The property market in London was slow in the summer of 2005, and it took around three months to sell my house. This was a blessing in disguise as it gave Annie and me plenty of time to feel happy we could handle the rigours of travelling together. We both felt our relationship was robust enough. I was slightly nervous about becoming an independent traveller. I had no experience and was apprehensive about backpacking alone. Plus, I'd never spent a significant period of time on my own. Both were well outside my comfort zone. As a businessman, I was used to being constantly surrounded by people and accustomed to having many of life's logistical matters taken care of. Annie was almost the opposite. She had plenty of experience solo travelling and knew how it all worked. She was fiercely independent. Sharing the journey with her would help me bridge my confidence gap.

We drew up a rough itinerary and plan for eighteen months. We'd travel around Asia for about a year, exploring Thailand, Laos, Cambodia, and

Vietnam. We had plenty of flexibility and figured that spontaneity would play a big part in our decisions. Maybe we'd want to stay longer in some places and cut short our time in others. Maybe we'd uncover some fascinating diversions on the way. We took any pressure off ourselves to rigidly follow our itinerary. One thing we knew for sure was that Annie's entire extended family would be in Perth, Australia for Christmas, 2006, which gave us just over a year to do our own thing before joining them for the celebrations.

After two months at my house, Annie left for Thailand. I remained to complete the sale and deal with loose ends, including shipping out items I'd sold. Our realities can shift in such a short period of time when we're truly open to and ready for change. Without any stuff, I felt so light, free, and optimistic. This was a truly liberating period. It felt like my new life was finally beginning.

Having been apart for a month, I felt thrilled to see Annie again and enjoyed those first four days at our luxury pool villa in Lamai. It was a bubble world for a moment, a brief time-out before my new life *really* started. There was plenty to embrace regarding lifestyle adjustments and each time I encountered an opportunity, it disturbed me. For example, the food in Thailand was nothing like I was used to eating back in England. I absolutely hate spicy food! The climate was uncomfortably hot and the atmosphere intensely humid. Massive thunderstorms and torrential rainfall frequently occurred, which led to flooding. That meant constantly getting wet and coming under attack from hundreds of mosquitoes.

If you've been to Thailand, you'll know the pace and attitude to life there is totally different to what you'd expect in a Western city. Unlike London, everyone is welcoming, friendly, and smiles at you the whole time. That's not the only difference. When I ordered food in a Thai restaurant, I rarely received what I'd actually asked for and that took a bit of getting used to. Often, the dessert would arrive before the main course. When Annie and I ate together, there was often a fifteen to twenty-minute gap between one meal arriving and the other. The locals calmly and happily accept this. In my first few days, I noticed how much these differences agitated or annoyed me, and I struggled to accept the reality. I wasn't used to this laidback way of life. Sometimes, the voice of my inner critic would protest. *Don't these Thai people know who I am? Don't they realise that I was somebody important in England?* These thoughts made me aware of how tightly wound I was. The unsavoury parts of my personality came to the surface more often than I care to admit. It quickly dawned on me that a different set of rules applied to virtually everything and that I'd have to adjust. I saw a need for some kind of psychological framework that would help me to accept and embrace a wide range of changes to my expectations and be at peace with it. Without it, I was going to struggle. With it, there was every chance that I could thrive during the next few months.

Transitions

If you've suffered a major loss, such as a separation or divorce, or been made unemployed, you'll know how challenging it can be to let go of your old situation, suffering the confusing nowhere of in-betweenness, before you can launch forth again into something new. This experience isn't uncommon. In his best-selling book, *Managing Transitions*, William Bridges, a leading authority on the subject, talks about the three stages of any transition: the ending, the neutral zone, and the new beginning. Bridges explains that each stage must be understood and embraced, and the worst thing you can do is to try and accelerate the process beyond the speed that naturally feels right.

That made sense to me. A caterpillar weaves itself into a cocoon to complete its transition into a butterfly. First, the caterpillar must bring an end to the form of life it's known. Then there's an indeterminate period of waiting, a neutral zone during which it appears as if nothing much is happening. Finally, when that period is naturally complete, a butterfly emerges and begins life anew. The whole journey has its own pace and can't be interfered with or accelerated.

According to Bridges, each transition in our lives can be experienced as a "mini-death." We need to let go of a part of us. As my life on the road started, my old personality was dying, which felt both frightening and liberating. I had no idea what would be on the other side of the transition or how long it might take. I sensed it was vitally important simply to recognise the process for what it was and honour myself fully by observing it without trying to interfere with it too much.

During my first month in Koh Samui, Annie volunteered most days at a yoga school run by her friend. I spent most of my time alone. My daily life consisted of hanging out, drinking coffee, and talking to other travellers. While it was enjoyable, I also felt an unexpected sense of worthlessness and guilt. I'd somehow managed to escape the mainstream life I'd had in England. I had no work to do, no deadlines to hit, no clients to meet, or targets to reach. I literally had nothing to do. So, I was no longer paying my membership dues to society through taxes. Neither was I contributing anything useful.

It was the first time in my entire adult life that I'd been in that position; totally free of any obligation and with one hundred percent discretion over how to use my time. It gave rise to a feeling of inertia. I was a well-funded explorer without a mission, compass, or map. I faced the future with a sense of huge uncertainty. With no need to conform to the rules that dictated my former life, I had no idea who I was.

According to Bridges, being in a transition is different from simply going through a change. Transition refers to the inner process through which people come to terms with a change. You let go of the way things used to be and reorient yourself to the way that things are now. In business, I'd helped many clients manage transitions at different times, supporting them to make that difficult process less painful and disruptive. Now it was my turn to navigate the same challenge. I felt a bit like a pro-golf instructor who suddenly finds himself competing in a tournament with top players. It's one thing to teach others, yet something entirely different to apply the wisdom to yourself.

Eighteen months had passed since my divorce, and I was living beside a beach in Thailand with a lovely new woman. You might say that should be more than enough to feel completely happy. Yet I was still haunted by my failure as a husband. Self-critical thoughts were going round my mind in a constant loop. *I should have done better at that. I am such a loser. I was the worst husband ever.*

Thinking this way made me feel anxious and the pressure heavier. I kept asking myself, *How can I get over this?* It literally felt like a high wall blocked my path, and I was struggling to climb over it. Since then, I've spoken to many people who have experienced a divorce or painful breakup, and many described it in similar ways—like a barrier across their path, a big hole open at their feet, or a disruption of their plans. All of us were looking for a way to get over it.

Support Structures
Fifteen years as an aircraft pilot taught me that it's vital to have procedures

and routines. Together, they provide a valuable support structure which ensures you always have safe and trouble-free journeys when you leave the ground. As the pilot in command, it was down to me to maintain a calm and resourceful state, if and when I was faced with a challenging or unexpected event. For example, if there's an engine failure during a flight, it's not an insurmountable problem. The worst thing you can do is panic and become emotionally charged as that would severely impact your ability to be rational and calmly figure out the best course of action. If you've seen the movie *Sully*, you'll know what I'm talking about.

All pilots learn how to remain calm in stressful situations through the disciplined application of two routines: procedures and checklists. Engine failure after take-off? Get out the checklist for that scenario and follow the procedure. Have to make a forced landing? Out comes the checklist for that situation. These procedures are drilled repetitively during training and give you a powerful psychological safety net. If something unexpected happens, you don't have to waste time or energy figuring out *what* to do. The checklists contain predetermined actions for each scenario. The pilot simply has to execute the sequence of actions for the safest outcome possible.

To create some order in my new life, I decided to apply this approach to my challenge as a nomadic traveller. I was terrified a letter might arrive for me in London to inform me that I'd failed to submit a form required by the government or had missed a vital payment back home. And faced with new and different routines, customs, social norms, language, culture, and environments in Asia, there was considerable potential each day for something unexpected to trigger a stress response. I wanted to be consciously prepared for these events. Otherwise, I might end up blowing my top and causing some serious trouble. I started to use checklists to manage my life on the road. It's worth mentioning that my journey began before social media had really taken off. In 2005, without Facebook, simply remembering the birthdays of all my loved ones, something I have always made an effort to do, was more logistically challenging than it is now.

Using internet café computers, I built an Excel spreadsheet to record everything I spent and kept it on a USB stick. That helped me to manage my financial resources carefully and be sure I kept within the budgets I'd set for myself. It gave me peace of mind and a sense of control.

LIFE WITHOUT A TIE

Not only that, I added up the total amount I'd spent each week, and it was generally less than I'd budgeted for. That made me feel optimistic, because accumulating a surplus meant I could put those resources to good use later, should an unexpected opportunity or emergency arise. In more recent times, many apps have become available to manage things like this, as the smartphone has become the tool of choice for people on the move. None of that was available when I began my journey.

Next, I built a checklist for managing tasks to remove any worry that an important action might fall through the cracks and cause me a serious problem overseas. The list included things like my driver's license and passport renewal dates, insurance policy expirations, and credit card information. My dormant consulting business still required some of my attention. It continued to function as a legal entity, and I received enquiries from potential customers for months after I departed. I put procedures in place to deal with those and to maintain contact with a small network of trusted associates to make sure actions were taken in a professional and timely manner.

My Excel spreadsheet worked so well, I continuously expanded it. Initially designed as a checklist to manage my expenses, it became the control mechanism for my entire life. Using a five-year rolling calendar, I created an inventory that contained every license, document, contract, subscription renewal, tax return, credit card, and key relationship for myself and my business. I made a note of any action that would be required for each in the future, as far out on the horizon as I could see. I updated it once a week, which took about twenty minutes, and I could then see any item that required an action for that week. It took a few days to identify and capture *everything*, and when it was done, my sense of relief was huge. I had virtually one hundred percent certainty that, logistically, everything needed to support the function of my life was taken care of and planned for.

Now I was completely free to allocate my attention to life in the present, to fully enjoy what was right in front of me without having to spend a single moment worrying. It was like having a personal assistant take care of every tiny detail regarding the bureaucracy, systems, and demands of the external world. My brother agreed to deal with all my physical mail in England. He scanned it and emailed copies of anything that needed my immediate attention, providing me with further relief from worry as he was a safe pair of hands I could rely on.

My support system worked well, and I still actively use it every day. If you're not the kind of person who is, or even likes to be, well organised, and all this sounds incredibly daunting to you, my intention isn't to scare you. I'm sure you'll inevitably find your way to take care of the bureaucratic infrastructure of your life. If you're able to cope with emotions that may arise from unexpected hassles, like the expiry of one of your key documents or credit cards, you may not need a system like mine. No matter where on Earth you go, it's virtually impossible in the digital age to untether yourself from all of the legal, financial, and logistical systems that we depend on for our mobility, and that has to be managed in whatever way works best for you.

With my logistics under control, my attention and awareness turned towards my inner world. My psychological needs weren't clear in the early days of my journey. There were few reference points for people in my situation, living without any aspect of my life tied down and with no obligations or commitments. I didn't know anyone I could relate my experiences to or turn to for advice when my internal state of mind was below par. I wanted to maintain my best and most resourceful state mentally. You can't underestimate how important this is during a major transition.

Any information I found on the internet on this topic was of limited use. Instead, I chose to rely on my own experience, my intuitive guidance system, or *gut feeling*, and construct a belief system that would support and empower me during my transition and help navigate the unknown future ahead. It was a tricky thing to do, like trying to draw a map of a territory I'd never visited or seen any images of. I felt like a scientist in a laboratory. My intention was to form hypotheses and use them to run behavioural experiments in my daily life as events unfolded. I wanted to observe the results, review and refine as necessary. It was a bit weird doing this, as I'd be the subject of the experiments as well as the observer. Have you ever experienced a time like this in your own life?

Australian blogger Lina Wynn articulated this beautifully in one of her posts. "Imagine driving at night in very thick fog with almost no visibility. It's certainly unsettling and scary to drive in those conditions. Attempting to see further by turning on your high beam lights only makes the situation worse, as it causes an instant wall of bright fog to be reflected in front of the car. You can't just stop because you might get hit by the car behind you. You have to move forward, slowly and cautiously. The way to get through the fog is to, in fact, use your normal low beam lights and just focus on what lies ahead, one white line at a time. Even if you can only see one metre ahead, as long as your car moves forward and your lights stay on, the next small stretch of road will reveal itself."

Ten Principles of Life Without a Tie

It was still early in my journey, and it dawned on me there was little point in worrying about what might lie ahead. Why not take one step at a time and trust the path will unfold? That seemed like a great experiment to conduct in my life laboratory. Framing it like that helped get my psyche under control, in the same way that the Excel spreadsheet had helped with my logistics. It's only in hindsight that I've been able to articulate the ten principles that guided me. They gradually evolved over time as I experimented with each one in different situations. You'll find stories with examples of how I applied these principles throughout the rest of the book but for now, let me explain what they are.

1. Presence

Whatever events were coming, I wanted to learn from them and be deeply changed by my journey. I committed to being fully present to each experience as they were happening, accept each one, and be grateful. I didn't want to be distracted by worries about the past, or the future, or fear of missing out on a different experience elsewhere. I'd always made long-term plans, set goals and targets, and worked tenaciously to achieve them, so I'd been used to living with my awareness and attention almost entirely on the future. My happiness had been dependent on the achievement of my goals. I'd rarely allowed myself to live fully in the present and simply enjoy it for what it was without any thought for what I might gain or lose. I recognised this was now a constraint. In your life, how often are you fully present in the moment without getting lost in thoughts about the past or the future?

2. Self-acceptance

People say we are our own worst critics, and that's especially true for me. When I left England, I was really hard on myself and felt ashamed

I'd failed as a husband. There was a huge gap between the perfect person I should be and the not-so-great person I thought I was. I committed to making no judgments about myself, no matter what I was thinking or feeling at any given moment. This was a departure in my thinking and especially important when things weren't flowing well. Can you recall a time when you experienced a similar gap in which you judged yourself as not good enough? How did it make you feel?

3. Non-attachment

In chapter four, you'll find out about a Buddhist monastery I stayed in, which was a significant event on my path. During a ten-day, silent meditation retreat there, I truly understood what the cycle of human anxiety, or suffering as the Buddhists call it, is all about. All human beings tend to seek pleasurable feelings or outcomes which lead to them. That leads to fixation on something specific, perhaps an object, person, or role which we crave. Craving leads to an expectation that our desire will be satisfied when we attain the thing we crave. In most cases, our desire is satiated only for a short while before more cravings arise as the effect wears off. The cycle repeats itself and is known in the Buddhist teachings as delusional thinking. Do you recognise this cycle? Can you think of a time recently where you were caught up in it? I committed to observe this in myself and let go of my attachments to specific outcomes as much as I could.

4. Wisdom

Rather than follow the guidance of others, I committed to trusting my own experience when making decisions. This way of life was unknown to me; I'd constantly referenced other people for their advice, opinions, thoughts, and ideas about what I should do as different decisions presented themselves. I sometimes felt dependent on others and a bit embarrassed that I couldn't resolve simple dilemmas myself. Seasoned travellers I met advised me to trust my inner voice in these matters. So I took it upon myself to practice turning up the volume of my inner voice, decipher the messages, and act accordingly. I'd actually been pretty good at doing this when I ran my business.

My intention for this practice was to expand my ability and desire to make choices where there was fear attached. Trusting and allowing others to help me had been important at the start of the journey. Yet even then, the voice of my inner wisdom was speaking to me and letting me know that there was a great opportunity to establish a stronger, clearer, and permanently accessible connection with it. Is there an area in your life right now where you could trust your own inner wisdom more than you do?

5. Lightness

Before this experimental journey began, I'd been through the toughest and most challenging period of my life, emotionally speaking. I felt tired from carrying the heavy burden of sadness, anger, and disappointment. I wanted to lighten up. So I committed to not taking myself, my physical journey, or my inner personal journey too seriously. By redirecting my attention towards the light, I could generate mindful energy, which would transform this feeling of heaviness. Pilots know that aircraft always take off into the wind for maximum lift. This was a perfect metaphor. Can you recall times in your life where you felt and/or chose to bring more lightness to your way of being? Can you think of an area right now where you could apply it?

6. Modesty/Frugality

You could have described my London lifestyle as affluent. I had a high income from running a profitable business and spared no expense on entertainment, buying clothes, household goods, meals out, gifts, and holidays. I was accustomed to the high life and the feeling of elevated status that gave me. As a traveller, I saw the need for greater consciousness around consumption and status. I wondered what conditions were essential for true happiness. I had already set a modest daily budget and was living within my means. I wanted to get by with a lot less money and still feel great on the inside.

This aspect of my experimental life also brought a kind of integrity to the experience, making it more authentic. I monitored my financial resources and scrutinised every single expense and checked inwardly to confirm if I genuinely needed whatever it was. Maybe you can review your consumer expenses and ask yourself what would happen if you were to reduce or even eliminate a couple of them? What do you truly need to spend money on, and what is taking more of your resources than necessary?

7. *Minimalism*

The experience of selling or letting go of all my worldly possessions before I left liberated me. For the first time in years, I owned virtually nothing except the gear I was travelling with. To preserve and expand that feeling, I committed to maintaining a pack weight of twenty-two kilos, max. I placed a self-imposed embargo on purchasing any unnecessary items such as souvenirs, fashion clothes and footwear, tech gadgets etcetera. The only purchases I'd allow were the replacement of items in my existing kit as needed.

I wanted to go through a kind of drying out process and permanently free myself from the mindless addiction to consumption I'd had in England. Instead, my focus regarding the acquisition of anything new would be on learning new skills, gaining knowledge, and creating new experiences. What are you addicted to when it comes to buying stuff? What items in your life would you consider truly essential?

8. *Connection*

In Bronnie Ware's book, she highlights that a common regret people have at the end of their life is that they hadn't stayed in touch with close friends who drifted away. I had a huge desire to remain connected with my most valuable friends and members of my family back home. The exchange of energy in those relationships was a source of power and aliveness for me. I committed to maintain a schedule of calls using Skype to connect with everyone on a regular basis. In the early days, it was more challenging than I'd bargained for. Not many people I knew used Skype in 2005, and even if they did, the seven-hour time difference between Asia and the UK made it difficult to reach many of them. That gave me a great opportunity to practice patience, understanding, and acceptance.

Relationships are a two-way thing and not everyone who knew me wanted to make the same commitment. It gradually became clear over time which relationships were sustainable and valuable. Later on in my journey, social media sites like Facebook completely changed the way we stay in touch. You may have lived as an ex-pat or travelled for long periods and be able to relate to this. Even if you haven't, was there a time in your life when you realised who the truly important people to you were, as opposed to those you were willing to allow to drift away from your path?

9. Contribution

I wanted to find at least one way to make a valuable contribution to others—my community of friends, family members, and people I met on the journey—and committed to writing a blog. My intention was to share the learning from my journey. I took plenty of photographs and posted updates on a regular basis. I carried a video camera with me wherever I went and spontaneously asked other travellers if they'd let me interview them. I asked them about what led to their decision to leave home and try life on the road, and how they defined a successful life. I learned a lot from their answers.

Later on, my commitment to this principle led to the creation of a global fundraising effort that continues to raise money for worthy causes around the world. I have written more about this in chapters nine and ten. This is particularly important to me, as I understand the power of generosity and kindness and how it can help people heal things that trouble them. My father went out of his way to help anyone he could during his life. It was only when he died that I truly appreciated that. He committed himself to contribute to others and inspired me to do the same. What part does contribution play in your life? In what other ways would you like to contribute more?

10. Health

If you're a foreigner abroad, medical issues can become very complex and expensive. I took out a medical insurance policy, which covered me for most eventualities and brought peace of mind. Maintaining my own health and physical well-being was something I hadn't been particularly good at in England. For years, I'd refused to accept that area of my life would require increasingly more attention, especially as I got older. In the year leading up to my departure, it had slowly started to change. I realised that my body wouldn't take care of itself. Shortly after my forty-third birthday, I'd started work with a dedicated fitness coach. I was about twenty-five pounds overweight at the time, with no real awareness about the effects that insufficient sleep, excessive alcohol, poor food choices, and virtually no exercise had on me.

Backpacking is intensely physical, especially trekking and climbing. I wanted to do a great deal of both, so I needed to continue the training regime I'd started in London. I committed to regular workouts, physical activities, and hikes. In towns, I walked or cycled rather than using motorised transport. Adopting a regular practice of exercise raised my awareness of my body and helped me avoid situations that might threaten my mobility. What steps could you take right now to take better care of your own health?

New Realities

As you'll discover in the pages that follow, I had plenty of opportunities to experiment with and apply these ten principles. An early test in the practice of frugality came in December 2005. Annie and I spent our first Christmas together on the island of Koh Pangan in the Gulf of Thailand. We found a tiny bamboo hut on the beach that was available for rent. It was relatively cheap at less than five pounds per day, and definitely at the low end of my budget. The huts don't have running hot water, which is one of the reasons they cost so little. To demonstrate to Annie that I was committed to live by my ten principles, I joyfully accepted our cheaper accommodation and consoled myself that at least we'd saved some money.

I faced the daunting prospect of my first cold shower that would be the first of many in my journey, and to my spoiled, over-privileged, self-important Western persona, that felt impossible to accept. I resisted it for a day, then two, and then three! Eventually, after nearly four days, I was repelled by my own body odour. I surrendered and reluctantly forced myself to endure the ice-cold water as it pounded my head and shoulders while I gasped for breath. Annie chuckled away as I cursed. In the days that followed, I was more able to enjoy it as my body adjusted.

Cold showers aside, I loved spending Christmas on the beach of a tropical paradise island. It was basic, yet beautiful, like a Robinson Crusoe experience. My inner hippy started to emerge. On Christmas Day, it felt liberating to sit on the sand in my khaki shorts and Christmas hat and exchange presents with Annie. We were living the dream. It was a million miles away from the traditional family events I'd been used to in England at my former in-laws' house in Surrey. The contrast confirmed I was truly on a different path now. Life was so simple; just wake up when the sun rises, sleep when it gets dark, and eat, drink, and play in between.

When you reflect on the ten principles I've listed here, you might notice that health appears at the bottom. To a certain extent, this reflected how much importance, relative to the other nine, I allocated to it when my journey began. After a couple of months, I was involved in a climbing accident on the island of Koh Tao. I fell and badly cut my left arm around my elbow. I wrapped a bandage around it and the following day, thought I'd cleanse the wound by taking a dip in the ocean. About four days later, I discovered that this was a terrible mistake. When I got back to my room after that swim, my arm began to swell and get hotter. At first, I didn't think there was anything seriously wrong. I put some ice in a towel and wrapped it around my arm. It continued to swell and twenty-four hours later, I felt sick and had a high temperature. Disturbingly, my left forearm was now nearly twice the size it should be. Clearly, something was seriously wrong, so I took myself to a small medical clinic on Sairee Beach. Koh Tao is a tiny island that you can walk around in a few hours. The medical facilities are limited, and there was only space for five beds in the clinic.

After being examined by a doctor, my suspicions were confirmed. Exposing the open wound to seawater had seriously infected it, causing my arm to swell. They advised me to check myself in immediately, which I did. The doctor told me that had I waited a day longer, an amputation might've been on the cards. When that sank in, I was shocked and grateful in equal proportions. I stayed in the clinic for four days. Fortunately, the expenses were covered by my insurance. That experience scared the hell out of me, especially as I had little else to think about as I lay in my hospital bed.

Up until then, I'd mainly thought about how to navigate the challenges to my psyche. This event made me push that to one side as it dawned on me just how precious my physical body was. It provided the base foundation for everything. Mobility was *the* most valuable commodity, more so than money or goods. Without mobility, the dream of being a nomad would remain just that. You may not be surprised to hear that after this insight, my health and well-being became a high priority and pretty much remains so to this day.

After my recovery, I thought more about ways to stay connected with my community of family and friends around the world. Getting injured made me realise my own physical fragility. The absence of anyone to look out for me, other than Annie, reminded me how far away from home and out of contact with my loved ones I was. I saw there were people writing journals on the internet. They were commonly referred to as bloggers, the first inhabitants of a new territory called the digital or online world that was unknown to the majority of people. These innovative pioneers had taken steps outside of the analogue world I was so familiar with, opening up the possibility of learning about people you'd probably never meet. The stuff they were publishing was so interesting and informative too.

In 2005, the internet was nothing like it is today. My only exposure to it had been in my business, which had needed a decent, usable website, and for ad-hoc access to personal banking, and one or two similar services. At that time, there were often days when it was completely unnecessary for me to go online. The internet had yet to become an integrated part of my life. It's hard to imagine life without it now.

To honour my commitment to contribute and stay connected, I decided to launch and write my own blog. I'd left my laptop in the UK, as it would have added two to three kilograms to my pack weight and been at odds with my commitment to minimalism. It's a reflection of that era that I'd deemed it a non-essential item. After several months on the road and the sheer frustration of using inadequate computers in internet cafés—most of which didn't have the software I needed—I had my laptop shipped to me from the UK. It became a necessary item, and it illustrates the fluid nature of how I applied my ten principles.

I spent a while examining other people's blogs, looking at the content, style, and presentation. I looked at the technical platforms they were using to host and present their blog posts and the kind of readers they had. I hatched the idea for my first blog, called *The Daily Lama*, in November 2005. Initially, learning how to use the tools felt like a huge ordeal. With no previous technical experience whatsoever, I was out of my depth and had to be patient, which was a great opportunity to practice self-acceptance. My intention was to provide a simple way for Annie and me to keep our friends and families informed of what was happening as we travelled.

We weren't interested in gloating about the wonderful places we were finding. We wanted to provide our global community with some inspiration, entertainment, and a perspective on historic events from whatever part of the world we were in. And we wanted to share our learning too. That's how we believed we could create value from the journey we were undertaking for our families, friends, and fellow travellers.

The feedback from our readers after our first few posts confirmed we were on the right track, which made us both happy. Unexpectedly, publishing *The Daily Lama* delivered a welcome gift to Annie and me too.

LIFE WITHOUT A TIE

To make it happen, we'd sit down and apply our creative thinking every week to craft words and select pictures for our audience. We had a kind of production meeting over lunch and really put our minds to how we could produce something of quality, but that was more quirky and irreverent than other blogs we'd seen. It became like a gym for us to train and improve our creativity. And it gave us some valuable time together, in which we could enjoy each other's presence. It enriched our relationship immensely.

Blogging to Connect

Annie and I determined that *The Daily Lama* should be written in the third person to give us more scope for humour and tongue-in-cheek silliness. We invented a few fictitious characters and gave them a contract to produce and publish our blog every two to three weeks. We came up with the names of our new editor and his assistant, which had us rolling around on the floor in laughter. Eventually, the job of editor went to Mozzie Byte, and we appointed Amber Solaire as his assistant. Initially, they wrote about our travel life and interviewed us for comments, which they quoted in their articles. They introduced themselves to our tiny audience of readers in our first issue in December 2005.

We decided to include a picture of the two of us holding a huge sign wishing our readers a Merry Christmas. I went off to find paper, card, and pens and brought them back to our room. We took turns drawing different parts of the card, arguing playfully about who should draw and colour each part of our artwork. We were like two five-year-olds watching television at home, arguing about whose turn it was to choose channels with the remote control.

Annie laughed as we played with the crayons. "Look at you! Were you really an award-winning businessman in England? If anyone could see you right now, they wouldn't believe it."

Her observation reflected a noticeable change in the rigid persona I'd built as a businessman. It was in the early stages of cracking, and I was relieved to see it happening. Rediscovering the ability to play like a child felt fantastic!

To give you an idea of just how tongue-in-cheek our blog was, here's the profile that was published to describe Mozzie Byte:

I'm Mozzie, editor of The Daily Lama. I trained in insect

combat at the Arachnid School of Martial Arts in Spain under the auspicious guidance of Master Juan Byte Toomenny. I graduated with a black belt in Swat and Squish. I currently hold the world record, swatting and squishing thirty-five mosquitoes in just under one minute. My record-breaking event took place in a restaurant in southern India in 2004. I'm thrilled to be on board with The Daily Lama and very excited about bringing you all of Ray and Annie's pictures and news.

Mozzie was later joined by a crack team of online journalists from around the world who reported on our travels through the different countries we explored. Included in this all-star line-up were Po Scard and Gran D. Tour, who wrote about our exploration of Asia. In Australia, Chuck Maboomerang provided similar coverage. Nick Elandimer joined the team to cover our travels in the USA.

Occasionally, we'd add specialist correspondents to write additional material. For example, when I started training for my first marathon, which you'll read more about in chapter ten, we gave birth to our Asian fitness correspondent, who faithfully reported to our readers from the gym where I did my workouts. He was flanked by our expert on diet and nutrition. All of these featured journalists had full profiles and pictures to maintain the illusion for our readers that it was being created for us. It may sound silly but doing this provided me with a great opportunity to practice lightness.

Surprisingly, *The Daily Lama* sometimes registered around two thousand page views a month once we were up and running. Not only did I discover that I enjoyed and had a talent for writing, we saw it made a useful and genuine contribution to others. One time, Annie and I were waiting in the queue for a taxi at Bangkok airport during the rush hour. We agreed to share a cab with an Australian couple heading in the same direction. On the way, I mentioned that we wrote a blog and what it was called.

"Really?" they said. "We've been reading that while we've been travelling. It's really good."

We were chuffed. People often say, "It's a small world" when events like that occur. They can happen at any moment in all sorts of different ways. Have you experienced this? When was the last time you did? What happened and how did it make you feel? Perhaps meeting this Australian couple was a confirmation signal from the Universe that we'd created something new and interesting and that people were actually listening. I didn't know for sure, but it was heartwarming to hear.

Caught in the Struggle

The two principles that I most struggled with in the early days of my journey were presence and self-acceptance. My head was constantly full of noisy, unkind, and relentless self-talk that was highly self-critical. In January 2006, after three months on the road, I received news that my ex-wife Charlotte had given birth to her first child, a lovely daughter. I was happy for her but at the same time, it threw me back into a negative spiral of thinking in which I berated myself for not being good enough. The voice in my head made itself heard. *Look at you. You've failed in your marriage, and now you've run away from your life. You should be the one starting a family, working and contributing like everybody else you know. Shame on you for not using your time productively.*

No matter where I was or who I was with, I was distracted and disturbed by these thoughts, like clothes in a washing machine stuck in an endless cycle of tumbling, agitating backwards and forwards. On the plus side, I had my logistics under control. I was getting used to living on a budget, and I'd adapted rapidly to the Thai culture. I'd also realised that my body and health were far more important than I'd first considered. Collectively, these changes helped me see the need for a psychological support structure to cope with the transition I was in, resulting in the ten principles I've described to you.

Nevertheless, they were still largely conceptual. I was in turmoil from processing so much change, and I struggled to apply all of them, all the time. Sometimes, when I was alone, I felt lost and even depressed. My body would actually contract, resulting in chest pains and a lump in my throat as if to confirm my sense of hopelessness. I felt unable to move forward with any confidence and unable to turn back and return to a normal existence. Can you recall a time when you felt like this?

Blog writing and creating short movies with Annie provided some relief from the turmoil, but they weren't an effective antidote. I was searching for something that would allow me to shift my inner state on a more permanent basis. I figured that if I could understand the deepest parts of myself better, I'd see what was keeping me stuck in those patterns of mental suffering, constantly being critical about my past, whilst not having a clear vision for the future. Then perhaps the incessant noise in my head would subside or even stop. And that's when I discovered Vipassana meditation.

Chapter Four
The Practice Of Mindfulness

"We live in a loud and distracting world where silence is increasingly difficult to come by—and that may be negatively affecting our health. In fact, a 2011 World Health Organization report called noise pollution a 'modern plague' concluding that 'there is overwhelming evidence that exposure to environmental noise has adverse effects on the health of the population.' We're constantly filling our ears with music, TV and radio news, podcasts and, of course, the multitude of sounds that we create nonstop in our own heads. Think about it: How many moments each day do you spend in total silence? The answer is probably very few. As our internal and external environments become louder and louder, more people are beginning to seek out silence, whether through a practice of sitting quietly for ten minutes every morning or heading off to a ten-day silent retreat."

Carolyn Gregoire,
Why Silence Is So Good For Your Brain

AT THE BEGINNING OF MY JOURNEY IN 2005, THE ODDS THAT I'D TAKE PART IN A ten-day silent meditation retreat were less likely than Britain leaving the European Union. Back then, mindfulness hadn't attracted anything like the amount of interest it currently does. Meditation was totally alien to me and I had cynical judgments about it, not to mention the kind of people who advocated it. I couldn't recall a time when I'd been silent for more than ten minutes. Not talking to anyone for ten days felt as impossible to imagine as walking across a ravine on a tightrope. Yet I was in Thailand and had committed to spending ten days at the Suan Mokkh International Dharma Hermitage.

This retreat was near Surat Thani in southern Thailand, and I'd been inspired to attend after an illuminating conversation with an Australian traveller called Callum. He'd suggested it as an antidote to the anxiety I'd felt after leaving the comfort zone of my life in London three months earlier. When he described what a Vipassana retreat was like, my body relaxed as I listened. Noticing that, I was keen to explore and learn about mindfulness. I wasn't doing it purely to find some relief from my stressful state, but to also gain insight into what living life true to myself meant. After all, Bronnie Ware had identified that in her book as the number one regret that people have when they die.

The International Dharma Hermitage was founded by a Thai Buddhist monk, the Venerable Ajahn Buddhadāsa in 1989 (the word Ajahn in Thai means teacher). He'd quit the monastic system in Bangkok, where he saw the temples were dirty, crowded, and corrupt, and returned to the south where he dedicated his life to following the pristine dharma. And he succeeded in his quest. The forest monastery he started has become one of the most famous meditation temples in Thailand.

What is dharma? At first, the word sounded strange, and I had no clue what it meant. It's difficult to provide a single, concise definition. According to Wikipedia, there is no equivalent single word translation in Western languages. The meaning depends on the context and has evolved over the centuries. My own definition of dharma is relatively simple. When we learn to drive, we study the Highway Code. It contains the information needed to be a good citizen on the road. Similarly, the dharma is a set of ancient and wise teachings that provide mankind with a code for living well. The code guides us to live our lives peacefully, in harmony with all beings, the planet, and without unnecessary mental suffering. Dharma encompasses ideas such as duty, rights, character, vocation, religion, customs, and all behaviour considered appropriate, correct, or morally upright. In Buddhism, dharma incorporates the teachings and doctrines of its founder, the Buddha. Annie and I came to study and apply those teachings.

About twenty-five thousand people from all over the world have been to Suan Mokkh since they began hosting meditation retreats. They offer a rare opportunity to withdraw from your usual daily routines and activities to a quiet and secluded place where you can devote time for study, contemplation, and meditation. It's set up in such a way that you don't have your attention on anything or anyone else for the entire period.

LIFE WITHOUT A TIE

You can devote the experience totally to yourself. I couldn't recall an opportunity like that when I lived in London. I don't think I'd have wanted it even if it had been offered!

Through learning and applying the practice of meditation, I began to explore and learn more about my inner world. I hoped to know myself better and possibly gain an insight into my fears and positive motivations in life. When I first told Annie that I wanted to experience Vipassana, she said it was her desire too. We'd heard there were strict no-speaking rules inside the monastery and understood it was an essential part of the experience. I was worried that if we were both there at the same time, it might contaminate the purity and power of our individual experiences. My inclination was to go to the monastery alone, as Annie's presence could be a hindrance.

"You know, Annie, if we do this retreat together, I don't want to interfere with or contaminate your experience of it or vice versa. Once we're inside, I think it's best that we don't look at or talk to each other. To get the most out of this, we should totally ignore each other until it's over. Would that be okay with you?"

In case she said no, I was prepared to go alone a month later. She understood where I was coming from and had no problem agreeing. Interestingly, during that conversation I noticed how uncomfortable I felt simply being honest about my needs and communicating them with her. Clearly, the decision to enter and raise my awareness about myself was already beginning, even though the formal retreat had not yet started.

We didn't need to take many things with us into the monastery. We packed some light, comfortable clothes for the meditation sessions, plus basic toiletries, a pair of sandals, and a torch. Mobile phones, music, and books or journals weren't allowed, and we handed them over for safekeeping on arrival. The prohibition of those items seemed harsh at first, but the benefits became clear when the retreat was underway. By fully choosing to consciously remove those distractions, I was more able to look deeply into my own mind. Can you imagine being in a place where it's nothing but you and your thoughts? How would you feel about that?

The accommodation was no frills, basic, and austere. I was given a small, single room with no furniture and a concrete bed covered with a thin straw mat. There was no mattress or cushions, and the pillow was a small, curved wooden block to rest my neck on. Having withstood the challenge of my first cold shower in Koh Pangan a couple of months earlier, I was shocked to discover there were no showers or hot running water of any kind. It was as if time had stood still. Bathing was done the old-fashioned, Asian way, using a bowl to draw water from a large, round Mandi reservoir, which you poured over yourself.

Fortunately, there was toilet paper, which was a relief to my pampered, Western personality! The monks know that most of the foreigners who come are used to their creature comforts and that the complete absence of these will be highly unsettling. By removing these, they intentionally push you out of your comfort zone, which is necessary for growth and a good thing in this context. The monks also forbid the consumption of alcohol or tobacco to ensure you don't intoxicate yourself. I quickly realised the conditions were in place for a powerful experience.

We weren't allowed to bring our own food into the monastery. Instead, two basic but tasty vegetarian meals were provided each day. The reason for this is quite profound. According to the monks, when you look deeply at the meal you are about to eat, you need to see far beyond the rim of the plate. Some types of animal foods can take a dangerous toll on our bodies. For example, processed meats increase the risk of colon cancer and the saturated fat found in meat and dairy products can lead to a higher risk of heart disease.

Then there is the equally dangerous and destructive toll that meat production and dairy farming take on our environment. Researchers at the University of Chicago estimate that switching from red meat and dairy to poultry or eggs for just one day a week could have a measurable impact on global warming and a bigger environmental impact than choosing locally sourced foods. It all sounded reasonable to me, except I was definitely not a vegetarian and actually enjoyed eating meat. Being completely honest, I hadn't bought into the liberal culture when I was a businessman. I hadn't felt a sense of wrongdoing when eating chicken or a well-cooked steak dinner. Going without meat for ten days felt like a big stretch, and I worried that I wouldn't be able to maintain my energy and strength.

The ground rules and daily schedule for the retreat were explained by one of the monks at the start. They'd seen many foreigners turn up over the years who hadn't fully appreciated the discipline that Vipassana requires. Inevitably, many visitors left before the end, depriving others of sought-after places. I quickly realised I'd need to get up early every day and adjust to less sleep. The schedule was mandatory for everybody, and it was slightly comforting to hear that it was gentle because we were beginners. When he said that, I thought, thank God! The daily routine was drastically different to the one I'd had in London just a few months before. Nothing we'd been asked to do sounded that bad to my slightly disturbed, comfort-deprived mind. Then, the killer blow came.

"You will have to deal with much bodily discomfort and will probably experience a lot of ups and downs emotionally during the retreat."

We were warned that we may react with discomfort, restlessness, boredom, doubt, feeling very tired, or any combination of these things. My agitation level rose a notch higher upon hearing this and for a moment, I had second thoughts. Who willingly goes into something knowing it's going to be physically uncomfortable, right? When was the last time you did such a thing?

World-renowned meditation teacher, S. N. Goenka emphasized in his teachings how important it is to get comfortable with one's discomfort without trying to fix it right away. I wanted to learn how to accept discomfort and get to know it closely, instead of pushing it away immediately. Avoiding or suppressing emotions that are seen as negative is a typically Western thing. We tend to think in black and white terms. Emotions we place into a category called happy are welcome, while the unhappy ones are not. I saw the truth of this in my relationship with Annie. When we were getting along well, life felt absolutely great. When we fell out, it was the opposite. At those times, I thought she criticised me, and I responded accordingly, which led to further problems.

The monk checked with me to see if I wanted to leave. I paused long enough to notice a feeling of certainty inside me. This was absolutely the right place to be. No doubt I'd be challenged, but I was ready for it. I confirmed my desire to continue and was taken to my sleeping quarters in the men's dormitory. Women attending the retreat had separate accommodation. I was glad this was the case as travellers tend to socialise in these areas, which might have tempted me to start talking. I wanted to honour the rules around silence.

In my tiny room, I felt a mixture of nervousness and excitement about the next ten days. Vipassana means insight, which one of the monks had described as "seeing things as they *really are*, rather than through the delusions we all have about the nature of reality." Understanding that is what led me to include non-attachment in my ten guiding principles. I wondered what my delusions were. How was I deceiving myself in the way I chose to perceive events and relate to others? What beliefs and attitudes were helping me in my life and which ones had been holding me back? One of the monks had earlier explained that insight meditation cultivates and leads to wisdom and permanent freedom from mental suffering (desire, aversion, and delusion). Hearing that made the effort worthwhile and lessened my fears about the challenge ahead.

Joining Annie and me were about one hundred and twenty people from countries as diverse as Australia, Germany, Israel, Canada, USA, and the Caribbean. We'd hardly any chance to talk to each other before it began. The period of silence maintained throughout the ten days began immediately after the introductory talk, which took place at four p.m. on the day of our arrival.

The Rules for the Retreat
We were asked to observe three basic rules for the benefit of everyone participating. They helped establish the right frame of mind for meditation and respected the way of life in the monastery.

1. Keep complete silence throughout the retreat. There were two exceptions to this. We were offered two allocated time slots of fifteen minutes each on day three and six for a one-to-one talk to one of the monks if we needed it. These gave us an opportunity to ask questions or tackle difficulties with the experience of the retreat. The second exception was in the case of an emergency.
2. Stay within the boundaries of the retreat centre at all times.
3. Abide by the Eight Precepts, which are to:
    - abstain from killing (unfortunately, this even applied to mosquitoes!)
    - abstain from stealing
    - keep your mind and body free from any sexual activity
    - not harm others by speech
    - not harm your consciousness with substances that intoxicate (no alcohol, no drugs, no smoking, etc.)
    - no eating after the meal at noon and before dawn
    - no dancing, singing, playing, or listening to music, watching shows, wearing garlands, ornaments, or beautifying oneself with perfumes

and cosmetics
- no sleeping or sitting on luxurious beds and seats (not that these were available! I think the purpose of this rule was to prevent participants bringing in mattresses and cushions from outside.)

These rules might seem a bit harsh, but they made complete sense to me, as they head off pretty much every possible distraction you could think of. There was no escape from any discomfort which might interfere with the experience of simply being still and observing one's self, ultimately preventing insight. The monks consider these rules essential to form the moral code for those who seek normalcy, and lightness and simplicity in living, so they sat well with my guiding principles. It didn't take me long to realise that learning meditation, like anything in life, takes energy, commitment, determination, and discipline, and it required a major shift in my daily routine.

For those of you who are interested in details, this is what the daily schedule looked like:

04:00 Wake up
04:30 Morning reading
04:45 Sitting meditation
05:15 Yoga/exercise: mindfulness in motion
07:00 Dharma talk & sitting meditation
08:00 Breakfast & chores
10:00 Dharma talk
11:00 Walking or standing meditation
11:45 Sitting meditation
12:30 Lunch & chores
14:30 Meditation instruction & sitting meditation
15:30 Walking or standing meditation
16:15 Sitting meditation
17:00 Chanting & loving kindness meditation
18:00 Tea & hot springs
19:30 Sitting meditation
20:00 Group walking meditation
20:30 Sitting meditation
21:00 Bedtime

21:30 Lights out

To signal the beginning of over half of these, one of the monks would climb the belltower and ring the enormous monastery bell. The truly beautiful sound reverberated throughout the compound, making it impossible to ignore. It was necessary because many of us had no idea what time it was. I loved the sound of that bell and actually looked forward to hearing it.

At four in the morning, the temptation to ignore the bell and sleep longer was *huge,* although the absence of a comfy mattress, soft pillows, and warm blankets to snuggle up lessened my resistance a little. Once the wake-up bell had been rung, I had about fifteen minutes to wash, get dressed, and slowly—mindfully—walk to the meditation hall. It was still dark, and I was guided by the light from my torch. One by one, the other participants silently and gracefully joined the flow of people on their way to the hall. Most days, I smiled in appreciation of all these people who'd come here to learn and grow just like me. I felt supported by their presence. Have you ever taken part in something where you felt the people around you were on the same path as you?

Ānāpānasati, or mindfulness with breathing, is the kind of meditation taught at Suan Mokkh. The first sitting meditation of the day lasted thirty minutes. I sat cross-legged and, as I inhaled and exhaled, tried to focus my attention on the area between my upper lip and my nostrils, observing and acknowledging every bodily sensation. Whether it was cold, heat, numbness, pain, tickling, tension, or throbbing, the goal was to notice them all and realise they are constantly arising and passing away. By meditating and observing my own mind, I began to know it rather than control it. Ten days is long enough to access the darkest roots of the unconscious and start to sharpen one's mind.

I'm not very comfortable sitting cross-legged for long periods, and we were doing it ten hours a day for ten days. To help us become more comfortable with these physical demands, there was a daily yoga practice session. The monks know that sooner or later, bodily discomfort in knees, hips, back, shoulders, and neck will affect most people. It was only the second time I'd practiced yoga, and it wasn't enjoyable. The stretches were physically demanding, and I was about as flexible as a steel girder. The best part of the session was the last ten minutes of guided relaxation when we laid on our backs with our eyes closed and carried out a scan of our body. This relaxed every part of my body and set me up for the rest of the day just fine.

Mindful Eating

I was definitely ready for breakfast by eight. I'd already been awake for four hours and done an hour of vigorous physical exercise without any coffee or food. I didn't like this regimen at first and was worried that I wouldn't have enough energy to get through the entire day, so I loaded my plate with extra food. Surprisingly, after three days, my body adjusted to this feeding routine. Whether it was due to the quality of the food or our early bedtime, I'm not sure. The hunger pangs I expected in the afternoon and evening never materialised, and that challenged my beliefs and patterns about food consumption. I saw that some of my desire to eat wasn't always based on hunger but two other factors: uncomfortable emotions and the desire to be regarded as sociable.

During the retreat, every meal was preceded with a prayer to draw our attention to five contemplations, read to us by one of the participants:

This food is the gift of the whole Universe: the earth, the sky, numerous living beings, and much hard, loving work. May we eat with mindfulness and gratitude so as to be worthy to receive it.
May we recognize and transform our unwholesome mental formations, especially our greed, and learn to eat with moderation.
May we keep our compassion alive by eating in such a way that we reduce the suffering of living beings, preserve our planet, and reverse the process of global warming.
We accept this food so that we may nurture our sisterhood and brotherhood, strengthen our community, and nourish our ideal of serving all living beings.

These contemplations made mealtimes special. I experienced the pleasure of eating food for sustenance, with gratitude, and without the need to socialise. I don't necessarily think that social eating, which is a big part of Western culture, is a bad thing or something to stop doing. But just think about it. How often do you get to sit with a bunch of people in total silence while you eat? How often do you eat alone without any distractions, without watching TV or looking at your smartphone? How often do you just enjoy the sensation of eating food and bring your full attention to the texture, smell, and flavours in your mouth as you chew? How much thought do you give to all the people and effort that went into bringing the food you're eating from the place it was grown, like the local farmer who grew your lettuce and tomatoes or the person who prepared the salad? Do you truly experience gratitude for it being there? And when was the last time you slowly enjoyed eating your food with no urge to finish quickly and move on to the next thing?

Vietnamese Zen Buddhist Monk and Teacher, Thích Nhât Hanh, who passed away recently, was a firm believer in mindful eating. Amongst other things, he advised people to refrain from arguing whilst eating. He advocated "chewing only your food, not your frustrations." In Vietnam, they never chastise anyone while they're eating, so as not to disturb their digestion. He also advocated moderation. Choosing smaller portions helps you avoid overeating and weight gain, and it's less wasteful of your household food budget and our planet's resources. If you use a small dinner plate, no larger than nine inches across, and fill it only once, you'll eat moderately.

We were encouraged to consciously take smaller bites and chew them well and to fully experience the taste of our food and improve our digestion, since the process of breaking down foods begins with enzymes in the mouth. We practiced chewing each bite until it liquefied in our mouth. I don't want to give you the impression this was easy. In the beginning, eating mindfully was a challenge. I arrived at the dining hall for both meals feeling hungry, and my tendency when I feel like that is to shovel my food into my mouth. I hardly chewed it at all and aimed to finish it as quickly as possible. This is a deeply ingrained habit. I had to consciously slow right down, talk to myself and instruct myself to take one bite at a time, place my knife and fork back down on the table, count the number of chews, swallow, and repeat.

When I put the first bite of food in my mouth, I was instructed to pause briefly before chewing and notice its taste, as though it was the first time I'd ever tasted it. You should try it! This felt strange and unnatural, yet after a couple of days of dedicated practice, I started to notice shifts in my awareness, and I felt expanded by it. Being fully present in the moment of consumption and experiencing all of the sensations with every bite made it a far richer, more colourful experience. With more practice in engaging all your senses, you may notice that your tastes change, increasing your enjoyment of what you may once have perceived as boring health foods.

After three or four days, I noticed that my appetite was totally satisfied with less food. Not having to be polite, make small talk, or pay attention to anyone else redirected more of my conscious attention inward towards my own thoughts, feelings, and observations as each day unfolded. Doing this didn't change my extrovert nature. If anything, it made me more discerning about who I choose to socialise with and when, and to be aware that being authentic in myself sometimes means saying no to invitations from others.

Meditative and Applied Practice
As well as meditating every day, we were required to contribute our energy in some way to keep the monastery running, which sat well with my guiding principles. For example, at mealtimes, we each took our plate and utensils from the table and washed them. After breakfast, it was time to complete your daily chore. We were allocated these after registration on the first day and had no idea what we'd end up with. Annie's task was to clean the toilets adjacent to the dining hall, whilst mine was to clean the huge dining hall floor after the breakfast meal, which meant waiting until everyone else had left. Being somewhat of a perfectionist, I actually loved the detailed meticulousness of my chore and took longer than most people probably would. I silently and joyfully cleaned every square inch of that floor. It was a wonderful daily opportunity to practice *applied* mindfulness as opposed to a *meditative* practice like sitting or walking.

The distinction between the two is important. These days, most of us heavily depend on our mobile phones. We install applications to get things done and charge the battery to create the energy to power the device. Both are required for the outcomes we need. Similarly, there are two types of practice required to live mindfully. The first is meditative practice. This is something you do alone to quiet your mind and relax your nervous system. For me, sitting in silence, walking in natural surroundings, and listening to soft music all accomplish that. Other people I know practice Qi Gong or Tai Chi, which are martial arts. When I become still and quiet, I become more aware of what I'm feeling and what kind of thoughts are most dominant in my self-talk. This meditative practice recharges my mindfulness battery and produces mindful energy for me to use in my daily life. This is mainly what we'd come to the retreat to learn.

The second is applied practice. In other words, how you direct your mindful energy in everyday situations. The aim is to be fully present and focus your attention on what you are doing for a richer experience. Examples include brushing your teeth, doing the washing up, cleaning your home, and spending time talking to friends. Sometimes in a conversation, the other person says something that ignites a strong reaction in me. Those moments can be challenging, and I've learned how to take a breath, slow down, and pause before I say anything in response, especially if I'm angry or upset. It helps me to remain calm, stay in rapport with the other person, and avoid becoming defensive, which is a pattern I'm aware of.

During the sitting meditations, which could last from one to two hours, I sometimes got a bit agitated. Just as the monks had predicted, my mind railed against the austere conditions. My thoughts drifted out of the present, and I felt restless and uncomfortable. Irrelevant thoughts flew around in my head like bees around flowers, completely out of control. In the relentless schedule, each minute that passed felt like an hour. Now and then, images formed on the inside of my eyelids. I sometimes drifted into sleep, only to awaken a few seconds later from the rapid, involuntary movement of my head dropping. Unlike life outside the monastery walls, there was literally no way of avoiding the discomfort. In fact, it was there to be observed and fully experienced. I'd momentarily forget what made me commit to the Vipassana retreat in the first place and looked to find someone else to blame for the pain and discomfort I was in.

Whenever I drifted out of the here and now, I was instructed to focus on my breathing and return to being fully present. Repeating this over and over again was the route to training our undisciplined monkey mind, as the Buddhists often call it. Just as a wild monkey has never been tamed, the human mind has been conditioned to be highly responsive to distractions, especially when we are emotionally charged. Think about it; what was the longest time you stayed with yourself, without *any* distractions?

What is Suffering?
To help us gain a better understanding of Buddhism and its place in the modern world, one of the monks would address our group every day at

ten a.m. and talk about an aspect of the dharma and the teachings of the Buddha. This was one of the daily highlights. It gave me a break in which I got to hear someone else speaking, as opposed to the voice in my own head. And he would typically share valuable knowledge and information that I used to help integrate the teachings as practices into my life afterwards. I was aware that continuing to be mindful after the retreat would be a major challenge without the support and the discipline of the monastics.

One of the most valuable insights of the retreat came to me during one of these daily dharma talks. Buddhism sees personal pursuit and attachment as a cycle. I became aware that we're all conditioned by society in such a way that we're stuck in this self-perpetuating cycle of mental suffering. There are many interacting elements that contribute to this condition.

At a subconscious level, we all hold a belief that we aren't good enough as we are. It can take many forms of expression, depending on who you are. Maybe you're not tall enough, not smart enough, not rich enough, not sexy enough—the list is endless and different for each of us. Take a moment and think about your own. You can just fill in the blank yourself: "I am not _____ enough."

To avoid experiencing the emotional discomfort that comes from buying into this belief, we create a desire for something or someone that will close that gap and make us feel good enough. We hope it will somehow fill the inner emptiness which is causing our pain and anxiety. In Buddhism, this is known as craving, and it leads us to grasp for the things we've determined will provide relief from the pain, even if it's not good for us in the long run. This is how addictions are formed. When we finally manage to obtain the thing we crave, it makes us feel better for a while, and we become attached to it. We fear the loss of it. Inevitably, we discover that the pleasure or relief is temporary. This is the true nature of all things. It can never be enough, so we crave even more. That's what keeps the cycle going.

After every cycle of wanting, getting, and loss, there is more emptiness, more disappointment. A sense of betrayal. And that makes us more desperate for relief. This cycle is known in the Buddhist teachings as delusional thinking. Becoming aware of and understanding it was a huge revelation to me.

"The Buddha said that craving is like holding a torch

against the wind; the fire will burn you. When someone is thirsty and drinks only salty water, the more he drinks, the thirstier he becomes. If we run after money, for example, we think that a certain amount of money will make us happy. But once we have that amount, it's not enough; we think we need more. There are people who have a lot of money, but they are not happy at all. The Buddha said that the object of our craving is like a bone without flesh. A dog can chew and chew on that bone and never feel satisfied.

"We all experience moments when we feel lonely, sad, empty, frustrated, or afraid. We fill up our feelings with a movie or a sandwich. We buy things to suppress our pain, despair, anger, and depression. We find a way to consume in the hopes that it will obliterate the feelings. Even if a TV show isn't interesting, we still watch it. We think anything is better than experiencing the malaise, the ill-being in us. We have lost sight of the reality that we already have all the conditions we need for our own happiness."

Excerpt from *Lion's Roar/Happiness in Every Breath*
by Thích Nhất Hạnh

When I'd been running my business in London, I'd often thought I wasn't good enough to be growing my company. I envied other people in the same position who seemed much more capable. I hid my pain and anxiety because I didn't really understand why I felt those emotions. To feel *good enough*, I'd go to a shop and buy expensive stuff I didn't really need, or I'd go to an expensive restaurant and stuff myself with hideously expensive, tasty, and unhealthy food. I drank expensive wine to numb the pain. These brought me some relief for a day or two. But it wore off, and I would repeat the cycle. My health suffered as I gained weight and stopped exercising, making me feel lousy about myself, which just led to more craving.

I set higher targets in my business every year to finance a life that required greater and grander material consumption than the year before, to justify all the effort and hard work I was putting in. There never seemed to be a moment in which I believed I had, or was, *enough*. It was like trying to score a goal in a football match but someone kept moving the goalposts. For the first time, I saw this cycle for what it was, without any judgment or self-criticism. I knew in that moment that I wouldn't have to repeat that cycle again unless I chose to. I saw that happiness was a choice. It was something I always had, if I chose to feel it, and not something to be *pursued*. It was a huge relief, and I felt a growing sense of ease as the retreat progressed.

Scriptwriters who create the storylines in TV soap operas exploit this delusional thinking for maximum dramatic effect. In the UK, there's a long running series called *Eastenders* about the community that lives in and around Albert Square in East London. Like all good soap operas, it's full of outlandish plots to keep the audience hooked. Something terrible often happens to one of the characters. They get dumped by their boyfriend, lose their job, or are betrayed by someone close. The writers can't apply the Buddhist doctrine and simply let them experience their emotional pain fully, without any drama. That would make pretty boring television. Instead, they script the characters to react and have them get drunk, start a fight, or unexpectedly start a secret affair with their best mate's husband or wife. Those scenarios are full of drama and much more exciting. The characters always feel better for a week or two. They're pumped up as they chase their lustful desires and hide their sordid secrets. Eventually someone finds out as it's all dramatically revealed in a cliff-hanger episode watched by millions. Then the scriptwriters start the cycle all over again. You may not realise just how conditioned to this kind of drama we are. It's conditioned us to avoid taking personal responsibility and encouraged us to blame circumstances, events, or other people when things don't go so well.

Marc Lewis, PhD, a neuroscientist and professor of developmental psychology at the University of Toronto, says that whether you crave success, material comfort, or prestige or heroin, cocaine, booze, or porn, it hardly matters. We believe that we've found an antidote to uncertainty, a guarantee of completeness though we never really become complete by chasing what we don't have. Incredibly, it's the pursuit itself that becomes the condition for more suffering, because we inevitably come up empty, disappointed, and betrayed by our own desires. This is addiction. Marc adds that Buddhists see that as normal seeking and suffering, a view totally contrary to the one held by Western medical practitioners, who regard addiction as something abnormal, a disease, and an unnatural state. The Buddhist perspective casts it quite differently as a particularly onerous outcome of a sadly normal process: our continuing attempt to seek fulfilment outside ourselves.

A friend of mine suffers immensely unless she has the latest version of a product. When a new iPhone is released, she has to have it. Her current phone may only be a year old and adequately meets her needs, but that doesn't matter. She's not happy unless she constantly upgrades. She somehow believes she's not good enough and that people will judge her in a bad light if she doesn't have the newest version. Of course, the companies that make these products understand human psychology extremely well and milk our tendency towards delusional thinking for all it is worth.

Michael Neill, coach and author of *The Path of Effortless Change*, has a wonderful take on this. He challenges people to consider how differently they'd approach their lives if they knew that nothing additional was needed for them to be happy and well. Well-being is our true, authentic nature. We spend so much of our time chasing after it like a dog chasing its own tail, we believe that the fact we're doing it proves it's a good idea. Neil says to take the idea that "life is a journey." This meme has become so embedded in our cultural mythology that we forget it's just a metaphor, and usually one used to counterbalance our overemphasis on goals and targets. We've become so obsessed with where we're headed that we don't notice where we are. It's as though being on the move is what's natural and being where we are is a skill we must learn. But actually, life *isn't* a journey. Life just *is*.

Re-entering the World
As each day passed at Suan Mokkh, the sitting and walking meditations became a little bit easier on my body, and I became more and more accustomed to just being in the present, without the desire to spend very long in thoughts about the past or the future. In February, the weather in Thailand is gorgeous, with high temperatures and glorious sunshine most days, which made my walking meditations even more enjoyable. I derived genuine pleasure from simply enjoying my surroundings, the healthy functioning of my body, the sustenance of simple food, and the energy of the monks. Every day, I would see Annie in the meditation and dining hall or see her walking through the monastery from a distance. I was glad we both took part in the retreat without the need to relate in the way we did normally. I couldn't honestly say I missed her, as I'd completely focused

on, and been absorbed in, my own learning process.

Eventually, the ten days were up and for the first time, we could hug each other and talk about our experiences. I felt excited and energised as we reconnected. I also talked to some of the other participants who I'd observed for ten days and knew nothing about. A few of us exchanged email addresses in the hope that we might see each other again. Two people I really connected with were a French woman called Danielle and an American by the name of Rosie. I had no idea that these two would reappear at a later stage in my journey. Our inability to predict the future, according to my way of seeing things now, is one of life's great pleasures.

As I left Suan Mokkh, I reflected on what I'd experienced. My outlook had fundamentally changed. My ego was less in the driver's seat now. I realised I'd spent years comparing myself to others as a businessman, husband, friend, and member of my community. That had kept me locked in a cycle of thinking and believing I wasn't *good enough*. Although it's become an overused cliché, the late George Carlin, a superb comedian and outspoken critic of the establishment, perfectly summed it up. "We buy shit we don't need with money we don't have to impress people we don't like."

I committed myself to separate as best I could from this egotistical mind, which was consistently making these comparisons. By detaching from the self-critical thoughts that accompanied some of these, I felt a sense of self-acceptance and peace. For example, it's hard to sit alone in a restaurant if you're constantly worried that people will see you as a loser because you're sitting by yourself. When I look at the raw facts, I see the reality is something different. Being fully present and alone is totally okay. There is no need to change it.

I also developed a limitless threshold for boredom, after sitting still for hours on end. I no longer needed constant input or entertainment when sitting silently. I'd learned how to remain in what Michael Singer, author of *The Untethered Soul*, calls "the seat of witness consciousness" and simply observe whatever is present without judgment. These days, I'm happy to sit and wait at an airport or train station through long delays without the need to go online, read a book, or any other form of distraction. I am fascinated with whatever I can see, hear, and feel all around me.

It's only in the writing of this story that I look back and see the clarity of the shift that took place for me during this retreat. At the time, all my energy was needed to simply process the experience, and it didn't make a lot of sense immediately. This is what happens sometimes. We need time to reflect on and integrate our experience to mellow us, in the same way that the waves of the ocean polish the stones on the beach over many years. I left the monastery committed to developing my newfound mindfulness practice and bringing this awareness and attention to every minute of my life. I no longer wished to dwell in thoughts about what might have happened had the past been different or what undesirable events might happen in the future. It felt more real, wholesome, and joyful to simply be in this moment now and fully accept whatever was happening from a place of wonder and curiosity.

In case you're wondering how any of this might apply to you, I've included a brief self-assessment questionnaire below. It's similar to one I give participants who attend my *Everyday Mindfulness* workshops. I suggest you select the last seven days as your timeframe as you consider each one. Provide an answer for every statement as best you can and try not to overthink it. It's best to be as honest and spontaneous as possible. There are no right or wrong answers, nor good or bad responses. You may find they help you to see where your ego may be locking you into the cycle of craving, desire, attachment, and addiction.

Give yourself an honest score for each question and apply a number between one and ten. If the statement never applies at all, then give yourself a one. If it completely applies to you all the time, give yourself a ten.

1. I am able to appreciate myself
2. I pay attention to what's behind my actions
3. I see my mistakes and difficulties without judging them
4. I feel connected to my experience in the here and now
5. I am conscious of an emotion the moment that I experience it
6. I accept unpleasant experiences
7. I am friendly to myself when things go wrong
8. I watch my feelings without getting lost in them
9. In difficult situations, I can pause without immediately reacting or becoming defensive
10. I experience moments of inner peace and ease, even when things get hectic and stressful
11. I am patient with myself and with others

12. I am able to smile when I notice how I sometimes make life difficult
13. I sense my body, whether walking, eating, cooking, washing, or talking
14. When I notice an absence of mind, I gently return to the experience of the here and now
15. I am consciously aware of my non-verbal communication with others
16. I am aware of my own thoughts and inner dialogue
17. I am able to understand and accept the morality and value systems of others
18. I know the difference between my own opinion and objective truth
19. In conversations with friends, I only offer my opinion or give advice when they invite me to
20. I am happy to help others without receiving any recognition or acknowledgment

There is no correct total score. Whatever yours is today, you can consciously develop new behaviours and habits using any of the applied mindfulness practices I touched on earlier. After a period of dedicated effort, assess yourself again and observe those questions where you've rated yourself differently. You can ask people in your family or community of friends, as well as colleagues at work, to assess you as well. By doing this, you may find you are more critical towards yourself than is necessary.

Finding My Sangha

After the retreat, Annie and I decided that we'd head north to Chiang Mai. It's the second largest city in Thailand, and we'd heard many great accounts about it from other travellers. As soon as we arrived, we instinctively felt at home. After the retreat, Annie and I had maintained our daily meditative practice and even though we were sitting for shorter periods, I noticed an increased ability to connect with my intuition. I felt a bit more distance in our relationship than before the retreat. I'd spent ten days in the monastery and hardly paid attention to her. I was also asking deep questions of myself about where this journey was now meant to take me.

Those ten days of meditation had created stillness and then clarity, like one of those snow globes people buy as a travel souvenir. Going back on the road felt like shaking the snow globe and obscuring the picture. I could no longer see as clearly. I observed some doubts as far as Annie and our future together was concerned. Just as I'd done when I was married, I chose not to pay too much attention to them in the hope that they would somehow disappear.

We liked Chiang Mai so much that we looked for a reason to stay longer. Eventually, we came across a course at the university for Teaching English as a Foreign Language (TEFL). Doing the course gave us our teaching certificates and opened up the possibility that we could work while we travelled. Whilst I didn't really need the money, I saw value in doing the course purely as a learning experience and decided to commit to it.

It was a great decision on the social front. We made more friends in Chiang Mai than anywhere we'd previously been, primarily because we stayed longer and were able to spend more time hanging out with people living there. That was how I came to meet Gaston Schmitz, an ex-pat from the Netherlands, living in the city with his girlfriend and working for an NGO (non-government organisation). Gaston was in his twenties. He was tall, and handsome, and open-hearted. He had a wonderfully calm presence which I loved. He had his own mindfulness practice and invited Annie and me to join the weekly meditation group he was a member of. It was called the Green Papaya Sangha, and they gathered every Thursday.

Sangha is a Sanskrit word that means company or community. I think of it more as a kind of family because it's a place where you can give and receive non-judgmental, wise, and loving support for your meditation practice. In those early days of my practice, I found it valuable and motivating to participate in the sangha and made many new friends there. I'm still in touch with and actually work with a few of them today.

During our weekly gathering, we did two sitting meditations and one walking meditation, each lasting about twenty or twenty-five minutes. The sangha follows the tradition of Plum Village, the monastery in France which was the home of Thích Nhất Hạnh for over forty years, until his passing in 2022. That's how I discovered his teachings. His community of monks and nuns are still there, and you'll read what happened when I attended a three-week summer retreat about five years later.

With the support of Annie and my sangha in Chiang Mai, my mindfulness practice constantly evolved, and my ability to maintain a mindful approach to life grew stronger with each passing day. That's not to say it was all plain sailing. On the contrary, there were often dark periods in which I forgot the essential lessons I'd been learning, especially when I was travelling alone in New Zealand. The more I practiced, the more insight and intuitive guidance came to me. It seems to me that we can tune in to obtain a kind of purer guidance than that which comes from our rational, thinking mind. But to access that frequency, we need to first train our mind to be quiet, as the noisy commentary it automatically generates tends to drown out our much quieter inner voice of wisdom. Even if we're able to hear the message, we may still doubt what it's telling us and hesitate to act on it.

It had been my feelings of stress and anxiety that had driven me towards the monastery to attend the Vipassana retreat. The prospect of some pain relief was behind that choice. But as time went on, I observed a far greater sensitivity and awareness to the suffering of others. My practice enabled me to generate a far more resourceful state within myself than I'd ever been able to before, at a time when I lived in total uncertainty. I could take care of my own psychological and emotional needs far easier, which left more energy to help and support others. As I travelled, I had many conversations with people who were searching for answers to their own questions about life. I gave those people my undivided attention and became a witness to their challenges. An ongoing part of my practice that has continued to this day is that of expressing gratitude, one of the five regrets that Bronnie Ware detailed.

> "In an eight-week study, brain scans of individuals who practiced gratitude had stronger brain structure for social cognition and empathy."
>
> Dr Emiliana Simon-Thomas, PhD,
> The Greater Good Science Centre

A number of brain-imaging studies have discovered that the brain's reward centre lights up when we feel grateful. This is the same neural circuit that underlies primal drives like feeding and mating. When we consciously practice an attitude of gratitude, things don't just look better, they actually are better. There is rarely a day that passes in which I do not name at least three or four things that I'm truly grateful for. As time has passed, it's become much easier to find these, and I appreciate small details I used to miss. For example, the communal garden area around an apartment I lived in was looked after by an elderly gentleman, who quietly and unobtrusively mowed the lawn, cleaned the stairways, made sure the trash was taken away, and did a bunch of other menial tasks that made the whole building more pleasant for me and the other residents. Some had no problem grumbling when something was overlooked. Others were totally unaware of how much work this guy did to maintain the standards that were expected by everyone. I marvelled at the guy for the amazing service he provided to us and thanked him whenever I got the opportunity.

Annie and I completed our TEFL course in Chiang Mai in June 2006 and travelled together for the rest of that year, traversing Cambodia and Vietnam.

> "Your vision will become clear only when you look into your heart. Who looks outside, dreams. Who looks inside, awakens."
> Carl Jung, *C.G. Jung Letters, Vol. 1: 1906-1950*

Chapter Five
Exploring Asia

THE COMPLETION OF MY TEFL COURSE IN CHIANG MAI MARKED THE PERFECT moment to make a two-week trip to England, where a couple of loose ends bothered me. Eight months earlier, when I'd minimalised my life and left, it had been impossible to know if I'd adapt to and enjoy the life of a traveller. As a precaution, I'd kept hold of two valuable possessions, my car and motorcycle, which I'd put into storage. If it were necessary to abandon my grand experiment and return to London within a year, it was convenient and financially pragmatic to have these ready and available. By keeping them, I'd avoided the effort and potential cost I would have faced if I'd sold and then had to replace them.

It wasn't purely a rational decision. My motorcycle was a rare Triumph Thunderbird in pristine condition, and I absolutely loved to jump on it and go for a spin. It was a stylish piece of chromed machinery, and I loved the deep, throaty sound it made and the sense of freedom it gave me. It was the only cherished possession I had left, and I was unwilling to let it go when I departed for my new life in Asia.

Sadly, the bike and the car were now liabilities, as they needed constant attention to stay operational. Finding a secure, dry place to store a motorcycle in London at a reasonable cost was as difficult as finding someone who hasn't heard of YouTube. I'd managed to, but I predicted that it was going to be harder and more expensive to keep doing it. After eight months in Asia, I knew I wanted to continue the fascinating, once-in-a-lifetime journey I'd started. There was no way I'd be coming back to London any time soon. They had to go.

They were both in great condition, so it was no hassle to find buyers quickly. Selling my car took a week and was painless, unlike the sale of my beloved Triumph, which I was much more attached to. When I watched the new owner ride it away, sentimental tears of sadness rolled down my cheeks. That bike had been a great source of pleasure, and one of the props that had identified me as Ray, the affluent London businessman. Funnily enough, I stepped back into that role for a moment during that trip.

A former client had heard I was in the UK and invited me to the Henley Royal Regatta with a bunch of corporate clients. Coming from Thailand, I only had shorts and T-shirts, so I dropped in at my mum's house to pick up something more appropriate. After six months as a backpacker, it felt weird to wear a suit again, like going to a fancy dress party in a costume. It was a pretence. I was worried these high-powered businesspeople would think I was strange when I told them about my new life and the Vipassana retreat. I was gobsmacked to find that they were riveted by my stories. It was a revelation, and I made a mental note of these observations. I had no idea at the time that I'd end up working with corporate executives to enable them to become mindful leaders, which I'll tell you about in chapter seventeen. I left that event with an emerging sense of liberation, joy, and freedom as I returned to Asia to resume my life with Annie. I gratefully added the money I raised from the sale of both items to my travel piggy bank.

Whilst away from Annie for a couple of weeks, I reflected on my experiences of travelling with her. The way things were going between us troubled me. After eight months of being together night and day, I was increasingly niggled during many of our conversations and largely blamed her for this. I was anxious and uncertain about our compatibility and questioned my commitment to her. We were having more arguments, and it was becoming harder to maintain harmony. Add it all up, and I'd begun to see Annie as less attractive than when we first met. I'd stopped appreciating her.

The judgmental voice inside my head suggested it might be better for me to go my own way. But I ignored that message, as I was scared about the uncertainties that a breakup with Annie might create. There weren't enough good reasons to justify such a radical decision. I was caught in a kind of emotional inertia, like when you hate your job but you really need the money. I was full of doubt. I couldn't really tell if these feelings were truthful or some kind of character deficiency in myself.

My self-critic took every opportunity it could to remind me that I wasn't good enough to be in a relationship. It had less effect on me after the Vipassana retreat. Although I'd had an amazing spiritual experience and developed a deeper awareness of this part of myself, I was still suffering from my own sense of inadequacy. As much as I'd like to tell you it was, ten days of meditation had not been the once and for all cure I'd hoped it would be. I still had my messed-up human experience as I struggled to relate to Annie, and it still bugged me. But it gave me a learning opportunity, a set of conditions in which I could observe my thoughts and emotions and eventually find a way to accept that part of myself.

The Gift

As luck would have it, Annie's birthday was coming soon. I put my feelings of doubt to one side and looked for a way to appreciate her. I wanted to make a couple of special gifts to give her in Bangkok a few days later. These gifts needed the involvement of her friends and family in England to make them possible. Luckily, Annie and I had combined our email contact lists when we started publishing *The Daily Lama* blog, so I had email addresses for most of them. I sent a message to them and asked them to take a few quiet moments to think about what they most loved or admired about Annie and send their thoughts to me in a message I could include in a book I was making for her. I begged all of them to keep my little project a secret until Annie's birthday.

Some people recalled the story of how they'd met her. Others told funny anecdotes. Every single one of the sixty-eight wonderful messages I received were from the heart. I compiled them into a beautiful, leatherbound book. I knew Annie would really enjoy reading them. What I'd not expected was how deeply moved I'd been by the loyalty, admiration, and appreciation being expressed in the words of her admirers. It was obvious that people saw Annie as an amazing, courageous woman. Seeing their perceptions of her enabled me to see her in a different way too. Making that book for Annie turned out to be a valuable gift for me too, as I became inspired again about our relationship. I headed back to Bangkok with a fresh sense of optimism and excitement. I realised that the best gifts we can give others are not always the ones we can buy.

As a special birthday treat, I secretly booked a room for two nights at the stunning Four Seasons Hotel in the heart of Bangkok. For those of you who haven't been, it's a beautiful, luxurious property with sumptuous rooms similar to the finest establishments in Mayfair, London or Park Avenue, New York. Annie knew I'd set aside a rainy-day fund for the odd occasion a special treat would be appropriate. This was one of them. When our taxi driver pulled into the hotel entrance and parked outside the lobby, she burst into tears of childlike joy!

We waited in the cab for a few moments so she could compose herself. After nearly a year of staying in cheap, basic hostels and budget guesthouses, this was a rare and welcome treat for both of us. We had the unadulterated luxury of room service, which threw me back momentarily to my life as a businessman. I glimpsed how far I'd come during my journey of reinvention. In Thailand, people asked me constantly about what I missed the most from my affluent life in London; sleeping in a comfortable bed with a great mattress and soft fluffy pillows was at the top of my list.

As you can imagine, Annie was thrilled to receive her tribute book. She repeatedly read every one of those heartfelt messages that members of her community had generously and willingly sent her. It reconnected her to her loved ones.

"There are many people in the world who I know and love," she said to me. "And when I read all of these messages, it feels like they're all in the room with me. This is something I could never have asked for myself. It's comforting to know that I'm loved by so many people."

The second gift didn't need help from anyone else. I'd been randomly filming Annie since we started travelling and had amassed quite a collection of video footage. She'd even asked me a few times if I was going to edit any of it whilst I was in London. "Not a chance," I'd said, which had been enough to keep her off the scent. In truth, I'd used my basic video editing skills to create a fifteen-minute movie. It reflected the best moments from our first seven months of travelling together, set to some thoughtfully chosen music. When we returned to our hotel room after dinner, Annie realised that something was going on. After she'd changed into her bathrobe, I took out a DVD and sat her down in front of the huge flat screen TV that was hanging on the wall of our swanky, five-star room.

"I made this for you while I was in England," I said and pressed play.

She absolutely loved the film and smiled like a ten-year-old kid watching *The Lion King*. In an interview with our blog correspondent, Po Scard, a couple of days later, she told our readers that she, "was blown away by the film, and I insisted on watching it three times." She added, "By making this film, Ray has given me a multimedia souvenir of our journey together which I will cherish for a long time." She completely forgave me for lying to her when I'd denied I would edit our footage.

My return to Bangkok had been triumphant, and the energy and aliveness in our relationship was restored. There was no need for the big, awkward conversation I'd imagined and feared while I was in London, and we continued from there. This feeling of renewal gave me a few months in which I parked my doubts about Annie. We celebrated our union by doing one of the most popular social activities amongst Thai people: we booked a private karaoke suite on the top floor of one of the mega shopping malls and sang our hearts out for a couple of hours, howling away to a few of our favourite tunes, safe in the knowledge that absolutely no one outside our room could hear us, which was probably lucky for them.

Cambodia

After the undeniable pleasure of our luxury break in Bangkok, we returned to our modest backpacker lodgings and the world of budget travel. You may recall that when Annie and I were getting to know each other at my house back in London, we'd envisaged travelling around Asia for about a year, exploring Thailand, Laos, Cambodia, and Vietnam. It was August 2006, which gave us around four months to make our way through Cambodia and Vietnam and make one further visit to Thailand before departing for Perth, Australia to connect with Annie's family.

We started in Cambodia. We left Bangkok by bus and headed for the border crossing at Poipet. The cheapest and safest way to reach Siem Reap, which is about eighty miles away, was to charter a clapped-out old taxi to take us about fifty miles to Bătdâmbâng. From there, we'd board a local bus to get to Tonlé Sap Lake, where we'd pick up a narrow boat that would take us all the way into Siem Reap. It was convoluted.

Cambodia had only been open to travellers for a few years, and there were hardly any decent roads, let alone public transport as you might understand it. Transportation for foreigners in many of these poor countries is in the hands of a few, grubby local businessmen, who actually looked more like dustmen! These guys run fleets of aging, dilapidated, and filthy minibuses and cars, which you can charter for a few US dollars. As I talked to these men and looked at their vehicles, I wondered if they were capable of making the journey. I had a moment of anxiety when I handed over our money to an unfriendly looking chap, whilst a rowdy crowd added to the prevailing sense of mayhem by screaming and shouting as their chickens ran around our feet in the mud. Minutes later, to my relief, our car appeared—a filthy, dented, and rusty twenty-year-old Toyota Camry that would have had a UK MOT inspector falling on the floor laughing.

The biggest joke of all was that we believed we'd negotiated exclusive use of the car, which was a long way from the truth. Shortly after we left Poipet, our driver stopped to pick up two huge guys who both squeezed into the spare front seat next to the driver and remained there for most of the journey. We made a couple more unscheduled stops so the driver could say hello to friends along the way, but we eventually arrived at our destination. The roads were full of potholes, and we were thrown around in the back of that car for about three hours. Annie and I could really see the value of our mindfulness training at Suan Mokkh. We'd been able to take a few deep breaths and stay calm as our driver constantly slammed the brakes, and swerved to avoid cattle, large trucks, and motorcyclists. This was the start of our basic education in how things really work when travelling budget in Cambodia!

It didn't end there. We quickly realised our driver had some kind of scam going with a couple of guesthouses he kept recommending in Bătdâmbâng. A lot of drivers receive commission for taking travellers to their friends' guesthouses, and even though we firmly refused his offers, we were still taken to the guesthouse he recommended. When we got out of the car, we hastily grabbed our backpacks and scarpered. The following day, we took the long boat for our lake crossing into Siem Reap. For a couple of hours, we felt like we'd been transported to another world. The lake was calm and peaceful, with fishermen's dinghies dotted here and there. I watched them cast their nets and enjoyed the morning sun.

Around the lake shore were many rickety homes, scattered throughout the long grass and reeds. Made from a mixture of bamboo and straw matting, most were sitting on stilts a few feet above the waterline. They looked incredibly fragile, as if they would collapse if a powerful storm came. In some parts of the lake, there were a few wooden shacks tied together, complete with ropes and makeshift boardwalks connecting them all. One had a small shop, which provided a floating mini market for the community living there. It was a far cry from the life I remembered in south-west London, and I loved the sense of adventure the contrast engendered inside me.

We arrived in Siem Reap a few hours later and were immediately besieged by an enthusiastic crowd of drivers and street sellers. After the tranquillity of our lake crossing, we were stunned to see the forceful and direct tactics they used to secure some business. Some of them leapt on to our boat before it had even docked and grabbed people's backpacks, hoping they'd hire them for a ride into town. Off the boat, we were surrounded by fifty or more tuk-tuk drivers and bike riders, who all wanted to help us get to a guesthouse. It was unnerving, as we were still part of the uninitiated. We had five or six of them yelling in our faces at the same time. It's the reason Annie and I made it our highest priority to learn the phrase "No, thank you," before we arrived in a new country!

We found a decent enough place to stay. We were there to visit the awe-inspiring Angkor Wat temple complex. It's ancient and it's huge, and it's difficult to convey in words the feeling of being there. The best way to give you a sense of it would be to ask you to close your eyes and imagine you're on a mission to find precious, lost treasure and ancient artifacts hidden in an ancient temple, deep in the jungle, like the ones from an Indiana Jones movie.

The ancient ruins at Angkor Wat have been reclaimed by giant trees over the past two hundred years. Their roots now grow through the roofs of these derelict buildings. Some are several stories tall, and the tree roots have made huge cracks between the giant blocks of masonry as they've forced their way down into the formidable structures and monuments. There are many individual buildings, all interconnected by a network of paths and roads. The complex covers an area greater than several of the world's largest airports put together. The scale and enormity are mind blowing, and I gasped for breath a few times as I took it all in.

The Lonely Planet lists a visit there as the world's number one sightseeing trip, and I'd be hard-pressed to disagree. My fledgling mindfulness practice gave me a deeper level of appreciation for the sheer wonder of places like this. I wondered how men with primitive tools could have fashioned something this intricate thousands of years ago. It would be virtually impossible to recreate today, even with all the amazing technology and resources we have. I also wondered what it might have been like to have been alive in an era when human beings dedicated their entire lives to the worship of higher beings and all that this entailed.

The thing I found most incredible was that this entire complex had remained largely unknown beyond Cambodia. It's a testimony to the spiritual concept of impermanence, and it reminded me that, in the grand scheme of things, even great empires don't last forever. As grand as it was, this place had untethered itself from the rest of the human race and faded into oblivion, at least for a while. Experiencing it helped me to let go of my sense of self-importance. Had I visited a couple of years earlier, I'd probably have been more blasé about being there. Now, it inspired me and fired up my imagination. I discovered they stage an International Half-Marathon race at the site every December, which attracts runners from all over the world. I've made a promise to myself that I will return there one day to take part.

In Cambodia, our *Daily Lama* travel correspondent, Po Scard, was busy writing blog posts to keep our friends and family connected with us. Being such a poor country, medicines and vaccines are in short supply. Annie and I found a small clinic on the edge of Siem Reap where they asked foreigners to donate blood. There was a chronic shortage, and we were both inspired to respond. There were two reasons that compelled me. First, after my accident in Koh Tao, I was aware how valuable it was if someone urgently needed a blood transfusion. Second, my father had been a champion blood donor when he was alive, and I'd forgotten that until I saw the notice outside. This was an opportunity to make my first donation and contribute to the citizens of the country who were hosting us. As I laid on the bed with blood being drained from my arm, I pictured my father beside me, smiling. I'd like to think that he would have been proud of me doing that.

You know when someone says, "I have good news and bad news. Which would you like first?" what do you normally choose? For visitors to Cambodia, if Angkor Wat is the good news, then the Choeung Ek Killing Fields on the outskirts of Phnom Penh are the bad news. Going there was a huge eye-opener for me and one of the first experiences in my journey that opened my heart. As a young teenager living in England, I had vague memories of hearing about Pol Pot and the Khmer Rouge on TV news bulletins. Pot led a genocidal tsunami of killing there during the 1970s. I had no idea why it had happened. At that time of my life I wasn't particularly interested in anything outside of my immediate circle of friends and paid no attention whatsoever to political events overseas.

Seeing firsthand what actually happened in the Killing Fields ignited a sense of outrage. It was there we came face to face with the remnants of a tragedy that cruelly claimed the lives of over two million people. Pol Pot had led an ultra-communist guerrilla group, and he took advantage of the vacuum left by the Americans after their withdrawal from Vietnam. He seized power, and it eventually ruined this poor country. Whilst it was truly shocking to learn about what happened, another part of me was keen to know more. I asked a guide to explain why these events had unfolded in the way they did.

What it came down to was that a relatively small bunch of people decided they wanted to create a society of equals, and they used fear, violence, and intimidation to force everyone else to agree to it. Anyone who refused was imprisoned, tortured, and eventually killed, including babies, children, adults, and the elderly. The Khmer Rouge murdered people if they didn't like them, if they thought they didn't work hard enough, if they were educated, or came from different ethnic groups, or if they showed any sympathy when their family members were taken away to be killed.

What I'd discovered appalled me. As I reflected, that feeling gave way to a deep sense of shame, for myself and the rest of the world. How often in our tethered lives, in our comfortable and safe bubble of reality, do we fail to notice suffering going on around us? Not just on an epic scale like this but with our neighbours or members of our own family? Even if we become aware, how often do we look the other way rather than take effective action to change it? I felt ashamed that I'd been aware of these horrific events and yet, I'd not paid attention. It must have been excruciatingly painful for the victims. Many were forced to dig the trenches or pits they would be buried in, before being lined up along the edge and bludgeoned or bayoneted to death. Some of the victims were still alive when they were buried. Can you imagine that?

Maybe ignorance of the horrific situations that take place in conflicts all over the world is a good thing? It releases you from feeling any pain or responsibility related to it. If there was a gift inherent in retracing the steps of history and acquainting myself with events in Phnom Penh, it was that seeing what happened raised my empathy level considerably. Crimes against humanity like this, on such a vast scale, make my own personal struggles in life seem truly pathetic. Looking back, my visit there planted a seed of compassion inside of me that came to fruition when I later became inspired to start my own charitable foundation.

In Cambodia, I had an opportunity to consciously practice lightness, one of the ten principles that were guiding and guarding me psychologically. In the face of all that human suffering, it was easy to be depressed and lose hope. I made a conscious effort to remember that, as awful as it was, it was just one book in the entire library of human existence, and there are many, many other books that are creative, inspiring, and uplifting too.

I've already talked about the mindfulness practice of expressing gratitude. As a result of many conflicts during the last sixty years, there are still tens of thousands of unexploded landmines in fields and forests all over Cambodia. Hundreds of innocent people are killed and injured every year as a result. I saw quite a few men and women who'd lost their legs from stepping on a mine. I'm truly grateful to be safe from the horror the citizens Cambodia have to contend with every day. I'm also grateful beyond words to have the full use of my legs. Later in my story, when I started my charitable foundation, the reason I'm so grateful will become obvious.

Vietnam

It was the Vietnamese who eventually invaded Cambodia in 1979 and liberated everyone from the Khmer Rouge, so it seemed fitting to spend a couple of months there. We travelled by road from Phnom Penh to Hồ Chí Minh City in the former South Vietnam. Depending on what movies you've seen, you might imagine that we'd taken a rickety old bus with open windows and luggage piled high on the roof rack, crammed full of hot sweaty passengers. If you did, you'd be a long way from the reality. As these so-called developing nations modernise and reach ever higher living standards that emulate those we enjoy in the Western world, older buses have given way to air-conditioned, luxury coaches that cover long distances easily.

Our six-hour journey was a feast for our eyes. We passed by hundreds of neatly layered rice paddies, beautifully cut into low lying, green rolling hills on either side of the road. The view was briefly interrupted here and there when we passed through small towns. When we did, I was struck by the number of motorcycles on the roads. There were literally thousands and thousands of them. They have been adapted for all sorts of uses, including carrying freight, and are the dominant form of transport in Vietnam. Many have sidecars, trailers, or specially constructed luggage racks. It's not uncommon to see more than two passengers, even entire families of four or five in some instances, on one bike.

If you've been an independent traveller for any length of time, you'll know how exciting it feels when you cross a national border in anticipation of the opportunities and new experiences that await you. I was still fairly new to it and felt apprehensive as we waited at the checkpoint. All passengers were required to hand over their passports to the driver without knowing what was going to be done with them or how we would get them back. I found that a bit unnerving, although it turned out there was nothing to worry about. Later in my journey, I became more and more comfortable with moments like that. I saw how to go with the flow and trust that everything would turn out okay, which it generally did. I put this newfound ability down to my meditation practice and to applying the principle of non-attachment, which led me to feel more and more relaxed in situations of uncertainty. Although I learned this as a traveller, it's a skill I've found useful in many ordinary, day-to-day settings. Can you think of a situation in your daily life where being more relaxed would be beneficial to you?

In Hồ Chí Minh City (formerly known as Saigon), Annie and I couldn't wait to get our first taste of pho (pronounced fuh). In its most basic form, a bowl of pho consists of rice noodles topped with thinly sliced raw beef and covered with steaming, spiced beef broth. Enhanced with a flurry of fresh herbs, like coriander and basil, crunchy bean sprouts, hot chillies, and tart lime, pho makes a restorative meal any time of day. To pay for it, we obtained some Vietnamese dong. Asian currencies were considered relatively weak when compared to harder currencies like the US dollar or British pound. We received over twenty thousand dong for every pound, which was a source of great amusement. It meant that for just under fifty pounds, we became cash millionaires, all the time knowing it was totally meaningless! In that moment, we were just like little kids playing. I loved that childlike part of myself when it came to the surface.

Still called Saigon by almost everyone who lived there, the city's character was essentially French, with wide boulevards, colonial villas, and a lively café society. Much of the old French colonial city had vanished beneath the rapidly rising skyline. Like many Asian cities, Saigon is dogged by traffic problems as more and more people want, and can afford, mobility. Some main roads were often gridlocked with literally thousands of motorbikes, scooters, bicycles and cyclos (rickshaws), as well as a few buses and cars.

All kinds of people travelled by bicycle or motorbike. There were women in their traditional áo dàis (a kind of tunic with long sleeves) and conical hats, and whole families—with the mother, father, and two or three children—squeezed onto one seat. Visually, Saigon and London were miles apart. It was like we'd been transported to another world. I'd seen so many movies depicting Saigon in the sixties and seventies, at the time of the Vietnam war. Being there and walking around was like walking on to the set of one of them. It was loud, vibrant, exciting, and visually captivating, with the delightful smell of street food permeating all my senses. I enjoyed the unfamiliar sound of the language and the chaos. It was a far cry from the serenity of the monastery where we'd been in a retreat a few weeks earlier.

To look for some budget accommodation, we ventured into the older parts of the city. Walking through District One, an area popular with travellers, we found a stark contrast to the clean, wide boulevards of central Saigon. In the older parts of the city, there's a high premium on space. As a result, the guesthouses were tall and thin concrete structures, packed together in tiny alleyways like giant dominoes. If a guesthouse had ten rooms, it probably had the same number of floors.

The alleys were too small and narrow to drive cars through. Guests looking out of their cramped bedroom windows on opposite sides almost had to take it in turns to avoid clashing heads! Despite this, it didn't feel claustrophobic. I practiced looking at this situation in a non-judgmental way. It wasn't necessary to decide if these buildings were something we liked or didn't like. I kept saying to myself, "It is what it is." I realised that events didn't always match with my expectations of what I thought they should be like, which was still predominantly based on my experiences of living in London. Not being attached to how things should be is one of the joys of travelling and something I was committed to keep practicing.

We chose a rather quaint little mini hotel called the Khách Sạn Mini Tân Mai Phai. Don't get the wrong idea; it was more like a basic hostel. Luckily, we got a room on the first floor and avoided carrying our heavy backpacks up and down the stairs. This may make me sound lazy but when you're on the move all the time, tiny benefits like this make a huge amount of difference to your levels of comfort, stress, and energy.

Our guesthouse offered food, and the kitchen was located on the ground floor. Because the building was so tiny, we literally had to walk through the kitchen to get in. We were fascinated as we observed the people working there. It was their chef who provided us with the inspiration for our *Daily Lama* food correspondent. In her next post, she wrote that Saigon was "teeming with food markets, crammed with tropical fruits, king cobras, and barbecued dogs. The pavements are packed with cafés, noodle stands, and vendors selling everything from baguettes to bottled snake whiskey."

Hanoi

Our flight to Hanoi in the former North Vietnam was simple and easy, apart from one tense moment when Annie was stopped by the airport security team and told to empty her bag for inspection. She'd inadvertently packed our vegetable peeler in her carry-on luggage, and it had been detected on the scanner, making her a security risk. We happily tossed it in the bin, boarded our aircraft, and joked about the incident for the next fifteen minutes. Just like young kids, we pretended to be super-tough, gun-toting, military-style, American airport security staff. "Excuse me, ma'am. Slowly put down your vegetable peeler, keep your hands where we can see them, and step away from the conveyor belt." We just couldn't stop laughing about it, until we reached the point when we thought our ribs would be crushed if we didn't calm down.

Things were going well between Annie and me. We enjoyed each other's company and laughed a lot, and we found some great places to explore together. We argued less and our connection enhanced our life on the road. We loved the city of Hanoi, which survived many American bombs during the Vietnam war. It had a timeless grace, and was full of Parisian charm, due to its history as a French colony.

Close to our guesthouse was a small, grubby, and exceptionally friendly street café serving a local dish known as bún cá (pronounced Boon Cha) which consists of fresh, handmade, white rice noodles served with delicious, barbecued pork meatballs, homemade spring rolls, and fresh salad greens and herbs. We loved it so much, we went back there for more several times. The family who lived and worked there took a shine to Annie; she'd found a way to connect with them despite not understanding their language. They invited her to try her hand at making their legendary meatballs. I hadn't eaten any meat since our retreat at Suan Mokkh, where I'd committed to a vegetarian diet. As with everything in life, there are always going to be exceptions and eating Annie's homemade meatballs had to be one of them. I'm happy to tell you it was truly worth it!

To keep ourselves fit, we got up early each day to run around Hoàn Kiếm Lake in the centre of the Old Quarter. It's one of Hanoi's charms. The lake was surrounded by a constant flow of traffic and drew hundreds of people from around 5:30 a.m., who came to exercise together before they started their long day's work. They congregated in small groups on the pavements and grassy areas around the lake to practice aerobics or tai chi. Some men lifted weights, while others played badminton on makeshift courts. Some people came to sit and meditate. Many of them were quite old, and the morning ritual seemed to be an important part of their social life. Despite their age, the younger people on the scene were engaged with them and appeared to respect and enjoy their older company.

It was uplifting and inspiring to witness. Sadly, I hadn't seen this kind of community spirit when I lived in London. None of these people would ever have belonged to the kind of posh, well-equipped gyms that I'd been a member of. We observed a complete absence of self-consciousness amongst these groups. Everyone joined in without regard for how they looked or what their level of ability or fitness was. Husbands, wives, friends, and neighbours. They all supported each other. People young and old made time to hang out with their friends for a while before their busy day started. It made me stop and think. How often do we consciously find time to socialise with people in our community around our busy work schedules? How might this approach foster more joy and lightness in our daily lives? It's definitely something you can experiment with, and you don't need to leave the country to do it. It occurred to me that life without a tie, for some of us, is as much about how we break the ties of our mental conditioning, beliefs, and habits as it is about geography, career, and relationships.

Annie and I relished the opportunity to re-establish a regular programme of exercise. We were constantly on the move and consequently, were never in one place long enough to get into any sort of routine. We decided to stay in Hanoi for about three weeks. It gave us an ideal opportunity to focus on our health and well-being for a while. Of my ten guiding principles, health had slowly climbed up the list in terms of overall importance to our safe travelling.

On a lighter note, our exercise regime gave us an excuse for our *Daily*

LIFE WITHOUT A TIE

Lama health and fitness correspondent to prepare his first post. He didn't have to wait very long to publish it either. Through a random connection, we met an English chap living there who was a member of the Hanoi branch of the Hash House Harriers (HHH). He invited us to join their group for one of their seven kilometre runs through the hills on the outskirts of the city.

The HHH are possibly one of the best-kept secrets in the world. I'd never heard of them. According to Wikipedia, hashing originated in Selangor, Malaysia back in 1938. A group of British colonial officers and ex-pats met on Monday evenings to rid themselves of the excesses of the previous weekend by going for a strenuous run. Hashing died out during World War II shortly after the invasion of Malaya but was restarted in 1946 by several of the original group. The objectives of the HHH, printed on the club registration card dated 1950, were:

To promote physical fitness among our members
To get rid of weekend hangovers
To acquire a good thirst and to satisfy it in beer
To persuade the older members that they are not as old as
  they feel

Astonishingly, there are almost two thousand chapters in existence in cities all over the world. Members distribute newsletters, directories, and magazines and organise regional and world hashing events. There are even two organised chapters operating in Antarctica! If you do a Google search, you'll probably find at least one chapter in your own town. Once you've joined, you can run with any chapter in any city you happen to find yourself in. It's like a huge, ready-made global social club.

Stumbling upon the existence of the HHH made me realise that our perceptions of the world and what we think we know can be incredibly narrow. This discovery, and others like it, was one of the reasons I loved travelling so much. It made me even more curious about what else is out there, waiting to be discovered. Looking back, I don't think it was an accident we found the group. It supported our focus on physical exercise and gave us a clear purpose for making the effort to do it. To get up at 5.30 a.m., we had to be motivated. Preparing ourselves to run six or seven kilometres gave us all the motivation we needed to run two to three times around Hoàn Kiếm Lake every morning. And it also sowed a tiny seed in my subconscious mind about becoming a long-distance runner. I'll tell you more about that in chapter ten.

The day of the Hash run came around and, despite our preparation, was pretty challenging for us. It was a dry, sunny Sunday afternoon. The trail was set through small forests and open fields in the Hanoi countryside. It was quite muddy in places from heavy rainfall that week, and we reached the end of the run in a state of mild exhaustion. We had big smiles on our faces, mainly because we managed to make it all the way until the end. In the aftermath, we enjoyed the age-old hash tradition of a drink and singsong with the entire group before heading back to town on the bus.

Sa Pa

We left Hanoi and took an overnight train to Sa Pa in the far north, close to the border with China. I'd never slept on a train before, and I was both nervous and excited in equal amounts. We were in a small compartment with four berths, two up and two down on either side, which meant we'd be in an intimate space with two strangers for a few hours. Fortunately, a charming French couple were allocated the other two bunks. We shared our travel stories and biscuits before nodding off to sleep. Any reservations I might have had about spending the night in a train were unfounded. I slept like a baby and was refreshed and ready to go on our arrival the next morning.

Sa Pa is a peaceful and beautiful place with millions of acres of rolling hills, rice paddies, and lush green vegetation. Compared with Siem Reap, it felt considerably less aggressive and chaotic and almost tranquil. A fellow traveller gave us a tip for a guesthouse, high up on a hilly road with great vistas, so we headed there and managed to secure a mountain view room for a few days for just a few pounds. At fifteen hundred metres' elevation, we were above the clouds sometimes. It made me feel like I was genuinely in heaven. Since my meditation retreat in Suan Mokhh, I'd felt increasingly grateful for the simple, natural gifts like this which life offered, ones I'd previously failed to notice. It lifted my spirit when I sat on the deck of the guesthouse, drinking my morning coffee as the sun was rising above the distant mountains, whilst a blanket of white cloud covered the small town below us. I'd take a few deep, mindful breaths as I surveyed the panorama, and feel expanded and energised. If you ever get the opportunity to visit

LIFE WITHOUT A TIE

Vietnam, this is one of the destinations I recommend, particularly for the hundreds of miles of trekking trails between and around the villages in the region.

It always amazes me how, when you have a purpose, the Universe helps you in ways you could never expect or plan for. I've experienced this many times in my life. Annie and I had met a couple called Darren and Rachael (from the USA and Australia respectively) in Hanoi. They'd recently been to Sa Pa and befriended a small group of Hmong children (an indigenous Vietnamese people) and had established a special bond with some of these kids. They had no idea where they lived, but they'd given us a photograph of two of these girls, so we emailed Darren and Rachael to let them know we were going to visit.

On our first morning there, armed with a map, their picture of the girls, and plenty of energy, we searched for them. We used the photograph to ask locals if they knew them. Because Darren and Rachael had told us so much about them, we felt we somehow knew the girls and were excited about finding them. Before long, we came across a small group of Hmong girls and showed them the photograph.

"I know her, and her," said one of the Hmong girls in the group.

We were fired up. We were on the right track and were thrilled that someone had confirmed their existence. She offered to take us to the local market to meet the mother of the two girls, and we gratefully accepted. This was a small town in the mountains ,and we had absolutely no way of knowing where these girls might reside. For all we knew, they could be miles away. We followed her to meet the woman she'd told us about. We quickly got the confirmation we were hoping for. The woman was definitely the mother of these girls. We explained to her that we were friends of Darren and Rachel and would love to meet her daughters, if it was okay with her. She was delighted her daughters would get another chance to improve their English, as well as eat some decent food at the market. A few minutes later, we were talking to them.

From that moment on, they accompanied us everywhere as we explored the town and the trekking paths. They didn't want to leave our side. As unbelievable as it might seem, there is a restaurant for travellers called Wish You Were Here! which I soon realised was named after the album by Pink Floyd. I grew up in the seventies listening to the *Dark Side of The Moon* and *Wish You Were Here* albums. Discovering this strange and unique place gave Annie and me a great opportunity to have some fun in our next blog post, which we published a few days later. In satirical style, Po Scard commented on the irony of finding a restaurant named after a British band in the northernmost region of Vietnam, and described in comical detail how guests were offered soup "Any Colour you Like", a hard bench to sit on making you "Comfortably Numb" and how, after dinner you could "Have a Cigar" if you fancied one. We also were told that staff don't fraternise with the guests; it is strictly "Us and Them." If you can think of any others, well done!

It's hard to convey how remote and medieval the villages are in the hill tribe regions around Sa Pa. It's like another world compared to the modern cities that many of us live in. We found a guy who owned an old military Jeep, and we paid him to take us to places that were off the beaten track for a couple of days. We stayed overnight in a small mountain village called Bắc Hà, with a population of three hundred people. During a perilous three-hour drive, our driver had to negotiate at least a dozen hairpin bends, on rocky tracks no wider than the Jeep, and with a sheer drop into the valley below, just to reach the place.

I walked around and came across a group of men gathered around an animal. From a distance, I couldn't make out what it was, but as I got closer, I could see it was a dog. The animal was obviously distressed and desperately struggling to get away from them. One of the men took out a knife and cut its throat, making sure that the blood flowed into a bowl that had been placed on the ground. Within a minute or so, the dog was dead. I'd never seen anything even remotely like this in my life, and it shocked me. Given the way I've been conditioned, it seemed outrageous and disgusting. Yet in this community, I realised it was regarded as perfectly normal. Dogs are routinely eaten, in much the same way as we eat pigs, cows, and sheep. No one consciously considers they're committing an act of cruelty. To these people, it was a totally normal thing to do. Not only that, they believe that drinking the dog's blood enhances their virility. Once again, it gave me an opportunity to observe my need to judge situations as good or bad, and right or wrong when in fact, it just is what it is.

The next morning as we were about to leave our lodgings, we observed a commotion going on nearby and asked our driver if it was okay to investigate. I was curious to understand what it was all about and could see a small crowd had gathered around a man with a trolley which was blaring out strange, loud music from a megaphone. On closer inspection, we discovered that the adoption of technology was happening slowly in these parts of the world. Behind the maniacal interest of the crowd was… a new laminating machine! We laughed. These days, we may take things like this for granted, but in the remote mountain villages of northern Vietnam, this sort of thing was cutting edge.

The DMZ

After Sa Pa, we headed back south along the coast of the South China Sea towards Saigon. The scenery in northern Vietnam is among the best that I've seen anywhere in the world and is absolutely stunning. If you ever want to visit a region that will literally take your breath away, then head for Hạ Long Bay in the Gulf of Tonkin. The bay has a dense cluster of nearly two thousand monolithic limestone islands, each topped with thick jungle vegetation, and they rise spectacularly from the ocean. It looks like something out of *Jurassic Park*. Several of the islands are hollow and have enormous caves. Annie and I spent three days exploring some of these, which made an indelible impression on both of us.

At this point, it dawned on us that we'd not spent any time lazing on a beach for months. Cát Bà island, one of many in the Hạ Long Bay area, had a great beach. When we heard about it, we started craving the idea of a lazy day in the sunshine, despite the fact that our mindfulness training had helped us to realise that cravings are the very things which create expectations and desires that ultimately lead to more suffering! You may think it strange that a full-time traveller wouldn't spend more time relaxing on beaches, but I wasn't really thinking about this journey as a holiday. Holidays come to an end. But my journey was continuous, with no end in sight.

To make the most of each moment, as per my guiding principle of presence, there was a trade-off sometimes between choosing a day to rest on the beach, which could be great for my overall health and wellness, or choosing a more active experience, which might broaden my mind and be more energising. Annie and I constantly reviewed our itinerary so we'd be clear about our options. We only had a limited number of days before our visas expired. If we made a choice to spend a day sunbathing, it had to be worth it. In the case of Cát Bà Island, it definitely was. Resting is an important part of life, and we'd needed that day more than we realised.

Exploring Asia

Vietnam is perhaps best known by older foreigners for its war, which ended in 1975. As a child, I grew up watching coverage of the fighting on TV news bulletins. During that conflict, as many as a quarter of a million American troops had been stationed there. These days, much of the tourism industry exploits this part of the country's history, and there are hundreds of tours which take you to the demilitarized zone (DMZ), underground tunnels, and famous battle sites like Khe San and Hamburger Hill. Those historical events have been revised and glorified in a stream of heroic Hollywood movies. Going there is the only way of grasping the reality of what really happened. And it's somewhat different from the stories portrayed in the movies.

A great example of this was the incredible underground labyrinth of tunnels at Vịnh Mốc, close to the DMZ, that used to separate North and South Vietnam. The tunnels are a monument to the determination of the North Vietnamese people to preserve and triumph at all costs and despite some incredible sacrifices in the Vietnam War.

In 1966, the USA began a massive aerial bombardment of North Vietnam. Just north of the DMZ, the villagers of Vịnh Mốc found themselves living in one of the most heavily bombed and shelled strips of land on the planet, and their village was almost entirely destroyed. The three hundred or so people who lived there started digging an underground network of tunnels and rooms by hand for the eighty-two families in their community. During the next six years, the underground population grew to around six hundred people, with seventeen babies being born inside the tunnels during that time. The Viet Cong (VC) found it useful to have a base at Vịnh Mốc and encouraged the villagers to stay. After eighteen months of work, during which the excavated earth was camouflaged to prevent detection from the air, an enormous VC base was established underground. There were one hundred and fourteen tunnels, with a total length of forty-one kilometres, built on three levels ranging between fifteen to twenty-six metres below ground. It seems to me that a lot of pain and suffering was endured by the Vietnamese people on the way to gaining their independence. Talking to many citizens about it helped me to understand more about their culture and way of life. Travelling is so brilliant for that kind of education.

Annie and I stopped in several towns along the south coast including Huế, Da Nang, and Hội An. But it was in Nha Trang that the Vietnam War ceased to be a story about other people and turned into one which we could connect with personally. Scanes Bentley, a former colleague and friend in England, is half American. His late father had been commander of the US Air Base at Nha Trang during the war. Scanes had never been to Vietnam and was keen to obtain more information about this part of his father's life. He knew I was there and asked me if I could find out if the base still existed. If it did, he wanted me to take some pictures for him. Armed with my camera, I went on a mission to find the base.

It turned out to be more difficult than I'd imagined. I asked a few locals about it but none of them seemed to know. Most of them were probably too young to remember 1968. Persistence is one of my strengths and after several hours, I eventually found something on the internet which helped me to establish exactly where it was. The next day, I went there to have a look and discovered that the former wartime US air base was indeed there. It had been used as a civilian airport for many years until its recent conversion back to a military training base. I wasn't allowed inside to get pictures, but I didn't want to disappoint Scanes, especially as I was aware he'd be celebrating his birthday in England while I was there.

Instead, I shot some video footage outside the base and edited it into a short movie, telling him the story of how I found the base. I searched the buildings around the airfield perimeter and managed to find an eight-storey guesthouse positioned within a whisker of the airfield. I politely asked if I could go up onto the roof, which they kindly let me do. I captured some great footage, which I edited into the movie and sent to Scanes via the internet in time for his birthday. This was exactly the kind of thing I had in mind when I included contribution as one of my ten guiding principles. It gave me an opportunity to share the benefit of being in these far-flung places with people who were unable to be there.

Further south, we stopped in Dalat, which was once called Le Petit Paris because it has a miniature replica of the Eiffel Tower which doubles as a mobile phone mast. The town is a favourite haunt of Vietnamese artists and avant-garde types, many of whom have made it their permanent home. We found the charming Stop and Go café there. It was a split-level, low-ceilinged, Bohemian kind of place. Mr Duy Viet, the owner, invited us in. A softly spoken, eccentric artist and poet, he wore a classic French beret, had a cigarette between his lips, and a cup of tea in his hand. With his thin, weathered face and long, greying goatee on his chin, he was the image of a gentle, revolutionary thinker, poet, or literary professor. He showed us his set of Japanese felt pens, with which he could spontaneously write, in flourishing style, poems in French, English, or Vietnamese.

Nothing can beat the call of nature. In Dalat, Annie and I trekked in some absolutely breathtaking places. When I lived in England, I hardly ever had the time or the desire to set foot in the countryside. In Asia, I'd discovered the unadulterated joy of walking through forests and rocky uphill paths to take in the amazing views. I loved it when I felt the sun and wind on my face. The pleasure of utilising my body fully, feeling my own power and strength through constant movement was addictive. In the hills and valleys of Dalat, we worked up a sweat and enjoyed a daredevil adventure, as we crossed a couple of long, swinging wire and wood footbridges, suspended with rope above a mountain stream. These dilapidated, rickety walkways sit about five or six metres above the rapidly flowing water and are only wide enough and strong enough for one person at a time. Stepping carefully on each one of the separate wooden boards, about half a metre apart, certainly got our adrenaline going.

We completed our tour of Vietnam with a fifteen-kilometre cycle ride from Di Linh to Mũi Né. The first section went through a coffee plantation and forest and included a five-kilometre uphill climb to get us warmed up. I knew it was going to be hard, and I was delighted they were able to rent us some decent mountain bikes with plenty of gears. At least Annie and I managed to complete the uphill phase without stopping, even though people walking overtook us once or twice! The rest of our route was mainly downhill as we made our way to the beautiful, red sandy beaches and dunes of Mũi Né.

Koh Samui, Thailand

Before departing for Australia for Christmas with Annie's family, we'd booked ourselves in for a week at The Spa on the island of Koh Samui in the Gulf of Thailand. After four straight months on the road, we'd returned there knowing that it would be good for our well-being to complete our first seven-day liver cleanse and detox. The Spa was launched in the nineties, and we'd heard from fellow travellers that their cleansing programme was excellent and cheap as chips, which suited my frugal budget. We also liked the fact their kitchen served some of the best vegetarian food in Thailand. If you're into a raw diet, they have one of the best raw-food preparation schools anywhere in the world.

LIFE WITHOUT A TIE

In case you're wondering why anyone might want to do a cleanse, Dr Rich Anderson, one of the world's leading authorities, answered that question in his best-selling book, *Cleanse and Purify Thyself*. When the bowel becomes clogged up like a blocked drain, the blood becomes filthy, and our liver is the first line of defence against toxic bowel particles that enter the bloodstream. When these toxic bowel particles accumulate over months and years, our liver can become challenged and over-exerted. Eventually, excessive proteins and fats cause the liver to lose its ability to function normally, and then toxicity begins to enter deeper areas of the body. According to Dr Anderson, eighty-five percent of the Western world's population have sluggish livers.

Obviously, Annie and I had no way of knowing exactly what state our bowels and livers were in. With one of my guiding principles being health, it made sense to check it out. We'd been living in Asia for about a year and mainly eaten in restaurants and markets, where we had no idea how our food was sourced or prepared. It was possible our internal systems were working under pressure, so we decided to give our bodies some internal maintenance. We were in reasonably good shape already, mainly from eating vegetarian food and doing tons of trekking.

After we'd completed our week at The Spa, we felt like a million dollars health-wise. It's incredible what eliminating all food and drink except pure juices and a couple of coffee enemas a day can do. Can you imagine how much better you might feel if you were to put yourself through a programme like that?

The peacefulness, inactivity, and rest those few days offered gave me a chance to connect with myself at a deeper level, and I unexpectedly became aware of a feeling of trepidation as the week came to an end. My life without a tie adventure was about to be indefinitely suspended, so that I could spend Christmas with Annie's family in the most conventional of settings. I wasn't excited about that, if I'm being completely honest. I've never been a big fan of traditional Christmas Day festivities in England. Excessive consumption of food and gifts that people often don't want or need, accompanied by over-the-top drinking of alcohol all seemed rather pointless.

When I was married, Christmas Day had often been spent at my in-laws' house, and their routine was the same every year. Of course, I wasn't sure if Annie's family celebrated Christmas in the same way, but I assumed it would be along the same lines, with the exception of being able to swim in the pool all day in the Australian summer sunshine.

From a selfish point of view, going to Australia meant that I'd be able to visit Matt and Elizabeth Taylor, who you may recall I'd stayed with in 2005 before taking part in *Out of Order*. They'd flown up to Cairns from Sydney for one of the shows, and I was thrilled about seeing them again. As we took off for Perth, I had no idea that for Annie and me, this trip was our last season together.

Chapter Six
A Fork in the Road

ANNIE WAS EXCITED THAT HER MOTHER, HER SISTER, ALL HER UNCLES AND AUNTS, as well as several cousins had gathered in Perth at the same time, an event that hadn't been seen in her family for years. In all, a total of thirty-five were there, including us. She was also excited to introduce me to all of them. She believed we'd been together long enough to consider our relationship to be serious and sustainable. Unfortunately, that wasn't true for me. The timing of this encounter, which I'd known about since the day I left England a year earlier, seemed all wrong…

In the fantasy romantic movie, *The Curious Case of Benjamin Button*, Benjamin is born as a tiny, aged, and wrinkled man, and subsequently abandoned by his shocked parents on the doorstep of an old folks' home. There, he fits in well, despite his small size, as he looks as old as the other residents. But unlike everyone else, Benjamin ages in reverse and grows younger every day. Early on in the story, he meets the love of his life, Daisy. She is a cute red-haired girl who becomes a beautiful woman, while Benjamin becomes a handsome young man. For a few short years, they are able to enjoy a close, romantic relationship when they are both about the same age. As she gets older, he continues to become a child. The longevity of the relationship is doomed, as both know they can only enjoy the few years in which their life paths overlap.

My relationship with Annie was similar. When we met, I'd just come out of a long marriage and was free again for the first time in nearly fifteen years. I wasn't ready to tie things down with her permanently. It was extremely hard for me to say this to Annie in a way she could understand and accept. To convey what that sense of freedom felt like, let me ask you a question. Have you seen dairy cows who, after years of captivity in small pens and being milked every day, are released into open fields again and retired? Once they realise they're free, they often start leaping for joy and running around in circles, grateful for the opportunity to rediscover the life they were born to live. Do yourself a favour and watch a couple of videos on YouTube and I guarantee you'll be moved by what you see. That's how I felt about my life in that moment.

By contrast, I believe Annie was ready to make a deep, heartfelt commitment with the right person to a lifelong partnership. She'd never been married and had reached a point in her life journey where doing that seemed like a natural and powerful development in her evolution. She wanted to make sure her investment in our relationship wasn't a waste of her time and effort and had patiently waited for me to come around to the idea of a committed, long-term partnership. Applying my guiding principle of wisdom, I couldn't take that step with her until I was sure it was a real and authentic desire for me and not just a way to meet her needs. I had no idea how much time I needed or whether I would ever feel that way. Naturally, Annie asked me when I might know, but I was unable to give her any reassurance as I literally had no idea.

I accepted the status quo that resulted and continuously reminded myself that everything I needed to know would reveal itself to me at the time it was meant to. For Annie, the uncertainty was difficult to live with. In that sense, our paths were different and diverging further with each passing day. This created tension and was a source of conflict between us, which couldn't be resolved. On the surface, everything was okay, and our day-to-day life continued to be fun and enjoyable. But below the surface, our relationship was in trouble in much the same way as a ship that has been holed by a torpedo under the waterline. As my whole journey was about discovering how to live life true to myself, I was unwilling to consider any decision that would compromise that. Annie knew this deep down, but it still caused her pain.

The day after we arrived in Perth, we checked our online stats and discovered that our *Daily Lama* blog had been viewed around seven thousand times during 2006, way beyond anything we'd hoped for or imagined. Given that I had no experience of blogging prior to this, I was pleased to see the positive impact we'd had. It was a confirmation signal from the Universe that I'd embraced my principle of contribution as I'd intended. Our arrival in Australia meant it was time to expand our team of special correspondents. Coverage of our travel adventures down under was going to be provided by master journo Chuck Maboomerang, naturally!

Annie and I loved that everyone in Australia could understand us. This may sound funny, but we'd become quite well practiced in overcoming

LIFE WITHOUT A TIE

the challenge of communicating with people in Asian countries, where we couldn't read the notices or signs and often struggled to have them understand or answer our questions. It was a welcome treat to speak in English for a while. Without the humidity and with the temperature being a few degrees higher than in Bangkok, our stay in Perth was even more pleasurable.

We stayed with Annie's Uncle Ron and Aunty Betty. They lived in an area known as the Perth Hills, with a sprawling home and vineyard in a beautiful green valley. Ron was a tall, bearded, burly man and a wine lover. He'd been producing small quantities of pinot noir for a couple of years. We made ourselves at home as more members of Annie's huge family arrived for the holidays. Annie has five cousins living in or around Perth, who all have children of their own, plus her family from the UK. Her sister, with husband and three children in tow, and her mum flew in from England. People dropped in throughout the day and evening, and it was pure chaos sorting out rooms and couches for so many people. It was incredibly noisy too; we'd come from the peace and tranquillity of The Spa in Thailand, so the raucous liveliness in the house was a bit overwhelming at times. To counter it, I went for little walks in the garden or sat out on the porch to regenerate my energy before engaging with the crowd again.

Annie's family were kind and generous. They had to be kind to Annie, but it was optional when it came to me, and I appreciated that a lot. One of Annie's cousins owned an apartment in a small coastal hamlet about half an hour's drive away, which they kindly offered to us for some peace and privacy. Ron let us borrow his old Toyota pickup so we could drive ourselves there and back. That gave us two quiet and restful days to ourselves before the joyful mayhem of Christmas with thirty-five people was in full swing. While we were there, we studied the map of Australia carefully and started to consider the possibility of making a once in a lifetime road trip from Perth to Adelaide.

Exploring the great Australian outback was something both of us were keen to do. We knew it would take longer to get to Adelaide by road than by air and cost a lot more. Yet, crossing the Nullarbor Plain really appealed to our sense of adventure. The more we researched and spoke to local people about it, the more concrete our vision became until we finally made the decision to do it. We booked a small campervan and arranged to pick it up after the Christmas festivities. Setting that up relieved my anxiety about handling the challenges of the family Christmas, as I now knew there was light at the end of that tunnel. After the Vipassana retreat earlier that year and with increased self-awareness, I had more clarity about my personal preferences and felt less tolerant about, or willing to participate in, superficial events, which is how I'd prejudged the imminent Christmas party.

Christmas Day morning at Ron and Betty's house was extremely busy. Feeding thirty-five people with a traditional Christmas lunch is no easy feat. With a willing crew toiling away in the kitchen, Ron kindly offered to provide newcomers like me with tours of his vineyard. He loved his forty-year-old red tractor and was grateful for any excuse to crank it up and drive it around with a trailer he'd attached for guests. Despite my earlier reservations, I managed to actually enjoy his tour, and I learned a few things about grapes too. Soon after, we all sat down for a sumptuous lunch. To my relief, it turned out to be far less of an ordeal than I'd imagined. After hours of stuffing ourselves, we retired to rest on the couches or in the garden. It was over ninety degrees outside, and there were plenty of chairs and towels around Ron's pool.

I stayed alert to ensure I participated according to my guiding principles. As an outsider, I found a great way to make a lasting contribution to everyone present and to repay some of the kindness and hospitality I'd received. I had my video camera and laptop with me. I made a short video of the family Christmas gathering and gave everyone a copy. I'd discreetly filmed people in and around the garden and house and had captured some delightful moments. I edited the clips together and chose some upbeat music for the soundtrack. To get the editing done, I had to isolate myself for a few hours. Nobody minded my absence, as they all knew I was creating a souvenir for them. Ron had one of those massive flat screen TVs which meant everyone saw it when it was finally ready on Boxing Day. They all loved it—mission accomplished!

Later that evening, after most of the kids had gone to bed and everyone was getting settled for the night, I wandered out onto the veranda for what unexpectedly turned out to be one of the pivotal moments of the entire trip and my relationship with Annie. It was dark. Most of the other family members had gone to bed. Ron was sitting with a brandy in his hand, quietly talking to Annie. There was no one else around. Although he'd lived in Australia for many years, Ron was from the north of England

and people from those parts are generally known for their forthright, unambiguous straight-talking approach. He was definitely no exception. He invited me to sit with the two of them and offered me a brandy too.

"So, when are you going to make an honest woman out of Annie?" Ron asked.

I was stunned. This phrase is a popular British euphemism for "When are you going to get married?" It was unexpected. He sat there quietly and looked at me as he waited for my answer. Annie looked just as surprised as I was, but nonetheless, was obviously interested in my answer too. The silence was deafening. It reminded me of awkward silences from my school days when a teacher would ask which person in the class had thrown a paper airplane across the room while their back was turned, and no one would confess.

I thought about what to say, all the while feeling Ron's eyes fixed on me like a missile locked on to a target. "I don't know. I haven't really thought about that yet. It's still early days." It was about the best I could come up with.

The honest truth was that I couldn't really imagine getting married to Annie, yet I felt ashamed to admit that. Ron was no fool and neither was Annie. My silent pause, followed by my less than enthusiastic answer, failed to convince either of them that I was in the relationship for the long haul. I'd been exposed. But at the same time, my answer to Ron's question allowed me to realise my truth. It was the first time I'd admitted it to myself. There wasn't a long-term future for the two of us. The hard reality about the gap in our needs was now coming to light. Both of us had chosen to overlook it until now, for different reasons, but neither of us had admitted the truth about it. The cat was now out of the proverbial bag.

Crossing the Nullarbor
I let that sink in for the next day or two. Neither Annie nor I talked about it for some time. On the surface, everything continued as normal, with the slight feeling of tension here and there. After the New Year, it was time to leave Perth, pick up our campervan, and get back on the road. Unlike hiring a car in Europe, there are unique hazards that drivers face in Australia. One of them is roadkill. In the outback, kangaroos freely roam everywhere and are often hit by cars and trucks when they cross the road. The guy at the hire company explained that if anything stepped out in front

of us, our safest bet was to hit it. He pointed to a vehicle in his yard that had been hired to a driver who hadn't followed this advice. That driver swerved off the road to avoid the animal, rolled the vehicle a couple of times and smashed it to pieces. He sustained serious injuries, as did his passengers. I made a mental note.

Perth to Adelaide is an 1,800-mile journey, and we reckoned we'd make it in seven days. It's a long distance to cover in that time, but we'd studied the maps, talked to people who had done the drive, and felt comfortable we could handle the challenge. The uneasy feeling between us was soon forgotten as the excitement of crossing the Nullarbor Plain, one of the world's biggest land masses, got underway. The journey took us through some of the most remote and beautiful parts of Australia.

To give you some perspective, driving from Perth to Adelaide is about the same distance as driving from London to Moscow, although you'd encounter considerably more traffic on the latter route. The modern campervan we had was designed to cram everything you could possibly need into a tiny, constantly interchangeable and functional space. Our first night in it had us both wetting ourselves with laughter. When I was a young kid, I played with a little square plastic puzzle that had room for nine tiles, but only eight were included which left a space so you could move them around, up, down, and sideways. Each tile had a number from one to eight, and you had to get them all in the right order. Accomplishing that was a lot harder than it sounds! Navigating a small campervan is the human equivalent of one of those puzzles. Annie and I had both underestimated the degree to which everything inside van had to be moved in a logical, sequential order. This was essential for us to choreograph our movement inside the van and avoid constantly bumping into each other. For example, to make the bed, the table first had to be stowed away. That meant the table had to be cleared, so the dishes on the table needed to be washed. That needed water pumped to the sink, which required the tank to be filled, and so on. Eventually, we found our rhythm and routine and had no serious problems with it.

It felt wonderful and free to be back on the road. This trip, my light at the end of the tunnel, had done its job of keeping me mentally well through the family Christmas holiday, and I was now running under my own power again, with all my energy back. Annie and I were aware that the conversation with her Uncle Ron had exposed a fundamental truth, but we somehow ignored it for the sake of the trip. It may have been irresponsible, but we both took the view that life itself would help us deal with that further down the road, and we'd face the issue at the time when it needed to be dealt with. For now, we just wanted to be present and enjoy what we were doing.

The Nullarbor Plain covers a total area of seventy-seven thousand square miles. The name comes from the Latin words nullus and arbor meaning no trees. The region starts in Esperance, and once we'd passed through, the landscape changed from Amazon-like rainforest to a barren, featureless wasteland. In order to arrive in Adelaide on time, we monitored our progress every day to make sure we covered the required distance. Once or twice, we routed along unsealed roads which were much slower, as the tyres kicked up loads of dust and stones. But it felt way more adventurous on those desolate, gravel roads. There were hardly any other drivers, and we enjoyed the safe isolation it brought. The downside was that everything inside the van got covered in a fine layer of dust that permeated through the vents and air-conditioning system. It only took a few miles on a dirt road before the van was filthy. It took ages to clean it up, so we limited taking these routes.

On the tarmac highways, there really isn't that much to see or do. The main route across the Nullarbor contains Australia's longest stretch of absolutely straight road. It's more commonly known as the Ninety Mile Straight. We were thrilled we could say we'd been there, done it, and got the T-shirt. It lived up to its name, in that it was long, straight, and had the potential to induce extreme boredom. We made the passage more interesting by inventing a new game, which involved spotting vehicles in the distance coming towards us and guessing how long it would be before they passed us. The closest guess won. That kind of thing is only necessary in a country which is so huge that you literally pass through different time zones every couple of days.

My favourite part of the journey, and certainly the most beautiful, came towards the end. The Great Australian Bight stretches for about six hundred miles and is thought to be the longest line of cliffs in the world. We parked the van and made our way on foot to the edge of the cliffs where we watched several huge schools of dolphins breaking the ocean's surface. It was incredible, and a treasured moment that we were extremely grateful for. It reminded us of the serenity and beautiful simplicity we'd experienced during our Vipassana retreat in Thailand.

Our final night in the campervan was spent in Mount Remarkable National Park in Wilmington. It was *so* remote. I'll never forget sitting outside after we cleared our supper away. It was well after dark, and there was absolutely no light pollution from streetlamps or anything manmade. We couldn't hear any traffic noise or aircraft overhead. Just a magnificent silence, punctuated with the sounds of a few wild animals. We marvelled at the sky above us, a pitch-black canopy with thousands of bright, shining stars and a half moon filling the darkness. We sat quietly for an hour or two to take it in fully and appreciate the gift we'd been given. The icing on the cake came when we were joined by a couple of possums looking for some morsels of food. We heard them before we could see them, which made us a little bit frightened at first, but not for long. They seemed completely used to humans and stayed for quite a while before scuttling off into the bush.

The Fork Appears
When we reached Adelaide, we'd covered a total distance of 2,260 miles. We'd achieved the crossing in seven days and come through it with hardly any mishaps. We crossed the water to visit nearby Tasmania, which had a compelling natural beauty and was packed full of gorges, mountain trails, rivers, and stunning countryside. It was during our visit there that Annie received a message from Steve Greenwood, who we'd met earlier that year in Hanoi. He worked with a non-government organisation (NGO) and invited her to join him and deliver a multimedia project in Cambodia that was in the pipeline. He wanted her to train a group of ten facilitators in the use of forum theatre techniques to raise awareness and debate around child protection issues.

Annie had used these in her work, but this was the first time she'd had the opportunity to train others to use them. It would also be her first time working with an NGO. The project was slated to start in a few weeks and required her to be in Cambodia for at least a month. It gave Annie a meaningful and exciting opportunity to volunteer for a programme in which she'd be helping underprivileged people develop their skills, and she wanted to take it. Since our Australian visas were about to expire, and we had to leave the country, like it or not, the timing was perfect. Life had stepped in to offer us the helping hand we'd hoped for when we left Perth.

LIFE WITHOUT A TIE

Whilst I was happy for Annie, the invitation from Steve triggered some discomfort and uncertainty. I had no fixed plan beyond Australia and could easily have gone with Annie, but a part of me didn't want to go. I kept thinking back to the realisation I'd had at Christmas on Ron's porch about not seeing a long-term future for us. There was also a growing sense in me that it was time to walk my path alone for a while. I wanted to follow my guiding principle of wisdom and honour that inner voice, although I was reluctant to do so.

Annie generated her own plans and set her agenda without hesitation. At least, it appeared that way. Whereas for me, it was an underdeveloped strength. Because of that, I noticed I'd tended to default to her decisions, like I'd done for the fifteen months we'd travelled together. It was the same during the seven years I was married to Charlotte. I realised that my programmed pattern was still running, and I knew instinctively it was time to transform it. I was caught between a rock and a hard place. If I chose to ignore this, I'd keep on defaulting to Annie's agenda, and if I chose to act upon it and travel alone, it could signal the end of our relationship, along with all of the emotional pain that would come from it.

In my inner world journey, I'd arrived back in the same place I was before I created the message book and video for Annie during my last trip to London. There was nowhere else to go from here, and the road was running out, literally and metaphorically. We talked about this, and we both knew the time had come for us to split. Sitting with that truth cast a dark shadow over our visit to Melbourne, a city that neither of us had been to before. Determined to enjoy our final weeks together in Australia as much as we could, we bravely put our unfolding personal stories to one side for the sake of the experience and focused on simply enjoying the present moment, as we'd learned to do during our Vipassana retreat earlier that year. As much as Annie hated the idea of me not going with her to Cambodia, she understood that my need to travel alone was a vital part of my personal unfolding, and she encouraged me to do it.

Our grand finale took place in the magnificent city of Sydney. There, I reconnected with my dear friends, Matthew and Elizabeth, as well as their seven-year-old son, Pete. Elizabeth was in much better health since her treatment for cancer in 2005. Annie and I stayed with them for a couple of weeks, and they had no idea we were heading towards an imminent separation, but it didn't matter. We were committed to staying in the present moment to enjoy each day for what it was. No more, no less.

One of the unique and truly spectacular experiences on offer in Sydney is the guided climb over the top of the iconic Sydney Harbour Bridge. It's been open since 1998, and we invited Matthew to do it with us as a thank-you gift for hosting us. The three-hour climb starts with a rigorous safety briefing. The highest point of the climb is about four hundred and fifty feet above the water, so they have to be certain that no one is going to fall off! We wore one-piece jumpsuits and a safety harness which tethered us to the bridge via a steel cable throughout the climb. I distinctly remember how windy it was as we moved slowly forward, one small step at a time, over that huge steel arch as six lanes of traffic roared across the road below.

Being strapped to the infrastructure brought a much-needed sense of safety and mental comfort. We stopped for a few minutes at the centre to take in the unforgettable view of the famous Opera House and the Sydney skyline. It was a breathtaking moment. The entire climb was an awesome experience and one of the last great adventures that Annie and I might have together for a long time. I felt a sense of gratitude for everything I'd experienced in my journey to this point, as well as excitement that I was about to walk my own path, without being subject to the gravitational pull of a significant other for a while. I don't know if that makes me sound a bit selfish. It was the first time in years that I'd really allowed myself to experiment with exploring life in my own way, without reference to anyone else's needs. It was a pretty exciting prospect.

On our last evening at Matt and Elizabeth's house, we created a surprise for our unsuspecting hosts and invited them to attend a special ceremony in their lounge before we sat down for dinner. Annie and I wanted them to feel appreciated for being such generous hosts and know the special regard we had for them because of it. This was a great moment to establish the first ever *Daily Lama Annual Global Hospitality Awards* evening! By a stroke of luck, they were our unsuspecting winners. I'd found a couple of small trophies in a local shop, which I had engraved with their names, and we prepared a little bit of theatre to give the evening a highly spirited feel.

After the rather short award ceremony, we presented our highly celebrated hosts with a wonderful Thai meal Annie had prepared. Elizabeth and Matt had welcomed us into their home, and we'd felt like extended family. We hoped that cooking for them would give them a chance to relax. Happily, we managed to pull it off, and it confirmed how well we'd worked as a

LIFE WITHOUT A TIE

team during the last year and a half.

The following evening, we booked a room in a hotel close to the airport. The end of the road for us had arrived, and there was no going back. We both had early morning flights to catch, with Annie headed to Cambodia and me to New Zealand. I'd always wanted to travel there, and this was the perfect opportunity, especially as it was relatively close. I felt nervous, excited, and sad in roughly equal measures. I knew that being without Annie was going to hurt for a while and that I'd miss her. Since we'd met, the longest time we'd been apart was six weeks. Now, we were going to be apart for a long time, possibly forever. Despite thinking that, I'd been through a similar experience with Charlotte, and I think that, coupled with my mindfulness practice, allowed me to be more at peace with it.

In March 2007, Annie and I parted company. I'd had an amazing time travelling with her throughout Asia and Australia. She was a brilliant person to have done this with. The invitation for her to take part in the NGO project came at just the right time. Isn't it amazing how the Universe provided exactly what was needed, as I had intuitively known it would? Just pause for a moment and think. How often has this happened in your life?

My trust in this guidance system was growing stronger with every day, week, and month of my journey. I'd never travelled on my own before, and I was curious to know how I'd deal with it. It was a vitally important part of my inner exploration. For the first time in fifteen months, I was about to face life on the road completely alone.

Chapter Seven
Travelling Solo

"Loneliness is the poverty of self; solitude is the richness of self."

May Sarton, *Journal of a Solitude*

I ARRIVED IN NEW ZEALAND MID-MARCH 2007. TRAVELLING ALONE, IT SEEMED like a great moment to revisit the reasons why I'd committed to this grand experiment called *Life Without a Tie*. Of the estimated 12,600 active days of life that remained, around five hundred were already gone. That didn't induce panic or a need to speed things up. Quite the contrary. My mindfulness practice had evolved in the past year, and I was able to remain more present than at just about any other time in my life. That brought with it a calmness and an inner peace which I enjoyed.

At the same time, most of those first five hundred days had been spent with Annie, and I hadn't really allowed myself to be entirely selfish in my choices. I really wanted to experiment and try that on for size. Before we go any further, let me explain what I mean by selfish. In my case, it meant consciously and unashamedly choosing to focus entirely on my own needs without any concern or consideration for others and how it might impact them.

I viewed this choice as healthy, great for my well-being, and entirely necessary as part of my journey of discovery. The absence of any distractions was something useful and helpful in these circumstances. For the first time in nearly two decades, I was untied from any obligations to other people and was determined to capitalise on it. Without Annie, my daily activities were totally down to me. Perhaps you've experienced times in your life when you knew you were denying some of your own selfish needs? In what ways do you currently sacrifice your own needs unnecessarily for the sake of others?

I was in New Zealand, and I was going to be selfish. I intended to do everything I wanted to do simply because I wanted to. The immigration authority granted me a visa to stay for six months, which gave me plenty of time to experience the range of things the country had to offer. I set a leisurely pace and improvised as the journey evolved. I loosely planned a basic travel route, mainly to give me a sense of direction but also to avoid wasting money on unnecessary backtracking between different locations. It wasn't a problem to stay longer in those places where it felt right to do that.

For those of you who aren't familiar with New Zealand, it's made up of two large islands (North and South). It's also isolated. It's twelve hundred miles away from Australia, and its closest neighbours to the north are New Caledonia, Fiji, and Tonga. Symbolically, it was quite literally on the other side of the world from the home I left back in England, the furthest away that it could possibly be. That reflected how far away my former life as a businessman was, which made me feel enlivened, free, and intensified my excitement.

New Zealand is one of the adrenaline hubs of the world, with numerous opportunities for those who want to move outside their comfort zone. I was definitely ready to touch the edges of mine. It was a perfect time to tick off a few items on my personal bucket list. Bungee jumping from a suspension bridge, glacier climbing, and freefall parachuting were all available, and I was open to other extreme experiences I might find. It probably sounds a bit clichéd, but here I was at forty-six years of age, excited about doing things that most people might try in their late teens or early twenties. The pursuit of these challenges gave me a useful and necessary orientation for a while. I could scare myself half to death whilst I contemplated and reflected on the deeper question, the theme of my entire trip, at the same time. What would living a life true to myself mean or look like in practical terms?

I still had no idea. However, I believed that a cherished life partner would be a key part in the eventual picture. I'm not sure if this was coming from the heart. If I'm really honest, it was more of an unquestioned assumption or a craving that needed to be satisfied. When I observed happy couples, the critical self-talking voice in my head would quickly pipe up. *Look, everyone else has a partner, and you don't. What's wrong with you? You're not normal if you don't have someone.*

The only conclusion that led me to was to continue with the pursuit of my dream relationship. Even after the Vipassana retreat, in which we were encouraged to become more aware of our delusional thinking, I was still pretty much in the dark. My belief system around this part of my life wasn't well examined. I operated on the basic assumption that all my troubles in life would definitely be sorted by the presence of a great girlfriend. If and when she showed up, I'd be the star in my own romantic movie. Clearly, this thinking was not in alignment with the principles I'd forged to guide my journey. But I wasn't really ready to face up to that yet.

A quest to find true love started to take shape, at least in my head. I'd sit and daydream about her. Perhaps I might meet her unexpectedly in New Zealand and fall deeply and madly in love. Maybe we'd forge a shared life and live happily ever after. Some years ago, a friend shared some pertinent wisdom with me. "People will come into your life for a reason, a season, or a lifetime. When you know which one it is, you'll know what to do for that person." When someone comes into your life for a reason, it's usually to meet a need you've expressed, outwardly or inwardly. They might come to assist you through a difficulty, provide you with guidance and support, or aid you physically, emotionally, or spiritually. It may seem they're a godsend, and they are because they appear for the reason you need them. Then, without wrongdoing on anyone's part, you or this person will say or do something to bring the relationship to an end. One of you might walk away. One of you may die. They may act up and force you to take a stand. Whatever happens, we must realise your need has been met, your desire fulfilled, and their work is done. The prayer you sent up has been answered and now it's time to move on. Can you think of someone who appeared in your life for a reason?

Some people come into your life for a season because your time has come to share, grow, or learn. They may bring you an experience of peace or make you laugh. They may teach you to do something you've never done. They often give you an unbelievable amount of joy. Believe it, it's real. But only for a season! I consider Annie to be one of those people for me. Can you recall someone who was in your life for a season? What did you learn from them? And did they teach you to do something for the first time?

Lifetime relationships teach us lifetime lessons, things we must build upon in order to have a solid emotional foundation. Your job is to accept the lesson, love the person, and use what you have learned in all other relationships and areas of your life. It is said that love is blind but friendship is clairvoyant. My ex-wife, Charlotte, occupies a place on my list of lifetime relationships. How about you? Who would you include in yours?

The List
The search was on to find the woman who could be my lifetime partner. Of the four life ties—a partner or spouse, career, house/home, and community of family and friends—it was this one which stood out and grabbed my attention. I didn't think about my career, my friends back in England, or where would be a good place to live next. Those had seemed too abstract and too far into my future, and they didn't warrant serious consideration. Instead, I became somewhat fixated on finding this special person, and it influenced my direction on the road to a large extent. Despite the fact that my experiences with Annie had left me feeling relieved to be alone, which seemed like a contradiction, I still believed I was open to partnering with someone else, as if they were the determining factor and not me. The perfect woman had to be out there somewhere, and I had the time, the interest, and the intention to find her.

Well before I left England, and a year before Annie showed up, I'd sat down with a blank sheet of paper during a period of introspection and crafted a list entitled, My Ideal Partner. It was about two A4 pages long and contained an imaginary description of the elusive perfect woman *for me*. I'd done that to transmit my desire to the Universe energetically, and I believed that if I was intentional and gave the Universe a clear brief, it would find this imaginary person and ensure we would eventually meet. This way of thinking is depicted to some extent in a charming romantic movie called *The Adjustment Bureau* with Matt Damon and Emily Blunt.

My description included some basics, like her age, height, weight, the colour of her hair and eyes, and such-like. I didn't want to be prescriptive with these, but merely state preferences. The basic details were only a small part of the overall picture. I went beyond physical attributes and assigned criteria to her personality and character too, knowing they would be important to create a feeling of attraction. I visualised how she might dress, considered what her professional life experience had been, her lifestyle, education, and her level of income. I imagined she would have a generous spirit, be open, honest, and communicate with kindness. Last but not least, she had to have sex appeal and be open and curious about life.

LIFE WITHOUT A TIE

Not too much to ask for, don't you think?

It may sound a bit crass, but I wanted to be clear and honest with myself and really identify the kind of person I thought I was looking for. Once my list was made, I took a mental snapshot of it, filed it away in my laptop, and forgot about it until I reached Wellington when a surprising encounter with someone inspired me to retrieve it. You'll hear more about that later.

The North Island

My journey through New Zealand started in Auckland. It became clear it would be more convenient to have my own transport than have to rely on buses and trains. A car gave me maximum freedom and flexibility, hands down. I'd heard from other travellers that there were a handful of rental firms in this part of the world that had a good stock of old bangers or crates for hire at reasonable prices. I managed to find a seven-year-old car belonging to one such company. They were happy for me to drop the car off in Wellington at no extra cost. Perfect!

Auckland provided my first extreme experience of the trip. I spent the first two nights in the waterside city at the funky Surf 'n' Snow Backpackers hostel. It was one of the few remaining low-rise buildings left in the Central Business District (CBD). As luck would have it, the building was one block away from the iconic Sky Tower, which meant I could never get lost! The Sky Tower is the tallest structure in Auckland and has a great observation deck. I went without hesitation to see the aerial view of the city and surrounding areas. It gave me a better orientation and intensified my desire to explore the place further.

Standing at over one thousand feet tall, the Sky Tower is slightly higher than the Eiffel Tower in Paris and is actually the tallest structure in the Southern Hemisphere. I reached the observation deck and was in for a surprise. Unbelievably, they offer visitors the chance to jump to the ground from up there. The deck is 722 feet above the ground, making the Sky Jump the highest tower-based jump in the world! How cool is that? My first opportunity to do something ridiculously scary, and it turned out to be a record breaker.

I accepted the invitation willingly, and it was not lost on me that once again, I'd put an idea out into the Universe, without knowing how or when it would happen, and in virtually no time at all, an invitation effortlessly opened up right in front of me. My faith in navigating life in this way was constantly strengthened by such unpredictable, magical events. Before you rush to the conclusion that I was stark, raving mad for doing this jump, it's what is known in extreme sports as a controlled descent. Once you're harnessed, the fan descender cable system is connected to sophisticated computer software that controls your fall at varying speeds all the way down until you reach the ground. The technology is the same as they use in movies for stuntmen falling from tall buildings.

I put on a blue jumpsuit and was taken outside to a small deck, where there was a steel gangplank. It was about four metres long and edged out from the tower. The whole bloody tower was literally swaying in the wind as I nervously edged my way to the end of the gangplank. Adrenaline furiously pumped through my veins. One of the staff saw my anxiety and tried his best to help me remain calm. I was excited but also frightened, which made me hesitant to let go and jump. Even though I knew in my mind I was safe in my body harness, I froze and couldn't take my hands off the safety rails on either side of the gangplank. The ground looked *so* far away, where city dwellers were going about their busy lives completely oblivious to this terrified traveller hundreds of feet above. The safety supervisor was incredibly patient with me. Eventually, after some reassurance and gentle coaxing, I summoned up my courage and dived off the edge.

In that moment, I immediately became aware of a fabulous, serene silence as I fell through the air. Then came the thrill. Picking up speed rapidly, I descended as smoothly as an arrow (at about 50mph) for around fourteen seconds. The software programme then kicked in and started arresting the cable, slowing me down progressively so that by the time I'd reached the last few feet, my speed was virtually zero, and I was able to land gently on the ground, standing upright. The design of the whole experience was brilliant and quite breathtaking.

Back on my feet, I couldn't stop smiling as I reflected on what I'd just done. I was proud of myself. I thought about other times when I'd faced a difficult and scary challenge and chosen to go for it, and one or two when I hadn't. Completing that jump imprinted a new and powerful *I can do it* reference in my brain, which I still use today. Everything transformed in those few seconds after I let go, turning my fear into sheer exhilaration. Can you recall a time when you let go of your fear and leapt? Are there situations in your life where you would like to do that more often?

LIFE WITHOUT A TIE

When Annie and I separated, we agreed to bring publication of *The Daily Lama* to an end. It had been our joint creation, and it seemed unfair to both of us that only one could inherit it. Letting go of it also meant I had practiced the art of non-attachment, which I had learned about during the meditation retreat and was one of my guiding principles. As an aside, my writing had improved (in my opinion, at least!), and I felt more creative. I wanted to continue learning and growing those skills, so I started a new blog called *The Daily Explorer*. I conjured up a new correspondent, Seymour Peaks, so he could write about the sky jump in the next post.

During the next couple of weeks, I made my way around the North Island. If you've been to New Zealand, you'll know how green and beautiful the countryside is. Most days, I'd drive in the warm sunshine with clear blue sky overhead. The windows were down, and I played my favourite music. There were hardly any other cars on the road, and it was as if someone had unrolled a long, smooth, undulating black tarmac rug with a dotted white line in the centre across the hills, just for me. I felt sublimely content.

When I reached Cape Rienga, the most northerly point of the North Island, a signpost at the lighthouse pointed in the direction of Sydney, which it showed as being 1,200 miles away. It's where I'd been with Annie just a couple of weeks earlier. There was also a signpost pointing to London, some 11,000 miles away. It was the furthest I'd ever been away from home both physically and emotionally. In that moment, I remember feeling nervous and anxious about the uncertain future ahead, but there was also an underlying sense of joy and excitement that I'd made it this far in one piece.

It was a great decision to rent the car for a couple of reasons. For a start, it meant that nowhere was off limits. I could reach any place of interest, especially the ones that were difficult or inconvenient to get to using public transport. It certainly would have been cheaper if I'd joined a tour group, which is what many backpackers do. But I didn't want to be tied to a fixed itinerary, so I chose to stretch my budget temporarily to gain more freedom. It made me aware how much I value my autonomy and made me question how often I'd honoured my need for it in the past. I made a commitment there and then to ensure I did this in all my choices, both professionally and personally, from now on. Bit by bit, as my journey evolved, I was getting to know myself better. Being aware of that strengthened my resolve to continue observing my thoughts and feelings and examine the hidden gems of information they revealed to me.

Having the car also gave me an excuse to interact with local people. This was well before Google Maps or satellite navigation was in widespread use. I stopped a couple of times a day to ask people for directions or to get suggestions for local places I could visit that weren't well known to tourists. As a result, I made some incredible discoveries. Let me share three examples of this with you.

Number one, there are something like forty million sheep in New Zealand (about ten sheep per person) The country produces thirteen percent of the world's wool. The tiny town of Te Kuiti is known as the shearing capital of the world, and I discovered this from talking to a chap at the gas station. He informed me that the annual Sheep Shearing Championships were happening at the Civic Centre, and they attracted hundreds of competitors. It was the sheep shearing equivalent of the Olympics! It was most likely the only time in my life that I'd have an opportunity to see such a spectacle, so I made my way there immediately and entered the packed arena.

On the stage were eight burly men in a line, each with a number pinned to their chests. They were all skilfully holding a sheep with one arm, whilst quickly shearing off their thick and valuable coat of wool using an industrial electric razor with the other. They worked frantically, shifting the animal's position every twenty to thirty seconds to make sure they got every last piece of wool. They were timed against the clock and observed by a referee and a panel of judges. Whatever the rules of this fascinating contest were, I didn't really understand them. I was just thrilled to see it and to feel the energy being created by the raucous crowd, who were shouting and cheering the contestants on. The sound cranked up a notch whenever a sheep was finished and sent to the holding pen, like when a goal is scored in a football game.

These guys were unbelievably fast! The best of the best can shear upwards of seven hundred ewes in a nine-hour period. That's more than one a minute. This spectacle continued throughout the day and evening. What I loved about it most was getting totally lost in the excitement of it all and hanging out with some of the most colourful members of the New Zealand farming community, with whom I couldn't have had less in common.

My second example was a discovery I made via a chance conversation

LIFE WITHOUT A TIE

when I arrived in Gisborne, which is nestled on the east coast of the North Island. Because of its closeness to the International Date Line, it is the most easterly city in the world and the first on which the sun rises every day. On January 1st, the inhabitants of the town are the first people in the world to see in the new year too. What's less well known is that it has a prison which was decommissioned in 1993. I know this because I was looking for a place to stay for a couple of nights and a local guy told me the prison had been converted into a one-of-a-kind backpacker hostel in 2003. It was undoubtedly the most unusual place in town, if not the entire country, to spend the night. I decided to give it a go.

I'm genuinely fascinated and often inspired to find out how people get such entrepreneurial ideas. When I checked in, I found the owner and asked him. He told me that after the prison closed, the building had become derelict, and people kept breaking in so they could sniff glue. He already had one successful hostel in the town and was looking for a second site which had bedrooms plus kitchen and bathroom facilities, and the idea just clicked. He approached the council, who gave him the thumbs up, and the rest was history. Amazingly, he'd renovated the whole place in such a way that it remained true to the original set-up. The communal shower block was in the courtyard, and the twelve cells were now used as single-person private bedrooms.

Drifting off to sleep in one of those former prison cells was an exercise in gratitude. The tiny space was cold, as the cool night air permeated through the barred windows. I had two fan heaters in my room and slept with half my clothes on. There was just enough room for me to lay flat on the small, hard bed. I imagined what life inside a real prison might be like and appreciated how lucky I was to have my freedom. I felt extremely happy that I didn't have to watch my back in the shower room every morning! The novelty of it all made it fun. Many of the travellers staying there were seasonal farm workers, so the kitchen was well stocked with fresh juicy apples and kiwi fruits.

My third example occurred when I visited Waiheke Island. About half the size of the Isle of Wight, you have to take a forty-five-minute ride on a car ferry from a small port a few miles south of Auckland to get there. I turned up one sunny morning and joined the small queue of cars waiting for the next departure. As I wandered over to the loading area, I spotted a rather attractive woman in her early forties, with long, strawberry blond hair and an hourglass figure. She was wearing an elegant, tight-fitting black summer dress with spaghetti straps and was sitting alone on a bench. Curious to know who she was and learn something about her life, I decided to take a seat on the bench next to her. I wondered how to start a conversation. I had a map of the island in my hand, which gave me an idea. "Good morning. I'm travelling through New Zealand, and I'm looking for some help with my route. Are you from this part of the country?"

She gave me a warm smile. "Actually, I live in Auckland, and I'm going to a wedding on the island. She's one of my best friends. What about you? How long will you be staying?"

Mission accomplished: ice broken. What followed was forty-five minutes of great conversation, lots of storytelling, and a few laughs. This is what makes solo travelling so exciting! Being alone made it so much easier to start conversations with strangers and engage with them for as long as I wanted to. When I started my tour in Auckland, I'd been slightly worried that it might be harder to approach people than it actually turned out. Connecting with Teresa spontaneously lifted my spirit and created a sense of expansion. She worked as a GP just outside Auckland and, like me, had a bucket list of sorts. I asked her which of the things on her list was lined up for her next challenge.

"I've always wanted to do a tandem freefall parachute jump. There's a place not too far away from here where you can do it."

"You're not going to believe this, Teresa. I've already booked myself in at that place two weeks from now. Let's do it together."

She accepted my invitation. After her friend's wedding, Teresa went back to her home in Auckland, and I continued travelling south until our rendezvous on the day of our jump a week later. But first, I need to tell you about an important conversation I'd had during that week which will become important later in my story. I left Waiheke Island and headed for Tauranga to meet with a girl called Katy. She was a Kiwi, and Tauranga was her hometown. Annie and I had met her whilst travelling through Thailand. The last time I'd seen Katy was in a hospital in Koh Samui while having her appendix out. If you've been a traveller, you'll probably appreciate how good it feels when you reconnect with someone you crossed paths with at another place and time.

During a couple of wonderful days in her neck of the woods, I was happy to hear she'd made a full recovery from her operation. She also told me about an orphanage in Pokhara, Nepal. She'd volunteered there and was massively enthusiastic about the kids as well as the people taking care of them. It sounded incredible. She asked me to promise that if and when I made it to Nepal, I'd visit that orphanage and do something to help them. They obviously meant a lot to her. I gave her my word I'd do that. Never did I believe that a year and a half later, I'd end up in Nepal where I'd fulfil my promise to Katy.

The Jump

Filled with joy and excitement after my brief reunion with Katy, I drove back to Auckland to team up with my newly made friend Teresa to fulfil the crazy pact we'd made to parachute jump out of an airplane. The airfield was about 35 miles south of Auckland at Mercer, and as luck would have it, the weather that day was literally perfect. Blue skies, sunshine, and scattered clouds. We were introduced to our tandem jump partners, who asked us to put our suits on and made sure our harnesses were properly fitted.

My jump partner was a friendly, laid back, cool looking, and slightly built guy in his twenties called Won. We waited for our call to board the aircraft, and Won explained the safety procedures to me, telling me how it was all going to work when we reached the designated jump height. He had thousands of hours of experience and made me feel extremely safe, despite my nerves. The maximum height for tandem jumps in that area was 16,000 feet, which gave us a freefall time of around eighty seconds!

The high-powered, gas turbine aircraft took off and climbed for about fifteen minutes to reach the jump altitude. My heart rate increased the closer we got, and my nerves kicked in big time when we were two minutes away from launch. Won tightened and checked the straps and clips that held me to him and made sure I was comfortable. It was hard to hear him over the noise inside the aircraft, so we kept our talk to the minimum. My mouth was bone dry, and I could feel my pulse racing as adrenaline flowed around my body. The voice inside my head was squawking. *This is a really bad idea, Ray. You should have stayed on terra firma.*

The aircraft reached jump altitude. This was it. Time to fly. Won pointed towards a light inside the cabin, and it changed from red to green. We were cleared to exit. Won manoeuvred us to the wide-open door, smiled at me, and threw us out into the warm slipstream outside. We were tumbling through the air, spinning for about three or four seconds until we stabilised in the classic free-fall position, horizontal with our legs spread, knees slightly bent, arms out wide, and our heads straight, facing downward. The air pummelled my face, spreading my cheeks as if someone had gripped them with clamps and was pulling them apart. My mouth distorted, and my lips were vibrating like crazy as the air rushed past. Despite my ears hurting slightly from the pressure of the wind, I felt amazing, freefalling through the air.

With Won in control, I was able to just relax and enjoy it as he took responsibility for everything. We'd been hurtling through the air towards Earth for a minute or so when Won pulled the ripcord on his suit which released our parachute. When the parachute deployed and we suddenly decelerated, I felt a strong, jerky pull upwards. The change in our descent speed was abrupt, as if you were cruising in your car on a motorway and changed from top gear to first gear in a couple of seconds.

I'll never forget that moment when the canopy opened and the roaring wind noise immediately stopped, like someone had pressed a mute button. We were now in an upright position, gently flying in absolute silence. With two or three minutes to go before touchdown and everything as it should be, Won took my camera and snapped a photograph of me. It was the most audacious picture of myself I'd acquired in my journey so far. We softly approached the ground, and Won gently took a couple of steps forward before we came to a complete stop. I was absolutely elated.

Teresa landed with her jump partner about one minute later. She had a beaming smile and was clearly thrilled. We gave each other a huge hug and returned to the clubhouse to celebrate our achievement over a much-needed beer. All of that had occurred as a result of a random conversation with a stranger. The *reason* we'd met each other had been fulfilled. I realised that we'd probably never see each other again, and I was okay about it. In that moment, I made a commitment to myself to continue starting conversations. The potential for hidden magic was infinite.

Wanganui

I met many fascinating people as I made my way further south, and some directed me to some pretty peculiar places. On White Island, I found New Zealand's only active marine volcano. Whitianga, in the Coromandel, was home to Hot Water Beach, where I experienced a free, totally natural, miniature hot spa. I rocked up at low tide, joined a few in the know individuals and dug my very own bath-sized hole in the sand. It filled with the steaming hot water that constantly runs under the surface and was so hot that I couldn't touch it for a while. In Matamata, I spent a couple of hours exploring a huge, twelve-acre farm which had been used as the filming location for the Shire in Peter Jackson's *Lord of The Rings* movie trilogy. Now known as Hobbiton, the massive outdoor set has been preserved for the pleasure of visitors, and it gave me a fascinating insight into how much effort went into creating the fantastic, other-world realities in the story.

If any of you are Elvis fans, you may be pleased to hear that in the tiny hamlet of Hawera, Elvis is alive and well! Actually, it's one of his die-hard fans. Kevin D. Wasley had been an avid collector of Elvis records since 1959. I'd read about him and decided to call him personally to see if we could meet. I was thrilled when he agreed. He was about six feet tall, and although he looked nothing like the King, he wore his hair teddy-boy style as an homage to his idol. He gave me a personal tour of his unbelievably huge collection of Elvis memorabilia, which is the largest collection of its kind in Australasia and possibly the world.

Leaving the world of rock 'n' roll, I headed for Wellington, New Zealand's capital city. I stopped en route in Wanganui. The office manager of my consulting business, Jann, was from there. She'd told me stories about growing up there, and she'd captured my imagination in the way she described it. I'd promised her that if I ever made it to that part of the world, I'd drop in and take a look, and now here I was. It was like the Universe had eavesdropped on that conversation all those years ago and now deemed it important enough to guide me there. When I'd made the commitment to Jann, I never would have thought in a million years that it would happen. It was clearly meant to be, even though I was totally unaware of the thread that connected the present moment to a previous event some four or five years earlier.

It was Steve Jobs who famously said, "You can't connect the dots looking forward; you can only connect them looking backwards. So you have to trust that the dots will somehow connect in your future." I decided to keep placing my trust in this phenomenon. I sensed that my future well-being depended on it.

Meditation teacher Tara Brach said, "We each have the evolutionary potential built into our brain of waking up the prefrontal cortex and integrating our brain in a way that we can directly experience our interdependence, our connectedness, and the unitive quality of the universe—oneness. We have that capacity. And the teachings of the path are to wake us up so that we can sense who we are in that. That there's not this separate self—that there's a resting in something larger."

I knew exactly what she was talking about and had felt it strongly when I was in my twenties. I realised that reconnecting with that feeling was one of the reasons I'd taken this journey and as each day went by, glimpses were occurring with greater regularity.

Wanganui was a picturesque, sleepy little place, and there wasn't really an awful lot to see or do there. It was so quiet and uneventful, the most interesting attraction on offer to visitors was a three-hour ride with Noel, the mailman, to deliver the post. I kid you not! Noel was a contractor for the New Zealand Post and was contractually allowed to supplement his income by taking passengers on his mail run. To his credit, he's figured out a way of giving an amusing and informative tour of the region, which made this a real find. And I got to meet some of the town's residents, who offered us tea and a couple of stories to boot. Noel is on first-name terms with everybody who lives along the river, and they all greeted him as if he were family. My own experience of living in London had been the complete opposite. There, hardly anyone even knows their next-door neighbour, and there's a complete absence of any sense of community. It was heart-warming to experience its clear existence in Wanganui and to see how people cared about each other. The fact that I seemed to care about this was an interesting revelation, and I made a mental note of it.

As my journey progressed, some of the best encounters happened when I least expected them to. One evening at my hostel, I was cooking supper in the communal kitchen, and I struck up a conversation with a couple of women staying there. Unlike me, they weren't travellers. They were sales reps who'd travelled from Wellington to meet some of their customers. It said a lot about the high standard of that hostel that they regularly chose to stay there. One of them was called Mary, and I instantly liked her. She was tall and slim, with dark hair and brown eyes, and she was stunning. I was like a moth to a flame, though I did my best to act as cool as possible. Her company sold health and nutritional products, which interested me and had initially got us talking. She asked me where I was headed next, and I told her that my destination was Wellington.

"That's great," said Mary. "You must come and visit me when you arrive. There's lots going on. I'd be happy to show you around and introduce you to some of my friends."

That sounded brilliant, and I couldn't quite believe she was inviting me to hook up. Of course, I assumed she was just being friendly, as was typical of the people I met in New Zealand, although I obviously hoped there might be more to it. The quest to find true love had well and truly been kicked into play, and I enjoyed the sense of optimism I felt after our encounter in Wanganui.

Most solo travellers will tell you that, for all sorts of reasons, it's a wonderful pleasure to be hosted in a strange city by people who live there. Local residents tend to know about the most interesting places that never feature in guidebooks, so they're excellent informants. It also feels good to know that as you arrive in a strange, new place, there will be at least one friendly welcome. That's what made things like couch surfing and Airbnb so popular, especially in the United States. It required an openness to strangers and new experiences, which usually turned out to be enriching and something I encourage you to try.

Wellington

When I reached Wellington, Mary kept her promise. She took me to a couple of parties, where I met many of her colourful friends. This was a first for me in New Zealand, and I was grateful for the chance to meet real, local people. After several weeks on the road, it was a welcome change from meeting and talking to other travellers. There's nothing wrong with that per se, but it'd got a bit boring asking and answering the same old questions over and over, like where are you from, how long have you been travelling, where are you headed, yada yada.

Mary was really well-connected and everyone liked her. She was also a bit of a dark horse. I discovered she sometimes worked as a model and was a fully trained stuntwoman! She'd stopped working in movies due to injuries, and her journey of self-healing was what sparked her interest in health and well-being. We got on really well. The conversation flowed easily, and we laughed a lot. On my last evening in Wellington, she invited me to her home for dinner. It was during that conversation that she revealed she'd been single for a couple of years and had recently reconnected with a guy called Alan, whom she went to school with twenty years ago. I could sense from her energy that she was excited about the potential this fledgling, four-week-old relationship held for them both.

As I listened, I went into inward conflict with my wish for her to be happy on the one hand and my growing desire for intimacy with her on the other. Her new boyfriend didn't live in Wellington, and we were alone. I didn't know what to do. Late into the evening, we'd both had a couple of glasses of wine when she moved towards me and offered her sweet, soft lips. We kissed and it was beautiful, like a dream come true. I couldn't quite believe it was happening. Mary invited me to stay the night, which I hadn't expected.

As if that wasn't shocking enough, something else took me completely by surprise. I'm not sure what to put it down to, perhaps it was my evolving mindfulness practice and my higher state of consciousness. Maybe it was pure nerves. My voice of inner wisdom spoke to me and warned me not to go any further. Whatever the driver was, I knew in that moment that I had to say no. I was truly surprised; I couldn't have imagined declining the advances of such a beautiful woman back in the day when I was a single guy. I would've jumped at the chance, no matter what the consequences. Here I was, just like that single guy in London, but there was something that didn't feel right about this situation. I firmly believed she had a genuine opportunity for lasting happiness with Alan, and I didn't want to put myself in the way of that, not even for my own pleasure. If I had, and it turned out that it had spoiled it for them both, I'd regret it. The right thing to do was to step aside and go back to my hostel.

That was an important milestone in my journey for a couple of reasons. Firstly, it reaffirmed my belief that the Universe always sends us the people we need to meet in order to evolve our consciousness. Secondly, it prompted me to remember my ideal partner list I'd made way back in London, which was buried in a folder somewhere on my computer. Mary had appeared to be a close match to the description of that imaginary person, and I wanted to check to see just how close. When I'd written that list, I'd made an assumption that if someone more or less matched, I'd feel a sense of happiness or rightness about it. That feeling was absent with Mary, so I wanted to understand why. I scanned down the pages, checking for clues. Nothing. I couldn't find anything that might be a reason. She appeared to be, by my own criteria, the perfect match. Then it dawned on me. I had left one vital data point out of my original description. And it related to her availability. I swiftly added it to my list.

Availability: must be free, available, ready, and willing to be involved in a relationship with me!

I added the asterisk to remind me that this was added in May 2007, some three years after I'd created the original document. After this encounter, I realised that the more specific we are with the Universe, the more able She will be to provide what we're looking for or what we need. I'd often heard people say, "Be careful what you wish for." Now the truth of that proverbial wisdom hit home, and I took the lesson on board with gratitude. I was potentially one step closer in my quest to find true love. Whilst things didn't quite pan out with Mary romantically, the reason she was sent to me was crystal clear. It had been a great thread to weave into the tapestry of my great adventure. I felt empowered with an increased appetite for more moments like this. We formed a close bond and remain friends today. Looking back, I discovered how positive human connection with strangers is the secret to happiness, well, one of them at least. The experience of meeting new people, getting to know a little about them and connecting, as my guiding principle required, started to have a profound effect on me. It inspired me to go to sleep with excitement for the next day...to live fully.

With no one around who knew me, I was in my own tiny, social vacuum. Stripped away from the group norms of my social circles back in London—the silent rules of engagement, shared experiences and in-jokes that quietly guided my day-to-day interactions—there was nothing left except me. Sometimes I liked what I saw, sometimes I questioned it, and sometimes it came as a surprise. Either way, exposure to my true self felt informative and important. I used my reflections about my inner journey to improve my ability to connect with others. After all, many of them were in the same boat as me. Over time, I experimented and asked questions that really got people talking. Here are some that worked well:

What are you most excited about at the moment?
What are you looking forward to?
How would you describe your year so far?
What are you currently reading?
What's your story?
What's your dream?

These were open-ended enough to elicit some intriguing stories. The questions seemed to let people speak from the heart. I found that when I dropped the usual, "What do you do?" type of question and spoke to people's values and what motivated them, they responded from a deeper place. Sometimes, I'd come across a person who wasn't happy in their job. By being curious about that, I was able to help them. It gave me an opportunity to work on my coaching skills and honour my principle of contribution.

In two months, I'd driven about 3,500 miles and visited every corner of the North Island. As I drove through the city for the last time, I saw hundreds of people buzzing around in what looked like a typical working day for them. Some were sitting in cafés, sipping their lattes and taking a break from the nine-to-five, and I remembered when I'd been doing that myself back in London a couple of years earlier. For a split second, some anxiety rose, but it was quickly replaced with the much stronger feelings of joy and pride that I was free from that previous role, in which I'd played the businessman.

The South Island
I dropped off my rental car and took the three-hour ferry to Picton on the South Island. We sailed via the narrow Cook Straight and slowly navigated through a huge network of sea-drowned coastal valleys known as the Marlborough Sounds. It was June, and the Southern Hemisphere winter was approaching. The temperature had dropped rapidly, and much of my kit was only suitable for the much warmer, Asian climate. A brief shopping spree addressed this, and I purchased thermal underwear, long-sleeved shirts, a fleece, and a windbreaker. I wasn't taking any chances because I can't stand being cold. My twenty-two kilos of luggage increased to twenty-five for the next couple of months.

If you're looking for a place in the world to visit that isn't crowded and has natural beauty in abundance, New Zealand is a strong candidate. The South Island is home to some amazing trekking routes, including the highly acclaimed Abel Tasman Coastal Track. Many travellers describe it as one of the best coastal walks in the world. It's over thirty miles long and quite a few people walk the whole thing. I wasn't interested in camping out overnight, because I didn't want to carry food supplies and equipment.

Instead, I chose a couple of sections which I could do as one-day hikes.

LIFE WITHOUT A TIE

Being close to nature, especially when it's coastal forest, which has such a beautiful combination of sand, sea, rivers, and trees, replenishes my soul. I spent much of my time on the trails meditating to maintain the mindfulness practice I'd started over a year earlier. In order to improve your ability to be in the present moment and maintain non-judgmental awareness, it's vitally important to recharge your mindfulness batteries every day, and meditation is one of the ways that works well for me.

Another experience which feeds my soul is being in the presence of wild animals. As a young child, I was totally enraptured by the story of *Moby Dick*. The classic seafaring tale revolves around Captain Ahab and his obsession with a huge, white whale. It caused the loss of Ahab's leg years before and left him to stomp the wooden boards of his sailing ship on a peg leg. Ahab was so fixated on his desire to kill the whale, he was prepared to sacrifice everything, including his life, the lives of his crew members, and even his ship to find and destroy his nemesis. It's a powerful and tragic story.

The image of that enormous, monstrous creature rising out of the water has always stuck in my mind. I'd always dreamed that one day, I'd see one for real and experience it firsthand. When I discovered there was a daily ocean sailing that departed from a small coastal town called Kaikoura to watch sperm whales close up, I had to go. I found a bed for the night in a nearby hostel, hilariously named The Lazy Shag and cooked a hearty supper to fuel myself for the next day. There was a boat which departed at 7:15 a.m. the next morning, and it had a limited number of places. I was both lucky and grateful to secure one, as I knew quite a few people were vying for them.

Unlike the Pequod in *Moby Dick*, the modern boat was equipped with sophisticated sonar and radar. The skipper could hear and see the movements of these huge mammals over four miles away and track them. The crew on the boat had done this many times, so they knew that sperm whales feed offshore, where the ocean floor suddenly drops to about three miles. We were shown some stunning graphic images on a huge flatscreen monitor inside the boat, so we could see this huge drop for ourselves. The sonar equipment was also able to pick up the sound of the whales as they fed, and when it was relayed over the PA, it was eerily distinctive. It was a bit like the sound of screeching brakes, played in slow motion.

Sperm whales only feed in deep water, where they can harvest enough microscopic plankton. As a watcher, great patience is required because a typical feeding dive can last around an hour. After that, the whale will surface for up to ten minutes to replenish oxygen supplies before diving again. That was the moment we were all hoping to witness. Suddenly, the PA went quiet as the feeding sound stopped, meaning that a whale was about to surface for air.

The skipper, who gave us a running commentary, opened the throttle to full and started speeding towards the area where the whale was most likely to surface. We all stood on deck, watching and waiting, fingers tightly crossed. My thoughts momentarily returned to Captain Ahab and the crew of the Pequod. The nervous tension I was experiencing may well have been similar for them as they patiently roved the sea in search of Moby Dick.

The captain called out on the PA to look into the distance. We saw spray blowing vertically up, coming out of the air hole in the top of a sperm whale's head. It was coming closer and closer to the boat. Our skipper carefully manoeuvred the boat to stay behind the whale, as they get uncomfortable if approached from the side or the front. He skilfully took us to within a hundred and fifty feet. One hundred and fifty feet! I'd never in my life thought or imagined that I'd get this close to one of the biggest creatures on Earth. When about ten percent of its long body was above the water, we gasped at the sheer size of this magnificent animal as it blew gallons of air out of its giant lungs at roughly thirty-second intervals. This went on for a couple of minutes until it had completely replenished its air supply.

Then came the best treat of all.

When the whale was ready to dive, it arched its back, which gave us a signal it was about to be push its massive tail fin vertically out of the water for a steep dive down to the ocean floor. Its tail majestically rose up a couple of seconds later, and then the creature was gone for another hour. Being in the presence of such a huge and entirely peaceful creature filled me with a sense of awe. We live in a truly incredible world with so many things we take for granted. This amazing, powerful animal could have knocked our vessel right out of the water and all of us with it. Yet, we were invited to gaze at her as she came to the surface, and we were granted the trust and intimacy of proximity. It prompted me to examine how often I allow people to get close to me and afford them the trust and intimacy we were being treated to. I was deeply grateful for the gift of this insight.

More Ticks on My Bucket List

New Zealand's South Island is a paradise for travellers. Glaciers are one of nature's phenomena and I'd never seen, let alone climbed one. Some are literally thousands of years old. Through these experiences, I learned a lot about the natural world and that inspired me and intensified my soul connection to life. Much of my time back in England had been spent living in the city, often working at the computer. I'd lost my connection with nature. I noticed how energising it was to recover that sense of realness the exposure gave me. How often do you get back to nature? How does it affect you?

Despite the fact I'd already jumped from the top of the tallest structure in the Southern Hemisphere and jumped out of an airplane from sixteen thousand feet, my need for massive adrenaline rushes wasn't fully satisfied. When I got to Queenstown, I was ready for my pièce de résistance! At four hundred and forty feet from the ground, the Nevis bungee jump was the second highest in the world when I did it—it's now ranked fourteenth. Way back in 1987, I'd heard a story in the news about an adventurous Kiwi by the name of A J Hackett, who had famously entered the international spotlight for the first time, using an elasticated rope to leap (illegally) from the Eiffel Tower in Paris. He gave birth to the bungee jump. I'd known since that day that I eventually had to try it and was thrilled that my one and only jump would take place in the centre he founded back at home.

I'll spare you the details and simply say that, with 8.5 seconds of freefall time before the cord reached full extension, jumping from that platform was the scariest and most exhilarating thing I've ever done. It stretched the edges of my comfort zone further than anything else ever had. I watched the person before me get ready. They jumped off the platform, and I watched the way they dived. I tried my best to copy their style and movement, spreading my arms wide, dropping my head forward, and keeping my feet together.

I pulled it off. I've watched the video of my jump many times since and still find it hard to believe that it's actually me in the film. Back on solid ground afterwards, my thirst for adrenaline had finally been quenched, so I headed for Christchurch. It's the largest city on the South Island and reminded me of Oxford and Cambridge in England, with similar architecture and green rolling hills in the countryside surrounding it. That made it a fitting finale and brought my trip to New Zealand to an end.

After sharing the first part of my self-discovery journey with Annie, I'd been worried I might not handle the solitude of solo travel well. Research confirms that human beings generally dislike solitude. It's been observed that people would rather administer mild electric shocks to themselves than just sit and be quiet. That's right, in studies where participants were asked to spend between six and fifteen minutes in a silent, windowless room without any stimulation, a significant portion (67% of men and 25% of women) opted to zap themselves just for the sake of breaking out of their boredom.

My mindfulness practice saved me from that fate. I discovered that solitude, or being alone, isn't the same thing as being bored or lonely. Loneliness increases feelings of isolation and depletes the spirit. Solitude increases self-awareness and ultimately makes us feel more connected with the world. We are never truly alone, although it's hard to really know this without sufficient time to reflect on it. When the word alone was coined in medieval times, it referred to a sense of completeness in one's own being, according to Ester Buchholz, a psychologist and psychoanalyst, and author of *The Call of Solitude*. Buchholz, as well as many other psychologists, say that solitude is an important, and normal, part of human existence. And it's also essential for our best creative work.

In today's age of social media and constantly available technology, I wonder if we've actually lost our sense of solitude and at the same time, increased our sense of isolation. There are now books written about how to break up with your mobile phone. Many people have an expectation they should get immediate replies to electronic messages, no matter what time of day or night. It means we have less time to reflect on and filter what's happening. It's an interesting paradox that can be hard to battle against, given that it's intended to connect you to the world. How is it for you? When and how often is solitude valuable to you?

Being on my own allowed me to develop the habit of setting the pace of my own journey, as opposed to letting others dictate it. Those few months in which I made my own plans and determined my own schedule sharpened my instincts and intuition, which I'd included as part of my guiding principle of presence. It also allowed me to absorb far more in the external world than I had when I'd travelled with Annie.

LIFE WITHOUT A TIE

I sensed, felt, and learned more than I'd ever anticipated. Other people are sometimes distracting. That can be a good thing, and there are times when connecting with another person is one of the great joys of life. But I found that walking up hills, through city streets, and along beaches with no conversation expanded my awareness of the quiet mutterings inside my head and gave me the space to make more observations. It felt healthy for my ego to recognise that although I'm not the centre of the universe, I'm very much connected with it and can participate in the world with humility and openness. What Henry Miller said is true: "One's destination is never a place but rather a new way of looking at things."

Above all, I knew at a deep level that I didn't need someone else to be around to be okay, which connected me with my inner resilience. Other people—those who helped me with problems, or became temporary roadtrip friends, or shared small moments with me around bowls of food—were an added bonus that I was really grateful for. But my quiet, inner voice that reminded me, "No matter what, I'll be okay," had been strengthened. It was an important gift I gave myself and that I keep giving myself.

Many people I've spoken to find the idea of taking off and travelling alone pretty scary, some even impossible, and I understand that. I had no experience of independent travel myself when I left England and was perhaps fortunate that Annie was a seasoned solo traveller. My year and a half with her was perfect training for me. How about you? If travel is something that calls you, what might keep you from doing it? And is there some way you could work around that?

There would be more solo travel to come as my quest to find true love continued with a trip to the Caribbean and the USA, which you'll read about in the next chapter. Later in my journey, I made trips to Tibet, India, Nepal, and China, all of which I'll talk about later. Now, it was time to fly back to the relative familiarity of my friends' house in Sydney for a couple of weeks and get ready to go halfway around the world to the tiny Caribbean island of Sint Maarten. A traveller I'd met in Thailand at the end of my Vipassana retreat had been in touch and made me an offer I couldn't refuse.

Chapter Eight
Keeping the Faith

BACK IN SYDNEY, I STAYED WITH MATT AND ELIZABETH AND THEIR SON, PETE. You may recall how Elizabeth's cancer had been the catalyst for my visit a couple of years earlier and how that had triggered a series of events which led to my journey. I was delighted that her health had significantly improved since then.

I was somewhat sheepish as I arrived and felt uncomfortable to ask for their hospitality, because I had no idea how long I needed to stay. I had no destination or exit plan in mind. Luckily, they understood and were compassionate. They kindly said I could remain as long as I wanted, which was a great relief. It didn't escape my attention how extremely fortunate I was to have such close friends in that part of the world, and I was grateful to them for providing me with a temporary space in which I could reflect on my journey and envisage whatever was coming next.

I still felt dizzy from the adrenaline that flowed as I ticked off the items on my bucket list in New Zealand. I wanted to be still for a while and reconnect with a sense of calm I'd strongly felt in the Thai Buddhist monastery. It was time to redirect my attention to, and explore, my inner world again and conjure up the next stage of my journey. This had become a necessity, because I was struggling with my motivation to get anything done. This was partly due to the total absence of any kind of normal routine in my daily life. I'd made no commitments that forced me to be somewhere, like a gym membership or study group, and I idled away hours and days. It had never been like that when I was a full-on businessman, driven by my goals and targets. I felt like I was floundering because of this dynamic.

It dawned on me how much my former life had been shaped by default and how little I'd noticed or questioned it at the time. Now it was more obvious and apparent. Can you imagine how different your life would be if you suddenly decided to question even one or two of the routines you have or any habitual commitments you've made? Since I left England, there was no job to do, no commute to work, no familiar social patterns, no weekly shopping and so on. That felt somewhat disconcerting. The absence of my own base meant there wasn't any place on Earth to return to that felt like home, and that worried me.

This feeling was something I hadn't foreseen or expected when I left, and it impacted me in two ways. The first was my mental health. No matter where I was, I didn't belong there. This gave rise to a sense of constant isolation even if there were other people around. The emotional discomfort led to constant doubts about the continuation of my grand nomadic experiment. I tried to avoid these unpleasant feelings as much as I could. But it was virtually impossible because each step I took was so transitory. For example, I packed up my stuff every couple of days, constantly left newly made friends behind, and wasn't regularly training in a gym.

This uncertain way of living was wearing me down, and the nomadic way of life seemed to have a unique set of psychological complexities. When I spent time with friends who shared my former lifestyle, like Matt and Elizabeth, it made me feel even worse. Observing them with their routines, circle of friends, predictable social life, and secure incomes threw me into self-doubt and was quite paralysing at times. And it was in moments like these that I took refuge in self-acceptance, one of my ten principles. I practiced being non-judgmental towards myself, no matter what I was thinking or feeling at any given moment.

The second way it impacted me was less of a problem, but it *was* a problem. It was my one bag and a laptop lifestyle. That imposed a huge constraint on new items I could acquire, carry, and use as I made my way around the world. With a maximum luggage capacity of around twenty-two kilos, I couldn't buy anything bulky or heavy, or things that weren't absolutely necessary. For example, people suggested I could save money on haircuts by purchasing a pair of men's electric clippers. The problem with those was that the power packs were extremely heavy, a couple of kilos in some cases, which made it impossible.

I met holiday-makers who had bought things for their home to remind them of their visit. When they saw I wasn't purchasing anything, they'd encourage me to change my mind. They told me I'd regret it in later years if I didn't keep any souvenirs. Compared to the beginning of my journey some eighteen months earlier, my thinking around this had shifted, and it disturbed me. I managed to maintain my discipline anyway.

Some comments left by readers of my blog posts gave me the impression that my nomadic lifestyle looked and sounded perfect to many of them, and I wrote in a way that maintained this illusion. But it wasn't the whole truth. Yes, I'd had a fun time in New Zealand and met some great people. But I'd also had days and weeks on my own and felt lonely at times. Wise teachers I'd met often talked about the joy of living in the present moment, yet despite being more mindful, I wasn't evolved enough to fully live that way without having any anxiety about the future. It definitely wasn't all a bed of roses.

Don't get me wrong; I felt truly grateful for the freedom I had to move around the world as I chose and for the privilege of not needing to work. Compared to many people I knew, I was lucky. But this gap between my own dissatisfaction and other people's positive perceptions of me had caused me so much unhappiness when I was a businessman in London. A few days after I came back to Sydney, I had a long conversation about it with Matt, and I reflected on how I felt most days when I ran in the nearby park. I was worried I was repeating an old and familiar pattern in my new nomadic existence. Different circumstances, same paranoia.

When I identified that possibility, it was a useful realisation. Being aware of it made me feel a bit dumb and self-critical. I wasn't at peace with myself and wanted to understand why it was happening and what I could do about it. But it also motivated me to continue with my grand experiment. I had yet to answer many of my deep, burning questions about the nature of happiness and living life true to myself. I knew there was more to discover. I decided to look for guidance and lo and behold, I came into contact with the perfect person in a matter of days.

The Dalai Lama

That perfect person was none other than the Dalai Lama himself. By chance, he was scheduled to be in Sydney that week and was giving a public talk in the heart of the city. I'd never met him or heard him speak, but I couldn't wait to hear what he had to say. If you want more inner peace, there is perhaps no one more fascinating to listen to than the Dalai Lama. I stood in the pouring rain for an hour, and his message contained exactly what I needed to hear. He told the drenched audience that the way to create world peace was first through every individual finding the way to their own inner peace. And then, peace with their spouse. Then their family, their community, and so on. His message made total sense and felt like a great starting point for reflection.

You might find it worth reflecting on too. Is there something happening in your life that prevents you from being at peace in yourself? And how does that affect the way you relate to the people you care about?

I was fired up and found a new level of self-acceptance. By practicing that and reflecting on what he said, I was able to quieten my doubtful thoughts and choose more positive ones, especially those related to the continuation of my journey. I accepted that doubts would creep in from time to time and if that happened, it was okay. There was no need to go into an internal conflict or berate myself. Travelling felt exciting and alluring again. I recommitted to exploration and life on the road, knowing that at any point I could easily change my mind and root myself if a project or special person materialised and it felt right to do so.

My two immediate questions were where do I go next? And more importantly, why?

I'd been travelling for just over eighteen months, and a part of me had an urge to use my business knowledge again. I had explored teaming up with an executive coaching organisation in Sydney. I figured I could establish a base of clients there without fear of losing my freedom. I wouldn't be permanently tied to living in Sydney like I'd been in London, and I could come and go as necessary. But on closer examination, there was no likelihood of that happening in the short term, which meant it was time to leave Sydney.

So, where to? A female traveller I'd met a year earlier whilst meditating in Suan Mokkh had reconnected with me via email. Nicole had become friends with Annie and me, and we'd enjoyed travelling with her through Laos some weeks later. She was a few years older than me, and I was attracted to her. She knew that because I'd admitted it to her in a moment of unguarded honesty during our trip. She'd said that spark of attraction was there for her too.

Nicole lived in Sint Maarten. When she invited me to visit her, I recalled that conversation months before and gave it serious consideration. Rationally, it seemed illogical to go halfway around the world for a woman I barely knew. My pause in Sydney had barely lasted three weeks, and I judged that thinking about travelling over ten thousand miles in pursuit of love and romance was complete idiocy. I'm ashamed to admit that, when it came to women, I was like the silver ball in a pinball machine, bing-bonging around randomly wherever there was some action possible. At some level, I believed that the answer to my problems lay in finding a new girlfriend. Financially, it was stupid and out of alignment with my commitment to frugality, one of my guiding principles.

Yet something about the risk inherent in that invitation was compelling. After a long Skype conversation with her, I decided to throw caution to the wind and go. Perhaps Nicole was the person who'd mark the end of my quest to find true love. I had to find out. "You only live once," I said several times a day until any lingering doubts had subsided.

Stopover in London

Even by today's standards, it's a heck of a long journey from Sydney to Sint Maarten, so I made a short stopover in London. It gave me an opportunity to meet Charlotte. By now, we'd been divorced for three years. I wanted to connect with her and check she was okay. Because she knew me well, I hoped she might give me some feedback about the changes she'd noticed in me. She had always been one of my greatest advocates for this experiment, and I trusted she'd give me her honest observations. It'd been over a year since we had seen each other, and this was a great moment to ask for her input.

"Since I saw you last year, you seem to have calmed down a lot," Charlotte said. "You're much more relaxed, certain of yourself, and laid back in your approach to life. You sound capable and confident of taking what comes and not so worried about the past or future. I also sense you're searching for your unique path. I think you're on the brink of an important personal discovery."

Interestingly enough, what she said challenged the doubts I'd sat with in Sydney. It made me adjust and recalibrate my reality slightly. It was an enormous dose of encouragement when I most needed it. It boosted the surge of energy I'd felt after hearing the Dalai Lama and strengthened my resolve to continue onward. Charlotte knew that living life true to myself was something that mattered a great deal to me, and she confirmed I had her full support.

Her feedback was immensely valuable. In fact, there was no one else who could see me like she did. She understood how challenging it was for me to stay positive sometimes. She'd witnessed how I'd ridden the waves of catastrophe and navigated a major transition without becoming the least bit cynical or damaged. In her opinion, I'd matured and softened in the process. She saw that I'd looked deeply into myself and was learning to open my heart. I was joyfully happy to hear that and relieved that the work I'd done to improve my self-awareness since our divorce had been worth it.

In the previous chapters in this story, you may have noticed I've touched on a particular theme a few times that not only influenced my entire journey but also continues to influence my life today. The theme I'm talking about is my belief in the notion that there are no such things as coincidences. For example, I held on to the wisdom from an old friend that when random people enter your life, it's for a reason, season, or a lifetime.

To strengthen my case and present some hard evidence, let me share what happened during one evening in my brief stopover in London. Omerli Cohen is an old friend who knew I'd be in town for a week and kindly invited me to a dinner party at her home in West Hampstead. I discovered to my delight she'd also invited another old friend and former colleague called Jelly Blount. If it hadn't been for that event, I doubt I'd ever have been in contact with Jelly again. The reason I say that is because soon after that encounter, she told me that she had cancer. It shocked me to my core. Her ensuing struggle with the disease, which she tragically lost, was a major catalyst for my decision to run my first marathon and launch a global fundraising effort, which you'll read more about in chapter ten. Clearly, we'd bumped into each other for that *reason*, only I didn't know that for at least another year.

Camembert and Baileys
Soon after, I headed for Heathrow airport for my flight to the Caribbean. Even though the island of Sint Maarten is tiny, it's divided into two parts, Dutch and French, which reflects its long history of colonisation. The average annual temperature is eighty degrees, and it has beautiful, white powder sand beaches lined with palm trees. What's not to like? If things worked out well between me and Nicole, I might literally be living in paradise, all loved up, for the rest of my life!

I arrived in Sint Maarten around Sunday lunchtime, in early July 2007. Nicole came to meet me at the airport. She ran a scuba diving business.

LIFE WITHOUT A TIE

She had blond hair, an athletic body, and was extremely fit for a woman in her early fifties. I'd seen pictures of her modelling a leopard skin wetsuit and looking like the love interest in a James Bond movie. During the year that had passed since we'd last met, I'd developed a romantic fantasy about her, which repeatedly played out in my thoughts. In that fantasy, she desperately waits for me on her sunny Caribbean island to make her life complete. I fly in and find her. We instantly fall deeply in love and live the rest of our lives together in bliss, taking daily walks on the pristine, sandy beaches and swimming in the ocean!

Back in the real world, I was feeling anxious about reconnecting with Nicole in this tropical paradise. We didn't know each other very well at all. What was she really like? Would there still be any chemistry between us? Would we eagerly run into each other's arms, embrace passionately, and dash off to her home to make love for the rest of our lives? I'd cast aside the wisdom I'd gained during my ten-day Vipassana retreat which had brought me a new perspective on living in the present moment and not having any expectations. There was some weight of hope that this encounter would unfold like my fairy tale. It's a paradox, I know, but life is full of those, isn't it? I still considered my life to be experimental, and it wasn't always desirable to be so present. I felt unable to maintain that level of awareness and gave myself permission to make mistakes and exceptions.

As I walked towards Nicole in the terminal, I had no idea that life was about to teach me a lesson about the dangers of having such lofty expectations. I came through the door from the baggage hall and there she stood. We nervously greeted each other. My much fantasized about welcome didn't materialise quite as I'd imagined. She took me to her small apartment in Pelican Key and warmly invited me into her little home. I could see she'd gone to some effort to make the space work to include me. It was essentially a tiny studio, and it looked like we would be sharing everything, including the bed. This felt slightly awkward, as we'd not been physically intimate in our brief, shared history. We hadn't explicitly spoken about our living arrangements either, and I'd assumed that Nicole wouldn't mind me moving in with her for a while.

In hindsight, I shouldn't have overlooked that. It was a dangerous assumption to make at any time, but had we not been on the same wavelength, it could have been far worse. We weren't speed dating; it was more like speed relating. Somewhat fortunately, a friend of Nicole's had gone away for a couple of days and had asked her to house-sit for her. So, she stayed at her house for the first couple of days while I occupied the studio, which relieved some of the pressure. Despite the initial awkwardness, we managed to create a warm connection, and things seemed to work well for the first couple of days.

I hoped that Nicole would want me to stay for the long term, so I started to look for opportunities that would enable me to sustain myself financially on the island, just in case that scenario transpired. Nicole helped me familiarise myself with my new settings and took me anywhere she thought I might enjoy. She knew anyone who was worth knowing and introduced me to a bunch of interesting people. With my long-term vision in mind, I asked loads of questions of every single one of them. I was fascinated to know what they did and the path which had led them to choose it. Every conversation I had with a new person gave me more data about island life and opened my mind to new possibilities.

Nicole put me in touch with a friend who ran a sports adventure business, and they invited me to join a half-day hike around the east coast of the island. Their business served the needs of the hundreds of visitors who come on cruise ships every week during the tourist season. They organise kayaking, cycling, and hiking tours for passengers who come ashore. With the high season fast approaching, they needed an extra guide to lead some groups and asked me if I was interested. That was exciting for two reasons. It was the first time in nearly two years that I had an opportunity to do some paid work, which gave me a confirmation signal I was living creatively and that my guiding principles were working. Secondly, it offered me the chance to do something I might really enjoy with a group of people who would be fun to work with. There was no way I could see myself relaxing on a beach all day at this stage of my life.

The next person of interest appeared at Nicole's local gym. I was introduced to a personal trainer called Mark. He was extremely fit and passionate about supporting people to excel physically. He was born in France and raised in America, and he'd trained Denzel Washington to prepare him for his role in *Training Day* and Leonardo diCaprio for his role in *The Beach*. He was an intriguing guy, and I was grateful the Universe made our paths cross. Even before my arrival in Sint Maarten, I'd felt a growing desire to build up my level of fitness. I'd been regularly hiking and backpacking, but I hadn't made any serious investment in muscle development, and I wanted to push myself to the next level. I had toyed with the fantasy of training to run a marathon but had pushed that aside. Instead, I chose to re-establish a discipline around strength training and making some tangible progress with that. If I eventually took up the offer of becoming a hiking guide, I'd need to be fit and strong.

The third example came from a daring move on my part. You may recall that back in 2002, I'd been the recipient of a business leadership award in England. I figured that if I connected with the right people, there might be an opportunity to coach and support some local business owners. That appealed to me, because it gave me a way to honour my guiding principles of connection and contribution and could also provide a source of income at the same time. I wasn't quite sure how to find these people. Then I remembered a story from way back that involved a friend of mine.

Back in the 1990s, whilst on a sailing holiday with a group of friends in Tahiti, my dear friend Nick Vesey, who was a great copywriter, concocted a fake press release and sent it to the tourism board ahead of their arrival. He was trying to secure VIP treatment for him and his friends. The carefully worded message announced that a flotilla of yachts carrying members of the Royal Willesden Yacht Club were headed their way. For those of you who aren't familiar with England, Willesden was a rundown area of North West London (at the time) and not only is there no yacht club there, it doesn't even have a lake, river, or any other kind of water!

Nick wanted to see if the recipient would fall for it. To cut a long story short, they bought it hook, line, and sinker, and a royal welcome was indeed awaiting them when they finally arrived a few days later. Taking inspiration from his success, I penned a press release and circulated it to the editors of the two or three newspapers on Sint Maarten, announcing my arrival on the island and the beginning of a year-long Caribbean Tour.

Award Winning Business Leader to visit Sint Maarten: Having spent twenty-five years advising senior executives in Europe, Martin wants to find out more about the issues people are facing in organisations in the Caribbean. He wants to understand the management and leadership problems that people in commercial business and public services encounter. He also wishes to establish how 'Best

Practice' knowledge from other countries can be used to the benefit of Caribbean communities.

In my case, it wasn't much of a ruse as I genuinely had the experience I claimed and knew I'd be valuable to business owners who were interested. Much to my delight, I got a call from a reporter at *Today*, one of the island's daily papers, who decided to print the story on page three. I was totally chuffed. Seeing it in print, I realised that life will give you anything you need if you're bold enough to ask for help. The article prompted a couple of business owners to contact me. I met them to discuss their issues and concerns and was able to help them. That press release was one of the most successful bits of seat-of-my-pants flying I've ever done and much to my surprise, it worked rapidly. Perhaps the islanders were just short of interesting news stories. I'm almost certain I wouldn't have been so lucky in London.

The more time I spent with Nicole, the more my feeling of unease grew. The red flags had started when she'd spoken about her disastrous marriage with her husband, who basically walked away years ago, leaving her to raise her child alone. She had an unfavourable view of men, to put it politely, and I found myself in the firing line of her vitriol. I'm not sure she was aware how negative the impact of that was. Her anger about that, together with her insistence on complaining about people and situations on the island, tired me out. Bit by bit, the reality of being with Nicole became further and further away from the fantasy I'd cultivated before my arrival. To be clear, I'd no desire to judge her because of it. I'm very much a live and let live sort of person, but I'm also aware how other people's outlooks and energies affect me.

One evening after an early meal, we were sitting in her lounge, talking. It got quite late, and I was a bit peckish. Without much thought, I said I was going to the kitchen to make a snack for myself and asked her if she wanted me to bring her something back.

"What are you going to have?" she asked.

"I think I'll have some of that Camembert cheese in the fridge on some Ritz crackers."

"And to drink?" she asked.

"Oh, I'm going to finish off the Baileys I brought with me."

Suddenly, there was silence, and I sensed the atmosphere had changed.

LIFE WITHOUT A TIE

Can you recall one of those moments when you've been with someone and everything was fine, then you suddenly become aware you've stepped on a landmine, but you're not sure how? This was one of those moments. I cautiously returned to the lounge with the Baileys and crackers on my tray. I looked at Nicole's face. She had a scowl so large you might've thought that I'd strangled her cat or set fire to her leopard skin wetsuit. "What did I say?" I asked.

"Camembert and Baileys? Camembert...and Baileys? I cannot believe it! How could you ever have these two things together?" Her cute French accent thickened, and her volume and incredulity increased with every word she uttered.

I was shocked by her venomous explosion and didn't know whether to laugh or cry, because her rant was hilarious despite her remarks being sharp.

"You are a stupid, ignorant moron. Don't you know anything about the food combining? I cannot believe it," she yelled.

Judging by her disgust, this moment seemed to mark the end of her version of the romantic dream, as well as the end of the world, apparently. It occurred to me that she'd been fantasizing about the two of us spending hours in the kitchen together. In her fairy tale, we'd taken it in turns to lick the wooden spoon during our romantic "food combining" sessions. Both our realities and fantasies were miles apart.

There are many reasons why a relationship between two people may not work out, but I have to admit that I'd never in a million years have thought that "food combining," or the lack of interest in that, might be one of them. Under aggressive verbal attack, I was defensive and tried to explain why I didn't share this passion and why I'd never developed an interest in it before. It was pointless. Her illusions were shattered. Her version of the fairy tale fantasy in which we both lived happily ever after had me cast as a gourmet chef, and it was non-negotiable, which pretty much meant the end of our little liaison. I found a temporary place to stay on the island and swiftly made arrangements to leave. Putting the fiasco with Nicole aside, Sint Maarten wasn't the kind of place I could imagine building a satisfying life. I knew in my bones it wasn't where I was meant to be.

This had been a harsh lesson in seeing things as they really are, rather than through the rose-tinted glasses I'd arrived with after months of fantasizing. I revisited my guiding principles and saw I'd lost touch with being fully present, had been attached to a specific outcome, and hadn't brought lightness to the encounter. On the other hand, I had practiced my guiding principle of self-acceptance and been compassionate towards myself about my shortcomings. The time I'd spent with Nicole had been a failure and a great learning opportunity to take with me into whatever was coming next. Events like this can be extremely valuable when you review them consciously. Perhaps you can recall a time when you made plans or set some expectations which didn't turn out quite how you envisaged, and you used hindsight to see where you went wrong. What was the lesson you received from it?

Ironically, as this was unravelling, I was reading a wonderful book called *Start Where You Are* by Pema Chödrön. It's about awakening one's heart and learning how to be more compassionate towards people you meet, especially those you don't easily get along with or those who have judged you in a way that has hurt you. Can you think of people like that in your life at this moment? I focused my practice on Nicole as best as I could and tried to be compassionate towards her. I could see we were both hurting from having unfulfilled fantasies. It was hard for me. A big part of me wanted to blame her for unfairly judging me in the way she had. Maybe you find it as challenging as I do in situations like these.

Nicole could be quite harsh when she spoke, and I actually cried a couple of times in her presence because of it. Even though we met in a meditation retreat, it didn't seem like she practiced what she'd learned, in the same way I had. It reminded me that it's not the acquiring of information that transforms one's life. Applying it every day, the *practice*, is the most important thing. Understanding good practice is quite different from practicing what we understand.

The bursting of the Nicole fantasy bubble was a cue to learn more about myself and the limiting beliefs I hold on to. I reflected deeply on the experience and gracefully moved on, making a note to pay more attention in future to the vision, needs, and dreams other people have when getting to know them, whilst checking that they truly align with my own. Three years after my divorce, this was something I still wasn't particularly good at.

I decided to head back to London temporarily. My experience with Nicole was unsettling and caused me to doubt some major decisions I'd made, including my separation from Annie some months ago. After the charity project in Cambodia, she had returned to Thailand to undertake some part-time teaching and training work. Even before I met her, she'd had a vision of her life taking shape there, so I was truly delighted to hear that she'd created a business partnership with a friend, and they were starting to create work opportunities on a regular basis.

Clearing the Air

Back in London, I discovered Annie was also there for a brief visit. She'd come back to obtain a long-stay Thai visa to continue living there. I got in touch and asked her if we could meet. When she accepted, I grabbed the opportunity with both hands. I felt lonely and needy and was in pursuit of some comfort after my episode with Nicole. I was hoping that Annie may provide it. I'd missed her loving, playful nature and wasn't sure how she still felt about me and about *us*.

When we split, we'd framed it as a trial separation and had given ourselves the option to meet up again in Asia later that year. During that period, although we'd stayed in touch via Skype, many of our conversations had been tense and emotional. Once again, even though I knew about mindfulness and the importance of kindness and compassion, I often forgot to practice what I knew when under pressure. At those times, getting my personal needs met superseded my commitment to being mindful. I hadn't worked out how to integrate both of those into my normal way of being.

Consequently, we never met up in Asia. Our relationship effectively ended over Skype, which was a new and dissatisfying experience. In hindsight, I regretted not making the time to go to her and complete things properly in person. With both of us in London, it felt like this was a perfect moment to make things right. There were things we both needed to say to and hear from each other.

Our conversation gave me a new-found sense of inner peace as we took the opportunity to speak from the heart and listen to each other about the hurts we'd felt before we separated. Parts of that conversation were awkward and uncomfortable, but I was happy we'd made time for it. At least we could both continue our individual journeys without any distractions or concerns about the past. That felt wholesome and gave me a sense of completion. I also had a hidden agenda, which was to sow the seed of an idea to leave the door open for later. I was uncertain about what was coming next and knew Annie was returning to Thailand. I wanted to know there might be a way back to her. Even if that didn't happen, our conversation cleared the air and brought us up to date with each other.

How difficult do you find it to stay up to date with close friends? How easy is it to not go there and leave your assumptions, judgments, fears, and concerns unacknowledged and unexamined? How might you feel if something terrible happened to you, like a fatal accident, and you died knowing you hadn't cleared the air with people you had unresolved issues with? It's one of my greatest fears and troubles me deeply sometimes. As I've got older, I've made more of an effort to clean up those kinds of things with others as I go along, at least as much as I'm able to. Whilst that choice has been challenging, and time-consuming, and requires courage, I have much preferred it to carrying the heavy burden of unnecessary emotional baggage brought on by things left unsaid.

The conversation with Annie also showed me that she'd moved forward with her life and things had worked out well for her, especially around her vision for her work in Thailand. It felt good to see that happening for her. It supported my belief that, if and when I was ready to take similar steps, life would somehow work out for me too. Perhaps you can recall a time when hearing someone else's story of overcoming a challenge empowered you in a similar way? It's one of the reasons we need each other. Knowing the details of what Annie had done to build a path for herself and what steps she'd taken helped me construct a vision for myself. It was all useful data.

I considered my next step. Where to pick up the trail and continue my nomadic journey? I had three choices. The first option was Australia. Every time I'd been there, I'd loved it. Living and working in Sydney for a while could be cool as a lifestyle. I talked to three or four contacts about different work opportunities there, including one which involved launching a new business with someone I knew. The downside of that choice would be giving up my freedom and committing again to hard work. I knew I wasn't quite ready to do that yet. Nothing in my conscious awareness called me in that direction, and I instinctively knew my journey needed to continue. My soul somehow knew I wasn't done yet.

A second possibility was to continue what I referred to as pure travelling, without a work element. I had enough money saved and was aware that a part of me didn't want to entertain this option because of my own guilt. I was holding a belief that travelling for its own sake was considered by many to be some kind of cop-out, that it wasn't challenging enough for the high-achiever friends in my life, and they disapproved of me doing it. I was buying into that belief to some extent.

The third option was to take a risk and embark on a completely new path around work and life by becoming a filmmaker or writer, for example. To explore this further, I booked a place on a two-day filmmakers' course in San Francisco to find out about the realities of that world. That might sound like even more illogical ping-ponging around the world, but it's not true in this instance. As luck would have it, a former business associate of mine in England had contacted me out of the blue whilst I was in London and offered me an opportunity to do some work with him in New Jersey, USA. It was timely and gave me the opportunity to connect with a friend in New York and attend the filmmakers' course in San Francisco with minimal additional travel costs. Once again, the Universe stepped in to provide me with what I needed at the right moment. Despite my uncertainty, it was still orchestrating things on my behalf. I made arrangements to visit New York in November 2007. America became country number eleven on my journey.

Joining The Dots

Remember the quote from Steve Jobs about trusting the dots of your life to connect? When I'd met Jelly Blount by chance in West Hampstead, I'd unwittingly stumbled upon a dot. It made no sense at the time, but it had a huge impact much later. When I left London for New York, there was no way I could have known that during my trip to the USA, three more dots would be revealed to be woven into the tapestry of my epic journey. As Steve Jobs pointed out, we don't necessarily recognise these moments as events or co-ordinates at the time, let alone appreciate their importance.

The first of these dots surfaced upon my arrival in New York. I'd arranged to connect with Angie Riley, an English friend of mine who lived and worked in Manhattan. We hadn't seen each other for over three years so had a lot of catching up to do. We spent a couple of wonderful days eating, walking, and talking together. On one of those days, the 2007 New York marathon took place. Paula Radcliffe, who was a superb English long-distance runner, took part in the women's race, and I'd heard there was a chance she'd break the world record. Being Brits, we wanted to witness this historic moment.

We made our way to Central Park and stood in the crowd where we could see her run the last stage and take the tape. In case you're interested, she won, in a time of two hours, twenty-three minutes and nine seconds, which was one second faster than her 2004 win but not quick enough to break her own world record time. She'd taken ten months off to have a baby, so that was still pretty remarkable!

Whilst we waited for Paula to run past, I distinctly remember having a Walter Mitty moment and imagined what it might be like to be a top marathon runner myself, winning the biggest race in the world in New York. It felt amazing. I must have drifted off for a while. I remember Angie was perplexed and asked me where I'd gone.

"If I ever run a marathon one day, which I doubt I will," I said, "I'd definitely want to do it right here in New York." I immediately forgot about it and carried on with my day. I mention it here because when you get to chapter eleven, it will all make sense. I'll get to the other two dots a bit later in this chapter.

Sightseeing in New York with Angie was followed by a short cab ride to New Jersey to meet my work colleagues. It was the first time I'd been in a business environment for over three years, and it felt both familiar and strange. I was there to run an experiment and explore the reality of building a global portfolio of clients. I wanted to get a sense of whether this could be a part of my future. I attended a three-day workshop, run by my colleagues, to observe them deliver a programme for executives in a global pharmaceutical company. It showed them how they could be more effective at building and managing partnerships and alliances. I didn't have any responsibility for the outcome of the workshop, which was a relief as I wasn't ready for something serious like that.

I reflected on my experience afterwards and knew instinctively that I wasn't ready to return to the corporate world just yet, despite the considerable financial benefits it promised. I didn't feel inspired or excited by it; I felt more like a fish out of water. I packed up my stuff and flew to San Francisco. Once I was back on the road, life felt creative and uncertain, as if it was a script being written one adventure at a time. That felt way more exciting than what I'd observed in New Jersey. Imagine leaning out over the front of a moving train to lay the next piece of track, one sleeper at a time, and you'll understand the feeling I'm describing.

In San Francisco, I stayed with an old friend called Michael Banks, and his charming partner, Karin. They lived just north of the city on the other side of the Golden Gate Bridge in Mill Valley. Michael had decided to attend the two-day film school with me. These two were playful, fun, and engaging. They were the perfect people with whom to celebrate the completion of two full years on the road. They understood what the experience of this journey had been like for me, with all its shocks, disruptions, and adventures. Their curiosity and empathy about it created a wonderful, deep connection between us.

The filmmaking course was illuminating and gave me information and insight as to what life in that world could entail. The highly regarded program was run by a guy called Dov Simens. He was an experienced Hollywood movie producer and perhaps the best teacher in the world for anyone wanting to know what it takes to make, sell, and distribute a successful feature film. The opportunity to dream about and glimpse an entirely different life, even for a couple of days, felt like a gift. After my acting turn in *Out of Order* earlier in my journey, I found it fascinating to look under the hood at the job of making movies from a technical perspective. I'm glad I explored it and saw enough to know that it wasn't a road I wanted to go down any further.

Trying things out is often one of the best ways of testing a desire or interest. I often suggest it to people I coach. Are there any opportunities in your life which you could investigate in a safe, bite-sized trial? Something you may be passionate about? What could unleash your energy or set your creativity free? What would it be like to give yourself permission and have a go? Who might you be if you weren't trapped by your current identity?

Rosie

In 2007, British visitors to the United States were automatically granted a ninety-day visa, and my return airfare to London had been paid by the company that ran the workshop in New Jersey. Because of that, I'd decided to stay in America for three months, which meant I'd be there over Christmas. The question I'd asked myself in Sydney about where to go next seemed like it had been answered for now. My worries about not having a base had also subsided. I'd recovered from the fiasco in Sint Maarten and was even comfortable again with my self-imposed, twenty-two kilo limit on stuff.

After my Vipassana retreat, I'd stayed in touch with a couple of people after I left the monastery. One of them was Nicole, and you know how that turned out. The other was a woman called Rosie, who lived in San Anselmo. It's only a few miles further north from Mill Valley, where I'd stayed with Michael and Karin. It would be an understatement to say we didn't know each other very well. We'd sat at a distance in the meditation hall without speaking for ten days and broke the silence with a brief conversation over lunch on our day of departure. We'd shared basic information about our lives and swapped email addresses.

I'd made an effort to regularly email or message people I'd met on the road. If I had to guess, I'd stayed in touch with about ten to fifteen percent of them, and I could see the potential for a real, lasting friendship with maybe ten percent of those. I wasn't sure which group Rosie might fall into. We initially met for lunch in her neighbourhood, and we got on pretty well. Lunch turned into a whole day and evening, and we were both up for spending more time together during the coming weeks. Being with Rosie was pretty easy and before long, our relationship became intimate.

In the life of a traveller, timing can be a matter of luck. Inadvertently, I'd picked the perfect time of the year to be in California. It was Thanksgiving, a traditional American holiday that takes place on the fourth Thursday in November. The purpose of the holiday is to give thanks for everything that one has at the conclusion of the harvest season and for most people, it's a big family event. I'd never been to a Thanksgiving dinner, so when Rosie invited me to join her and her brother's family in Oakland, it was a special treat, and I was extremely grateful. She cooked a fantastic meal of chicken in red wine and persimmon with sweet potatoes, vegetables, stuffing, cranberry relish, and buttermilk biscuits. As if that wasn't enough, there was also pumpkin pie and apple pie for dessert. We ended the day feeling a bit like beached whales.

The days flew by as Rosie and I got to know each other. If you're a foreigner, America is one of those countries where you can't play it by ear regarding how long you stay there. Once your ninety-day visa runs out, you must leave immediately or have what the authorities consider to be a damn good reason as to why you should be allowed to stay longer. Getting married to a US citizen in order to obtain a Green Card is common. That wasn't something I was ready to entertain, though I liked Rosie a lot. She was keen to start a family but I definitely wasn't ready for, or interested, in that. For the second time in three months, I had broken up with someone, and it felt lousy. As I lamented the loss, even though I knew in my deepest wisdom it was the right thing to do, I couldn't help thinking that I should never have separated from Annie. I wondered what might have been if we'd worked through the problems we'd had.

The Prophecy

My discomfort about the breakup with Rosie was soon to be relieved. I'd arranged to spend my last thirty days at the ranch home of one of my best friends, Nic Meredith, in Penryn, near Sacramento. You may recall that he'd been my companion on a road trip in Arizona at the time of my separation from Charlotte. We'd visited Sedona, where Nic met Regina. Their instalove story confirmed that meeting that special someone by chance *was* possible and could happen anywhere.

It was in their home where the other two dots appeared. I checked my emails each day and was somewhat surprised to see a message from a woman who'd been a former client. I ran the company virtually as the office had been closed for three years and there were no active clients. Camilla had written to let me know that she'd decided to leave the corporate world and start her own consulting business, just like I had. She asked if I might consider being her mentor for a while.

It was one of those confirmation signals. It was totally in alignment with my vision of blending work and travelling. Camilla needed me to do the kind of work I'd had in mind when I was weighing up those options in London. I felt confident that she'd receive the value she needed from me. She wasn't aware that my circumstances had changed radically, so I wrote her a message to update her about my nomadic existence. Back in 2007, the concept of remote working wasn't widespread. Without realising it, this was an opportunity for me to be a pioneer.

I let her know I was in the USA and that I wasn't sure when I'd be back in England. I asked if she was open to working remotely via Skype rather than face-to-face. If I did a great job supporting Camilla, she might recommend me to other people. It brought a sense of reality to my vision. I set out how it could work and waited for her to respond. We had a phone call shortly afterwards to discuss the details, which resulted in an agreement to work together for a few weeks. Not only was it completely unexpected, but I'd also never have thought of contacting her, even if I'd been proactively trying to make such an outcome happen.

That's the difference between using your will to push everything into existence as opposed to relaxing into whatever you are doing and trusting that the Universe will, when it's necessary, bring you precisely what you need for your soul's evolution to continue. Nic and Regina celebrated this welcome development with me and saw firsthand how experimental my road trip around the world actually was. My mentoring contract with Camilla was exactly what I needed to step into a new way of living. I had no idea that a few months later, things would escalate to another level in a way I couldn't have anticipated. I'll come back to that in the next chapter.

It felt uplifting to be with my friends in their California home. I practiced my guiding principle of lightness and soaked up the love and playfulness that was a feature of our daily lives during those precious days and weeks. At weekends, we sometimes went further afield and made overnight trips in their RV, which were great fun. During one of those trips, Regina said we were heading for Sonoma County, and that if I was interested, I could have a reading with a renowned astrologist by the name of Walden Welch. Both she and Nic had readings on previous occasions, and they advocated his abilities, wisdom, and insight with so much enthusiasm that I couldn't resist.

In his sixties, Walden had been doing psychic readings since the age of seventeen and used astrological charts for more accuracy in the timing of his predictions. He'd studied with well-known astrologer Gavin Arthur and hosted his own television shows. He'd also appeared several times on *The Merv Griffin Show* and *The Hillary Rose Program*. This guy had some serious street cred and seeing him in person sounded pretty exciting. Besides, to get an independent view of my future would be hugely beneficial as we were about to enter 2008. I sent Walden the personal data he needed so he could work on my chart. I know plenty of people who are cynical about astrology. I'd had limited exposure to it, although I'd had my palm read a couple of times in Thailand, which was enlightening at the time. I was happy to take whatever clues Walden might provide about what was waiting to happen next.

It was in my session with him that the third dot revealed itself. Our session was scheduled for an hour and in the first thirty minutes, the information that Walden shared with me was boring and inconsequential. Then the energy suddenly changed. He revealed something in my chart which startled me.

LIFE WITHOUT A TIE

"This is going to be a very lucrative year for you financially," he said.

I laughed and could see that Walden didn't know what to make of my reaction. "I'd love to believe that were true, Walden. The thing is, I have no business income or job, and I'm travelling and spending money with no intention of changing that this year. So, unless I win the lottery or find out that I'm going to receive an inheritance, I can't really see any truth in what you've told me."

He paused for a moment, as if to consider what I'd said. "Well, you know, Ray, you may be right. All I do is read the chart and let you know what it tells me, and it says that this is going to be a good year for you around money."

When our time was up, I thanked him for the session and left to meet Nic and Regina in the RV. I told them what had happened.

"He's been right so many times with us," Nic said. "You're just going to have to wait and see what transpires."

So that's what I did, although Nic and Regina's comments didn't entirely assuage my cynicism about Walden's prophecy. I left the sunny state of California to head for London, doubting that any of it would come to pass. It wouldn't be very long at all before I would be proved wrong and start to see a picture of my future emerging from joining the dots I'd uncovered.

"The only thing that is ultimately real about your journey is the step that you are taking at this moment. That's all there ever is."

Eckhart Tolle,
The Power of Now: A Guide to Spiritual Enlightenment

Chapter Nine
Finding More Dots

APART FROM MY MUM, AT LEAST ONE OTHER PERSON WAS HAPPY I CAME TO London in 2008, and that was Camilla. While I'd been in America, we'd had a couple of virtual working sessions to support her as she evolved her growing business. In a meeting with her in London in February 2008, we discussed the growth challenges she faced, and it suddenly dawned on me what Walden's prophecy was all about.

I had mothballed my business, but it still had loads of commercially valuable intellectual property, tried and tested tools, systems, and processes that had taken years to build. As I mentored Camilla, it became obvious that she'd generated plenty of demand from clients and consultants in abundance who could deliver projects. But there was an absence of infrastructure, which is essential for the profitable operation of such a business. Time was of the essence, and it occurred to me that a merging of our two businesses could be beneficial. She knew from direct experience that the quality of what she'd acquire was sound, which made the possibility of a deal easier than I thought. All she needed was a realistic and affordable price.

As I was moving in a different direction energetically speaking and couldn't see any further use for my business, I was happy to monetise it. We seemed to have a perfect match in terms of needs. I'd forgotten there was over £50,000 sitting in the business bank account. Selling the company to Camilla would release that money and supplement whatever she agreed to pay for the business. Walden had literally been right on the money in his prophecy, and I'd been a chump for doubting him.

To cut a long story short, I made Camilla a proposal and after a brief negotiation around the price, we shook hands on a deal. It was March 11, 2008—exactly four years after Charlotte and I had closed our doors to new business. First Place Consulting came to an end, and I felt a sense of jubilation about that. I was thrilled that Camilla, who held similar values to me, had acquired the materials that Charlotte and I had so lovingly crafted. I was also excited that she would take them back into the business world and use them well.

The sale gave me closure with that phase of my life and a satisfying final exit from the role of businessman that I'd played for so many years. One of my life goals had always been to create and sell a business, and although it was on a smaller scale to what I'd envisaged when I was younger, it was still immensely satisfying to have done it. Another goal I'd been driven by, and now achieved, was to create something that would outlive me and be useful to others.

In the four years that had passed since closing First Place, I'd particularly enjoyed having a break from the relentless need to generate more business. Finding and winning new clients for substantial contracts requires tons of energy and focus. I'd taken ownership for that during our eight years of operation and had also been responsible for that in my previous job, with huge targets to meet every single month. Although I was extremely capable in that role, it was exhausting, and I'd had enough.

For the first time in twenty years, I didn't have that pressure. I was free to focus on different things, like what I wanted to learn. I made a promise to myself, which I've kept to this day, that any work I did going forward in the field of coaching and leadership development would be on a freelance basis, either on my own, or perhaps as a member of a team for an established consultancy or coaching company. Maybe you've experienced a time when you felt that something you'd done for a long time was no longer working for you and called you to make a change? Was it difficult to do? Could you do it now?

As part of the deal with Camilla, I agreed to continue in the role of mentor for the remainder of 2008. I asked Charlotte to help transfer some of our delivery systems, which she willingly agreed to do. Looking back, I was deeply grateful for her unconditional cooperation. I'd conducted myself honourably throughout our breakup and divorce and was delighted that she reciprocated in a positive way. We were both so happy that our shared work had found a new home.

The question of how to define myself now was still to be answered, but the sale gave me another powerful confirmation signal from the Universe that my life was unfolding perfectly.

The signing of the deal marked another anniversary. It was one year since Annie and I had separated. Despite the energy and excitement around the sale of my business, I missed her. A part of me was craving the intimate connection that relationships allow, and the feeling drove me to find Annie again. It had been so good to touch base with her in London. I wondered if there might be a way back to her. The arrival of Valentine's Day presented the perfect opportunity to let her know how I felt. I spent several hours making a video celebrating what I liked and admired about her. I knew how much she appreciated thoughtful gifts, like the birthday book I'd compiled with acknowledgments from her family and friends. The video was well received, and with Annie's approval, I headed to Thailand to see her.

As I was about to leave, yet another dot appeared on my radar of awareness when I met with a former colleague called Julian Hartley for a catchup. Have you ever experienced a time when dots appeared? How long was it before you were able to join some of your dots? If you look back now, can you see how things were linked?

Julian and I had worked together many years ago when I was in my twenties. He now worked for ING, who were sponsors of the London marathon. I was fascinated when he described his experience of running in the race. He outlined his training programme and as I digested what he was saying, I noticed a twinge of excitement rising inside me. That was probably the first moment when I seriously considered running a marathon myself. I'll come back to that later.

Second Time Around

I was happy to set foot in Chiang Mai again. It was Annie's base now, and she'd built a life that seemed to be working well for her. We had one month to reconnect before I had to fly back to Europe for the first experiment to test my vision of integrating occasional freelance work with my nomadic journey.

We'd started healing our wounds when we'd met briefly in London, after my disastrous couple of weeks in Sint Maarten. We had a few more openhearted conversations which enabled us to clear the air and establish a new way of being together. I felt as if we'd created a newfound intimacy and a feeling of closeness which was a great development and a lovely step forward in our shared journey.

Within a week of my return, Paul Smith, who we'd met during our TEFL program, was getting married. Paul was a likeable, energetic English guy who'd stopped in Thailand to do some volunteer teaching and had met a lovely Thai woman. He was smitten and moved to Chiang Mai to become an English teacher. He'd invited Annie and me to the wedding without realising that we'd been apart for some time.

I'm not sure a wedding was the right kind of environment to be in whilst getting to the bottom of what I wanted from my relationship with Annie. It was easy in that setting to view life through rose-tinted spectacles (once again) and see a fairy tale outcome, as I'd done with Nicole. I was haunted by memories of the tensions and arguments that had led to our separation. It was confusing, to say the least.

The wedding took place in Nakhon Si Thammarat, which is in the southern half of the country. We flew down there and after the celebrations were over, we were in no rush to go back to Chiang Mai. Instead, we took a detour and headed for the tiny, exotic island of Koh Lipe, about three hours away by car and speedboat. We found a small resort beside a white sand beach and rented a tiny hut for a few days to continue our ongoing conversation and explore what we both needed and wanted.

After the disappointment with Nicole and the short romance with Rosie, I realised that Annie was special in a way that I hadn't fully appreciated before. I still had doubts about whether a committed relationship with her was what I wanted, authentically. I wondered how it might impact my solo travelling in the future. I worried that my need for comfort and intimacy was keeping me stuck in some form of codependency. I was concerned that getting back together might be a backward step. If I was playing out a pattern, I didn't have any support to break it. I felt frustrated, and confused, and unable to reach clarity about it. Despite all of that, we both decided to recommit to our partnership.

That decision helped solidify my vision, of travelling with some occasional work thrown into the mix, as I could now see the feasibility of that, with Annie back on the scene. Strangely, the work part didn't seem as desirable as it had when I'd first contemplated it in Sydney. Ironically, I'd read a book whilst in Koh Lipe, called *Courage*. It was written by the Bhagwan Rajneesh, or Osho, as he was better known. He described what it takes to live one's life outside of peer pressure and explained how to let go of the need to conform or seek approval. It resonated with me deeply, as did the way he spoke about making choices based entirely on what most energises you as an individual. I knew I didn't want to return to what

LIFE WITHOUT A TIE

I used to call my 'normal' life but had not yet grasped how to redefine myself. I was being mindful and consciously working on it, paying close attention to my thoughts, actions and my energy whilst in the process.

Back to Business

My first opportunity to work in a freelance capacity as an associate for another firm, with two four-day events in Singapore, came in May 2008, a year that had begun well and was unfolding nicely. I'd sold my business and topped up my bank account, which extended my financial runway and my nomadic journey for a much longer period. I'd reconnected with Annie and recommitted to our partnership. If I could find a way to re-engage professionally in the corporate arena and be valuable in a way that felt good, it would be the icing on the cake.

Annie didn't want to join me for the trip. She was immersed in her own projects in Asia and had no desire to leave them just to be with me while I worked. She was aware how important this experiment was to me and backed me totally, even though it meant that we'd be apart. We both realised that if it worked out, there would probably be more projects down the road and that separations would be inevitable. Nonetheless, we both accepted a non-conventional construct in our partnership and had chosen to unconditionally support and trust each other.

I returned to London to get myself ready. I'd be part of a small team delivering a training program to a global pharmaceutical company. It came about after I'd spoken to Steve Thomas, a friend and former associate, a year earlier. I'd told him about my nomadic journey and my freelance vision and mentioned that I'd be interested in doing some work in Asia. Luckily for me, he'd paid close attention and remembered that conversation. He called me to let me know there was an opportunity in Singapore, and I bit his hand off. I wasn't sure I had the competency to do what was required, but Steve assured me that I'd be given whatever support I needed.

Unexpectedly, Steve's client then decided to change the program. They postponed the events planned for Singapore and set up two new events in Switzerland and America. It was a bit ironic, because Steve had invited me primarily because he needed someone based close to Singapore. Now I was being sent to those two countries instead, which meant leaving Asia to fly to the other side of the world. That fitted nicely with my vision of having a portfolio of work around the globe and opened up the possibility of some free travel, as the flights were always reimbursed.

The commitment I was asked to make to this program was twenty days of the year ahead, which was perfect. There was no risk of getting pulled back into the kind of regular working routine I'd been used to when I was a CEO, and it felt like a small, yet positive step forward. I'd be working with some great people in an interesting environment where I'd learn and contribute, which aligned well with my guiding principles of connection and contribution. It also gave me an additional income.

I'd like to take a moment and underline the perfection of this development, and the growing sense the Universe always seemed to have my back. Basel, which was one of the venues chosen to replace Singapore, is only about fifty miles from Zurich, which in turn is a few minutes' drive from a small village where Charlotte now lived. I could have been sent anywhere in the world, yet I was going to be on her doorstep. I couldn't let the opportunity to see her and her family go to waste.

It wasn't the first time I'd seen her or her daughter since I left England. But I hadn't met her son, who was born just a few weeks earlier. It was also my first opportunity to see what her home life was like and meet her husband, which I was decidedly nervous about. I'd prepared for some hostility or awkwardness from him, as I was on his turf. However, he was welcoming, friendly, and hospitable, and I felt quite comfortable being there. Slowly but surely, I was healing from my past with Charlotte and fully embracing the new realities of our friendship.

I observed Steve and his colleague deliver the training in Basel and saw how the programme worked. The next venue was in New Jersey, USA. I spent a long weekend in London, rested a little, and prepared for the flight to New York, where I was expected to deliver the training with a colleague. I remember feeling somewhat overwhelmed and anxious about that as I made my way there. I was so unaccustomed to work after two and a half years of backpacking.

The particular course we had to deliver was designed for trainers who had an extensive background in techniques derived from neurolinguistic programming, or NLP for short. Whilst I'd received some training in NLP many years ago and was familiar with the main concepts, it quickly became obvious to me and my colleagues that my ability to work with and facilitate groups in these techniques wasn't as refined as it needed to be.

Following a review afterwards, I agreed to step down so they could replace me with someone more qualified to work on the next event. I had felt completely out of my depth in the workshops in New Jersey. In fact, I was so inexperienced that it was terrifying. In terms of my performance, I was ineffective and incompetent. At one point, I stood at the front of the training room with every single one of the thirty delegates looking at me, waiting for me to speak. My mind was off-the-charts noisy, and my body was filled with fear. I forgot everything I'd prepared, was tongue-tied, out of control, and sweating. I could hardly breathe. My co-facilitator saw what was happening to me and stepped in to take over. The whole thing traumatised me.

Worse than that, it really pissed off my colleagues, who had to compensate for my inability throughout the four-day event, as I simply couldn't handle what was expected. All of this put my friend and associate, Steve Thomas, in an awkward position with them, not to mention the client who'd hired us. Steve had vouched for me and assured everyone that I'd be a great addition to their team. Now they were essentially saying, "Don't ever send us an idiot like that guy again."

As I reflected on this horror show, I realised I hadn't been that great at listening to, and acting on, my instincts when I'd first been approached about doing it. As we'd prepared, I'd definitely had my doubts. After I'd observed a couple of events, I was a million miles away from feeling confident enough to take control of one. I'd ignored these thoughts and stayed silent, because I hadn't wanted to reveal my fears to my team members in case they took the opportunity away from me. The damage I'd caused from my lack of transparency was plain to see, and I took some very tough lessons from it. I realised that if work was going to become a feature of my travelling life, I either had to seriously invest in learning some new skills or stick to things I already knew how to do well. It was obvious that I couldn't just turn up and be paid without the right kind of experience. I'd thought I was smart enough to wing it, but the reality was that probably no one could do that, at least not me.

Whilst my self-judge chastised my behaviour, my self-coach acknowledged the courage I'd had to take on the challenge in the first place. If I'd not leapt in, I wouldn't have known what I didn't know! In the coaching work I do with senior executives in business, one habit I encourage people to adopt to become an extraordinary leader is to "Fail forward, fail fast." The more failures you have and the quicker you recover from them, the more you will grow. It's simple and easy advice to give someone else. In this instance, I had to be my own coach and realise that this episode had helped me see where to go next in terms of my professional learning and development. It had pushed me in the direction of genuinely wanting to learn how to become a much better facilitator and coach. Even though it put me off doing any further work for a while, the seeds of my desire for improvement were sown in that moment. I decided to learn how to become great at it, and trust that the Universe would send me the right teacher at the right time so that could happen. You'll hear more about this in chapter fourteen.

It was Steve Jobs who famously said, "Your work is going to fill a large part of your life, and the only way to be truly satisfied is to do what you believe is great work. And the only way to do great work is to love what you do. If you haven't found it yet, keep looking. Don't settle. As with all matters of the heart, you'll know when you find it."

As I left New Jersey for London, I'd reached the end of my horizon of certainty. As a perpetual traveller with no permanent base, committed to experiment with choices that felt right as they presented themselves in the moment, I'd got more used to living with the uncertainty of what might be coming next. If I looked in my diary at any moment, I'd see actual commitments or obligations I'd made for that week or possibly the next. There was nothing beyond that at all! For example, when I made the commitment to do the corporate training work I've just talked about, it was December 2007. In that moment, my horizon of certainty expanded to just the end of May 2008.

When I got back to London, my horizon of certainty had compressed again to around one week, the length of time I'd arranged to stay at my brother Paul's house, before I decided where to head off next to continue my nomadic journey. I liked that feeling of uncertainty at times. It reconnected me with the enormous sense of excitement I'd felt at the start of this adventure in 2005. Despite some doubts in Sydney, living with uncertainty and mastering that ability was becoming part of my new identity. I decided to head back to Thailand to see Annie and plan a solo trip through the central region of Australia. We'd talked about the possibility of trekking in the Himalayas towards the end of the year, and we'd be able to flesh out that reality and what it would take to organise it.

LIFE WITHOUT A TIE

Home with Annie

Before I left London, I met a guy called Nathan. He worked for a training company that had a few global customers, and they wanted to expand into the Asia Pacific region. To keep the dream of blending working and travelling alive, I took every opportunity to open discussions about the potential of enrolling as an associate, as long as there would be a good fit with my experience. We spoke for about an hour and whilst nothing was possible at that time, my interest was registered, and we left it there. Many months later, that conversation turned out to be more significant than I realised, and I'll come back to that in chapter thirteen.

I went back to Chiang Mai in mid-June. Annie was waiting for me in the arrivals hall at the airport. Her beautiful, beaming smile lit up the terminal building, and it felt wonderful to receive her loving energy and tight, warm hug. Out of respect for Thai culture, neither of us wanted to be too passionate in our greeting as the locals don't indulge in such behaviour. I don't know about you, but when I'm asked what one of the best experiences of my life was, I'd say that arriving at a foreign airport and being met by someone close to you is one of the most joyful experiences you can have. I was elated Annie had made the effort to be there.

The month we'd spent together in March felt like ages ago. Annie, who now lived more or less permanently in Chiang Mai, had cultivated a few friendships with other ex-pats in the city. One, a guy called Andy, was a yoga teacher. He'd lived there for five years and had his own studio, which came with a small, separate cottage. It was in a secluded, leafy, and relatively quiet compound inside the old city. Andy had gone back to the UK for a couple of months and invited Annie to house-sit while he was away. Once again, the Universe had stepped in; the timing of his trip was absolutely perfect for us and gave us a cosy little love nest for our exclusive use.

It was almost one thousand days since my grand experiment began, moving from one accommodation to another and living out of the same holdall. Staying in Andy's house gave me the chance to unpack my ten kilos of clothes and put them into proper drawers for a few weeks. It was also a rare treat to take a much-needed break from repacking every few days. Being there with Annie, I experienced having a home for a little while, which I'd been craving when I was in Sydney a year earlier. The house had its own kitchen, which meant we could prepare fresh juices and cook our own food, as there was an abundance of delicious and cheap fruit and herbs. I really appreciated these simple things and felt extremely grateful for them.

For the next two months, I enjoyed being around Annie and slowed right down. I practiced meditation most days, went for massages, met friends for coffee and went to a few social gatherings. I was thrilled to be with Annie for my forty-eighth birthday and delighted when she arranged a surprise treat for me. It turned out to be a visit to the Elephant Nature Park, which is a unique project set in a natural valley in northern Thailand, about forty miles outside Chiang Mai. The founder, Sangduen "Lek" Chailert, had legendary status and ran the park along with her American husband, Adam. Her nickname (Lek) means small one in Thai. We really wanted to meet her to see what she'd created. At the time, I had no idea that my visit there would be another one of those dots that would result in a radical shift in the purpose of my nomadic journey within a few short months.

Heaven for Elephants
The Elephant Nature Park was established to provide a sanctuary for over thirty distressed elephants from all over Thailand. Lek and her staff of mahouts (elephant handlers), veterinarians, and volunteers tended to the growing family of elephants that reside there. Some had suffered wounds or abuse by their handlers. I saw a female who'd had her eye poked out by her owner after she'd refused to work. Another male had his foot blown off after he stepped on a landmine in the rainforest. Lek has created a two-thousand-acre retirement home in which she hopes they'll be able to live out their days in peace. Since its inception, the park has received numerous awards from institutions, including the Smithsonian in the USA. And Lek has become affectionately known throughout the world as the Elephant Whisperer.

We met Lek when she interrupted her work to tell us about her background. Her maternal grandfather was a shaman in north-eastern Thailand, and he'd once received an elephant as payment for saving a life. She grew up with the animal and treated it as a member of the family. Over time, she adopted a characteristic commonly found in female elephants, the willingness to treat another's offspring as their own and to protect them fiercely. This affection led to her working with elephants in the forests. Against a backdrop of poverty, she managed to obtain a university education, something remarkable considering her circumstances. She became friends with a vet and together, they provided medical care to sick elephants in remote areas, which often involved hours of walking narrow jungle paths inaccessible to vehicles.

This was the first opportunity I'd ever had to get up close and personal with wild elephants. First, we were invited to feed these giant, docile creatures. Fruits and vegetables that could no longer be sold for human consumption are fine for elephants. We'd arrived with bucket loads of both, which we'd purchased in a Chiang Mai food market on the way and loaded onto a truck that followed us to the park. We carried it to a specially constructed feeding area for visitors, where I spent twenty minutes holding up huge pieces of melon and bunches of bananas for the elephants to grab with their trunks and place in their mouths. They had teeth the size of bricks and ground the food to a pulp in seconds. The intimacy of the feeding session was profoundly moving, and I was blown away when I saw the elephants totally trusted us. It staggered me when I found out they eat up to two hundred kilos of food per day. I started to get a sense of how much money would be needed by Lek and her team to constantly finance these supplies.

In 2008, it cost about $250,000 per year to run the sanctuary. There was no government funding, so every penny needed to be found by Lek and her team. She even had to negotiate fees with private owners so they would give their elephants up for a life in the sanctuary. They worked tirelessly on the funding side of things, which is why there was always a queue of people from all over the world who paid to volunteer there. Angela Botta, an American yoga teacher, was a great example; she'd travelled all the way from Brooklyn, New York to experience this amazing place. I had no idea at the time that our paths would cross again.

A river runs through the Elephant Nature Park, and one of the highlights was when we were all invited to join members of the elephant herd and their handlers for bath time! You might think it's dangerous to wade into a river with a herd of giant elephants, but I can assure you it was incredibly safe. Lek has created a culture of love for these animals and as I witnessed her interacting with them, it was pretty obvious that they had an unbreakable bond and would do absolutely anything for her, including being gentle and friendly with her guests. Just like the elephant she grew up with, she treated them all like members of a great big family and gave them names like Hope, Liberty, Jungle Boy, and Pooky.

I grabbed a broom and a bucket and started washing one of them down. He seemed to love being scrubbed and playfully sprayed me and others in my group with water from his trunk as we cleaned him up. If I sound overly enthusiastic about this, it's because the closeness of it blew me away. Up until that day, I'd only ever seen elephants in a zoo, at a distance, or in man-made enclosures that were nothing like the conditions here. I felt truly blessed being there and was inspired by what Lek and her faithful team had managed to accomplish on a shoestring budget.

To put the magnitude of what Lek was doing into perspective, you need to understand that in Thailand, elephants aren't wild. They're all someone's commercial property and if you own one of these powerhouses, you expect some kind of return on your investment. Since logging in Thailand, which was the main work they were used for, is now illegal, many owners turned their elephants towards other forms of work in tourist resorts, like painting pictures with brushes held in their trunks, performing bizarre circus tricks, or giving rides to tourists. It's easy to see these as an innocent form of entertainment. You might not realise that to make an elephant do such absurd things requires the total submission of their will, which is accomplished through a process of cruel beatings, until the elephant is literally broken. Lek showed us video footage of this barbaric practice, and we saw the immense suffering the animals endured. Once I understood this, I felt sickened that this practice was still allowed and angry that there was virtually no momentum to stop it.

Hearing directly from Lek about the efforts she made to protect these animals and gain wider support politically had a powerful effect on me. For days afterwards, I let my imagination wander and thought about what I might be able to do to help her. I knew deep in my bones that I wanted to do something. I just wasn't sure how or what. I prayed that the next dot would appear so that a picture might start to emerge.

I didn't have to wait long for the Universe to respond. A couple of days before I was due to leave for Australia, Annie arranged for us to have dinner with a couple of her friends. Mel Campbell was an English woman living in Chiang Mai. Annie had attended yoga sessions with her at the same studio. She brought her husband, Matt, along. We met at a small Japanese restaurant in the Nimmanhaemin area of the city, which is a trendy, chic enclave full of quirky coffee shops and interesting places to eat. Annie and Mel were chatting away, so I found out more about Matt. He'd worked in London and installed financial trading software for huge banks. I'd had exposure to that world through our dealings with clients at First Place, so I could relate to his experiences, and we connected easily.

We talked about hobbies and interests outside of work, and he revealed he was a keen runner. He was about ten years younger than me and had run five or six marathons. As he told me about his training routines, the races he'd entered, and the effect it all had on his health and well-being, I was completely fascinated. "Matt, could anyone run a marathon?"

He seemed surprised and puzzled. "Well, yes, I suppose so, as long as they're prepared to do the training. That's the most important part. If you do the training properly, it's almost guaranteed that you would finish a marathon."

"Ah. I see. Can I ask you another question then?"

"Sure, go ahead," said Matt.

"Do you think *I'd* be able to run a marathon?"

Matt paused, in the same way a diplomat or politician pauses in order to ensure that what he said next wouldn't offend me.

"If you don't mind me asking, how old are you?" he asked gently.

"I've just turned forty-eight. Ideally, if I were to run a marathon, I'd like to do it before I'm fifty." I realised that my desire to do it was unquestionably there. I remembered standing with Angie in Central Park watching Paula Radcliffe and my brief encounter with my old friend Julian just before I left London. That's where the spark had been ignited. Running a marathon could underpin a fundraising campaign and enable me to donate much-needed money to the Elephant Nature Park. My adrenaline flowed at this exciting possibility.

"Well, you look pretty fit to me, so I don't see why not. If you decide to give it a go, I'd be happy to help you and share some tips."

That was as far as that conversation went. For the first time, it gave me a concrete option for something I could realistically do that would be life changing for me *and* life changing for Lek and her team at the Elephant Nature Park. It was another dot in the emerging picture of my future. I parked the idea in the back of my brain to let it marinate and continued to Australia, where I'd arranged to do some solo travelling. That marked a recall for the popular *Daily Explorer* journalist, Chuck Maboomerang, who'd be reporting on my encounters for my blog readers.

You may remember me talking about Mary, who I met during my trip to New Zealand. It had been over a year since our lively and sexy encounter, in which I'd been invited to spend the night with her and had declined. She now lived in Brisbane, so I chose to make that my point of entry to Australia so I could visit her and find out if I'd done the right thing. I hoped to God I'd find out they were happy together and it had worked out, otherwise I'd give myself a good, hard kicking for passing up such a wonderful invitation on my last night with her.

Since then, she'd given birth to her first child. He was a gorgeous boy. And she'd moved with her partner, Alan, to Brisbane, where she'd grown up. Seeing the three of them together, I felt like my decision was totally vindicated. I saw the value of personal sacrifice, and it made me realise that I'm not a standalone unit in this world. We're all connected. Every one of my decisions has direct consequences and either enhances life or it doesn't. In this case, it was clear it was the former. I left Brisbane feeling satisfied in the knowledge that I was living my guiding principle of wisdom. Next stop, Sydney.

The Impossible Dream
Matt, Elizabeth, and Pete Taylor once again welcomed me with open arms. I was last there a year before, when I'd reflected on the next big step in my journey and decided to head to Sint Maarten. This time, my direction was clearer and the road ahead was marked out, at least for now. Elizabeth had fully recovered from her cancer and had prepared my guest room beautifully. Coming from the tropics, I was shocked by how cold it was, as August is in the Australian winter. I asked if I could put the gas fire on within minutes of arriving and worried about how I'd survive a trek in the Himalayas, which is where Annie and I were headed a couple of months later. It was ninety degrees in Sydney, and I was freezing! If you're thinking of visiting Australia, I strongly recommend you give the period between July and September a miss.

With my business sold and the horrendous result of my first freelance experiment in New Jersey still haunting me, I was tempted to turn my back on that world for good. Yet I didn't really want to. Yes, I'd spent the last two and a half years being totally free, with no professional commitments or responsibilities. But now, I had a growing appetite for engaging in a limited amount of meaningful and challenging projects. I wanted to engage with bright, creative people, and I had a growing desire to learn some new approaches that I'd need in the future to guide and facilitate others. Gandhi said that if you want anything to change, you must first be the change you want to see in the world. So, I promised myself that I'd look, listen, and consider any opportunity that might help me grow into someone who would be skilful and competent to develop others. I had no desire to revert to the conventional working routine I'd had in England or endure the kind of ridiculous travel itineraries that are typically part of life in the corporate world. I knew enough about my soul to know that wouldn't serve my well-being. My intention was to maintain the freedom and mobility to take off and go anywhere at a moment's notice, whatever that took. I knew I had something valuable to contribute to people in the business arena, but I wanted to do it on my own terms.

When I sat down and imagined how that might look, I pictured having an associate relationship with two or three small organisations like First Place. The people in those businesses would regard me as a valuable addition to their team and would have no problem with me being available only for limited periods of time. Ideally, I'd visit Sydney two or three times a year, for a month at a time. That would leave me free to continue travelling in between. Whilst I loved thinking out of the box like this, I also believed it would be extremely difficult to find such relationships. This led me to christen this vision, "The Impossible Dream." I really wasn't sure if it would work out exactly how I imagined it, but there was no harm in trying. At the very least, I'd make a few new friends and enjoy hanging out with them.

My exploration started in Sydney, with the management team of Six Degrees, a coaching, training, and consulting company. I'd found them via a string of coincidences and chance conversations that had begun back in the UK a year earlier. Yet again, life had guided me towards the people I needed to meet for a reason. I had two similar conversations with people in other businesses after that, and each one helped me to understand where I could be most valuable and clarified what my ideal working relationship would look and feel like.

In 2008, there was a shift in where I directed most of my attention and energy in terms of the four main ties in life I described earlier. Unlike the first couple of years of my journey, my career was now under reconstruction. As I'd taken care of that for the time being, I felt ready to resume some serious solo travelling. I had about two months to spare before I met up with Annie in Bali, and I'd set my heart on exploring the central region of Australia. I planned a trip from Adelaide in the south up to Darwin in the north.

There were long periods in which Annie and I were apart, so we maintained our connection through Skype and email. We'd both developed an ease with the non-conventionality of our relationship. Exploration is one of my core values, and I found travelling so engaging that I didn't exactly miss her when I was doing it. Of course, I was happy she was in my life. I knew we'd be together in a couple of months and that gave me something to look forward to. One of my guiding principles was to be fully present to life in any given moment, and I did my best to maintain that awareness and mindset. It had become part of my daily practice.

It could be quite a challenge to simultaneously hold what felt like mutually exclusive realities sometimes. For example, how could I acknowledge the joy that the presence of another person brought me and at the same time, honour the commitment to my own path? I experimented with how to find the balance and didn't always get it right. Looking back, many of our virtual conversations while I was on the road were quite practical, especially as Annie had organised some of the logistics for our forthcoming trek in Nepal. I preferred to save the deep dives into the dynamics of our relationship until we were actually together.

An Invitation from the Tea Master
Before I set off for Adelaide, I had an unusual and exciting appointment to attend in suburban Sydney. In Koh Samui in the gulf of Thailand, I'd become a friend of a rather unusual and quirky gentleman called San-Bao, better known there as the Oolong Tea Master. Originally from Germany, San-Bao dressed in unconventional garb and looked like a Kung Fu master. He was a huge, burly man with a shaved head, gold-rimmed spectacles, and a wispy, white goatee about six inches long. He described himself as "a Chinese man in a Bavarian body."

A seasoned traveller and man of the world, he was one of the more interesting characters I'd met in Asia. He'd led what I'd politely describe as a colourful life, with at least one brief spell in prison for a minor infraction. His passion was the tasting of fine teas from all over Taiwan, which he brought to Thailand for guests at The Spa to try. I'd been to a couple of his legendary weekly tea ceremonies during a liver detox in 2006 and loved them. He had a light, non-serious approach to the rituals of tea tasting, and he showed me how to drink and appreciate it in the ancient way. He made it simple, flowing, friendly, and meditative. We'd got to know each other quite well.

San-Bao was an avid reader of my blog, *The Daily Explorer*, and he'd seen in my most recent post that I was going to be in Australia. He sent me an email saying I must meet his friend Gary. San-Bao convinced me that Gary had an unusual story to tell. He thought I'd enjoy hearing about it and maybe even write a piece about him in one of my blog posts.

"How do you know him?" I asked in a telephone conversation.

"Oh, I met him in prison," said San-Bao.

That was a surprise. I didn't even know that San-Bao had been to prison. As he was such a cool guy and an avid reader of my blog, I trusted his recommendation and agreed to visit Gary. I took the train from Circular Quay to a suburb called Glenfield, southwest of Sydney. As I knocked on the door, I felt my pulse speed up. I was dying to know what Gary had done that had led to him being incarcerated, but I was also scared that he might be a violent criminal. He opened the door, and he certainly looked like one. He was massive. About six feet four inches tall, with huge, tattooed biceps, and a six pack, he would have put most prop forwards to shame. He was the kind of guy you might run into at a grungy boxing gym where badasses work out with heavy weights. His hair was regulation army style, and his appearance was quite menacing. We sat down, and I asked him if it was all right to ask him questions about his past, in particular his conviction. He was fine with it, and I quickly discovered that he'd been convicted of attempted murder, for which he'd served eight and a half years of a twelve-year sentence.

After the shock subsided, I relaxed a little and saw that Gary was an articulate and gentle man. He struck me as open, curious, and totally transformed. It was hard to believe that he'd been convicted of attempted murder. He talked openly about himself, what he'd been through, and how he'd fallen in with the wrong crowd at an early age, and one thing had led to another. I realised that his life journey didn't look like mine or probably anyone else's, but it was just as valid and enlightening. It made me wonder how different my own life could have been if I'd not had the love and good fortune I'd received in my childhood and youth. Prison is still a taboo subject in our culture, and I was aware of the paradox I felt in his presence.

On one hand, I could see my own prejudices towards him and on the other, I could see he'd become a totally new and different version of himself. He'd spent five of his years in jail meditating daily. He became a yoga master and had more mental discipline than just about anyone I'd met. He'd rebuilt his life and had set up a centre to teach martial arts to young, underprivileged kids in his community. It was a gift to meet someone whose life had been so different to mine and to learn about it, and myself, in the process. I practiced my guiding principle of being present without making any judgments. Through moments like that, my journey gave me such wonderful opportunities to grow.

After that, I made a two-day stop in Melbourne, which is a wonderful cosmopolitan city and probably my favourite in Australia. It has a distinctly European feel to it in certain parts of town. It's also relatively close to Adelaide, where I intended to track the Stuart Highway during my eighteen hundred mile journey to Darwin. I reconnected with an amazing woman called Rachael Guthridge, who Annie and I had met travelling in Vietnam two years earlier. She generously picked me up at the airport and put me up for the weekend.

She told me about a community project she'd launched to support Melbourne taxi drivers to develop a collective voice and begin a dialogue with citizens to help foster a culture of collaboration and harmony. This project was conceived to shift fairly negative perceptions that people had towards taxi drivers, and it was clear from the results that Rachael had accomplished a significant shift in a few short months. It really got me thinking again about how I could raise awareness about Lek and her community of volunteers at the Elephant Nature Park, so they could be more financially sustainable.

I left Rachael feeling inspired, excited, and uplifted by her story. It never ceased to amaze me how lucky I was to find such solid people on my travels. I'm pretty sure that no matter where I was in the world, chances are that I've met someone who would offer me a place to stay.

From Adelaide to Darwin
In my previous visits to Australia, I'd been to Perth on the West Coast, travelled from Sydney up to the Daintree Rain Forest on the East Coast, as well as Melbourne, Adelaide, and Tasmania. On top of that, I'd driven

across the Nullarbor Plain with Annie. The only part of the country I hadn't yet seen was the huge section in the middle between Adelaide and Darwin. When you consider the abundance of natural beauty in that region, it was definitely a real treat to explore it and probably my last chance for a while to travel solo. I didn't know for certain that was the case; it was more of an unacknowledged fear I'd begun to notice since I'd recommitted to my partnership with Annie.

I'd started to worry that my life would become restricted again. I held an expectation as time passed that I should desire to spend more time with Annie, which ultimately meant we'd do everything together. Every time I noticed those thoughts, I suppressed them rather than explore them with curiosity. They were scary, and I gave myself a hard time about it. My inner critic had plenty to say about it. *You shouldn't have thoughts like that. What's wrong with you? You're sick in the head.* I reminded myself that I was engaged in a quest to figure out how to live true to myself. In that context, these thoughts were helpful warning signals that I might be off track and gave me an opportunity to talk with Annie and get a solid reality check about her expectations. Staying aware of this was an important part of my mindfulness practice.

The first stop on the way was in the tiny and virtually abandoned mining town of Coober Pedy. I'd never heard of the place before I started my research for this particular trip. When I read about it, and the extreme conditions there, I knew I had to go and experience it for myself.

Coober Pedy is about five hundred miles north of Adelaide and had a rawness I'd never seen before. Over the years, the only reason people came to live in this inhospitable desert outpost was to dig for opals. It had around three million, mostly redundant, drill holes dotted across its opal fields. Buses going there were few and far between. I took a flight from Adelaide in a small ten-seater aircraft that could land on the dry, compacted mud runway. The small town looks a bit like the end of the world, which is probably why it's been constantly chosen as a location for sci-fi films like *Mad Max 3* and *Priscilla, Queen of the Desert*.

Just under two thousand people live there. It's so hot, about fifty percent of them live underground. How fascinating is that? The temperature can rise to around one hundred and thirty degrees in summer. During my visit in August, which is the cooler part of the year, it was somewhere around eighty degrees. I stayed at an underground hostel called Radeke's

Backpackers. Martin, the eccentric Aussie chap who ran the hostel arranged to collect me from the airport, which is a couple of miles out of town. There were no taxis as such, so Martin—a classic, outback Aussie, with a bush hat and thick, messy beard, like a guy in a Crocodile Dundee movie—picked me up in his minibus. The narrow tarmac road we took was flanked on both sides by miles and miles of dry, arid, rocky soil with no trees in sight.

This was the first time I'd slept underground. From the reception at ground level, there was a narrow winding set of steps carved out of the rock. These descended to a labyrinth of rooms, including my dormitory, which had two sets of bunkbeds with an aisle in between. It looked like the inside of a cave, lit with miner's lanterns. Surprisingly, it was well-ventilated and cool, compared to being upstairs on the surface. Once I'd slept the night, I totally understood why the people there lived like this.

As ridiculous as it may sound, the town had an eighteen-hole, grassless golf course, which looked like one giant, sandy bunker with a few holes in it. If you're a golf lover, you'll know how much water is required to keep a course green, and it was impossible in a place like this. There wasn't a single blade of grass on the fairways, and the "greens" were fashioned from oiled sand. Ironically, golfers used a piece of artificial grass to tee off. The owners hadn't lost their sense of humour, and there were plenty of witty "Keep off the Grass" signs around. On my last day, I visited a couple of underground churches, and their existence, which I was surprised to see in a mining town, brought a whole new meaning to the term underground religious movements.

Uluru (Ayers Rock)
Uluru is the world's largest monolith and Australia's most iconic landmark. I'd seen it from the air on previous flights in and out of Australia, as it's clearly visible at cruising altitude. For most of my life, I'd known Uluru as Ayers Rock, which is how most people referred to it until 1995, when the government of Australia finally returned ownership of it to the Anangu people.

To get to Uluru from Coober Pedy using public transport, there's only one option. You have to take a bus to Alice Springs, which is miles past, stay the night there, and switch to a different bus that then takes you to Uluru. There appeared to be a much more direct route on the map if I was prepared to hitchhike, so it didn't make any sense to me to take the bus. It seemed such an unjustifiable waste of money, which didn't sit well with my guiding principle of frugality.

I took the direct route and for the first time as a nomadic traveller, tried my hand at hitchhiking. The bus from Coober Pedy stops at the turn-off for Uluru, right by the roadhouse in Erldunda. I knew there'd be minimal risk in hitching from there, because if worse came to worst, I had a bed for the night there and could get on the bus coming from Alice Springs the next morning. I expected the road to Uluru to be busy, with lots of vehicles heading out to the rock, which was about a three-hour drive away. To get the best results from hitchhiking, I made a couple of signs to hold up to attract the attention of drivers. I found two pieces of cardboard and grabbed the black marker pen in my rucksack for times just like this. On one, I wrote "ULURU, PLEASE." I figured that a neat, well-written sign stating where I wanted to go ought to do it. That was my plan A. I stood in a place where it would be easy for drivers to stop, held the sign up, and smiled. For the next ten minutes, no one stopped, so I decided to activate plan B. I'd been taught in both my flight training and as a businessman to expect the worst and have a back-up plan. I got my marker pen out again and made an additional sign marked "GREAT COMPANY."

If I made eye contact with a driver as I held up the first sign, I'd show them the second sign with my other hand. When I did that, they always smiled. The fourth time I repeated this little routine, a guy stopped and took me all the way to my backpackers' hostel next door to Uluru. David, a surveyor in his early fifties, was on his way to a construction site. His architect's plans, tools, and hard safety hat were on the rear seat of his SUV. He cleared the passenger seat for me, and I strapped in. One of my friends in England was a surveyor so I found it easy to ask him questions about his work and life. He was curious about my life and journey too. David had considerable knowledge of the Uluru region and gave me a few useful tips for my onward journey. The Universe had sent me the perfect driver.

Uluru, in physical terms, is a huge, elliptical-shaped sandstone rock. It's just over two miles long and one and a quarter miles wide. It rises over one thousand feet above the surrounding flat landscape. Energetically, Uluru is considered to be one of the seven most sacred sites on earth, and that's what drew me there. It's sometimes referred to as the Solar Plexus

Energy Chakra of the World. For indigenous people, it's the spiritual heart of Australia.

People come to Uluru from all around the world, just to walk around or climb it in the hope that they will be changed by its magical healing powers. The local custodians, the Mutitjulu people, asked me not to climb the rock. I thought they did that to avoid offending spirit beings and asked one of the elders if this was so. With a grin, he said "We don't want these white people killing themselves. As custodians, we're responsible for the welfare of those at the rock and when people die here, we are responsible for their spirit."

That made sense! So I chose to do my own slow, meditative two-hour walk around the five-mile base track and become fully present to the energies I sensed in this sacred place. Other people went ahead and climbed the rock, despite their request.

As I went back to my hostel, I felt a sense of calm, inner peace. There was no need for me to hitchhike back to the roadhouse, because the bus for Alice Springs came through Uluru the following morning. I spent a quiet evening alone, watched the sunset, and sat in solitude while I processed and reflected on the experience of being in this incredibly powerful, divine place.

I eventually made it to Darwin, which was bland and unimpressive. It had all the hallmarks of a typical Aussie backpacker town, which is to say it was really made for partying, with many bars booming out loud music into the small hours. Great if you're into that sort of thing, but there was little else if you weren't. I posted a blog and reflected on my sixty-four days down under. How satisfying was it? What had disappointed me? What did I enjoy about travelling on my own? Was there anything I wanted or needed to change in the months ahead? What were the life lessons for me during this period?

As I reviewed my experiences, I was aware a subtle shift was taking place at a purpose level. It no longer felt satisfying to simply be a tourist. Even though it was rough, the business trip to New Jersey had opened up a whole new possibility for a new dynamic in my great nomadic experiment. Don't get me wrong; some aspects of being a tourist were fantastic, like the variety and adventure, meeting interesting people, and seeing new parts of the world. The feeling I'm describing was beyond those things. It was a deeper need for meaning and purpose. I'd felt that strongly when I'd launched my business in London years ago and had consciously let go of it as I transitioned out of that world into my life without a tie.

I realised that I'd needed to be completely aimless for the last couple of years, and it had been a kind of total reset mentally. And as I sat in Darwin, it occurred to me that I was approaching the point where that phase was coming to a natural end. I wasn't quite there yet, but I could sense it was coming soon. I'd been collecting dots for months, but they didn't quite join up into a picture yet.

Maybe my coming adventure with Annie in the Himalayas would enable me to gain absolute clarity. I was excited by that but also slightly nervous about linking up with her again. I trusted it would all work itself out somehow. I was happy that Annie and I would be together for the next couple of months as we explored a part of the world that neither of us had been to before. It was the first time we'd travel together since we recommitted to our partnership a couple of months earlier, in Chiang Mai.

It was mid-October 2008. Annie was participating in a challenging yoga workshop in Bali, which was pretty close to Darwin. I headed there to meet her. We had a whole week of relaxation to enjoy and enough time to plan some of the fine details of our big adventure in Nepal that would take us through to the end of the year. The best time to trek in the Himalayas is October and November, and we'd timed it perfectly.

Chapter Ten
The Roof of the World

Turning up in a new and strange city in the early hours with no one to meet you can be a bit daunting. Annie had intended to meet me at the airport in Denpasar, but my flight delay leaving Darwin scuppered her plan. I should have arrived around eight at night but actually touched down just after midnight. So, there was no Annie and no driver waiting for me. It was a great opportunity to draw upon my mindfulness practice and accept the situation for what it was. I called Annie, and she waited in Ubud whilst I found a taxi driver to take me there (forty-five minutes by car). I prayed he'd be able to find our guesthouse in the pitch-black, middle of the night. I needn't have worried. It worked out fine to trust the Universe.

Being in Bali brought back an unpleasant memory for me. I'd been several years before in 2002. It was the last vacation Charlotte and I took together when we were happily married. The echoes of that trip, together with a hint of sadness, lingered in my thoughts for a few hours. Coming back gave me a valuable data point as I compared myself with the man I'd been six years earlier. Back then, I didn't have the appetite for, or appreciation of, independent travel that I'd gained from my two and a half years on the road. It's embarrassing to admit but I spent virtually the whole two weeks inside the hotel resort, which was only a short taxi ride from the airport. In those days, my frame of reference was totally different to my newfound life without a tie mindset.

That older version of me was blinkered, bordering on pompous. Everything I needed was inside the hotel and at the time, I'd thought that venturing outside the resort was a waste of time. I had little interest in understanding the country, its people, or the culture. This was my first *real* visit to the island as this new version of me. I was fully present in the moment, with an open, curious mind and a genuine desire to explore and discover everything there was to see and do. It was as if the Universe was giving me a second chance to make things right. I was determined not to squander it. Maybe you can think of a time or event in your life when you realised that a period of change had reached completion, and you had shifted from an *old you* to a *new you*.

In Bali, and Ubud in particular, there's a symphony of colour, fragrances, beautiful architecture, and amazing culture that impacts all your senses. Elizabeth Gilbert recorded her experiences there in her best-selling book, *Eat, Pray, Love*, published in 2006. She described Ubud as "a healing place with a spiritual energy, ideal for reclaiming one's sense of self." If you know her story, you may recall she also met and fell in love with a Brazilian hunk in Bali, so maybe her opinion is a tad biased. After a few weeks in the Australian outback and with our Himalayan trek looming, I was glad to have some downtime with Annie, and this was a great place to do it.

Undefended Love

Bali was country number thirteen in my nomadic experiment. If you're superstitious, you may think that might've made it unlucky. I'd say the opposite was true. Annie gave me one of the best invitations of my life that week, something that lit a tiny spark of curiosity, which eventually led to a significant unravelling of patterns of behaviour that had dogged me during my marriage and were still hampering me. Lounging beside the pool, I noticed Annie reading a book that absorbed her attention.

When she'd finished, she handed it to me. "I'd really like you to read this book. It helped me understand how I can show up better in our relationship, and why we argue sometimes. I think it would help you too."

Slightly stunned, I took it. "Okay, Annie. I will. Thanks."

The book was called *Undefended Love* by American therapists Marlena Lyons and Jett Psaris. They described the capacity we all have to love without defences or qualifications and know ourselves so deeply that real intimacy becomes a lifelong expression of our deepest nature. I liked the sound of that and was compelled to read more. I hoped to build a truly intimate relationship with Annie. In line with my guiding principle of connection, I wanted ours to be direct and heart-to-heart. Their book addressed how to create that. It gave me a powerful vision and contained information that turned the problems and conflicts which inevitably arose in our relationship into opportunities for deeper connection. Their words certainly resonated with me.

Although Annie and I were together again, there were tensions in our relationship. Many of those were down to me, as I could be closed and defensive when she said something I didn't like or want to hear. Reading the book gave me a genuine opportunity to garner some new information and insight that could help improve the dynamic between us. Whilst a small part of me wanted to defend the way I was and not even read the book, I saw that was the whole point of reading it. My voice of inner wisdom was just loud enough. *Stay open, Ray, and pay attention to what you read. Don't ignore this.*

Completely rested after our stay in Bali, we left for a three-day stop in Singapore on our way to Kathmandu, Nepal. By now, *The Daily Explorer Blog* readership had grown to around one thousand visitors per month, which I was delighted about. It validated my commitment to my guiding principle of contribution. I placed a high priority on producing interesting content, which required more and more of my time. I didn't mind at all, as it was amazing to see my global community growing with each month that passed, and it helped me improve my writing and photography skills.

I was gripped by what I learned as I continued to read *Undefended Love*. The authors laid out an inspiring and practical approach to create lasting, loving relationships. It made sense to me. I became more and more aware of my emotionally protective barriers and saw how I used them to create a kind of shield so nothing could ever get to me or change me. I was underlining ideas with a pencil on almost every page. I saw how I could liberate myself, to love Annie with an undefended heart. I could use my biggest challenges as the way to become more authentic and happily committed. I still had quite a bit of work to do to avoid repeatedly messing up relationships. But it was the first time I'd had a glimpse of what might be possible, an intimate relationship that nourished and sustained us both. Annie saw I was reflecting deeply about *us* and was open to learning. Neither of us imagined that less than six months later, I'd be going to San Francisco to meet the authors of that book. I'll come back to that later.

The Annapurna Circuit

For as long as I can remember, I'd wanted to go to the Himalayas. Once, I'd even fantasised about climbing Mount Everest. There's something alluring about extreme environments that have an element of danger and challenge your survival. There are only fourteen mountains in the world that are higher than 26,000 feet. Eight of those are in the Himalayas. It's just as well, because they provide a major source of income for the poor citizens of Nepal. At forty-eight years old, I finally had the chance to step into my Himalayan dream with Annie. We'd committed to complete the Annapurna Circuit, one of the ten most challenging and popular treks in the world. As we flew into Kathmandu and glimpsed the snow-covered mountain peaks poking through the clouds below, my heart pounded with excitement.

The Annapurna Circuit is a two-hundred-mile journey. At a steady pace, it takes around eighteen days to complete, and the highest point is a mountain pass at Thorung La. The start is located midway between Kathmandu and Pokhara. We'd based ourselves in Thamel to prepare for our expedition. We needed special clothing, sleeping bags that could handle minus twenty-degree temperatures, medical knowledge in case of altitude sickness, a guide, and a porter. Thamel was the centre of the universe for Himalayan trekkers. It's packed with shops stuffed with trekking and mountaineering gear and with staff so enthusiastic to help you that their kindness blew us away. The area is best described as filthy yet charming chaos. It's a labyrinth of narrow, muddy market streets, crammed with thousands of Nepalis with wrinkled, bronzed faces, cows and goats, and hundreds of motorbikes zipping in between.

Although we were drawn to Nepal for the trek, we wanted to familiarise ourselves with Nepali life and soak up the culture and atmosphere of Kathmandu before we left the busy capital for the mountains. We had virtually no time constraints and had purchased ninety-day visas, so we were relaxed about taking our time and being fully present to the wonders we were surrounded by. Some days, we'd sit on the steps of a temple and watch life going by and play with the street kids who seemed so curious about us. I enjoyed being fully present to the simple, vibrant life we encountered there.

Westerners have been going to Kathmandu for years, many of them with the dream of climbing, or at least seeing, the mighty Mount Everest. Consequently, that was the most popular name adorning shops, hotels, guesthouses, and products. We ate in the world-famous Everest Steak House and knocked back at least one or two Everest beers. Our guesthouse was just on the edge of town, about a forty-five-minute walk into the centre. The dust and pollution were pretty extreme on some days, and I was glad we'd soon leave it behind for some fresh, clean mountain air.

LIFE WITHOUT A TIE

The Daily Explorer continued to report on our adventures. Seymour Peaks, who'd last been seen in New Zealand, returned to faithfully track our progress. We hired Madan Gurung, a guide who had been recommended by a fellow traveller. He was from the Everest region and had led treks for folks like us around the Annapurna Circuit many times. When we met, we instantly liked him. He was friendly and spoke enough English to communicate well with us. He gave us confidence that we'd be safe in his hands and assured us that we'd remain in total control of decisions about schedules and stopovers en route.

It was invaluable to sit down with him and look at the map to see the options for our itinerary. After some deliberation, we chose what is commonly referred to as a teahouse trek. That meant we'd be sleeping in small, wooden lodges dotted along the mountain trails instead of sleeping in tents. Despite my three years on the road, I couldn't resist a little bit of creature comfort, especially in the sub-zero Himalayas. Once we'd agreed our plan with Madan, he asked his friend Kamal to be our porter.

With Madan and Kamal on board, we had a manic day in Thamel. We acquired all of our essential gear, stocked up the first aid kit, and made sure we had sufficient cash to last nearly three weeks in the mountains. There are no ATMs up there, and we needed to eat every day and pay for accommodation. Lastly, we attended a safety briefing at the Himalayan Rescue Association headquarters in Kathmandu. At 17,600 feet, the altitude at the Thorung La Pass is over half that of Mount Everest and about 3,300 feet above the highest mountain peak in Europe. Altitude sickness can affect anybody who ascends beyond ten thousand feet, which meant we might encounter it. Neither of us had ever attempted a prolonged, high-altitude trek that involved significant oxygen depletion.

At the safety session, we learned how to help our bodies adjust to these high altitudes. It's known as acclimatisation, and the rules were simple. Above ten thousand feet, you need to make sure your sleeping altitude is no more than fifteen hundred feet higher than the previous night. That ensures a controlled ascent and gives your body enough time to adjust.

Madan obtained all the necessary permits for us to start our journey, and we were set up and ready to go. We departed Kathmandu from the local bus station for a five-hour journey to Besisahar and the start of the Annapurna Circuit. We felt like two little kids in a sweet shop and could hardly contain our excitement. When we arrived at our first tealodge, the place was a total dump, but at a couple of quid a night, it was hard to complain. It somehow added to the colourful flavour and wackiness of the journey. The doors must have been designed for Nepalese men, who are much shorter generally, as I banged my head on the door frame several times.

We caught our first glimpse of snowy white mountain tops from the rooftop restaurant, which was actually more like a rooftop storage room for old junk! We were an awfully long way away, but we knew it wouldn't be too long before we'd be much closer. On our first full day of trekking, we walked just over thirteen miles, which took about seven hours. By the end of our second day, we'd reached a village called Bahundanda. Madan found us a bed for the night in a lovely place run by two brothers, who talked with us for hours, trying to improve their already pretty good English. We each took a hot shower, which are scarcer the higher you go.

In the mountains, Dal Baht is a traditional, tasty dish which almost everyone eats. It's made up of lentils, rice, curried potato, and spices. One of the challenges facing trekkers in Nepal is finding and drinking at least three litres of water every day. It's too heavy to carry that much, so we had to find it on the trail. Bottled mineral water is relatively expensive as it has to be hauled up to these places by mules. The street price in Kathmandu was about twenty rupees, whereas the price reached one hundred and sixty rupees a bottle in the higher, more remote places. Another issue that affected the supply of water was pollution.

Sixty-eight thousand trekkers visit the Annapurna conservation area every year. Each person consumes three bottles per day, so you can work out how many empty plastic bottles get left there. They don't decompose and can't be recycled in Nepal, so it's a serious problem. To counter this, the government (with financial support from New Zealand) introduced Safe Drinking Water Stations. They had all the filtration equipment needed to produce enough clean drinking water to meet the needs of trekkers and at considerably less cost.

After five days, we'd completed fifty of the two hundred miles and reached an altitude of nearly nine thousand feet without any problems. I made a conscious effort to maintain my mindfulness practice and embraced my guiding principle of presence. I wanted to fully enjoy every step and take in each beautiful, serene moment. It was easy to mentally rush off too far into the future, especially as we were driven by the desire to achieve the end goal at Thorung La. We can so easily shift our focus of attention to our goals and miss the journey on the way. This trek became a useful metaphor and reference point to help me remember that going forward.

To honour my commitment to lightness, Annie and I developed a few games we played as we walked the ever-ascending path. My favourite was called the racehorse game, which required a bit of imagination, a willingness to make up reality, and to act stupidly. I noticed one day that Annie sometimes walked a few steps ahead of me. I don't know if you've ever heard horse race commentators talk during a race. They tend to speak really quickly with no pauses, like a continuous monologue.

"And Annie is a couple of lengths clear as she crosses the bridge, closely followed by Ray, who is gaining ground," I'd say in my best race commentator's voice. "As we pass the fern trees, the gap is closing and Annie is looking a little tired, while Ray continues to close the gap. They're neck and neck, stride for stride, and Ray is now in the clear. He's fifty metres from the line, he wins the race!"

My playful commentary resulted in a gradual and then rapid quickening of our pace until we were both in an outright sprint. The end of the game came when we were puffed out and literally couldn't run any further. We collapsed on the ground laughing and then continued as normal adults would. It was so much fun, and I felt so childlike and free. I also felt happy in those moments and grateful that Annie was there to share them. My earlier feelings of uncertainty about our future together had disappeared and had been replaced with a sense of a deepening companionship between us.

The Only Way is Up

As we continued our ascent along the trail, we got to know Madan and our porter, Kamal, better. Madan was a talkative chap and used every opportunity he could get to improve his English. I had to explain to him that I sometimes wanted to walk in silence so I could be fully present and appreciate the awe-inspiring beauty of the mountains. I'm not sure he fully understood why but he was easy going, and it wasn't a problem.

When we got to Lower Pisang, my breathing became more difficult. The altitude was 10,500 feet and just like we were told, the oxygen level in the atmosphere started to drop. Normal walking now required slightly more effort. You may be surprised to hear that the temperature in the mountains during the day was relatively warm. It dropped off dramatically once the sun had gone down, which was usually around four o'clock. After that, it was fleece, scarf, down jacket, and hat time. We grabbed a front row seat right next to the burners that were constantly refilled with dried Yak dung to keep the fire burning inside. These were common in these ramshackle lodges along the trail and warmed us up before bedtime. After a week or so, we stopped taking daily showers. Hot water became hard to find, and even if it was available, it was just too damn cold to take our clothes off. We both decided we'd rather be a bit smelly and stay warm!

On day eight, we reached Manang, which had better facilities than a lot of the villages we'd already walked through, including a tiny makeshift cinema which was showing films about Mount Everest. Manang sits at around thirteen thousand feet. Unlike Annie, I started to experience some mild altitude sickness symptoms. We were still four days away from crossing the pass at Thorung La, which concerned me. Heeding Madan's advice, I rested an extra day and ate a big portion of high protein Yak steak to replenish my body with a much-needed boost of nutrition. It did the trick, and we were good to go a couple of days later.

While we rested in Manang, Madan took us on a slow, one-thousand-foot climb to a tiny Buddhist monastery at Praga Gunpa, nestled in the surrounding hills. The air had about 75 percent oxygen, so we had to take it slow. It took us around one and a half hours. The resident Lama there was ninety-two years old, and he'd lived alone for over fifty years. How often in life do you get a chance to meet someone like that? We made a donation of food, and he began his blessing, which I was deeply grateful for the opportunity to receive, believing it would be good for my well-being.

He washed my head with some kind of holy water. I couldn't understand what he was saying as he only knew one or two words in English. No matter, I felt his compassion and kindness as he looked deep into my eyes. He tied a shred from a yellow, Buddhist prayer flag around my neck. It felt surreal, and I took it as a confirmation signal that my nomadic experiment was right for me. That gave me a strong sense of confidence to trust my path.

The night before we reached the pass, Madan found us a room which came complete with one broken bed and an attached bathroom, with a squat toilet at an extra cost of fifty rupees (about fifty pence). In the Himalayas, leaving the warmth of your sleeping bag to go for a pee is bad enough in sub-zero temperatures. If you don't have a toilet in your room, you have to put on your trousers, socks, jacket, hat, and boots, and go outside. I was willing to pay almost any price to get a loo in our room rather than have to go through all that palaver. Why go outside to pee in a hole in the ground, when you can pay extra for a hole in the ground inside your room?

We rose at four a.m. the following morning for the sixteen-mile hike up to the Thorung La pass, the highest point on the Annapurna Circuit. Our moment of triumph was now within shouting distance. It was dark, snowing, extremely cold, and difficult to breathe. Despite all of that, I felt excited as we were so close to the top. Every step felt laboured, and I stopped every fifteen to twenty steps to catch my breath. Above sixteen thousand feet, there's only 50 percent oxygen in the air. You can imagine how hard it is to maintain a regular breathing pattern in the cold whilst climbing uphill. Weirdly, our travel insurance policy only covered us for mountain trekking up to heights of sixteen thousand feet, which meant we'd be uninsured for a few hours as we crossed the pass.

We finally made it at around nine in the morning. Those last 1,650 feet were intensely satisfying. After a much-needed rest, we took the obligatory souvenir photograph of the two of us in front of the traditional chorten and prayer flags. We were standing at 17,872 feet, the highest point I'd ever been. And I'd walked all the way there myself, although Kamal carried my pack for me which had definitely made it easier. The view of the mountains from the pass was breathtaking, and we were awed by the panorama of those Himalayan giants. Elated, triumphant, and exhausted, we gathered ourselves for the descent to Muktinath and beyond.

The feeling of elation wore off over the next couple of days as we made our way to Pokhara. We'd heard that businesses with powerful commercial interests had funded a road-building program, designed to give tourists rapid access to the Thorung La pass from a newly constructed airport at Jomson, about a day's walk away. Jomson had a five-star hotel and several fancy guesthouses in anticipation of the boom this new road would inevitably bring. Maybe I'm a traditionalist, but the idea that you could simply fly in, stay in a luxury hotel, and walk a couple of hours to reach the pass stripped out the guts and challenge of the entire experience we'd been through and seemed pointless. I wish there was a way to preserve the heritage of the area and the authenticity of this amazing trekking route.

I'm glad that we were able to complete it in the traditional way. We'd missed going to Everest Base Camp to do it, but I returned to Nepal two years later to take on that challenge.

Our distress about these economic developments brought a feeling of heaviness to us. We realised we weren't going to resolve the issue. Occasionally, we forgot about it, like the time we passed through the village of Kagbeni and spotted a small, run-down Nepali restaurant called Yacdonalds. The sign outside was painted in exactly the same red and yellow livery of its namesake. Yak meat was extremely popular in the region, and I'm sure it tempted many hungry and tired trekkers to drop in. I do my best to stay open to trying new things when travelling, because it's a great way to immerse yourself in the culture. When was the last time you tried something new from another culture?

Namaste Children's House

The final week of our trek around the Annapurna Circuit had been a breeze because we'd more or less descended all the way. Temperatures went up, and we could breathe normally. Eight days after we crossed the Thorung La pass, we arrived at our final destination of Pokhara. I was excited to arrive there for a few reasons, like decent hot showers, Western food in the town's many restaurants, and access to the internet, to name a few.

Pokhara is the perfect place for some rest and recovery time. It's visually stunning and is set beside the enormous and picturesque Phewa Lake, which gives it an air of calm serenity. I loved to sit by the water's edge and observe the sun rise over the Dhaulagiri, Annapurna and Manaslu peaks. They're all mountains over twenty-six thousand feet, and you could clearly see them from Pokhara, which gave the place a divine feeling. This was as close to heaven on earth as you might get.

Aside from the chance to rest, you'll recall I promised my Kiwi friend Katy that I'd visit that orphanage and do something to help them. It was called the Namaste Children's House (NCH).

Nepal is one of the poorest and least developed countries in the world. Forty-two percent of its population lives below the poverty line. That may not mean much when you read that, but being there, seeing the reality of that on the ground, right in front of us, was heartbreaking. If you've never travelled to places like Nepal, it may be hard to appreciate how challenging it is for the people who live there. Twenty-seven thousand children die of dysentery every year. Two and a half million children are engaged in different sectors of child labour. Nepal also has one of the highest rates of child disappearance in the world, many into the human trafficking network.

It wasn't difficult to see why NCH was not only needed but also valuable, not to mention worthy of our support. The organisation received no government funding and survived entirely from donations and volunteers. It was home to about sixty children from as young as four up to late teens. Some were orphans, and some had been taken in from poor families in the surrounding villages because their parents simply couldn't provide for them. I don't just mean food. These kids had no access to education and no support to enter the workplace once they were old enough. In many ways, NCH was like one huge family which constantly changed as the elder children left and younger ones were invited in.

Katy had connected me with Visma Raj Paudel, the founder of NCH. With his team of carers, he was responsible for the overall running of the place. I'd been in touch with him via email, so he knew we'd arrived and was keen for us to see what they were doing. Visma was an inspiring character, and it was obvious that he cared as much about every single one of these children as he did for his own three kids. He explained the purpose that drives him and his team. In the main communal area, painted in large letters on the wall was the following statement:

Childhood is the foundation stone upon which stands the whole life structure. The seed sown in childhood blossoms into the tree of life.

That sentence encapsulated everything this place was about. Visma described how they provided love, education, healthcare, nutrition, and a solid sense of family, community, and cultural identity to the orphaned and needy children of Nepal. He gave us a tour of the buildings, which included meeting rooms, dormitories, washrooms, a kitchen, and a dining area. We could see and feel that Visma meant every word he said. Despite inadequate funds, the buildings were in relatively good condition for Nepal, although one of the dormitories had a leak in the roof. It was home for around twenty boys, and there was no money available for repairs. They used buckets and moved beds around to lessen the effects of heavy rain. That stuck in my mind for several weeks afterwards as I went to sleep each night, grateful it was in a totally dry room. Despite these conditions, the boys had been remarkably playful, happy, and energetic beings who joyfully engaged with us and made us feel truly welcomed.

The Universe had guided me there for a reason. Guided by my principle of contribution, I asked Visma what we could do that would be most useful to the NCH community. Inspired by what we'd seen, we kicked a few ideas around and settled on organising a picnic for the children the following weekend. We donated around thirty US dollars to purchase the food and Visma and his team organised the catering for everyone.

When Annie and I returned, we joined an exuberant and excited group of forty children, plus carers and one or two cooks. We took a thirty-minute walk into the nearby fields and carried the stuff that we needed to set up a party on the grass, including something to cook the food and a way to play music for dancing. What ensued was a few hours of abundant joy as we ate together, danced wildly to Nepali music played by a couple of the cooks, and ran around chasing each other until we flopped on the floor, exhausted. For us, it was like being kids all over again, and the children wanted to hug us and sit with us. There are so many people in the world starved of the basic love and affection I take for granted.

I sat and reflected on that event for many days afterwards. I was gobsmacked how far thirty dollars went in terms of the joy and energy it generated for those children. To this day, I still consider that to be one of the best things I spent money on during my entire life without a tie adventure. The NCH team were doing truly brilliant work with these underprivileged kids, who definitely gained a sense of security and belonging as a result. I wondered how many would fulfil their potential as they eventually made the transition into adulthood. It got me thinking about what Visma and his team could do for this community if someone came up with a much larger sum of money. That thought churned over and over in my mind as my journey continued.

Christmas in Kathmandu
We went back to Kathmandu in mid-December, which marked the departure of *Daily Explorer* journalist Seymour Peaks for a while. He'd fulfilled his job chronicling our adventures in the Himalayas admirably. Writing the blog in the guise of these characters was something I'd loved

doing since the journey began, and it was even more rewarding now the readership had grown. Around twelve thousand visitors viewed my site in 2008, and while that may not sound like a lot when compared to someone who is a global celebrity, it gave me a deep sense of satisfaction. It confirmed I'd been able to use one aspect of my journey as a way of contributing to others.

Annie went to the UK during Christmas and New Year to be with her family, and I chose to stay in Kathmandu. I wasn't in the mood for another trip to England, given I'd been twice already that year, and I had no problem with being alone for a few weeks. Before she left, I wanted to be sure Annie felt good about our relationship and how it was going. We'd had a brilliant time in the Himalayas, and she deserved some appreciation and a special send-off. On her last night, I took her to a restaurant in Thamel for dinner. When we'd eaten and our table had been cleared, we sat and drank a glass of wine. I smiled at Annie and said I'd made an early Christmas gift for her. I asked her to sit and listen as I read her a poem I'd composed. The poem reflected my appreciation of her playfulness, warmth, and drama-free approach to life. It also gave me a chance to express the love I felt about her as a companion, friend, and lover and how her presence had made this particular outing so memorable.

She loved it! We parted with a wonderful, heart-felt connection between us.

Loosening My Armour, Opening My Heart

My guesthouse on the outskirts of town was lovely. Most days, I sat and drank coffee in the morning sun on the roof terrace, read books, and contemplated my incredible journey. Reading *Undefended Love* had enabled me to see myself in a new light, and I'd realised how defensive I was. I'd always thought of myself as easygoing, open, and willing to adapt to pretty much anything. I could now see that my behaviour didn't always reflect this.

When Annie tried to give me feedback about something I'd done that hurt her or that didn't serve our relationship well, it was virtually impossible to hear, let alone accept her view or consider a change in my behaviour. Instead, I'd blame her for her poor communication and use that as an excuse to dismiss her ideas, which were valid. I got upset over and over in these conversations, albeit we didn't have them that often. This was my version of being armoured up.

It had played out regularly in my failed marriage to Charlotte. Back then, I'd blamed her for everything as I genuinely believed it was her fault. Annie was an entirely different person, yet she caused me distress in exactly the same way. It was slowly dawning on me that the common denominator in both relationships was me. It was a eureka moment, and it propelled me to take concrete steps to understand why I was like that and to find a way to change it. Have you ever come across a book that affected you so deeply, it enabled you to look at yourself and life differently?

Undefended Love had been incredibly helpful. I had plenty of time on my hands in Kathmandu and researched online to see how I might build on what I'd learned. I discovered the authors planned to run a two-day workshop in Oakland, California. I assumed it would be prohibitively expensive to fly all the way to the USA for a two-day workshop and almost dismissed the idea. By chance, my brother called around that time to see how I was doing. He's a pilot at British Airways and had access to discounted fares for family members. I gave him the workshop dates, and he told me I could fly from Heathrow to San Francisco and back on those dates for less than a hundred pounds. It was a clear confirmation signal from the Universe that I was meant to go.

Not only that, I could afford to invite Annie and potentially create a tour with her. She'd never been to America, and I knew the prospect would excite her. I called her to ask, and she happily accepted. We booked to go in February 2009. I confirmed a place on the workshop and felt really excited about the chance it would give me to learn more about myself and improve my relationship with Annie.

My horizon of certainty was now set at just over two months and that brought a sense of calmness. Kathmandu was virtually deserted over Christmas, so it was just as well that being alone was something I was totally comfortable with. I'm aware that some people find it a struggle. But I'd learned from my mindfulness practice that being alone is different from feeling lonely. Maybe you can remember a time when you were on your own for a longer than normal period, without the accompanying loneliness or anxiety that you can sometimes feel. Time on my own gave me a chance to reflect deeply on what was occurring in my life and how I showed up in it. I'd rarely had time for that before I began my self-exploration. I felt expanded from my experiments with the balance of being with others enough to meet my need for love and connection and being alone enough to maintain my full capacity to be present to whatever or whoever came towards me.

One thing became clear as I reflected in Kathmandu; I was ready for a different kind of year in 2009. I wanted to feel more directed, more purposeful, and to use my energies in a different way and turn up the volume on my guiding principle of contribution to others. I reviewed 2008 and realised that taking the pressure off myself for the last three years and simply being there to experience life in the moment with no particular aim in mind had fundamentally altered my perspective.

I'd let go of identification with ownership, consumption, conspicuous luxury, and status. I'd tried new things out. I'd solo travelled and obtained my TEFL qualification. I'd rediscovered my curiosity. The combination of my visits to the Elephant Nature Park, and the orphanage in Nepal, had ignited my passion. My personal connection with friends like Elizabeth Taylor in Sydney and Jelly Blount in London, both of whom had suffered from cancer, invited my compassion. And I'd discovered Matt Campbell, who opened my mind to the excitement and challenge of running a marathon.

A vision started to emerge. With the right help, I could set up a global fundraising campaign to serve those worthy causes. I'd need to find some kind of challenge to do that would raise money. I'd actually done something similar five years earlier when I lived in London. I rode a Royal Enfield motorcycle 1,200 miles across Southern India from Kerala to Tamil Nadu and raised £14,000 for the Rainbow Trust and the World Wildlife Fund. There was no reason I couldn't raise a significant sum of money once again. It would most certainly be worth all the effort it would take. Not only that, I'd stretch my beliefs about what I'm capable of physically and mentally and learn a lot from doing it.

I started to think about what the ideal challenge would be. I briefly considered the idea of climbing Mount Everest. It didn't take much research to realise it was a non-starter. The cost of undertaking a summit attempt is somewhere in the region of $100,000 or more, depending on who your guide is. To do that, I'd have to raise impossible sums of money and donors would be extremely reluctant to fund such a costly adventure. As far as I know, there isn't a single guide on earth who will take you to the top of Everest if you haven't already summited at least five or six serious mountains. I had absolutely no mountain climbing experience at all, so I ruled it out. You may think I was silly to even consider something as outlandish as that, but I believe it's vitally important and creative to be open to any possibility to begin with and *then* rule things out, as opposed to not allowing yourself to even entertain the idea.

Eventually, I opted for running a marathon instead, which was challenging enough. All the money I could raise would go to my chosen beneficiaries. I was approaching fifty, so training for and completing the twenty-six-mile race would put me in great shape health-wise too. The dots were now lining up nicely. I decided to sit with that plan until after the New Year, to make sure it wasn't just a momentary impulse. That was critically important, because it would be an undertaking that would span the whole of 2009 and probably a few months beyond. One of my core values is integrity, which means doing what I've committed to. I needed to be certain I was ready and willing to take this challenge on. With that question simmering away in the back of my mind, I found a couple of Swedish travellers in Kathmandu who had planned a week-long trip into Tibet, and I decided to join them. Even when you're a solo traveller, if you're curious about others and engage with them, it's quite hard to be alone for long.

Tibet

If you're a foreigner, you have to jump through a few hoops to enter Tibet, or the Roof of the World, as it's sometimes referred to. It became my sixteenth country and the first one that absolutely prohibited independent travellers. The controlling Chinese authorities will only allow you entry as a member of a group, led by a licensed tour guide. My newly made Swedish friends and I found six other people, and we ended up in a group of nine for the road trip to Lhasa.

I wanted a firsthand experience of what life was like for the Tibetan citizens who'd remained there after the Chinese took control in 1959, which caused the Dalai Lama to flee to India with thousands of Tibetan monks. I'd heard many stories of oppression circulating in the Western media about their plight, and I wanted to know the truth about what was going on. My group explored the remote wilderness on the five-hundred and fifty mile journey to Lhasa in two four-wheel drive Jeeps. For most Tibetans, a four-wheel drive Jeep is a luxury that would be way beyond their means, and there weren't many of them on the roads. Instead, most people used a medieval-looking tractor that you'd expect to find in a *Mad Max* movie. They were like a horse and cart, but with a small petrol engine mounted on two wheels and an iron handlebar fixed to the wheels for steering. These contraptions were common in the few small, isolated towns we passed through. In December, the outside temperature during the day was under fifty degrees, dropping to around minus thirty at night. Unfortunately, the heating system in one of the Jeeps wasn't working properly, so we took it in turns to sit in the freezing cold. It was a pain in the arse, but a small sacrifice to make as a seasoned adventure traveller.

The crossing point between Nepal and Tibet is the Friendship Bridge at Kodari. At the border, we felt the tension level rise as we were eyed by heavily armed Chinese border guards. They searched our hand luggage thoroughly, thumbing through every single page of my Lonely Planet to make sure I wasn't trying to smuggle pictures or information about the Dalai Lama into the country. They also checked the digital images stored in our cameras. Photographs of the bridge, or any of the official government buildings, were not permitted.

Our Tibetan guide, Tenzin, was about five feet tall, with bronzed skin and a huge smile, and he was friendly and playful. He reassured the stern-faced guards that we were all okay, and we were soon on our way. For some reason I couldn't fathom, Tenzin had me pegged as a dead ringer for Barack Obama (which, quite clearly, I am not). He was so convinced of it that he got his driver to take pictures of us together so he could show them to his friends. Throughout the next week, he constantly called me Obama, to which I replied, "It's Mr President to you!"

Spirit in the Sky
Three days in, we arrived at the Nyalam Tongla Pass. This rather eerie place was a sky burial site. These are derived from an ancient tradition of ritual dissection, wherein a human corpse is cut into small pieces and placed on a mountaintop, exposing it to animals, especially birds of prey, and the elements. This has been a common funerary practice in Tibet for many centuries. The ground is too hard and rocky to dig a grave and with fuel and timber scarce, a sky burial is often more practical than cremation. The majority of Tibetans adhere to Buddhism, which teaches reincarnation, so there's no need to preserve the body, as it becomes an empty vessel in

death. Birds may eat it or nature may let it decompose. The sky burial is simply the disposal of the remains. There were smelly, decaying items of clothing like trousers, jackets, hats, and scarves strewn all over the place. These belonged to the people who'd been buried there as gifts to the gods. I felt distinctly uncomfortable surveying the site. It felt like a scene from a Stephen King novel and had a lifeless atmosphere that was haunting.

Tibetan people look fascinating to me. Their faces are a beautiful bronze colour, and they're always smiling. Sadly, hardly any of them understood English, so we didn't talk much to the people we encountered. In one village, a farmer proudly showed me the head of a freshly slaughtered Yak, which he'd parked on the floor beside the table where the rest of the animal was on sale. There's no way that would have got past the health and safety officers in England, and it was easy to imagine we'd been transported back a hundred years or more to this place. The farmer offered me a taste of the traditional and popular Yak Butter Tea, which is a combination of black pu'erh tea—a fermented dark tea from China—a spoonful of salt, a fat serving of yak butter, toasted barley powder, and milk curds. It was absolutely disgusting.

New Year's Eve in Lhasa
We reached Lhasa on December 31st, just in time to celebrate New Year's Eve. Tenzin had organised a hotel which had previously been a large, traditional Tibetan house. Amazingly and quite unexpectedly, there were fitted electric blankets on all the beds. It was minus thirty degrees in Lhasa, but these blankets meant we all slept without the need to keep all of our clothes on, as we had on previous nights. It felt like we'd arrived in the Wild West and were booked into the best saloon in town.

Tenzin came up with a couple of options as to how our group could see the New Year in. After a bit of deliberation, we chose to eat a meal together and visit a karaoke club. It was a surreal and bizarre choice. Who would have thought I'd spend New Year's Eve in Lhasa, Tibet, singing out of tune American and English songs with a group of semi-drunken fellow travellers? This was the sheer joy of living in the moment, going with the flow of life, and saying yes to whatever came my way. The hysterical singing was a great way to let our hair down, be vulnerable, and bond strongly with each other.

An hour after midnight, I called Annie in England to wish her a happy

New Year. Being several hours ahead, it wasn't quite the end of the year for her yet, but she was still happy to hear from me. Yes, I enjoyed life in the moment, being in Tibet, and doing my own thing, but at the same time, I felt genuinely excited about the way our relationship was evolving and what it was possible to create together in the year ahead.

On New Year's Day, we wandered around the impressive Jokhang in the centre of Lhasa. It's the most sacred and alive of Tibet's temples, although the old Tibetan quarter only makes up a small area of Lhasa these days. Despite Chinese oppression, this magnificent square and the surrounding area is still the spiritual heart of the city. I observed an otherworldly mix of flickering butter lamps, wafting incense, and prostrating pilgrims. The Dalai Lama and many Tibetan monks fled because of the oppression they faced trying to practice Buddhism. I was deeply saddened to see how an old and beautiful city like Lhasa could change so much. It was obvious the Chinese government wanted to eradicate the Tibetan culture and homogenize it to become part of mainland China. At least I'd managed to get a glimpse of how it was in days gone by.

Taking pictures of Chinese soldiers, of which there are hundreds in Lhasa, is strictly forbidden. Anyone caught doing so faces imprisonment. Two of the travellers in my group were stopped and their cameras searched by plainclothes police outside the Jokhang Temple because they'd taken shots of the building and inadvertently captured some soldiers in their pictures. They were ordered to delete the offending pictures and allowed to walk away. The heavy-handed treatment they received activated the rebel in me. I was determined to leave with a few images of my own, so that people who'd never been there would see the oppression the Tibetan people faced every day. Despite concerns I might end up in trouble, I managed to capture six usable photo images for publication in *The Daily Explorer*. As soon as I got them, I rushed back to our hotel, emptied my memory card, and breathed a huge sigh of relief. I can't imagine what it must be like to be a real journalist in places like this.

The Foundation Takes Shape

After my week in Tibet, I returned to Kathmandu. I had one final, significant pilgrimage to make and that was to Lumbini. It sits right on the border with India and is where the Buddha was born. It's considered to be one of the most important religious sites in the world. I wasn't especially interested in the ancient excavations, or the architecture, or anything to do with the physicality of the place, impressive though those all were. I wanted to go there to feel the energy of the place. Since I left the UK, I'd spent loads of time in predominantly Buddhist countries and had completed my first ten-day silent meditation retreat at Suan Mokkh, a Buddhist monastery. This had deepened my interest in the philosophy and way of life it pointed to, which had become a part of my own practice. I was humbled to stand in this place. It was worth two days on a rickety old bus to get there and back, and it was a fitting choice for my final excursion in Nepal.

I reflected on my journey afterwards and realised that my ten guiding principles were slowly becoming more integrated into my way of being. I regularly experienced the power of presence. My ability to live in the moment, accept each event, and be grateful for them, whether pleasant or unpleasant, had greatly improved. I accepted myself and all my shortcomings more, especially in relation to Annie. And I was better at trusting my own experience and using my instinct and intuition when making decisions. Going to Tibet had been an example of that. A couple of years earlier, I might have been tempted to go with Annie to the UK for Christmas, despite the fact I didn't really want to.

I returned to London in mid-January 2009 to prepare for a different kind of year ahead. Within a few days, I sadly learned of the death of my friend Jelly Blount from cancer. If there was one defining moment that signalled the launch of my fundraising project, this was it. After months of collecting many dots, they'd finally joined into a crystal clear, compelling picture. I knew what my next step was and made the commitment to start. For me to accomplish what I had in mind, I had to make sure I had the full support of two particular people.

The first was Annie. Organising a global fundraising campaign would require a massive amount of time and energy from me and would impact our shared life. She understood and appreciated that and gave me a massive thumbs up.

The other person was Matt Campbell in Chiang Mai, who I'd been introduced to a few months earlier before setting off for Australia. He'd run six marathons and indicated that he'd be willing to help me learn how to do it. It was time to call him. "Hi, Matt, it's Ray. Do you remember the conversation we had last August when we met at that Japanese restaurant?"

"Kind of," said Matt. "Just remind me what we talked about?"

"You told me about running marathons, and I asked if you thought I'd be capable of running one. Do you remember?"

"Oh, yes. That's right. Of course, I remember that," he said.

"Well, I want to ask you something. And before I do, I must tell you, it's a really huge ask, and it's something deeply important to me. I know we only just met, and you hardly know me, so I'd totally understand it if you said no to what I'm about to ask you." I could sense from Matt's energy that he was getting slightly anxious about the question that was coming. "The thing is, I want to take on a significant personal challenge, so that I've got a reason to ask people all over the world to make donations to a fundraising campaign I'm starting. The challenge I've got in mind is to run a marathon before I'm fifty. Would you be willing to be my mentor and show me what to do?" I held my breath and waited for his response.

"Yes, of course I would. I know what it means to you."

It was a huge relief to hear him say that, and I was able to breathe again. "Do you have any conditions?" I asked.

"Only one, really. You'll need six months to train. It would work best if you were here throughout that period so I can put a program together, show you the ropes, and make sure you'll be ready. We'll be entering a couple of shorter distance races to get you some race experience. When will you be back in Chiang Mai?"

"Early April. Annie and I are off to the USA soon. I've got a two-day workshop to attend, and we're going to travel with a couple of friends."

"Okay, Ray. See you in early April. Look forward to it."

And with that done, I was all set. The Calling All Angels Foundation was about to come into existence, and with it, a sense of purpose for the weeks and months ahead, which would be hugely challenging. I felt both nervous and excited in equal amounts. This project had the potential to be life changing in so many ways and I couldn't wait to get started.

Chapter Eleven
Calling All Angels

RUNNING A MARATHON AT ANY AGE IS A DAUNTING CHALLENGE. I WAS ABOUT TO turn forty-nine, with no idea what I'd really let myself in for. With Matt Campbell on my team, I took the first step and chose the race to make my debut in. It was an easy choice. In New York in November 2007, I'd stood in Central Park and watched Paula Radcliffe take the tape. I knew in that moment that my dream was to go to the Big Apple and participate in the premier marathon in the world. At the time, I believed this was going to be a one-off so it might as well be the world's largest and most prestigious event. I had no idea that I'd go on to run four more during this journey.

I made an online application via the ballot. To my delight and surprise, I was successful and secured a place. The organisers usually receive around half a million applications every year and only around forty thousand runners are selected. Clearly, the Universe was also on board with my plan, and I was deeply grateful. The race was scheduled for November 1, 2009. That gave me enough time to prepare myself for the monumental task ahead and complete the event successfully before turning fifty.

I went back to London to join Annie, and we left for the USA. What was originally a short solo trip had morphed into a spontaneous adventure for us. Annie had never been to America or done a road trip like the one I had in mind, and she'd jumped at the chance. We put together a month-long itinerary for a tour through Arizona and California, ending with me going to the workshop in Oakland.

Sedona
Our first stop was Sacramento, where my friend Nic still lived with Regina. They both worked in media and were involved in the annual Sedona Film Festival, so we tagged along with them for a few days. Nic had a large RV that became our base while we attended the festival. It was well-equipped, with a lounge, kitchen, toilet, shower, two double bedrooms, a TV, and DVD player. The kids I'd met at the orphanage in Nepal the previous year

would have probably thought they'd died and gone to heaven if they had the chance to live in one of these. That kept me focused on my vision for the year ahead and made me remember why I was about to undertake such an enormous challenge.

Sedona has a reputation as a spiritual mecca, like Byron Bay, Australia and Glastonbury, England. Vortexes, which are thought to be intense concentrations of spiritual energies, were identified there in the 1980s and have attracted many metaphysical believers to the town. It's visually spectacular, with plenty of red sandstone rock pillars—which appear to glow in brilliant orange and red when illuminated by the rising or setting sun—punctuating the desert landscape.

"It's even more beautiful than I'd imagined," said Annie while we were out hiking one sunny morning.

And it was impossible to disagree. We both appreciated the rugged, arid landscape and the profound sense of connection we felt with the earth beneath our feet as we hiked the trails scattered throughout those incredible sandstone rocks. That feeling reminded both of us of the beautiful experience we'd had during our Vipassana retreat in Thailand. Only now, we didn't have to slog it out in a monastery for ten days to feel the equanimity and inner peace. Here, nature was doing all the heavy lifting for us, and it felt heavenly to be exposed to it.

Coming to the west coast of America was a different kind of travel experience to Asia, in part due to the dry heat and because the USA is a driver's country. The road network is vastly superior to many Asian countries, with hundreds of routes that stretch for thousands of miles. In America, you can't get anywhere without a car. In some parts of California and Arizona, there's no viable public transport system. After five days in Sedona, the Film Festival came to an end, and we said our goodbyes to Nic and Regina. I'd loved hanging out with them, but I was excited about having some quality time with Annie without anyone else being around.

The Grand Canyon & Las Vegas
We headed for the mighty Grand Canyon and took the famous Route 66 to get there. Being alone with Annie was a chance to enjoy being in the present moment, together. We had a demanding year ahead that could create some relationship challenges for us. But that was in the future. Right then, I wanted Annie to feel she had my full, undivided attention.

LIFE WITHOUT A TIE

Presence was one of my ten guiding principles. I'd come to realise that principles only make a difference when they're practiced. In my former life, I'd rarely allowed myself to live fully in the present and enjoy it for what it was. I'd had too many concerns about what was coming next. I was determined to experience this time in a different way.

I consciously practiced self-acceptance and lightness, two more of my principles. I was a long way from being the perfect boyfriend, but I was committed to improvement in how I showed up for her, and I decided to give myself some encouragement about this. When I work with clients, I usually advise them to develop the habit of spending more time in self-coach mode than self-judge mode, because we tend to speak with a bit more kindness to ourselves from the former and more critically from the latter. I practiced lightness from simply enjoying Annie's sense of playfulness and engaging with her like we were a couple of kids in an adventure playground. We had loads of fun together when we abandoned our serious adult personas.

The Grand Canyon is one of the few places on Earth that literally takes my breath away. At two hundred and seventy miles long, eighteen miles wide, and one mile deep, it's considered to be one of the Seven Great Wonders of the World. Even though it was my fifth visit, I was utterly speechless for a few minutes when we caught our first sighting. The sheer, awesome wonder of the place literally leaves me with nothing to say, which I'm sure some of you who know me may find hard to believe!

Annie was a first-time visitor and was completely gobsmacked when we arrived. Having trekked in the Himalayas around the Annapurna circuit just a few months ago, we were keen to go down into the canyon on foot. We chose the Bright Angel Trail, with a descent of over three thousand feet that took us to Plateau Point, some seven miles from the south rim. The first part of the trail was slippery, as some of the winter snow had turned to ice. By the time we reached the second rest stop at three miles, we'd completed the descent. A further walk of around three miles got us to Plateau Point. We spent over an hour sitting in silence on the rocks as a few mighty condors circled around overhead. I felt a sense of absolute bliss being out in the wilds of nature with no other people in sight, nothing to do, and nowhere to be. It was incredibly difficult to tear myself away from that awe-inspiring place.

Travelling widely exposes you to experiences that vary in order of magnitude. Less than three hundred miles from the Grand Canyon, Las Vegas is a great example of a city of extremes. The so-called entertainment capital of the world is famous for its large number of casino resorts and associated entertainment. There's so much intensely bright, outdoor lighting that, when viewed from space, the Las Vegas metropolitan area is the brightest place on Earth. The Strip is the straight, four-mile stretch through the centre. I'd been there before, and I thought Annie would be blown away by the audacity, kitsch, and scale of it all. It was such a far cry from the beauty of the Grand Canyon and the Himalayas, and like a different universe from the one in which we both had done our Vipassana retreat.

A huge amount of money and effort has gone into creating the fantasy world that exists there. The casinos replicate some of the great iconic landmarks from around the world. The hotel, New York, New York, has replicas of the Statue of Liberty, the Empire State Building, and the Brooklyn Bridge. The irony of that wasn't lost on me, given I'd got a place to run the marathon in the Big Apple in a few months' time. The stunning Venetian hotel is based on the architecture in St. Mark's Square. The Mirage has an erupting volcano. Paris has a half-sized replica of the Eiffel Tower, in which you can ride an elevator to the top. And the Luxor is a twenty-seven-story hotel and casino, built to the same size and scale as one of the Egyptian pyramids.

If you simply want some fun and short-term distraction, it's an eye-catching world of fantasy that is second to none. I understand why so many people come all year round. The lights, the shows, the twenty-four-hour culture, and the millions of dollars per hour being spent is all quite fascinating but ultimately, it's hollow and devoid of any meaning. If you're curious about the world, this place is definitely one you have to see, but I'd limit your exposure to one or two days at best.

After forty-eight hours, Annie chalked it up on her list of unusual places with no return anytime soon and said, "Let's get out of here." I was happy to hear that, and we departed this weird fantasy world for something more real. We were grateful for the contrast it provided and felt more committed to our mindful path. It helped us appreciate the real, authentic relationships we both had in our lives. Our final stop before attending my Oakland workshop was Seattle.

LIFE WITHOUT A TIE

Fierce Conversations in Seattle

My first attempt at freelance work in New Jersey had been a disaster. In Seattle, I explored another potential working relationship. Fierce Conversations is a business that was founded by author Susan Scott after she published her best-selling book of the same name. I've used that book extensively in my coaching work over the years. The company was looking for independent coaches and trainers who wanted to become licensed partners who would use the material and ideas in Susan's book to run workshops in large cities around the world. I was curious to see if it might be a good fit for my needs.

Susan's philosophy is simple; whilst no single conversation is guaranteed to change the trajectory of a career, a company, a relationship, or a life, any single conversation can. I'm someone who has always loved the idea of being able to communicate authentically and powerfully, so her philosophy resonated with me. I'd achieved some good results in the past using a couple of the suggestions in her book. The possibility of training and facilitating others to improve the way they communicate was of interest to me and partnering with Fierce was one way I could potentially do that.

I left to reflect on it over the next few months. I could have jumped in there and then, but I wanted to sit with it for a while. A substantial commitment was being asked, both financially and energetically. The cost of the license had to be recovered, and I wanted to carefully examine the amount of work it would take to reach that point. More importantly, I wanted to assess the impact that focusing on that might have on my life. A part of me was worried about my future income requirements. But I didn't want to be driven by fear. I had enough money for now. I chose to embrace my inner wisdom, which guided me to take my time and remain unattached. Maybe you can think of a time when you took on a commitment impulsively out of fear and soon realised you may have been better to sit and wait a while.

Annie and I returned to my friend's house in Sacramento, ready to explore San Francisco, which was about an hour's drive away. It's one of the most loved, most photographed, and most visited cities in the world, with over fifteen million people paying homage every year. I'd been there many times and couldn't wait for Annie to experience it, as it was all brand new to her. She'd dreamed of walking across the Golden Gate Bridge all her life, inspired by countless glimpses in films and TV shows. We rode on the iconic cable cars, drove down Lombard Street, the most crooked street in the world, took the ferry out to Alcatraz Island, and finished off with a meal in a classic, old-fashioned American diner.

Taking the Mid-Life, One Leap at a Time
Our road trip was nearly over, save for my two-day workshop in Oakland, which is located on the opposite side of the bay to San Francisco itself. I'd gained many useful insights from *Undefended Love*, the book Annie had given me, and I was excited to take two days to explore my inner world under the authors' guidance. This was the information I'd received about the course that prompted me to register:

> "If you're between forty-five and sixty-five years old, you are undoubtedly attempting to navigate your mid-life passage. What makes this experience unlike any other is that it requires the death of who you have known yourself to be and promises the birth of who you could possibly become. Far too many people 'die' in their fifties and are not buried until their eighties because they did not take the full journey possible at mid-life. The whole point of midlife is to allow the construct of who you are and the life you have created to fail. It's not just an opportunity for a fresh start; it's a mandate for one."

I was about to turn fifty, which made the invitation to participate sound irresistible. This programme could help me reflect on my personal values and decipher what would be most important for me in the next decade. I was ready to build on the ideas in their book and continue the work of opening my heart. I sensed subtle changes in my perspective were already happening. I wanted to deepen my connection with Annie and free myself to experience greater love and intimacy with her. Above all, I wanted to make the right choices for myself so that I'd have no regrets later. I was surprised and reassured by many people that showed up (who seemed just like me), who were also curious to examine their lives in this context.

The weekend had a deep impact on me. I found a number of beliefs that it was time to let go of. Several patterns of behaviour that had been useful in the past now felt quite restrictive. I'd always seen being extremely dogmatic about decisions as a strength. I was a "Once I've made up my mind, that's it. I won't waiver" kind of person. Perhaps that wasn't as much of a strength as I'd originally thought. It stopped me from being completely open and curious and made it harder to discover a new way of looking at something. It made me closed and defensive when some of my assumptions were challenged by others, who invariably had my best interests at heart. And it compelled me to be right at all costs when I didn't see eye to eye with someone.

In the workshop, I had a chance to review some of the reasons my marriage failed, and that led to greater clarity and a deeper understanding of my values and beliefs. The result was a much-welcomed sense of freedom and inner peace. I still had work to do, to completely unarmour myself and open my heart not just to Annie but also to all my friends and family. I was moving in the right direction. I was leaving for Thailand the next day and was scared I didn't have the support around me that the other participants did. They all lived close to Jett and Marlene, which gave them easy access. I raised my concern with Jett and asked what I should do.

"The best way to support yourself, in my opinion, would be to join a program called The Hoffman Process," she said. "It runs in several cities around the world. If you take part in that, I'm pretty sure all your questions will be answered and your needs will be met. Are you familiar with it?"

Bizarrely, I had heard about the program, although I'd totally forgotten it. I came across it when I was starting my entrepreneurial journey as a fledgling CEO in 1999. I'd found myself a mentor, Derek Edwards, who'd been a senior executive in several global blue chip companies. He'd kindly agreed to share his experiences to help me grow and develop. He intrigued me. In our one-to-one conversations, he seemed to have an unusually kind and compassionate way of being that I'd rarely come across in business. I'd always assumed that corporate guys like Derek were your typical alpha-male type, brutal and domineering, with little or no sensitivity to feelings. He wasn't like that at all. One day, I asked him why.

He smiled, leaned back in his chair, and removed his glasses. "Well, a few things have changed me, but perhaps the greatest single event was when I took part in a program called The Hoffman Process."

He described his experience of this eight-day intensive personal workshop and talked about how it enabled him to open up his own heart and remove the traditional armour he knew he no longer needed. It was exactly what Jett and Marlene talked about. But at that time, his words hadn't resonated with me. I was nowhere near ready to explore that stuff. When I got divorced five years later and my life was in tatters, a friend invited me to an information evening at Regent College in London to hear about the Hoffman Process. Because Derek had spoken about it, I went along to find out more. I was interested but once again felt the timing was wrong, so I took it no further. Now I was one hundred percent ready, and I made a mental note to investigate it further once I got to Thailand.

Becoming a Runner and a Fund Raiser

After I'd taken a deep dive into my psyche, it was time to refocus my attention towards training my body. I had two aims in mind: to complete my first marathon in New York and launch my global Calling All Angels fundraising campaign. I committed myself to several months of intense training to reach a level of fitness I'd never known. Just like the Gandhi story about the boy eating sugar, I was doing something I'd previously thought of as virtually impossible. This added an element of excitement to my life for three reasons.

First, I was embracing my guiding principle of health. By applying a mental discipline and transcending some of my limiting beliefs around fitness, I'd cultivate a growth mindset. That would generate empathy and humble authority, which would make me more valuable and effective as a coach. Secondly, it was a major investment in my physical well-being as I entered my fifties. Putting in the hours now would be a good insurance policy against the effects of aging. Third, my fundraising campaign was a powerful manifestation of my guiding principle of contribution. The combination of these three perspectives truly motivated and energised me.

Chiang Mai was home for the next six months at least. Annie and I were both comfortable there and enjoyed the relaxed lifestyle. We'd made our initial visit there in 2006 for our TEFL qualification. With the marathon training and fundraising campaign about to start, we needed a solid base. We engaged the help of several property agents and spent several days looking for the right place, which in the scorching hot sunshine was pretty exhausting.

If you've ever searched for the perfect rented home, you may have reached a point where you felt like giving up. We certainly did. We lost a fabulous apartment to someone else. Looking back, I believe that must have been serendipity. A couple of days later, a friend of Annie's, who had a lovely, fully furnished, and secluded house in the old city (our favourite part), announced she was leaving town for four months and wanted someone to rent her home while she was away. It was perfect for us. Just as had been happening since I opened my mind to it, things were turning out well when I most needed it. I'm inclined to believe it was something to do with the purpose I was engaged with, but I have no idea really. What I observed at the times when I lived my life true to myself fully, the Universe inevitably stepped in to help during those moments.

New adventures, countries, or events in my journey often initiated a new *Daily Explorer* blog correspondent to join the team. And who else would be better qualified to manage my fundraising campaign than Ivana Getachek. My blog readers were going to see a lot of her in 2009.

The money raised from running the New York marathon would be split three ways. I'd chosen the World Cancer Research Fund (WCRF) after I'd met with a couple of their representatives in London. Several of my friends had struggled with cancer, and it was their stories, together with the untimely death of Jelly Blount, which inspired me to support the WCRF. The Namaste Children's Home in Nepal, and the Elephant Nature Park in Chiang Mai were the other two beneficiaries I chose.

Drawing on my experience from running my own business, I devised a marketing campaign for *The Daily Explorer* that ran throughout the year until November, when I would've completed the race. I set an ambitious target of $10,000, knowing it would be a huge challenge. I was a long way away from my friends and supporters back home, but I believed that with Annie's loving support and the Universe behind me, I'd find a way. I had no idea how all-consuming this project would turn out to be.

Once Annie and I were settled in our new home, I linked up with Matt Campbell, my new running coach. Time was of the essence, and we agreed on a training plan that would see me reach peak race condition towards the end of October. I was thrilled and grateful to have a coach at all. Most people I knew who'd attempted a marathon had done their training on their own and used books or other online sources to learn. When I learn something new, I thrive on the energy and connection that comes from the interaction with another person. It's no surprise that connection is one of my ten guiding principles. Matt's energy was vital to help me build momentum and maintain my motivation when things felt a bit difficult. He had a cool, even temperament and was rarely flustered by anything. That, together with his proven capabilities at long-distance running, made him the perfect coach for me.

One Step At a Time

My training plan covered a twenty-six-week period. At the start, Matt had no measure of my level of fitness, so he ran with me a couple of times and got me to do some training in the gym. I vividly remember the first timed run he asked me to do around a lake on the edge of town. It was about one and a half miles. I turned up in my shorts and vest at six a.m., and the reality of my challenge hit me in the face like a right hook from Muhammad Ali. I finished that run gasping for breath, exhausted, and about to throw up. Towards the end, Matt yelled at me to go faster. I know he needed to do that to accurately assess where I was starting from fitness-wise but that didn't stop me wanting to punch him in the face. I was at full capacity and running like a tortoise, which had me feeling quite dejected. Matt could see I was pissed off.

"I can't believe I was stupid enough to agree to this," I said. "I'll never be able to run a marathon. I can't even run one and a half stupid miles. I'm a total idiot for ever thinking I could." I was overcome with fear and panic. I couldn't see how I'd be ready for the marathon in the time we had.

"No need to worry, Ray," Matt said. "You'll be fine. Trust me. I know what I'm doing. Within twelve weeks, you'll be running a half-marathon, as long as you do what I tell you."

I was so glad to have such a mild-mannered, calm dude with me for this challenge. Matt asked me to set a target time for the race in New York. I was aware that elite athletes run marathons in just over two hours, and I wondered what sort of target I should aim for. It seems that most first-timers finish the marathon in between four and five hours. The holy grail for newbies is considered to be a sub four-hour time. That settled it. I set my target, with Matt's support, to finish in less than four hours. That meant running twenty-six miles at a pace of around nine minutes per mile. I had no idea if that was feasible for me, so Matt agreed to accept it for now and to re-examine it after a few weeks of training to see if my body was capable of performing at that level.

In the early days of my training, Matt's presence gave me a lot of encouragement. Even though he was primarily focused on my running, he related to me as a whole person and not just an athlete. It made a huge impression and caused me to shift how I perceived my own work as a coach.

"Don't worry," he said whenever I got anxious. "Just ease your body gently into the idea of running for the next two weeks. Sleep and eat well and have a massage or two."

He knew how to keep me in a positive state of mind. In my first week, I ran twelve miles and cycled twenty-two. In the second week, that increased to seventeen miles of running. Matt used my performance data to set targets for the next ten weeks, intended to build my endurance. During those ten weeks, I pushed myself harder than I'd done for years. Spurred on by my cause, I was determined to build my strength and endurance. Once we'd completed that phase, Matt explained he wanted me to undertake a time trial, which meant running over six miles within a time he specified. If I achieved that time, he could tell I was on track for a sub-four-hour marathon. If I failed, it was extremely unlikely my body would cope well with the intensity of the training yet to come. If that were the case, Matt felt it would be better for my well-being to aim for a slower time from the outset.

I was worried by that conversation. I'd identified health as one of my ten guiding principles, and I really wanted to be a shining example of what was possible for other people my age. I had an opportunity to demonstrate that, with the right effort, it was possible for anyone to roll back the years and enjoy a physically active, healthy life. This marathon was about so much more than simply completing the race. It was a chance to use my life to inspire others who face the same limiting beliefs about age and fitness as I did. I could transform those with the right mindset and lead the way for others. Once again, Matt reassured me it would be okay and that I should put my fears aside for the time being.

In case you're thinking, "Wasn't it too hot to run in Thailand?" you'd be right if I'd done it during the day, when temperatures soared. Instead, I started my runs before six in the morning, which meant the sun rose around the time I finished. I'd changed my lifestyle to suit, as I needed to be in bed by around nine p.m. in order to feel rested enough for those early starts. Typically, I'd eat my last meal of the day around six p.m. to help my body function as efficiently as possible. The more I got into it, the more my general level of well-being improved, which compounded my desire to keep going.

Matt had built in recovery days between each run to make sure I wasn't in danger of over-training, which might lead to injuries. On those days, I went to the gym to do weight training and core strength work, as well as a long, timed stint on the cycle machine. What had initially been born out of a heartfelt response to help others had become a massive physical re-education for me, and I loved how it felt to be given such great quality input from my coach.

After three weeks or so, Matt told me there was a six-mile race coming up in Chiang Mai that weekend and suggested that I enter it with him to gain some experience. I didn't feel ready. I'd never run in a competitive race over any distance. Nor had I run six miles in one go. I'm sure you can understand my reluctance. Knowing I'd only been training for two and a half weeks in total, I imagined he'd be sympathetic. But I know from my own work as a leadership coach that sometimes, to serve another person well, some radical challenge or radical support is needed.

"Trust me, Ray. This is a good idea. You'll get your first taste of race conditions, with no pressure on you to hit a particular pace. Just get used to the scene and get a feel for what the crowd and the atmosphere are like. We'll run it slow, around eleven minutes per mile, and I'll be with you all the way."

I relaxed and touched a bit of excitement. This was going to be a big moment for me—one small step on the road to my first marathon. On Saturday morning, at five a.m., I set off for the race with Annie in tow as my cheerleader. I got my race number and did my stretches. Matt explained that the presence of the other runners and the energy from the crowd would trick me into galloping off at the start at a faster pace than we'd planned for, which would have a detrimental effect on my overall time. I needed to be aware of that when it came to the New York marathon in November, and this was my first chance to experience it.

We set off, with Matt setting a comfortable pace for me to follow. I made no attempt to compete with anyone else but towards the end, Matt wanted to see what I had in reserve. He asked me to speed up a little and overtake a couple of runners ahead of us. To my surprise, I was able to do it and still keep going. I crossed the finish line with Matt in just under fifty-five minutes. I was knackered and totally chuffed. My pace was 9:03 minutes per mile, which was actually slightly faster than the speed I'd need to run in the marathon, but this race was less than a quarter of the distance. Nonetheless, it felt like a deeply encouraging moment.

Annie was delighted for me, and Matt was happy with my progress. My time predicted four hours and nineteen minutes for the marathon, so we knew we had more work to do.

Show Me the Money

I enjoyed the unmitigated focus that my goals for the Calling All Angels Campaign gave me. It was in total alignment with several of my guiding principles. My physical training improved my health. My fundraising efforts made a contribution to hundreds, if not thousands of people, and helped me connect with friends and family all over the world. I practiced self-acceptance when things didn't go well. And I remembered each day to keep my awareness and attention in the present moment. It felt like this was a prototypical period for living my life true to myself. It confirmed that such a life *was* possible.

Another newcomer to my Calling All Angels team in the first few weeks was a wonderful Thai masseuse called Jang. Annie introduced me to her in 2008. She was superb at releasing muscle tension, and she'd been a regular visitor in the past year. She was now anointed as my official physio. With the support of Annie, Matt, and Jang, my training went well. With sixteen weeks to go, a welcome distraction materialised.

Nic and Regina came to Chiang Mai. Naturally, we wanted to make sure their visit to the city was memorable and comfortable. I did most of my training in the early hours, so their presence didn't disrupt my routine. I was so excited when they arrived because they were my first friends to venture out to this part of the world to see firsthand the life I'd been living. I shared my excitement about my fundraising campaign with them.

The campaign had a simple, yet challenging aim. I wanted to raise over $10,000 dollars for the three worthy causes I'd chosen. The first donation had been made by my ten-year-old nephew, Daniel. When I was in London about to leave for Thailand, I'd told him what I was doing, and he contributed his own pocket money, which really touched me. I knew in that moment, with that kind of support, we'd be able to make a really big difference. It was another confirmation signal from the Universe that everything was as it should be.

I felt compelled to take Nic and Regina to the Elephant Nature Park to give them a sense of why I'd put so much energy into my campaign. Their business, the Conscious Media Network (CMN), was a popular video platform. They offered to interview the park's founder, Lek Chailert, in the hope it would generate some publicity in America and beyond. They had a global audience of three hundred thousand viewers. Lek granted them an interview and took us to meet the park's newest arrival, Faa Mai, who had been born just twenty-five days earlier.

None of us had ever been close to or played with a baby elephant. Lek's presence signalled to its huge and protective mother that we weren't a threat. She stood by quietly while we played with him. Despite being a baby, he already weighed over one hundred kilos and was a bit of a handful for tiny Lek, and for us. Nic loved him and played around until Faa Mai was tired out, which took some doing. We sat quietly and appreciated the soothing sound of a baby elephant snoring. It was a wonderful experience and galvanised me into action to get the money rolling in for Lek and her family of elephants.

Lek's interview was broadcast on the CMN channel within a few days. My passion for this project was being shared, first with my friends, and then with many more of their viewers worldwide. It nurtured a growing belief that we were on track, and it was definitely going to work. It strengthened my faith in what we were doing, and it deepened my resolve to make sure we smashed our target. That experience helped me realise how important it is to get other people involved when you're passionate about something. Can you recall a time when you've shared something that you're passionate about? How did it feel for you? Did it bring more people in? What happened as a result?

On Track in Pattaya
My friends returned to the USA, and my training intensified. By now, I was running up to forty miles per week and was far more comfortable with it than I'd been at the beginning. Slowly but surely, my heart rate had dropped as I ran at the same speed or slightly faster than when I'd started in April. Annie sourced large quantities of fresh fruit and vegetables at the local markets and made sure I had at least one litre of fresh, blended fruit juice every morning, which replenished my body with the nutrients I needed. She threw in a little bit of everything—bananas, mangoes, papaya,

dragon fruit, oranges, melon, pineapple, spinach, cashew nuts, bee pollen (a brilliant superfood) and kale—and they were delicious.

Matt was happy with my progress and saw I was ready for some hill runs and intervals. If you've tried it, you'll know that running up steep hills increases your heart rate dramatically and produces lactic acid in your muscles, particularly the ones on the tops of your legs, which feels like a burning sensation. Interval training is similar but on level ground. After a warm-up, I ran half a mile at a fast pace then slowed right down for two hundred metres to catch my breath. I repeated this cycle five times, a total of three miles at speed, without stopping. By the end of the fifth set, I was exhausted. Both hill training and intervals are designed to work the heart hard and increase your lactate threshold. Basically, that means you can run longer without your legs feeling heavy or tired from too much lactic acid.

My fundraising campaign was going well, and donations were being made. In the first few days alone, I received money from people as far afield as the UK, USA, Switzerland, Canada, Thailand, Uganda, Australia, Spain, France, Sweden, and Germany! By the end of the first week, well over $1,000 had been raised. With all my business contacts and the people I'd met in the fifteen countries I'd travelled through, I was grateful that I had so many friends to turn to for support.

By July, I was ready to enter the first of two half-marathon races. Matt signed me up for the Pattaya International half-marathon. It's one of the major sports events in Thailand and attracts hundreds of runners from around the world. They come for a chance to compete for the first prize of two hundred thousand Thai baht, which was worth about $6,500. Unbelievably, but as Matt had predicted, it had only taken twelve weeks from my first day of training in April to be fit enough. I was relaxed about the race in Pattaya. I'd run the thirteen-mile distance twice in my training, so I knew I'd finish. The real test was whether I could run it fast enough to indicate I was on course for a sub four-hour marathon. To be on track, I had to complete it in two hours or less.

Pattaya is a coastal town. Annie came with me, as she loved the ocean, and it gave us an excuse to have a couple of days there. I'd been totally focused on the marathon, not just the training but also the fundraising for the last three months. I'd hardly given Annie much attention. I was on the phone morning, noon, and night so I could call people in different time zones around the world and ask them to donate. She'd been sympathetic as she really wanted my campaign to be successful. I hate to admit it, but even though I knew she was suffering, I carried on without responding to her needs. With regard to Annie, I wasn't living my principles. I was totally focused on myself and wasn't there for her. It seems there are times in which we don't live our principles or stay true to our values. Have you ever found yourself in a situation like this with someone you care about?

The half-marathon started at five in the morning, which meant getting up at 3:30 a.m. The route had a couple of hills and steep inclines. In training, my best time at this distance was two hours and seven minutes. I psyched myself up to go one hundred percent all in for the fastest run of my life. I carefully stretched my legs for the last time and joined the vast group of runners that were penned in, eagerly waiting for the race to start. As well as coaching me, Matt was training for his own marathon in Bangkok, and he set off with the intention of running a much faster pace. He was an inspiration, finishing about fifteen minutes ahead of me.

Matt had taught me that it never works to run faster than your plan, even if it feels easy. I managed to stick exactly to mine for the first eight miles. I passed the halfway mark and was feeling optimistic. At this point, I paid the penalty for drinking too much water before the race. I desperately needed to take a pee but didn't want to stop and waste precious time. I tried to run through the discomfort for a mile or so, but it became too big a distraction. Eventually I had to stop, and it cost me about thirty seconds. I made up for it as best I could.

After nine miles, there was a half-mile incline. I was getting tired and struggled to maintain my race pace. I gave my all in the last mile and approached the finish line exhausted. It was great to see Matt at the end in the recovery area waiting for me. He'd been instrumental in getting me this far, and I wouldn't have got this result without his knowledge, input, and guidance. I was full of appreciation for him and immediately wanted to discuss the race. At the organisers' tent, we got confirmation of my official time, which was two hours and fifty-eight seconds. It was great news for two reasons.

Firstly, my personal dream for New York was well and truly alive. Until now, running a full marathon had been a fantasy, but now I was convinced I would be ready and able to complete the full distance in New York. I could see it was possible to do it in under four hours. Second, sharing this piece of news would hopefully inspire more blog readers to make a donation to the campaign. In eight weeks, we'd raised $3,234. I was gobsmacked that people had been willing to make these donations, and this positive response gave me a lot of encouragement to keep putting one hundred percent into my training. It was like I had the energy of a huge, global team of people behind me, which was an empowering feeling.

My marathon training programme continued throughout August, and I ran one hundred and eighty miles. At the start of the month, Matt reviewed my performance and established I was on track for a time of four hours and fifteen minutes. We still had a few weeks left to go, and I was optimistic that I could close the gap.

The training and running the global fundraising campaign had effectively become a full-time job. Ten weeks after the launch, we'd raised $7,612. Through the *Daily Explorer* blog, emails, and phone calls to people around the world, money was consistently pouring in. With a couple of months still to go, I raised the target to $12,000. There was loads of support for what I was doing. I worried sometimes that my friends might be irritated by me bombarding them with communications about the fundraiser. When I meditated, I ended with a prayer asking for forgiveness from them for continuously banging the drum. I trusted they would appreciate that Lek, the kids in the orphanage in Nepal, and cancer sufferers needed our collective help. If they had seen firsthand the amazing work going on in these places to alleviate suffering with such limited resources, I was certain they would feel exactly the same sense of passion and intention that I did.

Last Try at the River Kwai

In September, I ran in the River Kwai International half-marathon. It gave me and Matt a final checkpoint to gauge my finish time in New York. To keep my dream alive, I had to run a sub two-hour time. I was worried about my body. I'd run over eight hundred miles in total and for the first time, I experienced physical problems in my left hip, which had been quite sore in the week leading up to the River Kwai race. No matter how much I stretched, the pain wouldn't go away completely. With my body not quite right, I knew that maintaining the required pace would be quite a challenge, particularly since the first three miles of the course were uphill.

Despite the six a.m. race start and the nagging pains in my left hip in the last six or seven miles, I registered the fastest time I could. If there was a single moment in my entire training journey where the stabiliser wheels came off and I earned my runner's badge, this was it. This was character-building stuff, as I was alone and in pain. I tapped into a state of inner resourcefulness I didn't know I had until that day. It was too scary to contemplate the idea of giving up on my dream.

I returned to Chiang Mai triumphantly, clutching my official time printed on a sheet of paper: a blistering 1hr 59min and 46secs. The dream was well and truly on, and I couldn't wait to tell Annie, Matt, and Jang. I'd come such a long way since my twenty-six-week training programme began. Back then, even contemplating a half-marathon seemed absurd. Now, thirteen miles felt like a short run. It was incredible how my body had adapted to what I'd asked of it.

A Lesson in Surrender
As pleased as I was with the result in the River Kwai race, I continued to suffer physically. I dropped my training to one hundred and twenty miles in September, which troubled me as the trend was going in the wrong direction. There were only six weeks to go before the race in New York and within a couple of days, my worst fear materialised. Five miles into a twenty-mile run, my left calf muscle tightened in a severe cramp that wouldn't release. It was so tight, I couldn't even walk. I went to see a physio immediately and discovered that I'd suffered a grade-two calf strain injury. The only recovery route was a complete rest from training. With five and a half weeks to go until the marathon, this was a lesson in surrender and a real opportunity to go with the flow and trust the Universe. I hoped and prayed that I had enough time for nature to do its work and for my body to heal. Of course, I did everything I could to help, including icing, massages, and stretching every day. The rest was out of my hands.

My global fundraising campaign, which had been underway for sixteen weeks, had smashed through the new target. There was now over $13,500 in the pot. I felt overjoyed. At the same time, I felt an immense responsibility to be well enough to run in the race. After all, that was the reason my donors had been willing to contribute. I felt I simply had to keep my end of the deal and make it into the race. Dropping out was not an option. I took some comfort in knowing that if I could make it to the start line, there was over five hundred dollars in the bank for every single mile I completed, a powerful image that lifted my spirit.

Chiang Mai had been the perfect base for the entire campaign, so it was a fitting finale to hold a spectacular, sell-out fundraising evening for people in the community there. I gave lots of thought to planning the event. The owners of a huge, popular vegetarian restaurant, aptly called Taste from Heaven, gave me exclusive use of it for the night. They had close personal ties to the Elephant Nature Park and were happy to offer their support. We generated some publicity to let the people of Chiang Mai know about it. The local newspaper, the *Chiang Mai Mail* ran a story about it too. I managed to persuade a handful of local businesses to donate some fantastic prizes for the raffle, including free meals at restaurants, free treatments at a spa, and a day at a jungle canopy adventure centre. We had over fifty prizes to give away, worth well over £1,000 in value. By the time the event started, we were sold out. Around seventy-five people came, and we raised another five hundred dollars to add to the pot.

One of the highlights of the evening was speaking to everyone there about what had made me decide to take on the goal of running a marathon. I told them the same story you've been reading. I really wanted them to feel happy about where and how their money was going to be used and gave them my word, as I did with all my donors, that every single cent collected would make it into the hands of the beneficiaries I was working on behalf of. Integrity has always been one of my core values, and it was vitally important to me that everyone trusted that would happen.

The icing on the cake was the appearance of Lek. She'd just flown back to Thailand from Canada the previous day, so I only expected her to join us for about fifteen minutes. To everyone's surprise and delight, she stayed for the entire evening. In fact, she was so excited when she saw how many people had come, she spontaneously invited every single person, free of charge, to spend a day at the Elephant Nature Park so they could experience it for themselves and spread the word about it.

Matt Campbell and his family were there too. He'd been such an incredible coach. I'd achieved way more than I could ever have imagined and don't think I could have done it without his support. He's a brilliant mentor and an exceedingly kind man. His way of being had such a positive effect on me, and it inspired me to bring more of that to my own work as a coach. We had an emotional farewell and naturally, he wished me the best of luck.

One woman I met through the Chiang Mai fundraiser was a delightful New Yorker called Libby Turnock. She was a marketing specialist who'd been in town for a few weeks volunteering at the Elephant Nature Park to help them promote it. When she found out what I was doing, she kindly helped me craft a press release that I sent to the *New York Times* and other US media outlets to create a buzz in New York ahead of my arrival. Being an optimist, I thought that maybe something magical could happen if we put some energy out in that direction. In the end, nothing came of it, but Libby, who'd run the New York marathon five times, offered to host an after-race party at her Central Park apartment for me and the small group of my friends who were attending as spectators. The marathon finish line is in Central Park. Once again, the Universe had done a marvellous job in ensuring I had everything I needed, and more.

It was time for Annie and me to head for New York City and take up my place for the greatest marathon on earth. Despite my injury, I knew I was ready for it. With a couple of weeks to go, I chose to believe that it would all come good on November 1.

Chapter Twelve
The Hoffman Process

An elderly Chinese man had two large pots, each hung on the ends of a pole which he carried across his neck. One of the pots had a crack in it, while the other pot was perfect and always delivered a full portion of water. At the end of the long walk from the stream to the house, the cracked pot always arrived half full.

This went on daily for two years, with the man bringing home one and a half pots of water. Of course, the perfect pot was proud of its accomplishments. But the poor, cracked pot was ashamed of its own imperfection and miserable that it could only do half of what it had been created to do. After all this time of what it perceived to be bitter failure, it spoke to the man one day by the stream.

"I am ashamed of myself, because this crack in my side has caused water to leak out all the way back to your house."

The old man smiled. "Did you notice that there are flowers on your side of the path, but not on the side of the other pot? That's because I knew about your flaw, so I planted flower seeds on your side of the path. Every day while we walk back, you water them. For two years, I've been able to pick these beautiful flowers to decorate my table. Without you being just the way you are, there would not be this beauty to grace the house."

WE HAVE OUR OWN UNIQUE CRACKS AND FLAWS. BUT IT'S PRECISELY THESE THAT make our lives together interesting and rewarding. As Annie and I made our way to New York, my attention was firmly focused on our relationship. She'd given me an immense amount of support over the last six months as I trained for the race and doggedly pursued my fundraising goal. It had come at a big cost to her, as I had increasingly been less available to join her for social activities or to give her my undivided attention at times when she really needed support herself. Years before, when I was married to Charlotte, the same thing had happened. I'd been aware of the unsatisfactory status quo and had chosen to ignore it. With Annie, I inappropriately and irresponsibly justified my inaction with the excuse that I was performing a noble and heroic act of charity out of service for the truly needy people of the world.

Despite everything I'd learned through the failure of my marriage and my mindfulness practice, I'd ended up repeating the same pattern. It created an uncomfortable tension and distance between us, and I judged myself harshly for doing it. Understandably, Annie was frustrated. She'd let me know in no uncertain terms that if nothing changed by the time the marathon was over, she'd leave our partnership for good, and there would be no way back. I was in a state of numbed paralysis about it and wasn't sure what to do. It dampened the excitement and energy I felt about my Calling All Angels project and the forthcoming marathon. But not enough for me to take decisive action.

We'd stopped in London for a few days on our way to New York. Back on familiar ground, my main concern was to fully heal the calf muscle injury I'd left Chiang Mai with, in order to stand any realistic chance of achieving my sub four-hour goal in New York. It had been improving but was still damaged. I'd managed to find an excellent physio who did some massage and gave me ultrasound treatment and some guidance on stretching and icing my leg to assist my recovery. I did everything I could think of, whilst I knew that to some extent, the outcome was out of my hands. I reluctantly accepted the possibility that I might not run the whole distance, or even start the race at all. The imagined scenario was one of immense disappointment. It would be a major blow and extremely cruel if I missed out after all the training I'd done. Despite my mindful approach to life, I couldn't find a way to let go of these strong, negative emotions and simply be in the present moment to take one minute, hour, and day at a time and trust it would all work out.

About ten days before the race, I began to wonder if the Universe had my back this time. I didn't want to face the possibility of dropping out and letting down the three hundred people who'd made donations to my campaign. The tension was all-consuming. In my coaching work with clients, I often talk with them about thought spirals, the kind of thinking that can descend during dark times, when you can only imagine the most pessimistic scenario and the negative consequences you believe will follow. In my case, I thought I'd get angry calls and messages from donors, who would accuse me of being a scammer or let me know they felt badly let down. It depressed me and consumed a lot of my energy. It also gave me further justification to ignore the cracks that had appeared in the vitality of my relationship with Annie.

The Light of Hope

With just two days to go before our departure to New York, I managed to complete a ten-mile run in London. It was a good sign that my recovery was happening as fast as I'd hoped. I'd actually planned to run twelve miles that day, but I'd felt my calf muscle tighten after ten, so decided to play it safe and stop. That left me in a peculiar place. On one hand, I still had niggling doubts. On the other hand, I'd clearly heard my inner voice speaking to me as I felt the muscle tighten, and paid close attention when it said, "Stop now and wait until you're in New York to test it once again. You'll be okay."

Observing one of my guiding principles, I decided to let my inner wisdom guide me and totally complied with its instruction. In the five weeks that had passed since my injury, I'd lost some of my peak fitness because I hadn't trained. Matt encouraged me to believe I could still achieve my sub four-hour goal, as long as my leg held up. We'd have around five days to spare in New York before the race, so that my body could fully adjust to the different time zone. That affects your bodily functions, like when you need to go to the toilet. It may sound funny, but I'd prepared well and left nothing to chance. The last thing I wanted to deal with was having to excrete in the middle of the race! Knowing I had those extra days helped keep my hope alive.

Just before I left, I got my name printed in large letters on the front and back of my running vest. If you're wondering why runners do that, let me explain. The New York marathon attracts around two million spectators, who line various parts of the route. Most of them bunch up around the last mile or two, where the runners reach Central Park and head for the finish line. That final part of the race is when novice runners struggle the most, as they move closer to exhaustion. Spectators know this and take an active role in coaching tired runners by yelling out their names as they run, or walk, past. This gives the runners some much-needed energy and encouragement. I'd seen it work firsthand when I'd been a spectator here.

I contrasted that with my experience of running the River Kwai half-marathon whilst training in Thailand a couple of months earlier. I'd run most of it in pain and was struggling to maintain my pace towards the end. How wonderful and energising it would have been if some of the spectators had called out my name and cheered me on in those final, gruelling twenty minutes. I sincerely hoped that I'd get that level of support in New York.

Come Fly with Me
My brother Paul is a captain with British Airways (BA), and he'd kindly helped us procure our flight tickets to New York. He knew the captain responsible for our flight and messaged to ask him if he might be able to get us upgraded. It's one of the busiest routes for BA, so Paul warned us not to hold out too much hope or expectation. The day before we left, Paul gave me the name of the captain flying us.

"Make sure you dress appropriately," Paul said. "If there are any spare seats in business class, they won't upgrade you if you look like shit. And if you do get upgraded, make sure you thank the captain in person before you disembark the aircraft."

It made sense. Pilots often pulled favours for the friends and families of their colleagues, so it felt totally right to show some appreciation. Annie and I packed our bags and said goodbye to Paul, who was digging up weeds in his garden as we left.

He stopped and wished me good luck in the race. "See you in a week!"

A couple of hours later, we reached the departure gate to board our aircraft. The agent asked us to step aside and wait for the flight dispatcher, who wanted to have a word with us. I'd been upgraded before, so I knew this was a kind of code for saying, "You're about to be upgraded." A couple of minutes later, he showed up.

"We'd like to make your journey to New York more comfortable. Would it be okay with you if we moved you to different seats?"

I looked at Annie and winked. The journey would be way more comfortable than in economy. Annie hadn't flown business class before, so I was thrilled for her. As we were shown to our newly designated seats, I realised we hadn't been upgraded to business class but first class. We were both stunned, and I remember thinking that I really owed my brother for this. We were settling in to our sumptuous flat-bed seats and marvelling at our good fortune, when one of the cabin crew came towards me.

"Our captain today knows your brother Paul, and he'd like to come and say hello. Would that be okay with you?" she asked.

I remembered what Paul had said about thanking the captain and was pleased to accept. About a minute or so later, the captain walked into the first-class cabin and came over to us—it was Paul! For a few moments, I was speechless and scratched my head as I tried to make sense of what was going on. It just didn't compute. "Oh my god," I said, and we hugged! It was unbelievable, and it took my breath away.

He'd set the whole thing up from the outset. He knew the details of our trip well in advance, and he'd been able to swap places with the original captain. It was brilliantly concealed and executed by Paul and the rest of my family, who were all in on it. We'd stayed at his house for a week, and no one had let on about it. I'll probably be telling this little story for years to come. Going to New York to take part in the marathon was special enough but to be flown all the way there in first class by my own brother brought a level of joy that I don't often touch.

In New York, we stayed with our friend Angela in Brooklyn Heights. Weirdly enough, Annie and I had met Angela the first time we visited the Elephant Nature Park a year and a half earlier. We'd hit it off straight away. Seeing the park firsthand, Angela understood what my fundraising campaign was all about and generously offered us accommodation in her apartment for the week. I walked around her neighbourhood and looked for places where I could load up with carbs. I found a couple of fantastic restaurants that served massive plates of pasta and vegetables. Three or four days before a marathon, it's essential to consume as many carbs as possible, to be fully loaded for the start. I expected to burn more than three thousand calories over twenty-six miles, which meant stuffing down around four thousand calories a day for the next two days.

While I worked on my food intake, my cheerleaders, Annie and Angela, made a bright yellow banner and painted an elephant on it so I'd be able to spot them more easily in the crowd on race day. Nic and Regina also came to New York to lend their support. At the NYC Marathon Expo, I collected my race number and the electronic shoe tag that tracks your time. My official race number was 32,548 which gives you an idea of how far back I was placed amongst the forty thousand or so runners in the starting lineup.

The 40th ING New York Marathon
Sunday, November 1, 2009 was one of the most challenging, memorable, and blissful days of my life. Injury aside, I felt absolutely ready for it. I woke up at around five a.m. and felt a mixture of excitement and fear. I checked online to see how much my campaign had raised, and it was over $15,000 from people in eighteen different countries. Matt emailed to warn me one last time about going off too fast at the beginning of the race, which was now four hours away.

When I lined up at the start on Staten Island, I was well-hydrated, fuelled up, and buzzing with adrenaline. I'd trained hard for six months and completed two half-marathons and three six mile races. I knew I could do it. Now it was showtime. We slowly began to move en masse and within a couple of minutes, we were off.

To make it a bit easier to run at the correct speed, I joined a group of runners following a pacer, a person who runs at a constant pace for other runners to follow. I made it comfortably to the eight-mile mark in about one hour and ten minutes. There, I saw Annie and Angela's bright yellow poster in the distance and headed towards it. The crowd was huge and densely packed on the sidewalk. They were both surprised to actually make eye contact with me for a second as I passed. In that moment, everything about my life felt perfect. I was in New York, living my dream, running a marathon, listening to my favourite music, and supporting great causes while doing it. It's what I'd describe as a peak moment.

I reached the halfway mark in exactly two hours, which was on target for my sub four-hour finish. By the time I reached mile sixteen, my calf muscles had tightened, and my legs began to feel tired. In the mayhem at the start, I'd lost the carbohydrate gels I'd brought with me so hadn't been able to re-fuel my body. My energy level had dropped, and I couldn't keep up with the pacer. No matter how hard I tried, the pack of four-hour runners were getting further and further away, disappearing into the distance.

It was agonising to accept that I wasn't going to run my first marathon in under four hours. The feeling of disappointment dragged me down further, and I still had ten miles left to go. I dug deep and found a way to keep myself going, for the elephants, the kids at the orphanage, and Jelly

LIFE WITHOUT A TIE

Blount. I downgraded my objective to run the race, rather than walk it, due to the tightness in my legs. In the final three miles, I slowed down considerably. *Come on, Ray, you can do this. Only thirty more minutes and this will all be over. You can do it.* My voice wasn't the only one I could hear. Shouts of encouragement from the sidewalk were bellowing out with "Go, Ray, awesome!" and "Come on, Ray! You're nearly there!" and "Good job, Ray!" and "Ray, Ray, Ray, yeah!" and "Keep going!"

Hundreds of total strangers were shouting my name. It was humbling and brought tears to my eyes. This was humanity at its absolute finest. They showed up and supported all of us to do our best. It was almost like being given a fresh pair of legs, and the extra energy carried me towards the finish line. When I started the final mile, I knew I was going to finish the race. I felt slightly faint and on the edge of exhaustion, and my legs felt heavier than a ton of bricks. Waiting in the bleacher seats at the finish line were Annie and Angela on one side and Nic and Regina on the other. Annie raised the camera to take a snapshot of me as I approached, and I summoned one final burst of energy to smile at her. She had no idea how tired I was.

I crossed the finish line, in an official time of 4:16:29. Not bad for a first marathon at forty-nine. It marked the end of six months of demanding physical training, in which I'd run eight hundred and fifty miles. My disappointment about the time gave way to a sense of relief that the ordeal was finally over. All I wanted to do was sit down and get something to eat and drink. About half an hour later, I left the recovery area for an emotional reunion with Annie, Angela, Nic, and Regina. I was also delighted that Angie Riley could join us, as it was during my visit to New York in November 2007 that the seed of an idea was planted, which ultimately led to this magical moment.

Annie was thrilled for me and rushed to congratulate me. Nic kindly gave me his coat and cap to keep me warm. My body temperature was quickly dropping, and I could hardly move my legs. Slowly, we made our way across the street and walked a couple of blocks to Libby's apartment on Cathedral Parkway.

I hadn't drunk alcohol at all during training, so my first glass of champagne was exhilarating. Finishing the marathon wasn't the only reason to celebrate. It was also Nic's birthday, which made the day even more special because we could share it together. Knowing how hard I'd worked to achieve my running goal, Nic asked me how I felt about missing it by only sixteen minutes. I sensed he wanted to console me a little, as we tend to do with friends when we see that they're disappointed.

"Never mind, Ray. You did really well to finish at all, given it's your first time," he said.

"Maybe I'll have another go at some point but for now, I'm glad it's over. I wouldn't be too upset if I never had to do the training again," I said, though it wasn't the truth. Deep down, I was totally committed to that goal and gutted that I'd failed. Yes, the Calling All Angels Campaign had been a huge success and I'd honoured my guiding principles by making a contribution to everyone who benefited. The sub four-hour goal was different. That wasn't for anyone else. That was purely for my own satisfaction. I knew, to honour my guiding principle of health, that I wanted to persevere with that goal. Besides, any future attempts would be another fundraising opportunity. Perhaps it was meant to be this way. I did eventually run a sub-four-hour marathon at my fourth attempt six years later. I'll tell you more about that in chapter seventeen.

Giving Back

As I recovered in London, I devised a plan to distribute the money. The World Cancer Research Fund, one of the three beneficiaries, was based there, which meant they would be the first recipients. I presented their Director of Fundraising with a cheque for £2,200, which included a donation from a company in the UK called Brewin Dolphin. That was largely down to the sterling efforts of a guy called David Quintrell who works there.

In the early days of the campaign, I'd asked every person I came into contact with to give me their support. I didn't know David well at that time. He managed my pension, so our relationship had been purely professional. When I told him about the Calling All Angels campaign, he was genuinely interested and said he'd get back to me. My cynicism got the better of me, because I'd assumed he might make a small personal donation to get me off his back. I was completely wrong.

A few days later, he called and said he'd mustered a lot of support within his organisation and that they would contribute a total of £500! I was in my tiny, hot windowless bedroom (which served as my campaign HQ) in Chiang Mai when I heard this, and I punched the air with my fist clenched as I yelled, "Yes!" at the top of my voice. That had given me a massive boost of confidence in the early stages. People like David have strengthened my faith in humanity throughout my journey. At the presentation, a photographer took some publicity shots for *The Daily Explorer*, and we all took a few moments of silence for Jelly Blount, who lost her life to cancer. I wished she could have been there to see it.

By sheer coincidence, Visma, the founder of the Namaste Children's House in Nepal, also happened to be in London for a few days. He'd flown over, courtesy of one of his long-term financial supporters, to meet potential donors. He was passionate about the work that his team were doing, so was virtually guaranteed to enrol them. With great pleasure, I shared my experience of running the marathon with him and that $5,000 had been raised for his organisation. You can imagine his reaction! He was overjoyed.

I asked him to think about what they most needed and discuss it with his colleagues in Pokhara, prior to my return there. I'd planned to go back in the spring of 2010 with their share of the money. I decided to do that in person, rather than simply transfer the money. I'd promised my donors that every penny raised would be utilised to the greatest effect on the ground, and by working with Visma and his team in a hands-on way, I could make sure of it. I'd no experience of doing anything like this before, so it also gave me a great learning opportunity and I trusted that my business experience and common sense would guide me through any challenges that surfaced.

Hell Hath No Fury Like a Woman Scorned

It was the first time in five years that I'd be in the UK for Christmas, and I decided to spend it with my family. Annie decided to return to Chiang Mai. In mid-November, during her last evening in London, the tension between us came to a head. Leanne, one of Annie's friends, came to my brother's house. She was single and wanted Annie to help her create a profile on a dating site and set up some dates. Annie pulled out her laptop and took Leanne into another room to browse the profiles of men on the site.

About thirty minutes later, Annie returned with an expression of smouldering anger on her face. "Guess whose profile we've just been looking at?" she asked.

I felt decidedly awkward. When Annie and I separated in 2007, I'd updated my profile and I'd left it active, even though we'd got back together in 2008. She was absolutely furious to see it there and demanded to know why. I tried to dismiss her anger and claimed I'd forgotten it was there and that I'd paid no attention to it. But it wasn't true. I had been in contact with one woman and had brief chats with one or two others. Receiving messages via email had given me a bit of a buzz. I'd indulged my ego and looked at the sender's profile, then entered into a dialogue, even though I knew that nothing would come of it. I didn't think I'd committed a serious offence but that didn't make it right, and I knew it. Still, I pleaded this defence, but it cut zero slack with Annie, who was severely upset by what she felt was an act of betrayal.

"That's it. I'm so done with this. We're over. And this time, I'm not coming back."

It was the final snowflake that started an avalanche, and it drove a massive, fatal wedge between us. We'd had many difficult conversations about our future whilst we were in Chiang Mai and more recently, New York. They were never fully resolved. Dazed, shocked, and full of guilt and shame about my deceit, I watched Annie as she left for Thailand, knowing it could be the last time I'd ever see her as my partner. We were both in tears during our last evening together in London. I felt heartbroken it had come to this and at the same time, stuck in some sort of mind trap. It was painful and frustrating, and I wanted to find a way to make things right. I'd got her back once; surely there was hope that I could do it again? I didn't know what needed to change in me, but I was fully engaged by the question and looked for help to answer it.

It was a déjà vu moment. I'd been here before with Charlotte. She'd been important to me, and she'd also left. I was troubled by this and couldn't help wondering if that memory affected me at a subconscious level, like a kind of trauma, or if I was simply incapable of making a commitment with my whole self. Or perhaps there was another possibility. Perhaps the relationship with Annie was simply not the right path for me. I was worried, confused, and somewhat bewildered by my lack of clarity about it. As I compared the event with Annie with the end of my marriage, I saw that some of the details were different. This time around, I was the betrayer. But it started to dawn on me once again that there was one common denominator in both scenarios—me.

LIFE WITHOUT A TIE

When I coach clients, I usually advocate the adoption of specific behaviours or habits that are conducive to building a growth mindset. One of the habits I encourage is to remember that you can only change yourself. Honouring my guiding principle of wisdom, I looked through that lens and reflected on what had happened. I saw that I'd been a primary cause of the relationship breaking down in both situations. I could no longer blame the other person, partly or entirely, or criticise them for their shortcomings, even if there was a sliver of truth in that. I squirmed with discomfort as I clearly saw that I'd repeated the same patterns. Unless I understood why, and more importantly how to change them, there was a chance I'd ultimately destroy every new relationship for the rest of my life. I genuinely wanted to face this head on and explore it deeply before I continued my journey, so I could rest in some clarity and peace around the issue. Someone once said to me, "No matter where you go, you always take yourself with you," (originally said by Neil Gaiman, I believe) and it's hard to fully enjoy life when you're suffering under the weight of knowing you have something fundamental to change about yourself. Maybe you can recall a time when you experienced something similar.

I thought about earlier that year in San Francisco, when Jett Psaris suggested the Hoffman Process as a way to keep my journey of self-discovery going. It takes a huge commitment, as it's an eight-day, fully immersive experience with a considerable amount of preparation. You have an interview with one of the Hoffman teachers before they'll accept you on to the programme, as it's not for the faint-hearted. You've got to have pretty good reasons for doing that kind of deep work. For the first time, I did. But the fear of what I might discover about myself, not to mention the sizeable fees, were holding me back. I needed a confirmation signal from the Universe that signing up was the right thing to do.

Right on cue, it came that Friday evening whilst I had a drink with an old buddy at the Electric Club in Portobello. Brian was a playboy in his early fifties, who owned a successful graphics business in London. We'd met a few years earlier, during a fundraising expedition across southern India. Brian was rich, handsome, single, and looked a bit like George Michael. He was a lady's man and exuded charm. On previous occasions, he'd enjoyed telling me stories about his alcohol- and cocaine-fuelled sex romps with women half his age. At the start of our friendship, they'd been titillating, but they'd become boring after a while, as it appeared that was all there was to him. I'd waited and hoped we'd eventually connect at a deeper level. It hadn't happened in the previous five years, so when we arranged to meet this time, I fully expected that the leopard would still be wearing the same spots, and I'd have to endure his lewd stories once again. I decided if he behaved in the same way as he usually did, it was the last time I'd meet up with him. Annie and I had just broken up, and I felt raw and upset about losing her. I was not in the mood to hear him gloating about his sexual conquests.

When I arrived, his greeting took me by surprise. He stood up with open arms and embraced me in a firm and long hug. It was so unusual for him to do that. We sat down and ordered a couple of drinks, and I asked him what had been happening recently in his life. He described a challenging relationship with his girlfriend and actually shared how he felt about what was happening, acting out of character again. He was vulnerable, transparent, and honest. For him, that was a transformation. In the past, he would have bantered, focused on the events that were fun or sensational, and made revelations about his lovers. He wouldn't have said anything deep or meaningful about his inner, emotional world. I was struck by the difference I saw in him.

"If you don't mind me asking, Brian, you seem really different from the last time we saw each other. What's happened to you?"

"I'm not sure what you mean, Ray. It's hard to say. Perhaps it's down to a programme I took part in a few months ago called The Hoffman Process. Have you heard of it?"

I had goosebumps. There was no way I could have predicted he'd tell me that. It filled me with awe and gratitude, as I was being guided by the Universe yet again. We talked about the programme, what he'd experienced, how it affected him, and the difference it had made in his most important relationships. He was hugely positive about it. If he'd been changed that much, there was a strong possibility I would be too. I called the Hoffman UK office the following Monday to find out when the next eight-day programme was starting and if there were any places left. There were, and I booked my place on the January 2010 course.

Participating in the Hoffman Process was a great way to begin the New Year, especially as I was turning fifty in a few months. It had taken four signals from the Universe over ten years to get me there. We genuinely have no idea how the world actually works. It's deeply mysterious and humbling to realise just how little control we have over events that deeply shape who we are. It felt like it was meant to be. Can you recall a time when you experienced something similar? What was the meaning of that event for you?

Eight Days in Sussex
The Hoffman Process is an eight-day residential course that leads to deep personal discovery. It's considered by some to be one of the premier personal development experiences available. During the intensive process, you examine and better understand your life by gaining new insight into why you behave the way you do. Hoffman graduates aren't allowed to tell you the details of what goes on during those eight days. The programme relies on the element of surprise to catalyse insight and change. If you knew what was going to happen in advance, it wouldn't be as effective. I signed a confidentiality agreement and promised not to disclose the contents of the process or anyone else's private stories.

It gave me a chance to gain some valuable self-knowledge, shed some destructive patterns, and create a vision of the life I wanted in the decade to come. Ten years is a long time and hugely difficult to conceptualise what might happen to us during such long periods. If you'd said to me in 2000 that within ten years I would have done the following things, I wouldn't have believed you:

ENDED my marriage
SOLD my business
BURIED my father
BECOME an actor
LET go of my permanent base in London
BECOME a global nomad
BUILT a monthly readership of over fifteen hundred people who
followed my journey
RUN the New York marathon
LAUNCHED a charitable foundation

But that's exactly what did happen. I was turning fifty in a few months and could see no reason why the next ten years wouldn't be just as unpredictable, or more so, with similar unexpected outcomes. If that were the case, I wanted to be ready on the inside for the inevitable ups and downs and emotional twists and turns that accompany those kinds of changes.

The Hoffman teachers use various techniques, drawing on Eastern mysticism, deep meditation, Gestalt and group therapy, and visualisation. The skilful combination of these modalities can condense a lifetime of analysis and therapy into eight days. Journal-writing, drawing, and a few group sessions were included too. Renowned clinical psychologist & author Oliver James described the Hoffman Process as "the most systematic method I know for properly exploring the role of childhood as well as offering a motorway back from the past."

The process started to work before I'd even arrived. The twenty-five-page pre-work questionnaire enabled me to reflect on my early childhood. Fortunately, I was staying at Paul's house when I did this. With some of those questions, I drew a blank. I asked Paul if he could remember anything about that time. For example, I was asked if our parents showed any favouritism towards me or my siblings? The pre-work was a critically important part of the process, as it started to unearth information that I'd held subconsciously and brought it to my conscious awareness.

It's an observed fact that when we are young, too young to consciously remember, we adopt many of the negative traits exhibited by our parents. We do this in the belief that if we're just like them, we'll be guaranteed a supply of love and nurturing that's critical to our survival in our early life. This is an inbuilt, natural process which should become obsolete as we grow up. The tragedy of this conditioning process is those patterns continue to run subconsciously well into our adult lives and result in a great deal of suffering for some. For others, it can also mean difficulty in creating viable, truly authentic relationships.

After I'd spent nearly six hours doing the pre-work, new insights began to surface for me. I gained a new perspective on a pattern of unsavoury behaviour I'd repeated for many years, in which I became inexplicably angry whenever I felt I was being ignored. It happened if I walked into a shop and no member of staff paid any attention to me, or if someone stepped in front of me in a queue, or when I was not offered service promptly in a restaurant. It would also happen in conversations with Charlotte or other close friends if they didn't listen to me or understand me when we didn't see eye to eye on something.

LIFE WITHOUT A TIE

As irrational as it may seem, these small and relatively unimportant events sparked a volcanic anger that had me shout and act aggressively, often to the embarrassment and discomfort of the people I was with. And then, as if by magic, a few minutes later I'd be as calm as a monk. I'd have totally forgotten the eruption that took place just a few minutes earlier. My massive overreaction puzzled everyone, including me. Although I wasn't so quick to fly off the handle anymore, I wanted to get under the skin of that pattern once and for all.

On a freezing morning in January 2010, I headed for Seaford in East Sussex. Inside Florence House, I handed over my mobile phone and laptop and met the other twenty-two participants. There were businesspeople, musicians, and writers, as well as a software engineer, a student, an actress, and a couple of mothers. I shared a room with two guys. To respect and give space to each other's process, we agreed not to utter a word to each other at certain times of the day and evening. We occasionally spoke during these periods of silence and sometimes burst out laughing when we were behind the closed doors of our room.

On the first day, we sat in a large circle. I looked around the room and made a judgment about each person: he's an attention-seeker, she's a woman who doesn't like men, and so on. This was part of the learning curve too. Nothing was as it seemed. The readiness to judge everyone and everything was inexorably linked with the negative patterns we'd all come to lose.

Before I began, my friend Brian said, "I recommend you don't judge or intellectualise everything. They'll ask you to do some stupid stuff. Your brain will say: 'I'm not doing this.' But just do it. There is a reason. And remember, it works."

We were directed to bash a pillow with a baseball bat until the point of exhaustion in order to connect with and let go of any deeply held negative patterns that we'd inherited from our parents during childhood. It's one of the hallmarks of the Hoffman Process. Externalising positive and negative emotions was intrinsic to the course. I was astonished as I addressed my negative demons, both by the way we did it and also because it unleashed loads of suppressed grief, anger, love, hate, and pure unadulterated rage. It poured out as I acknowledged all my negative patterns and pounded them to smithereens. The days were long, starting at eight a.m. and finishing around ten p.m. There was no time to read, walk, or watch TV.

After a couple of days, I realised that everything related to our sessions was intentional, including where we sat, our roommates, and our teachers. It takes about four years to qualify as a Hoffman teacher, and I could see and feel that they really knew their stuff. They had carefully read our histories. Occasionally, my teacher Simon came over and whispered something in my ear to support me during some of the more challenging moments, or we'd have a five-minute chat when there was a break. He was hugely supportive and kind. The first half of the process was excruciating and exhausting. In the second half, it became easier. Every day unearthed a new layer, which brought more lightness and ease to the work. In the last couple of days, we learned how to take our insights and learning into the outside world in a sustainable way.

We were advised it was best to spend the weekend after The Hoffman Process by ourselves. I followed their guidance and used the time to reflect on my experience and appreciate the insight and understanding I'd gained, which I've summarised in these five areas below:

1. An expanded capacity for self-love and self-acceptance

> "How much we know and understand ourselves is critically important, but there is something that is even more essential to living a Wholehearted [sic] life: loving ourselves. Knowledge is important, but only if we're being kind and gentle with ourselves as we work to discover who we are. Wholeheartedness is as much about embracing our tenderness and vulnerability as it is about developing knowledge and claiming power."
>
> Brené Brown, *The Gifts of Imperfection*

Perhaps for the first time, I knew what it was like to love myself unconditionally and truly forgive myself. I'd understood how automatic and unstoppable it is to adopt the negative patterns of our parents and how it starts at an early age. Even though I refer to myself as grown up, with the confidence and control that implies, I'm able to admit that I often feel like a small child on the inside: frightened, lonely, and struggling to learn when challenged, as well as petulant, belligerent, defensive, and righteous. I found new ways to let go of my self-critical inner dialogue, which had worn down my sense of optimism and creativity over the last few years. I left knowing that it's definitely okay to not feel okay sometimes, and I had a renewed desire for more playfulness, which aligned with two of my guiding principles, self-acceptance and lightness.

2. Deep insight into and appreciation for my parents' childhood

Until I did the process, I'd never stopped for more than a few moments to consider what the childhood experiences of both my parents, who grew up during the Second World War, were actually like. This realisation gave rise to a sense of shame initially, followed by curiosity to find out more. My father passed away in 2004, so it wasn't possible to speak with him, but my mum was alive and well. I hate to admit it, but I didn't even know her father's first name. He'd died before I was born. She knew I'd been doing the process but didn't know that we'd been invited to both prosecute our parents and then cathartically defend them during it. The experience of forgiving them was truly liberating, and I felt a physical release as well as an emotional freedom. Given my parents' level of education, poor upbringing, and the conditions they'd lived in as kids, it was nothing short of miraculous they'd found the wisdom to raise me and my brother in the encouraging, unconditionally loving way they did. I saw my mum a few days afterwards and had one of the best conversations we'd ever had. I realised just how much she'd always loved and encouraged me throughout my life. I also filled in some of the gaps in my knowledge of her life and listened to a few of her childhood stories. It honoured my guiding principle of connection.

3. An expanded awareness of my trigger patterns and how to shift them

I effectively reset my pattern of expressing volcanic anger whenever I was ignored. The culprit was a feeling of being disregarded I'd experienced as a child. Once I'd named it, I wore this word on a badge so that the other participants were aware of it, and I could take full ownership of it. It was obvious I'd installed this pattern as young as three years old. It arose when my parents interrogated me or my brother when a serious mishap occurred at home, and Paul would point the finger at me. Consequently, I'd be punished, which usually meant I'd be sent to my room. Naturally, I protested, but it fell on deaf ears as my parents disregarded anything I said and refused to let me speak again until my emotional outrage had subsided. All of this was buried in my subconscious and unknown to me for nearly fifty years. Now, it was in my conscious awareness. I had the tools to change my response and choose different behaviour when that feeling was present. Ten years on, I hardly ever react in the same way anymore. I follow my guiding principle of non-attachment when strong emotions are present.

4. A clear and simple vision for my life
In my twenties and thirties, I had tons of ambition and a clear vision of what I wanted to accomplish. Approaching my fifties, I no longer had the same drive. I'd been aware of this void for some time, especially since the sale of my consulting business. In the process, I spent time visualising and confirming what I wanted to create in four key parts of my life; how to show up in the world (self), the kind of relationship to manifest, my life's work, and my ideal home. What you're about to read about is the life I imagined, which I telegrammed to the Universe to start the inexplicable process of manifestation. With dreams like these, it's not enough to just know it or what it looks like, just for yourself. You have to actually say it, as if you're casting a spell. By openly declaring it, I committed to doing the necessary work going forward to make it a reality. I left with a clear manifesto and aspirations that still guide me today.

Self
* I am in excellent physical health and have a high level of fitness
* I love the way my body looks and feels
* I have a great sense of inner peace
* I feel completely present in the company of others
* I am truthful, soft, warm, kind, and compassionate towards others
* I don't feel the need to judge anybody
* I am thoughtful and creative
* I am able to connect with everyone I meet
* I create lasting and fulfilling friendships
* I am comfortable in myself and able to know what's going on inside me
* I love myself and forgive myself
* I am able to totally trust my inner guide
* I am strongly directed by my spirit self and well-balanced

LIFE WITHOUT A TIE

Relationships
* I love deeply and connect on an emotional level with my partner
* I am unconditionally supportive of my partner
* I am loyal and committed to my partner
* I feel a strong sense of trust and friendship
* I am real and don't feel any need to play roles or pretend
* I am always honest in a way that's kind
* I experience the deepest possible intimacy
* I am in a deeply committed relationship, with a joyous, loving connection that feeds my soul
* I am enjoying and loving all of my friends, family, collaborators and co-creators
* I am a generous, forgiving soul with infinite capacity and patience
* I love the outward expression of the love I feel inside and get great pleasure from loving people

Life work
* I am speaking to groups, teaching, facilitating and entertaining
* I am able to help people feel great about themselves, and help them find their strength and courage
* I travel frequently around the world
* I love my work and feel fully engaged by it
* I am constantly learning and growing as a result of my work
* People seek me out constantly
* I turn work down (when I have too much or it doesn't feel right)
* Money flows easily to me—I always have plenty, and I am well paid
* I create high income per day, so I am able to work less hours
* People value me highly and appreciate my contribution
* I don't need to sell hard; it's what people want and what they ask me for
* I am admired by many in my field and acknowledged by clients
* I have no desire to be perfect and no struggle to be great
* I have access to all of my inner wisdom and experiences

Home
* I live in a clean, simple, and beautiful apartment/house with a garden, plants, and trees inside and out

* There is lots of white space with colours here and there that make it homely
* My home feels like my place, my sanctuary
* I love just being at home
* It is warm and comfortable
* It's well organised, minimal, and uncluttered, with high ceilings and spacious rooms
* People love hanging out in my home when they come to visit
* The kitchen is the best room to be in
* It's luxurious, yet humble and unpretentious

If and when you do any vision work of your own, you'll probably find that it helps to give yourself plenty of creative license. Give yourself time to imagine loads of scenarios without censoring, as it will help you discover what feels most real for you. When I work with clients, I encourage them to brainstorm and write down all of their thoughts. Eventually, a picture will emerge and when you see it, you'll know where you're headed. You'll also need to describe your vision to someone else, as that makes it far more likely to manifest.

5. A renewed desire for commitment to intimate relationships, with Annie in particular

During the process, I uncovered the limiting beliefs that helped me understand why I'd felt unable to make a powerful commitment to my partnership with Annie. Until then, I hadn't been aware that I perpetually experienced myself as not being lovable, not being good enough, and not being creative enough, plus a couple more to boot. These fears had distorted my behaviour in relationship to Annie and also affected relationships with other partners in my past. I can see this with clarity now, but it was never obvious to me before. Have you ever had a powerful insight or made a vital discovery about yourself that you weren't aware of? What was the catalyst that brought it to your awareness?

I realised that Annie had given me her love and support throughout our entire time together, whilst I'd worried about being exposed as not being good enough or worthy enough. Consequently, I'd been constantly on the lookout for someone who would see me and accept me as good enough, just the way I was. Whoever did that would be the perfect person.

LIFE WITHOUT A TIE

That belief had driven my decision to leave my dating profile online even though I was in a committed relationship with Annie. I saw the futility and destructiveness of that. You can imagine how excited I was to discover this. For the first time, I took ownership of my own inadequacies. I stopped the endless search for a perfect imaginary person and saw I could fully enjoy and accept Annie, without any need for her to be more perfect than she already was.

Back to Life

I'm often asked if the effects of the Hoffman Process last and if you permanently change. According to clinical psychologist Derek Draper, M.A., it's the equivalent of about one year's worth of weekly psychotherapy. He did the process and experienced a sense of wholeness that, several years later, gives him a benchmark for how his life can be at its best. My own experience is similar. A decade later, I reckon I show up in the world better than I've done at any time previously, and the more I put into practice what I learned, the better things get. Of course, life itself is the real process and that will last for the rest of my time here.

Above all, the Hoffman Process gave me the confidence to trust that my true spiritual self is the ultimate director of my life, relieving me from an inappropriate dependence on my intellectual self or my emotional child self to make all the big life decisions. This never worked out well in the past. I dropped the need to feel certain when it came to making choices, as long as they felt instinctively right. The clarity and peace of mind I found is what I'd been searching for in the past four years, as I'd wandered around the world. It was a huge relief.

When the Hoffman Process was over, I was excited to engage with my journey again. I was desperately keen to get back to Chiang Mai and find Annie, despite the fact she'd made it crystal clear that our partnership was over. I believed that, perhaps for the first time since we met, I was genuinely ready and able to build the kind of committed relationship she'd always spoken of. I wanted that too, and I wanted to convey that certainty to her in the hope she would change her mind. My attempts at doing that in a couple of awkward and uncomfortable Skype calls hadn't gone well, as I sensed she was cynical and apprehensive about the idea of getting back together. That was understandable, given my previous behaviour.

I had to get back to Chiang Mai and be with her for a deeper and more transformative conversation. If I was there, I was sure she'd forgive my shortcomings from the past and see that my desire for the future was genuine. With the energy and clarity of the Hoffman Process alive in me, I was convinced I could find a way to inspire her about my newly formed vision of life and change her mind about us. I arranged my departure for Thailand as soon as I could.

Chapter Thirteen
Spreading the Love

I RETURNED TO CHIANG MAI IN FEBRUARY 2010, WITH $10,000 TO BE distributed from my Calling All Angels campaign. But that could wait. The much-anticipated conversation with Annie consumed my thoughts for the entire twenty-four-hour journey from London, and I urgently needed to find and reconnect with her. I imagined our conversation going really well and hoped for a happy outcome in which we fell into each other's arms and rekindled the passion for our partnership and onward journey together.

When we met, it was clear from her energy and presence that she wasn't open to me. We'd spoken about the Hoffman Process in a Skype call, and I'd got the distinct impression I was way more excited about the changes in me than she was. Nervously, I asked Annie if I could set out my case for why we should be together. I let her know I was now more capable, ready, and willing to enter into a long-term commitment with her than I'd been at any point since we first met. I emphasised how excited I was to have reached this moment. I assumed by sharing that with her, she'd be delighted, as she'd waited over four years for me to say it. Tragically, just as it was with Nicole, the reality was different.

As a storyteller, I'd love to say this tale had a happy ending. But I'm afraid it doesn't.

"There's no way I could imagine being in a relationship with you. I've thought about this a lot and reflected deeply on what's happened. To be blunt, I don't trust you anymore. I should have known better when I agreed to get back together last time. I was foolish and regret that I let you talk me into it. I know you've done some deep work, and I appreciate the courage that must have taken. But as far as I'm concerned, that's not enough to change my mind. We're done."

It was obvious and heartbreaking that her intention was clear. Tears rolled down my cheeks as Annie spoke. There was no wiggle room at all. I felt devastated, and it was extremely painful to be present. I sobbed and pleaded with her to reconsider, but to no avail. She'd let go of any notion of *us*. Her vision of life going forward included a return to the UK in a few months and a partnership with me wasn't in the picture. The huge epiphany I'd had wasn't going to open Annie's heart to me once again. I'd been totally wrong about that, and I cried myself to sleep that night.

Over breakfast, I reflected on our conversation. The strong emotions had passed through, and I calmly understood where she was at. Her vision and needs made sense. I didn't blame her for the way she felt and saw that it was my actions during our four years together that were responsible for it. As I took ownership, the pain of loss intensified again. Yet there was also a strange and unexpected sense of relief too. A part of me, the part that can look at the raw facts when feelings are running high, acknowledged that Annie appeared in my life at a time of great change. She had lovingly supported me during those first few nomadic years, and I was grateful for the experiences we'd shared. Her decision didn't mean I couldn't create an intimate, loving relationship which I'd envisioned during the Hoffman process. It simply meant it wasn't going to be with Annie. Perhaps that was a good thing. Time would tell. But in that moment, it felt like my heart was ripped in two.

As time passed, the pain subsided. Any relationship of substance is built on truth, integrity, and open, honest communication. From a place of calm, I saw that to love someone unconditionally, it was necessary to deeply understand what *they* need—not just what *I* want or need. That insight made it easier to accept this new reality. I consciously mourned the loss of our relationship and the closure of a memorable chapter of my life. In retrospect, I believe that even if our partnership had continued, our individual visions were so different, it's hard to see on a practical level how it would have been sustainable.

It had taken me five years to create a compelling vision for our relationship and to be ready and able to do the work, but timing is everything, and it was too late for Annie. It was a bittersweet irony. With her gone, I consoled myself that I'd reflected deeply on those parts of myself I wanted to change for many years so that I could show up better in future relationships. That would serve me well for when the time was right and a new person appeared. Looking back, I've changed the most after some of the romantic losses in my life. In that sense, the conclusion of my relationship with Annie was a defining moment. It's sometimes easier to recognise our defining moments when we look backwards. Perhaps you can recall something that may have been pretty rough at the time but felt like a gift later on.

Return to Elephant Heaven

Lek Chailert is an amazing woman who I really admire. I was excited to see her and to ceremoniously hand over the huge, three by four foot cheque that I'd had specially printed for the occasion. Pictures of the handover were later published in *The Daily Explorer* blog so that all three hundred donors in twenty different countries could see the impact of their kindness and generosity.

Lek and her wonderful tribe of volunteers received $5,000. The money was used to construct a water system for a new and much more robust elephant shelter. It provided these amazing animals with access to water during the night when they were unable to reach the river. The new shelter was constructed from steel and saved Lek and her team a huge amount of wasted effort from the constant repairs the cheaper and weaker bamboo shelters needed. I felt a deep sense of peace and contentment about the difference this money made to their programme.

If I'm completely honest with you, my return visit to the park wasn't entirely altruistic. A few months earlier, a baby elephant called Faa Mai had been born. When I'd visited, I'd been blown away getting up close and personal with a twenty-five-day old baby elephant. I wanted to see him again, for what would probably be the last time in quite a while. He was now seven months old, and although he'd put on a ton of weight, he was still off-the-charts cute. We played together for about twenty minutes, after which he went to sleep. I quietly sat beside him as he lay on his side, under his mother's watchful protection, and I gently stroked him as he snored away. It was a magical connection, which as you know was one of my guiding principles for this journey. That day was also the full realisation of the twelve-month period in which I'd physically trained and campaigned hard on Lek's behalf. I couldn't have done it without the generous support I received from people all over the world, so a huge thanks to those of you who stepped up!

The one beneficiary left from the campaign was the Namaste Children's House orphanage in Nepal. My plan was to return to Nepal in early April 2010 with their funds. The weather conditions at that time of year were favourable for the high-altitude, two-week trek to Everest Base Camp, an experience that still sat on my bucket list. I'll come back to both of these stories later. In the meantime, I was about to make my first visit to mainland China. Holding the vision of doing part-time, freelance coaching work as I travelled, I made my way to Shanghai, to explore and establish a working relationship with an Asian business called Progress U. They provided coaching and leadership development across the region, with similar services to those my own company delivered in the UK. I'd had a virtual meeting with both partners and had been impressed by them.

The Red Dragon
Like so many events that took place during my fourteen-year nomadic journey, an unexpected chain of connections led me to them. About a year earlier, a woman called Joanna Thumiger contacted me out of the blue and asked if I might be available to do some executive coaching in Thailand. She'd got my name from a guy called Nathan who I'd met in London in 2008 and told him about my vision of working part-time. Nathan had remembered me and told Joanna I was looking for one or two part-time associate relationships. That illustrates the power of setting an intention *and* telling people about it. Joanna explained to me that any work they might ask me to do would initially be in Malaysia or Indonesia, as their sales efforts were being made there. On paper, it seemed like a perfect match for both of us.

Progress U had offices in Hong Kong, Singapore, Tokyo, and Shanghai. The two partners were based in the latter, and they invited me to take part in a four-day advanced masterclass in coaching. They wanted to see how I'd handle typical situations and scenarios their corporate clients face, through a series of role plays. For them, they'd discover if they were comfortable with the way I work and if I'd be a good fit with their team of coaches. For me, it was an opportunity to practice with and refresh my twenty-eight years of knowledge and experience acquired in the business world. I also wanted to explore how my four-and-a-half-year nomadic journey had influenced or changed my style of coaching.

I went to the Chinese Embassy to submit my visa application and stopped in at one of my favourite eateries on the way for some breakfast. It was a sunny morning, and I sat alone at a small table outside, next to an attractive woman in her early forties at the next table. We smiled at each

LIFE WITHOUT A TIE

other and eventually started talking. Her name was Christine. She was from Vancouver, Canada and was travelling alone. We struck up a great connection with ease. She had loads of questions about Chiang Mai, and as I knew the lay of the land pretty well, I offered to take her to one or two places.

Inwardly, I was still grieving the loss of Annie, and my confidence had been knocked by that. It felt safe to befriend Christine, as I was about to leave for Shanghai, and I couldn't imagine anything developing between us in just a couple of days. Having said that, one thing I noticed, apart from the fact I fancied her, was that I liked how *I* was being with her. That may sound like an odd thing to say, but I'd been practicing what I'd learned during the Hoffman Process, and I could swear I was being a better version of myself already after only a few short months. I felt present, with no need to gain her approval, and I was truly engaged and curious about her at the same time. Feeling that, I felt uplifted and motivated to stay conscious and keep practicing.

China became country number seventeen as I continued my great nomadic experiment. In my research for one of my blog posts, I discovered that Shanghai is the largest city in China and the third largest city in the world, with a population of over twenty-four million people. As I wandered around, I couldn't believe how packed the streets were. Citizens literally forced their way onto buses and trains, often being pushed from behind by overzealous transport officials. Everywhere I turned, there were thousands of people. It was challenging to function, as there were no signs in English, apart from on the metro. Virtually no-one spoke English or seemed interested in helping me. I stood out like a sore thumb; I'm tall, fair-skinned, wore my backpack and carried a map which clearly marked me as a tourist. Consequently, I was approached in the street by no end of shady characters, who offered all sorts of things, from cheap watches and bags to massages and gay sex!

Even though I thought it could never happen to me, I fell victim in Shanghai to the first professional scam I'd encountered in my journey. It was on my second evening in the city, when I walked around People's Square for a bit of sightseeing and to get a feel for the place. I looked at my map as I came out of the metro station, to figure out which way to go. A group of four students, three girls and a guy, approached me.

"Are you lost?" asked one of the girls.

"Do you need any help?" asked the guy.

Immediately, I relaxed. They spoke English. I engaged with them in what was a friendly and interesting conversation. They'd come to Shanghai to get jobs at the forthcoming World Expo and were happy to talk to me to practice their English. I felt good hearing that and continued chatting. I had the time, and no one else to meet. After twenty minutes or so, they invited me to join them for a traditional Chinese Tea Ceremony nearby, and I gladly accepted. We walked a couple of blocks to a nearby building and entered a small room, presided over by a traditionally dressed tea server. I'd attended a similar ceremony in Ko Samui, Thailand.

For the next thirty minutes, we chatted and sipped a few different teas and were then offered a chance to buy souvenir packs of tea. These students purchased what seemed like an awful lot, and I remember feeling it was strange. Something didn't fit. The products were expensive, and these kids were students. How could they afford it? My suspicions were aroused further when the bill came. It added up to about three hundred US dollars. I hadn't purchased any gifts and asked to pay just for the tea I'd tasted. There was an awkward moment of silence as they looked at each other and then back at me. One of the girls then told me it was customary for the guest to pay the entire bill, which made me feel uncomfortable at first and then, angry.

"You should have told me this before we sat down." I really wasn't sure if she was being straight with me. "This is a huge amount of money, and although I don't wish to offend you, I'm definitely not paying this bill," I said.

They knew I meant it. To cut a long story short, I paid for the few sips of tea I'd had and left sharply. Somehow, they managed to make those sips come to forty-five dollars. To put that into perspective, a full-time waiter in a Shanghai restaurant in 2010 earned around one hundred and fifty dollars per month. A take of forty-five dollars from one mark was a pretty good return for them for one hour of work. After I left, I still had my doubts about whether or not I'd been scammed and wondered if I'd been insensitive to their culture. I checked with my colleagues the following day and told them the story. They laughed!

"Ah, Ray! You fell for the old tea ceremony scam!"

Apparently, this was a common sting; students, who really work for the shop they lure you to, pretend to be tourists and spend lots of money on gifts at the ceremony, which they aren't really buying. I got the joke. Those sips of tea were damned expensive! I was truly grateful it was the only time this had happened during my experimental journey. I wondered if the Universe sent me that event as a reminder that travelling isn't always as easy and without risk as it might seem.

The four-day coaching masterclass with Progress U went well. I handled each of the role plays I took part in to the best of my ability. I listened carefully, as everyone in our group gave me their feedback about what I did that worked well and what I could improve. I enjoyed meeting everybody and the chance to learn and be challenged. I'd missed the focused energy you encounter in the business world. I met a cheerful Belgian guy called Raf Adams, who was in his early thirties. He'd lived in Shanghai for about five years and worked for Progress U in business development and marketing. Outside of work, he was writing a book about spirituality. We had a long, deep conversation about why he was doing it and the key ideas he'd included. It was the start of a close friendship that we still enjoy today. I had no idea that we'd eventually collaborate around our work.

I could easily imagine joining the team. The foundations were laid for a great working relationship, and the fit on both sides was excellent. My vision of freelance work had started to materialise. Of course, I'd have to wait and see if the demand for Progress U's services would increase in the region. That would trigger the need for self-employed people like me to supplement their small, full-time team. To increase the chances of that happening sooner, I agreed to visit their office in Hong Kong the following month to be trained to deliver their consultative sales programme.

In the meantime, I returned to my makeshift base in Chiang Mai and made final preparations for my return trip to Nepal to take the money that was set aside for the NCH orphanage in Pokhara. I also wanted to see Christine again. We'd stayed in touch via Skype, and I'd had a few hour-long conversations from Shanghai in which I'd felt our connection become stronger. The physical attraction was undeniable. I paid conscious attention to things she said that triggered an impulse to react. I applied what I'd learned during the Hoffman Process and the Vipassana retreat, noticed negative feelings as they arose, and remained calm. The more I did that, my ability to maintain my state of equanimity improved. In that sense, my conversations with Christine were like a life laboratory of experimentation. Every day was an opportunity to be more aware of myself and understand her better, which allowed me to bring my best self to our fledgling relationship. It may sound a bit serious or intense, but it was also a lot of fun. Choosing to embrace my guiding principle of lightness also helped.

Christine believed in personal growth and knew I wanted to improve myself, as I'd been transparent about my history. She empathised with my challenges and was supportive. We'd both ended long relationships in the relatively recent past and as a consequence, were okay with a somewhat casual arrangement, with no expectations or obligations. That was common for people living a nomadic life. I was about to leave for Nepal, without a clear return date and wanted flexibility and freedom with my schedule. Likewise, Christine was a free bird who had several different options too. It felt somewhat at odds with the vision I'd created during the Hoffman Process of what my ideal relationship might look like. At the same time, applying my guiding principle of non-attachment, I was okay to go with the flow, allow things to unfold in their own time, and simply be present to each moment as it happened. I'd formed an affectionate bond with her, and we agreed that when my Calling All Angels campaign work in Nepal was done, we'd do some travelling together in Asia.

Training in Hong Kong
On my way to Nepal, I made a five-day stop in Hong Kong. It gave me an opportunity to reflect on how much I'd changed since my first trip there eleven years earlier with Charlotte, well before I became a global nomad. We had a contract to train a group of junior managers at Goldman Sachs, which meant spending a week in the Mandarin Oriental Hong Kong. It was one of the finest and most luxurious hotels in the city. I remembered two things from that visit. The first was how vertical the city was. Due to a lack of available sprawl space, there were at least seven and a half thousand skyscrapers. As a result, more people live or work above the fourteenth floor than anywhere else on earth.

The second thing, which I saw again when I returned, was that consumerism was really aggressive. Just like in London, the lifestyle of people in the corporate world in Asia was affluent with a capital A. All the global fashion brands competed for a share of their spending power. I'd minimised that in my life and spent nearly five years as a budget traveller, so I was seeing it all through completely different eyes. I booked in at a guesthouse, tucked away in a lively, narrow street in Causeway Bay. It was the tiniest hotel room I'd ever seen in my life, though it was a little like the prison cell at the hostel in New Zealand. My budget of twenty pounds per night was around five percent of what it cost for the room at the Mandarin Oriental in 1999. But I enjoyed it a hundred times more because it was totally authentic and gave me exactly what I needed and nothing more—a single bed (which took up literally half the room), a toilet, and a sink, which took up the rest of the space save for a spot on the floor for my bag. The contrast was astonishing, and I could see in hard terms what the need for status truly costs.

Raf Adams was also taking part in the training at Progress U, and it was great to see him again. He'd made slow, steady progress with his book, which he'd decided to call *The Suited Monk*. Along with ten others, we spent two days listening, learning, and practicing our delivery of Progress U's consultative selling training course to inspire confidence in the founders that their clients would all be in safe hands. It remained to be seen whether they would generate the sales they hoped for. Even if they did, there was no guarantee I'd be available. We agreed on a flexible arrangement that was perfect for me, and I liked how relaxed it felt, with an absence of the tension and pressure I'd experienced during those frantic days running First Place in London.

Everest Base Camp

When the training was over, I exchanged the high life, glitz, and opulence of Hong Kong for the dirt, poverty, and calmness of the beautiful Himalayan mountains. It was the end of April and with the heavy rains of the monsoon season approaching in early June, it was the perfect time to fulfil an experience on my bucket list and complete the trek to Everest Base Camp. I'd been in touch with Madan, who'd been my guide when I'd tackled the Annapurna Circuit. He was free to join me again, which I was delighted about. Of course, I paid him to be there, but we'd become friends during the seventeen days and nights we'd spent together, and I was happy to see him again. He found a porter called Onil, and the three of us prepared our gear for the gruelling journey ahead. Having done one high-altitude trek in Nepal, it felt much easier to pull everything together this time around.

Having said that, there'd been political unrest in Nepal for several weeks before I arrived. Word of that had filtered out through a number of alternative media websites. The coalition government was failing, and protests had been staged to force their resignation. I knew something was wrong as soon as I landed at the airport. I'd expected to be swamped by taxi drivers and hoteliers, all looking for business, but there were none to be seen. A general strike started on the day I arrived, and it paralysed much of Kathmandu and Nepal for six days.

It was fortunate I'd pre-booked a room in a guesthouse in Thamel, Kathmandu. A guy there messaged me to confirm he'd come to the airport and collect me. My flight arrived around ten thirty p.m., and I was relieved to see him, especially as Thamel was over four miles away. The problems arising from the strike had to be faced, but my first night was sorted. I've come to realise there's never really a problem when you live fully in the present moment. As I went to sleep that night, I thought how nice it would be to have breakfast the next morning at one of my favourite restaurants and hoped it would be open, as they catered entirely for tourists and would not be expected to join the protests and close their business.

No such luck. When daylight broke, I was shocked to discover I was staying in a ghost town, and absolutely everything was closed. If you've been to Kathmandu, you'll know the streets of Thamel are where all the trekking groups source their supplies, and they're usually jam-packed with hundreds of people, rickshaws, motorbikes, and cars. You can hardly move. With the general strike in full swing, many of the shops and restaurants were boarded up. There was an eerie silence. The Maoists intimidated everyone with a business into supporting their strike, threatening to destroy their property if they tried to open their shop or drive a vehicle on the road. I felt sad and angry that ordinary Nepali people, who are relatively poor, were coerced to close their businesses. They desperately needed the income from travellers and tourists. The world is not a fair place sometimes.

Even though I applied the principles of frugality and minimalism throughout my journey, I was always grateful that I had savings to fall back on, especially when I saw this kind of hardship. In Kathmandu, no buses were running and only a handful of the ATMs were working, due to the banks' concerns about looting and rioting. The latter could potentially have been a serious problem for me. In the Everest region, you need a stack of Nepalese rupees to pay for food and lodging on the way to base camp. I needed enough for me, Madan, and Onil for seventeen days. It was another one of those opportunities to take a couple of deep breaths, relax, and trust the Universe. Madan managed to find one bank that had a working ATM before we eventually left.

With everything in Kathmandu at a standstill, it dawned on me that the best thing I could do was to get out of the city as fast as possible and head for the mountains. Madan managed to pull forward our date of departure so that we could leave within forty-eight hours. We headed for the airport and made the forty-minute flight to Lukla, which was the starting point for the trek. It's a tiny airstrip cut into the side of a hill at an elevation of eight thousand two hundred feet. The gutsy pilots who fly the small, twenty seat aircraft all day long brave all sorts of weather to ensure the flow of trekking groups is maintained. The weather plays a critical factor as you can't fly safely without clear visibility. It's often touch and go as to whether the flights will happen at all.

Everest Base Camp is around sixty miles from Lukla. Madan said we needed around eight days to reach it, depending how I coped with acclimatisation. Going up into mountains has to be done gradually because above ten thousand feet, your body needs time to adjust to a much less oxygen-rich environment. You should only ascend a maximum of 1,500 feet per day and take a rest day when you've climbed three thousand feet. Some people do go faster because they can handle it okay, or they're not aware of these guidelines and start having problems as they go higher. In some rare cases, people have died through ignorance. Having previously trekked around Annapurna, I was familiar with the brief and knew exactly what to expect.

For the first couple of days, we trekked along the lush green bank of the Dudh Kosi river to Namche Bazaar, where Nepalese and Tibetan traders exchange provisions. It's still the central trading post in the Khumbu region and has an almost medieval feel to it. It's also the gateway to the high Himalaya. We were at an altitude of eleven thousand feet. As we continued our ascent to the village of Syangboche, the price of food and drinking water increased steadily. Everything had to be carried up by a yak or a porter, which made it more expensive than in Kathmandu.

One Nepali girl was loaded up with at least thirty kilos, and a small, slightly built man carried an eighty-kilogramme refrigerator all the way from Lukla to Namche. These people were tough and resilient. I found it tiring carrying my small rucksack, which only weighed about six kilos. The guy with the fridge strapped to his back arrived in Namche only two hours after me, despite the fact he was carrying nearly double his own body weight.

After a day's rest in Syangboche, we continued through the tiny village of Tengboche to reach an elevation of 12,600 feet. I was surprised to discover sixty monks lived in the remote Temple there. I happily stopped for an hour to join them for meditation and chanting. After that, we pushed on to Dingboche, where we ascended above 13,200 feet. Madan excitedly, and quite unexpectedly, banged on my door at around 6:15 a.m. the next morning, urging me to come outside to look at something. I rubbed the sleep out of my eyes and saw that the clouds had virtually disappeared, the sun was shining, and right in front of us was the tip of the mighty Everest. It was my first sighting of the mountain in Nepal, having first seen it from Tibet. It was an incredibly exciting moment, and I felt a powerful sense of aliveness and gratitude.

It was noticeably harder to breathe at this altitude. I continued to take ibuprofen to ease the constant headaches which were common amongst most foreign visitors. A seven-mile hike from Dingboche to Lobuche, which sits at an elevation of sixteen thousand feet positioned us within four hours of Everest Base Camp. Lobuche is a particularly busy place every April as hundreds of porters and sherpas from the region pass through on their way to Base Camp. They move supplies for various climbers and expeditions in preparation for the Everest climbing season in May, which has the perfect weather—typically between the 15th and 25th—for summit attempts.

Along the trail, the lodges are primitive, consisting mostly of stone huts with shared bunk dormitories. It's a bit like the kind of towns you may have seen in old spaghetti Western movies—just a handful of buildings either side of a muddy path, with a saloon, a small hotel, and jail, plus accommodation for mules and horses—except in Lobuche, the landscape looks more like the surface of the moon, with thousands of small grey rocks scattered everywhere and no vegetation in sight. Towering in the background are the snow-covered peaks of the highest Himalayan mountains.

Reaching Lobuche, I was both excited and fatigued. The high altitude made my kidneys work overtime, as they compensated for the lack of oxygen. I passed a lot more water than usual and was constantly on the lookout for signs of dehydration. At five the next morning, we headed for Gorak Shep to eat breakfast and to drop off our bags. We were just under two hours away from Everest Base Camp and the realisation of a dream I'd envisioned for many years. The trail into the camp is on a high ridge for most of the way. From a distance, we could see the enormous Khumbu Glacier, and we recognised the tiny specks of colour dotted around beside it as the temporary village of tents at the base camp.

Luckily for me, May was the best month to go in terms of the atmosphere, as the village swells with hundreds of climbers in expedition groups, creating a real sense of camaraderie and excitement. After eight days and around sixty miles of seriously tough trekking, we finally made it to Everest Base Camp. It was around noon, and the sun was shining brightly. We hugged each other, and I fully enjoyed what we'd accomplished.

It felt like a defining moment, what I sometimes refer to in my coaching work with clients as a peak moment. These can give rise to a sense of bliss and will likely remain imprinted forever. If you aren't sure whether or not you've experienced a peak moment, think back over your life to any event in which you've thought, *Life does not get any better than this*, or *I could stay in this moment forever*, or *I'm going to remember this moment for the rest of my life*, and so on.

My peak moments were usually accompanied by feelings of deep satisfaction, happiness, contentment, and peace. They don't necessarily need to be grandiose events, like reaching the summit of a mountain. One of my most powerful peak moments, which occurred when I was seventeen, was the most ordinary event of passing my driving test. The intense feeling of elation came from knowing my life would immediately, and radically, change. It gave me the freedom to venture out from the tiny, boring town I lived in and go to London and other happening places. That's what made it such a big deal. Can you recall a peak moment and how you felt? Or perhaps imagine an experience that you believe would result in it becoming a peak moment for you.

After the euphoria of our achievement had passed, Madan, Onil, and I headed back to our lodge at Gorak Shep for some much-needed food and rest, with huge smiles on our faces. By embracing the principle of presence, I'd been deeply changed by this journey. I consciously chose to be present in every step and simply enjoy it for what it was, without any thought for what I might gain or lose. When I'd been a businessman, those moments were practically non-existent. My happiness had been entirely dependent on the achievement of targets and goals. I'd always made long-term plans, set goals, and targets, and I'd worked tenaciously to achieve them, so I'd lived with my awareness and attention almost entirely on the future.

In the Himalayas, the natural environment is truly awesome. The air is fresh and clean, the sun warms your skin throughout the day, the terrain is fascinating and constantly changing with steep, twisting, inclined paths, and rivers and ravines draped with makeshift wood and rope bridges here and there. The sherpas are wonderful, hardy, spirited people who are happy to share whatever they have. There's a total absence of urban noise too. No industry, traffic, planes, crowds of people, or loud music. Just the sound of birdsong and the wind. How could you come close to fully experience or appreciate all that if you were in your head and lost in your thoughts?

Choosing to experience it all fully gave me a new and clear insight into this. I felt joyful, light, free, and expanded, with less interest in following rules that might inhibit my spirit. I said a little prayer of thanks and committed to staying present in my ongoing travels. It's challenging, yet extremely satisfying and rewarding psychologically. In your life, how often are you fully present in the moment you're in, without getting lost in thoughts about the past or the future?

Going down is obviously easier in terms of physical effort and much quicker as a result. Our walk to Pheriche was the first day of the trek that was entirely downhill, or at least flat! It was a relief to get the help of gravity for a change. Over the next couple of days, we made our way back to Namche Bazaar. There, I had my first hot shower in thirteen days, and I *really* needed it. Climbers and trekkers rarely shower every day, as there is limited or no hot water in many of the lodges. Plus, it's always cold, so you don't sweat as much as you would at lower altitudes. Having said that, this was a new record for me, and I was filthy. It was probably the best shower I've ever taken and reminded me of the joy of something as simple as being clean and warm.

The downhill journey from Namche Bazaar to Lukla took us less than six hours, compared to the two days it had taken us on the way up. As we walked, I reflected on and celebrated what we'd accomplished. I'd ticked off a major item on my bucket list and added it to the unique collection of events acquired from this incredible nomadic journey. I'd run my first marathon, done a four hundred feet bungee jump, leapt off the top of the tallest building in the Southern Hemisphere, parachuted out of an aircraft from sixteen thousand feet, spent ten days in silence in a Buddhist monastery, started a successful global fundraising effort, and acted in the lead role in a play in Australia. I felt truly blessed to have done all this, and now I'd set foot in the base camp of the world's tallest mountain. Eventually, Madan, Onil, and I boarded a plane at Lukla and returned to Kathmandu.

Before I finish the story of my trek to the base of Mount Everest, I have one final story to share with you. Many people know the first man to reach the summit in 1953 was Edmund Hilary. But not many are aware that he dedicated himself to improving the lives of the sherpa community in the Khumbu region. I saw some of the schools and hospitals he'd helped to establish, as we passed through Khumjung and Khunde, and I was inspired about what he'd done. I was on my way to Pokhara and the NCH orphanage to do something similar, and it vindicated the effort and hard work that had gone into my Calling All Angels campaign. The difference we can make to other people's lives when we choose to shatter the mindset engendered in our highly individualistic societies and get involved is truly amazing.

The Angels Come Home

After a week of rest, much-needed Western-style food and some decent coffee in Kathmandu, I boarded a bus for Pokhara and the Namaste Children's House orphanage. A year and a half had passed since I was last there. I'd fallen in love with all of the kids and felt thrilled to go back, especially as I was bringing them $5,000 to buy things they needed. With some careful thinking, that money could do a lot to improve the lives of these kids. If it was spent wisely, the benefits could even be sustained long term. The challenge was to make these limited funds go as far as possible.

I'd never done anything remotely like this. I was making up every step as I went along, relying on my experience as a businessman and following my intuition. I'd researched stories about people who'd been in similar situations, especially in Nepal. I'd also reached out to people in my personal network and picked the brains of one or two who worked in NGOs. I soon realised that corruption was rife. There were instances of unscrupulous people in Nepal who'd set up charities to extort cash from Western tourists. Little or none of the money they handed over ended up being used for a purpose with a good intention behind it. This discovery worried me, despite the fact I'd been to NCH and directly experienced the founder and the community.

For my own personal security and protection, I'd brought the money in travellers' cheques, and I needed to exchange them at a local bank for Nepalese rupees. I'd been carrying them for weeks and was relieved to finally be free of them. Being such a prolific campaigner and fundraiser himself, Visma Raj Paudel was well connected with many people in Pokhara, in banks and other financial organisations. We wanted to obtain the best exchange rate we could for what was a relatively large sum of money there, so he found a bank that would do the exchange for us.

I checked the prevailing exchange rates beforehand to be sure we were being offered a good deal. We sat in a small, poky, and somewhat dishevelled office at the back of the local branch, with the windows wide open. A ceiling fan whirred away overhead. *Wow. I'd never have imagined in a million years that I'd ever be in a scene like this, for real.* There were a few onlookers in the room who watched me hand over the cash to the manager. For most of them, $5,000 was more money than they'd ever seen or were likely to earn in years.

There was a moment of tension when the bank manager explained to me there was a daily exchange limit of $2,000, which seemed ridiculous. I explained that meant I'd have to come back on three consecutive days simply to change money that was earmarked for donation to their local orphanage. When she understood that, she responded brilliantly. After a brief discussion in Nepalese between Visma and her, she said the bank would allow me to exchange all of it in one go. I'd like to think it was my persuasive charm that did the trick, but in fact it turned out that she was married to Visma! He'd failed to mention that his wife was the manager, which is why she fully understood how the money was going to be used. We left with 368,000 rupees, and we were ready to agree on a plan to spend it.

I chaired a meeting with Visma and his management team to discuss and agree on an investment plan. They came up with a few ideas regarding what was most needed and the priorities. In my view, it made sense that any money spent should enable NCH to ultimately reduce their dependency on donations and become self-sustaining in the long run. We included that as one of several criteria to explore and assess each idea. We eventually agreed to focus on a handful of projects.

The first one to get a green light was at their rehabilitation centre, five minutes down the road from the orphanage. Many of the children NCH take in are street kids, usually homeless and outside of the education system. The rehab centre provides twenty-five of them with temporary food and shelter, while either their parents are traced or a place in a better home is found. It's basic, but it's a better option than the alternative. There isn't a great deal of space inside the tiny dormitories, so the kids sleep in bunks of up to eight per room. The building was in a poor state, with many holes in the roof. Water leaked into the dorms whenever it rained. With the monsoon season already underway, urgent action was needed to prevent the children from getting soaked every night. We organised a carpenter/roofing specialist to be available for two days and went to purchase some sheets of tin roof material.

Despite these conditions, the kids at the rehab centre were in great spirits and happy to lark around with me. Their infectious energy and carefree way of being lifted my spirit and reminded me that happiness is a choice, rather than a consequence of external circumstances. It's something that I still forget at times. The local carpenter toiled for two baking hot days to get the job done. Mangal, who managed the rehab centre, was so happy that the leaking roof was fixed up and the damp ordeal they'd endured for months was over, and it meant the kids were guaranteed to remain dry during the rest of the monsoon season. The total cost was three hundred and thirty dollars, so there was plenty of money left in the pot.

Visma had a truly inspiring vision for NCH, and it made me feel good about working alongside him. In my work supporting people to create clarity around, and take positive steps toward, their vision is something I'm quite used to. Visma didn't have a coach; he'd been driven to create the vision by himself. In six years, with paltry sums of money but bags of energy and enthusiasm, he'd opened two further houses to accommodate around one hundred and twenty children. He'd also established a scholarship programme for kids to attend a local secondary school. And he'd set up a handicraft centre to make products that could be sold to reduce their dependency on donations. What he'd already achieved was awesome, but he wasn't stopping there. Eventually, he wanted to build a children's village and create a proper community. By owning the property, they would remove the threat of eviction from their existing houses, which were rented to them on a short-term basis by private landlords. It was an audacious plan, but it was certainly possible.

We also picked the NCH Scholarship Programme for investment. It would sustain long-term benefits in their community, so I was particularly excited about it. Visma wanted as many children as possible to get access to a proper education to increase their chances of a better quality of life. The programme had paid for over one hundred and twenty children to attend the Step by Step secondary school in Pokhara. The cost for each child was around fifteen hundred rupees per month or about twenty-five US dollars, and the money came entirely from donations received. It was a huge stretch for them.

I met Sumeru, the manager who ran the programme, and heard how he regularly visited homes all over the Pokhara region, including some over one hundred miles away, high up in the mountains, to interview families and find children who are suitable. He had a clapped-out, ten-year-old, rusty 125cc motorbike that had seen better days. It was unreliable and constantly required repairs, and therefore, money. It was time to replace it with a new machine so that Sumeru could reach these places quickly and easily. It would save NCH money, because a new bike would need considerably less maintenance for at least two or three years. I teamed up with Sumeru and went to one of the dealers in town to see what we could afford.

We eventually opted for a 150cc Pulsar, which came with a full warranty and free servicing for a year. Sumeru could hardly contain his excitement. He gave the new bike a test drive and gave us his thumbs up. Visma and I sat down with the manager of the dealership and thrashed out a deal, which included a part-exchange for the old bike to make our funds go even further. A joyful Sumeru returned to NCH with a smile as wide as the road outside. I was truly happy for him. He'd endured years of poor performance and unexpected failures with the old bike. He'd never made a fuss about it and was humble and enthusiastic about his work. It only cost around $1,900, but the value was immeasurable, making an investment in the new motorbike was a worthwhile choice.

I took great delight in walking to school with the kids on the mornings when I could. It had to be one of the most beautiful school walks in the world, through lush green fields at the foot of the mighty ice-capped, twenty-three thousand-foot-high Machapuchare, an awe-inspiring Himalayan peak in the Annapurna range known as Fishtail Mountain. Knowing who I was, and how the money from my campaign supported them, the kids and the house mothers who looked after them all welcomed me into their family. A few enjoyed practicing their English with me. I don't have children of my own, so I made the most of the opportunity to connect with them and get to know more about each one of them. Seeing their energy and joy for life made me realise how valuable the NCH Scholarship Programme was for them and the wider community they'd eventually go into.

The rest of the money was earmarked for technology, land, and basic necessities. They had a small amount of aging computer equipment and no access to the internet. With over sixty of them living in the house, more computers were needed. Visma and I agreed they deserved to join the rest of the developed world and have access to the internet. At the very least, it would support their learning and give them access to email. They'd also be able to use global platforms like Facebook, Google, and YouTube, just like kids all over the world do every single day. I went with Man Singh, the Administrative Director at NCH to buy two new high specification PCs, a printer, and the equipment needed to get the children online. Three hundred dollars was set aside to pay the connection costs for the first twelve months. In total, we spent around $1,200.

At NCH, there is a tradition. When someone donates equipment, such as a computer, they're invited to an official handover ceremony so the kids can thank them personally, and I was no exception. I was embarrassed at first to receive such an acknowledgement, as I hadn't expected it. I much preferred to direct any attention of this kind to my donors instead. But Visma was insistent, and I'm glad he was. It allowed me the opportunity to explain to the children that the new computers and internet connection were there to enable them to learn and grow, and so they'd have the same facilities as more advantaged children in the developed world. I asked them to take good care of the stuff and make the best possible use of it. Of course, they could always use more help to learn about and master life online. After reading this, if you feel inspired to volunteer, let me know, and I'll be happy to help you organise a visit.

With a few dollars still left in the pot, I talked to the house mothers and made a list of basic necessities which I could purchase before I left.

These were growing kids constantly in need of new clothes, including underwear, socks, and even raincoats and umbrellas during the heavy rains of the monsoon season. We'd directed most of the investments towards major items that would make NCH more self-sustainable in the long run, but there was also a clear and obvious need for a few less expensive, basic items in the short-term. We took the money left over and went on a shopping spree.

We're talking about kids here. They need to have fun, not just survive. At NCH, there was rarely any money available for things that might be fun, so I insisted that we used a small proportion of our fund for just that. Not everything had to be a necessity. After some creative discussion, we decided to purchase some cotton and sewing materials. The ladies at the house used these to make some traditional Nepali saris and kutas (clothing) for the boys and girls to dance in at a weekly event they all referred to as Fun Friday. We found some beads and plastic gems so that they could make some jewellery for the girls.

Going shopping isn't one of my favourite things to do, especially for clothes, but as it was all for such a good cause, I was determined to enjoy it. Manju, one of the house mothers, and I went to the centre of Pokhara. It's full of dusty shops and market stalls selling merchandise of all kinds. Like most traditional markets I'd been to in Asia, it was a noisy, chaotic experience. We spent the best part of a day picking up everything we needed to replace a lot of worn-out smalls and to create some amazing costumes for the next Fun Friday. We threw in ten plastic raincoats, thirty umbrellas, and a few pairs of jeans for good measure. These are basic and essential things that many of us take for granted. Here, they were just as essential but unaffordable without projects like the Calling All Angels campaign.

Soon, it was my last day at the orphanage. When I'd arrived, I had no idea how long it would take to accomplish everything I wanted to. But I knew I couldn't leave until I was totally satisfied that my work was complete and the best outcomes had been achieved. When I first met these wonderful kids, it had started with a picnic, so I thought it would be fitting to end this visit with another one. Like before, everyone got involved in creating the day, especially around the food preparation. A few of the kids performed songs and dances and seeing them enjoying themselves filled me with a profound sense of inner peace and happiness too. I thought of

LIFE WITHOUT A TIE

Annie, who'd been with me when we came for the first time and felt sad that she wasn't there to see the difference that had been made.

We returned to the main house at NCH later that day for the immensely popular weekly Fun Friday event at six o'clock. I was moved to see the kids dressed up in their new traditional Nepali costumes, performing dance routines and their own comedy sketches. I couldn't understand the words as it was all in Nepali, but it was obvious they were poking fun at one or two of the country's politicians. One boy pretended to be a TV interviewer asking questions of the Maoist leaders who'd incited the recent general strike, and it caused hysterics. My parting gift for Visma was the last five hundred dollars to put towards the children's village project. With that, my fundraising programme, which began a year earlier in May 2009, had come to an end.

Being at NCH for those few weeks was a grounding and humbling experience. I'd become emotionally attached to the kids, and I knew it would be hard to leave when the moment came. Ganesh, a nine-year-old boy, had a story that was both tragic and miraculous at the same time. The tragic part was that he was there because his father tried to kill him, after murdering the boy's mother and his sister. Despite serious head injuries, Ganesh survived and made a full recovery, although he had scars and disfigurement to the right side of his head. The miraculous part of the story was that he was one of the most loving children I've ever met. We spent quite a bit of time together, during which he mainly wanted me to hug him. I'll never forget him.

As I departed, I reflected on the months of training I did for the marathon, the hours and hours I spent emailing or phoning people around the world at various times of the day and night, and all of the kind people who gave their generous support to my campaign. Seeing these children having such a lot of fun and pleasure as a result, and to know what a difference it would make to their lives in the future, made every minute absolutely worth it. There's so much we can do if we put our minds to serving other people.

Another Transition Begins
I've already referred to the book, *Managing Transitions* by William Bridges, and that the three stages of any transition have to be understood and embraced, rather than rushed through. As I left Nepal, I recognised I'd entered a transition again, psychologically speaking. It was the end of

this incredible, purposeful, year-long phase in which I'd dedicated myself almost entirely to my fundraising campaign. It was an emotional time, as I knew that my job was done. I was totally satisfied that the money raised had been used well and that Lek's elephants, the Nepali kids, and the cancer sufferers all had a brighter future. *But*…I had no idea what was next in terms of my personal focus and direction, and I felt anxious about the coming void that was inevitable. I was in the neutral zone of transition. I wondered how long that phase might last and when a new beginning would make itself known to me.

Having lived through so many transitions, I've discovered ways to navigate them with more ease and less stress. Inspired in part by Bridges, as well as numerous teachers in the field, I've evolved the following checklist for such periods, and you're welcome to use it too. It's been my companion for many years. A neutral zone can last anywhere from a few minutes to several months. Following the guidance below has helped me pass through those periods with minimum pain and maximum creativity. If you're going through a transition, these are my recommendations for when you are in the neutral zone:

1. Take your time
2. Arrange temporary structures, e.g. living space, work. Don't try to create stability or permanency
3. Don't act for the sake of action
4. Recognise and acknowledge why you are uncomfortable i.e. which part of you is facing a "death"
5. Take care of yourself in little ways, e.g. eat good food, sleep, take bubble baths, walks, whatever you like to do
6. Explore the other side of the change ahead and what the outcomes could be, both positive and negative
7. Find someone to talk to who will listen, not advise
8. Explore what's waiting in the wings of your life. What wants to manifest for you?
9. Use this transition to look clearly at your experience and create new intelligence about your life
10. Recognise and understand that transition has a characteristic shape, and that you're in the middle of it!

I was about to turn fifty in a couple of months and felt it was important to periodically pay attention to all of the above, whilst remembering to do it through my self-coach lens, rather than judge or be critical towards myself. Maybe you're in a transition or have recently been through one. Do any of these suggestions resonate with you?

I headed for Kuala Lumpur in Malaysia to meet Christine, the Canadian traveller whom I'd met in Chiang Mai a couple of months earlier. We'd decided to team up and do some travelling together in Borneo. I liked her and felt there was potential for our relationship to develop into something special. At the same time, I'd done the groundwork for some freelance coaching and consulting work to come my way, so it was possible that my plans might have to change at short notice. I proceeded consciously with presence and non-attachment. Whatever would come next, I knew I'd be happy whichever way it turned out. With that in mind, I stepped into an uncertain future once again.

Chapter Fourteen
Turning Fifty

I ARRIVED IN KUALA LUMPUR TOWARDS THE END OF JUNE 2010. I MET CHRISTINE, and we drew up a travel plan that would take us through Borneo, Sarawak, and Brunei over the next two months. With my fundraising programme complete, at least for now, I had total discretion over my time and an absence of any deadlines or obligations. I felt relieved about that and happy to be an anonymous tourist again for a while.

Our first destination was Mount Kinabalu, in Sabah, Borneo. It's a strenuous five-mile trek to the top which takes two days. Botanist Dr Willem Meijer described Kinabalu as "a mountain of mist and rain" with swirling mists and puffy clouds that constantly change the scenery and visages. There is a myriad of vegetation and natural habitat and that has increased the variety of flora and fauna. According to Professor E.J.H. Corner, an eminent Cambridge University botanist, Kinabalu "has the richest and most remarkable assemblage of plants in the world."

Mount Kinabalu is near the equator and rises straight out of the tropical rain forest. The mountain is U shaped, with a bare rock plateau at just over thirteen thousand feet. It looks like two arms, with the infamous Low's Gully in between, which is half a mile deep in places. The trail we took to the summit wound up a steep staircase of gnarled tree roots to a mossy world of drifting clouds and orchid-draped trees, where pitcher plants and rhododendrons abound. At 8,200 feet was the fourth shelter which had wild begonias growing nearby. We stopped there to observe the squirrels, tree shrews, and birds, all of which seemed so unafraid of us.

The effects of heat and humidity made this steep, but fairly easy, walk quite a challenge. Having recently been to Everest Base Camp, it felt a bit like going back to kindergarten in trekking terms, but it was a great way for me and Christine to get to know each other. At the end of the first day, we reached the overnight lodge at just under ten thousand feet elevation, the level at which it normally becomes slightly harder to breathe. My body was still conditioned to function with reduced oxygen levels, so I avoided any problems. Christine hadn't been feeling well a few days before, and she used an inhaler, so I kept my eye on her. We rested at the lodge until three a.m. and set off for the ascent to the top, in time to arrive and see the sun rise. We sat quietly, watched the clouds roll past below us and the orange sun rise over the horizon. These were truly wonderful moments to share with Christine and set the tone for several happy weeks of travelling together.

It was the first time I'd been on the road with a companion since the breakup with Annie seven months earlier. Christine and I had virtually no shared history and no shared vision beyond the few weeks we'd marked out. It was a fantastic opportunity to embrace my guiding principles of presence and non-attachment. No expectations. No guarantees of any shared future. Just the joy of experiencing the life of a traveller with another human being.

Not only that, but it was also a perfect laboratory to apply much of what I'd learned during the Hoffman process and continue to improve the way I showed up in challenging conversations which gave rise to strong emotions. I didn't know Christine particularly well, and it's impossible to be around someone 24/7 without conflicts happening. That was certainly the case with us. Superficially, we'd disagree over meals, where to stay, what room to take, and other trivialities. At a deeper level, we clashed over opinions about the state of the world, the dynamics of relationships, the meaning of commitment, and other issues which didn't align with my values and beliefs. When this happened, I consciously welcomed it and practiced responding from an undefended, vulnerable, and curious place. That built a lot of trust and connection between us. I also noticed that I liked myself a lot more when I was being like that.

The nature in Borneo is spectacular. Clearwater Cave has one of the world's longest underground rivers and is home to over three million bats. I'll never forget the stench of the guano (bat droppings), which accumulates inside in huge piles over three hundred feet high on the floor of the cave. It's pretty dark, and as we shined our torches, we could see bats appear like a shiny mass covering the entire wall of the cave. They roost by day and leave the cave in what looks like a giant, swirling cloud between five and seven in the evening. It's an unforgettable, jaw-dropping sight to witness as the swarm follows an aerial path that makes them look like a celestial serpent in the sky.

LIFE WITHOUT A TIE

At the Sepilok Orangutan Rehabilitation Centre, we were virtually brought to our knees as we encountered the tragic plight of these animals whose rainforest habitats continue to disappear. It's happening at a rapid rate, aided by the government in an attempt to make a better commercial return from the use of their land. They have systematically replaced the rainforests with enormous palm oil tree plantations. This effectively guarantees extinction of the species. I'd never faced the reality of an issue like this before and doing so brought a whole new perspective. It was heartbreaking to see and hard to take in without feeling despair about our collective future.

A brief excursion into Brunei made it the eighteenth country I'd entered since leaving London nearly five years earlier. My brother Paul used to live and work there back in the eighties as a helicopter pilot for Shell Oil. In those days, I was so busy working on my path towards having a business empire that I never made time to visit him, and that had always sat uneasily with me. Earlier in my story, I wrote about Bronnie Ware's book, *The Top Five Regrets of the Dying*. She observed that the second regret for most people was working too hard. I stood outside the apartment where my brother, who's in his sixties, lived over thirty years ago and imagined what his life was like in his twenties. I silently acknowledged the guilt I'd felt, because I'd never made the time to visit him, and as I did, the truth of Ware's observation hit home in a way it never had before. Somehow, being there brought with it a sense of healing. I packaged up a whole bunch of pictures and images for Paul and sent them via email, so he could see me standing in all the places he was familiar with.

Birthday on the Beach
August 2010 was my fiftieth birthday. Before my journey began, I'd always imagined that I'd be in England, at home with my wife and family, throwing a huge party with my circle of friends and loved ones. My new life without a tie guaranteed that wouldn't happen, and I accepted this wasn't how it was going to play out for me. Christine and I were taking a chilled-out break in Cherating, on the east coast of the Malaysian Peninsula. It was the perfect venue—a remote, quiet, undeveloped, white, sandy beach with hardly any visitors. We rented a hut near a wonderfully simple, basic, and friendly reggae bar called Don't Tell Mama Café. Luckily, and unexpectedly, it had a free Wi-Fi network, which meant I

was able to upload the next issue of *The Daily Explorer* blog. We'd clearly stumbled on one of the best kept secrets in Malaysia.

Christine sensed I was sad about being separated from my family and friends back home. She kindly and spontaneously created a few games and treats for me in the hope I'd feel better. She had an incredible knack for being creative with virtually no resources and taught me a lot about creating gifts for others. For example, she wrote me a long letter from the imaginary Mayor of Cherating, in which he acknowledged my presence in their village and celebrated some of the qualities that Christine had observed in me in the relatively short time we'd known each other. I knew it was child's play, that she'd made it all up, and there was no mayor. But it didn't matter. Receiving that letter filled me with love, joy, laughter, and appreciation. I've come to realise that this heartfelt intention—that she modelled perfectly—is the most important aspect of any gift.

Christine gave my next gift to me over lunch at the reggae bar. She started a conversation in which she lovingly and skilfully guided me to articulate my theme for the year ahead. She showed up for me, with an intention to be valuable and kind, and gave me her undivided attention. It was really powerful. She'd prepared a carefully curated list of questions to ask. Each one made me pause and imagine an aspect of my life in the year ahead. She listened deeply when I spoke and sometimes asked me a further question, so that I could clarify my own thoughts. That helped me see what action to take, and it helped me connect with my motivation. Through her gift, I experienced what it must feel like for the people I have the honour to coach and saw how powerful it was to be asked the right questions.

I made a couple of promises to myself. The first was to work with people and businesses around the world as a coach or mentor on a freelance basis. This was more important now, as my all-consuming fundraising campaign was over, and there was a vacant space in my life. I instinctively knew my greatest contribution could be made by working with managers and leaders in business. It allowed me to draw on the wisdom I'd accumulated as a successful business leader and to make good use of the experience I'd gained from my years of travelling. The combination of these two chapters of my life gave me a unique perspective on the challenges those people face. My intention in my fifty-first year was to re-enter the business world and open the doorway to begin my life's work, as I'd envisaged it during the Hoffman process.

Christine worked online as she travelled, and I admired her focus and dedication to the life she'd built. She had clear goals and put in the hours when necessary, and she knew how and when to fully relax and take time out too. Her way of life inspired me and gave me confidence that I could make my vision around professional work materialise. Looking back, I was extremely grateful that the Universe brought Christine into my life to show me these possibilities, and I was amazed by the synchronicity regarding the timing of her appearance. After the global financial crisis in 2008, interest rates around the world had tumbled, and the flow of income that I'd received from investments started to dry up. I wanted to create additional income to mitigate that trend and allow me to safely continue with my grand nomadic experiment.

The second promise I made was to write a book. The fact that you're reading it now is testimony to the power of setting an intention. At the time, I had no idea what the book would be about. But I knew it was something I wanted to do. Can you recall something that you've imagined doing and set an intention around, then seen it come to full realisation later? Or is there something bubbling under the surface you might want to undertake at some point?

Christine found the most unusual way to round off what might be one of the weirdest birthdays I've had so far. A couple of miles away from Cherating beach was a Club Med resort, and it just so happened that my fiftieth coincided with the anniversary of its opening. They were holding a huge Michael Jackson-themed champagne party for all their guests, including a tribute concert to the late, great performer, who'd died in June 2009. She managed to obtain two tickets and arranged for us to have dinner in the hotel restaurant. Eating high-quality food and drinking a glass of red wine felt ultra-posh after the weeks of budget travel we'd endured, and I appreciated the treat. It brought the sense of occasion that Christine had aimed for.

Fortunately, I had a chance to reciprocate on Christine's birthday three days later. Taking a leaf out of her book, I'd secretly prepared gifts for her using the limited resources I had at my disposal. I made a four-minute video using photographs taken as we'd travelled together, set to music, to give her a permanent memento. For her second gift, I created a set of birthday vouchers, which I had laser printed in a shop in town. They were about the size of a banknote. I'd already had a conversation with her a week earlier about her vision and theme for the year ahead, which she said was about "discovering and loving her true self." Each voucher reflected that theme.

I made a total of twelve, each with different wording. They included things like a back rub, a cup of coffee and a chat, a foot massage, an uplifting conversation, a walk on the beach, watching a movie, an outdoor book reading session, a glass of wine somewhere special, and other nice things I'd thought she might enjoy. All of them had minimal or no cost, yet would mean a lot to her, especially if and when she really needed or wanted that. I even included a voucher that offered a thirty-minute negative emotional dump session (non-judgmental) for those tough times when she might need to rant. They were a massive hit.

Christine had said for weeks that she wanted to learn how to ride a basic motorcycle. I wandered into the village and found a guy who was willing to rent me his moped for the day. The car park adjacent to where we stayed created a perfect, safe venue for her to try her hand at riding. One of the vouchers in her pack was for a one-hour basic motorbike training session in the car park. She was absolutely thrilled.

I've found over the years that the gifts I've made for people, which include vouchers, awards certificates, poems, songs, and books with heartfelt messages and cherished pictures from their friends have always been warmly received, appreciated, and cherished far more than items I've purchased. That was fortunate, because as a nomadic budget traveller, I was usually miles away from any shops, and I had no room to carry heavy gifts in my twenty-two-kilo backpack.

Letting Go
My fiftieth birthday on the beach had been an exercise in my guiding principle of presence. I'd let go of expectations I'd clung to for years and accepted what felt right in the moment. I also wanted to let go of my expectations about relationships, especially the notion of the perfect relationship. I seriously questioned if such a thing even existed.

Christine and I continued travelling together for another three weeks. We left Borneo and entered Malaysia, to explore Kuala Terengganu, Kapas Island, and the huge tea plantations in the cooler and greener Cameron Highlands. We'd begun to talk about what we both wanted to happen after that and started to see our visions weren't compatible. I'd enjoyed our time together and had become quite attached to extending it into a sustainable, long-term relationship. At the same time, looking at it from my guiding principle of non-attachment, I knew she was on a quest to find her own happiness on her terms.

We met just weeks after she'd ended a ten-year relationship with someone who had betrayed her trust several times. She was on an inner journey to heal herself and felt she wasn't ready or capable of doing that with me. Applying the principle of wisdom, there was a bigger picture, and we were both contained within it. My desire to support her to find her way to well-being and happiness superseded my desire to tie her down for the sake of my needs. I liked and appreciated that wise part of myself, and it's an asset I use a lot in my coaching work. Despite this understanding, it was painful to let go and say goodbye to her. I wept during our final night together in Bangkok. She flew back to Canada, and I returned to console myself in Chiang Mai.

We'd spent five months together. I strongly believe there's a Universal intelligence that guides our lives beyond anything that our limited minds can truly understand. It seems to me that the Universe always provides us with what we need, when we truly need it or are ready for it. Christine and I found each other for a reason. She's a rare, one-of-a-kind, thoughtful, intelligent woman, and I was glad our paths had crossed. Our conversations were challenging sometimes, yet they helped me to get a better understanding of my needs from a relationship. Perhaps she came to teach me about that. Or to show me what life as a travelling, freelance coach could look like in reality. Or to share my fiftieth birthday and hold a space for me to appreciate the life I've had. I'm not entirely sure, but for whatever *reason* it was, I'm truly grateful.

For Christine, I may have been sent to her to create compassion and safety for her as she stepped into her journey to heal her past. I don't know. We were together for a moment in time to help one another heal and grow, and we'd done that. When that happens, I believe it's best to let go, as the Universal purpose has been served. I've learned to resist the temptation to hold on and trust the perfection of what is. I assume that things are meant to be exactly how they are, and it has released me from a lot of anxiety about the events of life.

I've said elsewhere that I advise my clients to develop the habit of spending more time in self-coach mode than self-judge mode, and I'd had a long, deep look at myself during the Hoffman process, especially how I wanted to show up and feel in a partner relationship. When I reflected on the five months I'd spent travelling with Christine, I saw clear evidence that I'd showed up with more kindness, compassion, patience, and ease than I'd ever been able to before. I noticed how much better I was at being open, curious, and non-judgmental, especially in conversations when we disagreed. I was encouraged by these self-observations and motivated to keep my experimentation going.

Learning Thai
Ironically, being fifty was a major advantage in Thailand, as I was eligible for a retirement visa. You can encounter all sorts of visa hassles as a foreigner. If you're old enough and can demonstrate that you can support yourself financially, Thailand will grant you a no-strings annual visa so that you can come and go as you please. Chiang Mai had become my de facto base in Asia, and I decided I'd take advantage of this privilege at my next renewal. I committed to learn how to speak Thai and attended a Thai language school twice a week for one year to reach basic fluency. I had no idea if I'd ultimately stay in Thailand and make it my permanent home. I knew I'd reached a point of frustration linguistically and wanted to engage more with Thai people but wasn't able to.

After a few weeks, I could read simple things slowly, order food, give directions, name the day, tell the time, and make a bit of small talk. Thai people seemed to appreciate me going to the effort of learning their language, even though many of them spoke English. They were especially tolerant as they knew how hard it was for me. Thai is a tonal language, and the pronunciation affects the meaning of the words. I didn't always get the tones right, so asking a question like "What are you doing today?" could end up sounding like "Is the lamp post blue!" to a Thai person. Many of the sounds in the Thai language simply don't exist in English. I had to learn how to make the sounds for the first time, and it felt weird. But it felt good to study a new language, and it felt far more satisfying to talk with local people in their own tongue as I became more engaged in the community.

In between language lessons, I started my research into the world of book writing. It seemed like a huge and impossible challenge to produce something that other people would read. Many people I'd met had asked me about my nomadic life and had been fascinated when I told them I'd been on the road. I knew absolutely nothing about what the life of a writer is like or what demands it would ask of me. I thought the best way to honour the commitment I made on my birthday and get started would be to attend a writer's course. It just so happened that a well-known and highly acclaimed writer from New York was running a five-day course in Chiang Mai the following January, and I signed up for a place. In doing so, I took the first, tiny step towards my big, ambitious goal to write and publish my story. The rest, as they say, is history.

Chuck Maboomerang Returns

Acting in the play, *Out of Order*, in Queensland, Australia had ignited the spark for my life without a tie journey. It was now five years later, and I made a Skype call to Elizabeth Taylor and her husband, Matt, to see how they were. They invited me to stay with them over Christmas and New Year. I hadn't seen them for two and a half years, so I joyfully accepted. Plenty of cheap flights were available from Bangkok and a day later, I had my ticket booked.

Readers of *The Daily Explorer* loved the Aussie journo Chuck Maboomerang, who'd carefully crafted the narrative when I last visited Australia. As I counted down the days to my departure, he made a well-received comeback about my plans to return to the land down under. My preparations were going smoothly when I received an unexpected invitation from Christine in Vancouver. It came during a call around the middle of October.

"You know, Ray, earlier this year, I said I wasn't ready to start a serious relationship. But recently, I've been talking to my therapist about it, and I've reached a place where I feel I might be ready now. I wondered if you'd be interested in coming here for a conversation about that?"

I was slightly taken aback and had mixed feelings about it. The last time I'd gone halfway around the world for a chance at love, it had turned out to be quite the disaster. I certainly didn't want to repeat that. But I liked Christine, and there was a chance we might be able to create a partnership, so it seemed unwise not to respond. I wasn't due to head for Australia for four or five weeks. If I'd been brutally honest with myself—something I'm great at guiding others to do but not as accomplished at doing for myself—I should have said no and had a few more virtual conversations before I leapt in. Deep down, a part of me knew that she wasn't really ready and that I wasn't the ideal partner for her. Despite that, I ignored my inner wisdom and accepted her invitation. In doing so, Canada became the nineteenth country I'd visited in my ongoing nomadic journey.

In hindsight, I believe my inability to look at myself with clarity and honesty at that time was driven by my need to avoid feeling disappointed. When I took part in the Hoffman Process, I articulated what an ideal relationship would look and feel like, probably for the first time. I opened myself to the possibility of meeting someone with whom I could create that and make it a reality. Being a nomad and living in constant flux, I thought it might take years to meet that person. But life hadn't gone according to that script. I met Christine three months later, and I instinctively felt it was significant. Once again, I became attached to a happy ever after fairy tale outcome. My ability to see things as they really are and remain unattached wasn't quite robust enough, given it's a foundation of my happiness and well-being. I was about to find out that this shortcoming had consequences.

During the fifteen-hour flight from Bangkok to Vancouver, I reflected on what could happen. Maybe I'd need to cancel my flight to Sydney and spend Christmas and New Year with Christine. Maybe nothing would change, and I'd leave things as they were and head for Australia. After five years of living in the moment, I was comfortable with such a high degree of uncertainty. Christine came to meet me at the airport, and it was lovely to see her again after two months apart.

The next couple of days were relaxed and pleasant. It's beautiful in Vancouver, and it was a great backdrop for us to enjoy each other's company and have some fun cycling, walking, shopping, and eating. As we spent more time together, our conversations inevitably turned towards what a shared future might look like and how we both felt about that. There was a noticeable shift in tension as I explored it with her, and our conversations were awkward. She appeared to have taken a step back and changed her mind. True or not, it was fairly obvious that a shared future wasn't going to happen. Part of me wanted to play the victim and blame her for getting me to travel all that way for nothing. At the same time, my inner voice of wisdom reminded me about something I touched on earlier in this story; everyone we meet is for *a reason, season, or lifetime.*

I believe our encounter occurred for a reason. In Vancouver, I'd heard what I'd needed to hear and could now let go. I gave myself a pat on the back for the progress I'd made in expanding my self-awareness in the past year. There may not have been a happy ending with Christine, but I left knowing I was more ready than I'd ever been for a committed relationship. I headed for Sydney with the sense it was inevitable that another person would show up. It was only a matter of time.

I was excited to spend the Christmas period in Sydney with my dear friends Matt and Elizabeth. Pete was now ten and had grown rapidly since my last visit in 2008. I felt like part of their family, which was a rare and welcome experience after five years away from my own kin in the UK. Sydney provided a pleasant contrast to my budget standard of living in Chiang Mai. The sunshine and high temperatures of summer mean that Christmas in Sydney happens on the beaches.

We went to sing carols at twilight on the beach in Balmoral. It was my first taste of "Chrissie" Aussie style and was quite surreal but extremely heartwarming to see hundreds of city folk picnicking in the late afternoon sunshine by the sea, whilst belting out some of my favourite yuletide anthems. The scene could not have been more different to the Christmases I remember from my years in the UK, where you're more likely to be standing outside in the freezing cold, wearing several layers of warm winter clothes.

Gifts From the Heart

I came up with some creative gift ideas for Matt, Elizabeth, and Pete. They had to be things I could make in the time and limited resources I had. One was an award certificate. I designed it, printed it out, and placed it in a five-dollar frame from the local Snappy Snaps. The Taylor family became the first recipient of the *Daily Explorer Hospitality Award*, in recognition of their kindness and generosity (a companion to the *Daily Lama* one they'd received a few years before). I also made them a keepsake chest, fashioned from an empty shoebox. I wrapped the box and lid in fancy paper, and I used coloured marker pens and stickers to make a label for the box. I wrote notes and placed them inside a gift card, which accompanied the empty box.

I've never been a huge fan of New Year's Eve celebrations, and when I was married to Charlotte, I'd looked for an alternative to the loud, boring conventional parties that would be more connected, private, intimate, and meaningful. I began an experiment on January 1 to ensure that each time we went out to the cinema, a concert, someone's wedding, a party, or sporting event etcetera, we placed the tickets, programmes, and invitation cards in a box when we got back home. On New Year's Eve, over a quiet supper at home, we took the box (which was full to the brim after a year of socialising) and tipped the contents out on the table. One by one, we consciously reminisced about each event we'd shared together, reflected on it, recalled what we loved or hated about it or how it had changed us, and let it go with gratitude for the experience. It took us a couple of hours to get through the entire box and by the time we'd reached the last item, we both experienced a fantastic sense of completion to the year, just minutes before it actually came to an end at midnight. You might want to try it one year.

Matt and Elizabeth loved the box and its brief, and she committed to starting the following day. Elizabeth, who is extremely creative artistically, had been thinking along the same lines as me. She was fully aware that my nomadic lifestyle meant I was unable to carry heavy or awkward items, so she made me a wonderful, small box with fifty-two hand-painted cards bearing different fishes, one for each week of the year. Inside the box were instructions on how to use the gift. Here is an excerpt:

Dear Ray,
I wanted to give you a gift that was easy to carry and would be with you all year. In this magic box, you will find a saying and a picture for every week of 2011. I wish the words were mine, but they belong to a mixture of wise and interesting people. The cards have been shuffled, and I trust that some greater power will ensure the next one in the pile is the right one for you for the week in question. However, the tiny paintings on each card are mine. This will be a little bit of me appearing in your space every week, wherever you are in the world. You'll see the painting and know I love you, am thinking of you, and wishing you well on your travels. I chose the ocean theme because I see you swimming as a fish in the sea—a great sea with boundless possibility. Nothing is tying you down, keeping you still; there is always a new vista. I've no doubt

LIFE WITHOUT A TIE

your journey has been daunting at times, but you have continued to bravely step forward, providing inspiration to me and others. You remind us all that we should not be still, stop learning or questioning."

I was overwhelmed and moved to tears. Gifts like this are so precious, as well as rare. We're all so busy, we don't have time. Elizabeth, who is a mum and a busy corporate executive, had spent hours making this for me, and I deeply appreciated it. I believe creativity is an expression of the soul, or God in action, which effectively means that through making the gift, she connected me with the source energy or God. Perhaps that's why the energy you feel when someone makes a handmade, crafted gift for you is of a higher quality and frequency than when they buy something from a store.

Arguably the best gift I received between Christmas and New Year came not from another person but directly from the Universe. I was scrolling down my Facebook feed one morning and saw that a friend of mine, Felicity, had posted a photo from a social event in Chiang Mai. The photo depicted her with a group of about eight people gathered together outside a yoga school which I was familiar with. I looked closely at the picture to see who I knew in her group. My attention was drawn to a good-looking woman, who appeared to be in her early forties, so I hovered my mouse over her and saw she'd been tagged. Her name was Sylvia. There was something mesmerising about her beyond her good looks that caught my attention, though I can't explain what it was.

I wanted to know more about Sylvia, so I looked at her profile. That's one of the great (and potentially creepy) things about Facebook and other social media platforms. There is a lot you can glean about another person and their life without even meeting or speaking to them. She hadn't posted that much on her Facebook page, so it wasn't easy to confirm if she lived in Chiang Mai all year round or was on a one-time visit. I considered taking a Machiavellian approach and asking Felicity to introduce me to her. I quickly dismissed that thought for two reasons.

The first was the practical matter of not knowing if Sylvia was already involved with someone. None of the pictures she'd posted showed that to be the case, but it was impossible to know for sure. The second reason was that I'd really enjoyed the mindful practice of living from my guiding principle of non-attachment. I'd got much better at allowing the Universe to guide me to whatever I needed, and I didn't want to undermine my trust in the power of my relationship with it. I decided to challenge myself. I sat still, closed my eyes, and set an intention. "Universe, please arrange for Sylvia and me to bump into each other in Chiang Mai when I return. And please make it happen easily." Once that was done, I trusted that somehow or someway, it would happen if it was meant to be.

The Universe Delivers
My daily routine in Chiang Mai started with a 5:30 a.m. training run on the track at the local football stadium, followed by a cooked breakfast at Blue Diamond, which had become one of my favourite neighbourhood restaurants. After that, I returned to my room to respond to emails and catch up with correspondence related to my Calling All Angels foundation. The rest of my day would vary, but would include meeting friends, studying Thai, reading, socialising, and watching the occasional movie.

About halfway through January 2011, after my training run, I decided to switch restaurants and called in at Nice Kitchen. It was a random choice. My inner voice called it out as I left the stadium on my motorbike. Trusting that, I duly complied. I arrived, sat down at an empty table, placed my order, and started reading the *Bangkok Post*. After a six-mile run, I liked to eat fried eggs and grilled potatoes, which were brought to me a few minutes later. I was halfway through my meal when two ladies walked in and sat at a nearby table. My pulse raced. One of them was Sylvia.

Adrenaline surged through my veins, and I started to sweat. You know that phrase, "Be careful what you wish for?" In the three and a half weeks that had passed since I'd sat in Matt and Elizabeth's house in Sydney and set the intention, I'd forgotten about it. But the Universe hadn't, it seemed. The Universe had delivered. The question now was how to deal with the situation. What would you have done if you'd been in my shoes?

It might seem like a dumb question to ask. I obviously knew who she was, but she had no idea I even existed. If I said that I'd been looking at pictures of her on Facebook and recognised her, she might have run a mile, or at least thought I was strange or possibly threatening. *Think, Ray. You could write her a note. You could go over and introduce yourself. Quick, come up with something. What should I do?*

Sylvia was with a friend of hers, so I ruled out approaching her at their table. It was too embarrassing, and I didn't believe I'd look or sound authentic. Before I decided what action to take, they stood up and headed for the cashier's desk to settle their bill, which meant they had to walk past me. As they did, I looked at Sylvia and she looked back at me. Maybe she picked up something from my facial expression, because she stopped.

"Do we know each other?" she asked.

Thank God! The ice was broken. The door was ever so slightly open. I panicked but wanted to play it cool. "No, I don't think so. Do you live in Chiang Mai?"

"Yes, for about five months of the year. How about you?"

It worked. Now we were talking. "It's more or less the same for me. By the way, my name is Ray. What's yours?"

Obviously, if I hadn't asked what her name was, it might have seemed strange. And if I'd said, "I already know your name as I've seen you on Facebook," it might have freaked her out, and I didn't want to scare her off. "It's lovely to meet you, Sylvia. Perhaps we'll bump into each other again at some point. I hope so."

"Yes, that would be lovely."

And then she left.

It didn't feel right to try to make a date with her immediately, and I trusted that things would work out the way they needed to even as we went our separate ways. Later that day, I connected with Sylvia on Facebook, which meant I could now message her freely. The Universe had done exactly what I'd asked and had us bump into each other. If anything was to happen beyond this point, it would be down to me. I sent her a message and invited her to have coffee with me.

She replied, "I'd love to. I'll be out of town for a couple of weeks, and I'll let you know when I'm back."

It was a great start, and I was happy to leave it there, especially as my five-day creative writing course was about to kick off, and I wanted to focus on that.

The Writer's Journey begins

The course was run by Wendy Goldman Rohm, an author and literary agent from New York. She had masses of experience and had published a controversial, best-selling book in the nineties called *The Microsoft File: The Secret Case Against Bill Gates*, about corruption within the software company. I was in a group with fifteen people. Some had published two or three books already. Other participants were complete newbies.

Unlike some business-related courses I'd attended, there was no set agenda. It was a fluid, improvised experience in which we were asked to write short pieces and read them to the group to receive feedback. I just about coped with some of the simple exercises and felt out of my depth with the more complex ones, which pushed me to the edge of my comfort zone in terms of learning. Whenever we attempt to learn something new, there are four steps that we all go through to reach mastery:

1. Unconscious Incompetence: we don't even know the full extent of what we don't know
2. Conscious Incompetence: we now know what there is to learn, have started to practice, and have no ability
3. Conscious Competence: we repeatedly practice, apply effort, and our ability steadily improves
4. Unconscious Competence: we don't have to think about knowing it. We can do it well and with ease

This helpful model was developed by Noel Burch in the seventies. Look back over your life and reflect on something you've mastered. You'll see these steps are simply inevitable and necessary. On the writer's course, I spent five days wading through steps one and two and wouldn't say I enjoyed it, as I felt quite stupid and incapable at times. It's the second step which is the most difficult stage, as that's when the real learning begins and when most negative judgments toward one's self are formed. Consequently, it's the stage where most people give up. I have to admit there were at least two or three moments when I felt like I wanted to walk out.

Despite my discomfort, I learned the important basics of genre, writing technique, and form, like constructing dialogue and writing in the third and first person. I played around with ideas and themes for my book, as well as different ways to structure and organise the contents. I found out how books get published and promoted. The net result was clarity that I wanted to write what's known in the publishing industry as a narrative non-fiction book, which means the story describes actual events that took place as well as the thoughts, feelings, and insights related to them.

LIFE WITHOUT A TIE

One thing I've learned about the creative process is that it's different for all of us. I took my first step and attended that writer's course at the beginning of 2011, but it wasn't until 2015 that my thoughts finally crystallised around the idea of *Life Without a Tie*, and I wrote the first words. I stayed in my creative cocoon incubating it for nearly four years! I guess we're ready when we're ready. At least I'd made a start on one of the two commitments I'd made with Christine on my birthday in Cherating.

A few days later, Sylvia returned to Chiang Mai, and we met for coffee. She was from Berlin and was a body worker, treating people who had injuries or problems, especially related to their back and spine. She stayed in Chiang Mai every year from September to March, then returned to Europe for the summer. We met again six times before she left for Germany, and I enjoyed getting to know her. Luckily for me, I had to return to London in April to renew my Thai visa and take care of a couple of administrative issues. It made it easy for me to see her, and since I'd never been to Berlin, it opened the door to another adventure.

Coach In A Box

The second of the two commitments I'd made with Christine was to start doing part-time coaching work. I'd set up a relationship with Progress U, having agreed terms in Shanghai and Hong Kong the previous year. No work had materialised yet, and it was unclear if or when it would. Once again, I turned to the Universe for help. I had no business contacts in Asia and no idea how to engage with the challenge of finding the right people. I was a member of LinkedIn and thought there could be a way I could tap into that global network. I went to the jobs page and entered the words coaching and Asia in the search box. A couple of hundred profiles appeared on my screen, and many of them were members of the Asia Pacific Alliance of Coaches (APAC).

I had to start somewhere, so I instinctively chose a French lady called Nathalie to send a message to as an experiment, asking for guidance and explaining what I'd like to do. Nathalie responded soon afterwards and answered my question. We arranged a Skype call and during our conversation, she told me there was only one man I needed to speak to, and his name was Woraphat. He was Thai and had been president of the APAC since it began. He spoke fluent English and had a huge number of connections in the corporate world. He knew everyone there was to know in the coaching community and had loads of influence within it. She agreed to message him on my behalf, which I was grateful for.

Like all great coaches, when I met Woraphat a week later, he asked me a lot of perfect questions to pinpoint exactly what I was looking for, so he could connect me with the best people in his network. He asked me to send him my coaching profile, as he knew two people who he thought would be a great match for me. One of them was a lady called Danielle Marchant, who was the head of a relatively new coaching business called Coach In A Box (CIAB). When Danielle received my profile from Woraphat, she contacted me via email almost immediately to invite me to meet her in Bangkok because she'd thought I sounded like a great fit for them.

As luck would have it, my next trip to Bangkok was coming up soon, as I was flying back to the UK to renew my visa. I met Danielle and listened carefully as she explained what kind of services CIAB offered their clients. To my absolute delight, I discovered their entire service was delivered virtually. This is extremely common these days but ten years ago, virtual coaching was in its infancy, and CIAB pioneered the use of the platform. With my business leadership background and coaching experience, there was a great match of needs. I could work from any location and choose how many or how few clients to work with at any time. Danielle offered me a place on the coaching team, and I accepted.

I was in awe of the miracle I'd seen unfold since I'd set my intention to do freelance work back in 2008. I'd got on with life in the meantime and allowed the Universe to determine how and when the opportunity would come. Now it was here, it struck me that it had taken virtually no effort. I'd imagined and often visualised it becoming a part of my life. I'd spoken to a couple of friends, an unknown French lady and a kind, well-connected Thai man, which resulted in me finding the perfect place to manifest my intention.

The thing is, the criteria I'd applied to what I was looking for—self-employed, working from any location, meaningful work, part-time only, maximum workload of twenty to thirty hours per month—made it virtually impossible to find using a conventional approach. Most of these criteria weren't terms you could search by on the main job sites. It was like looking for a needle in the proverbial haystack. If I wanted rock-solid proof that the Universe always delivers when you align your heart and your head, this was it.

LIFE WITHOUT A TIE

I learned from this experience that the starting point for manifesting is to know explicitly what it is you want or need, why you need it, and how it will look and feel when it comes. It's a practice I've become better at over the years and one that I often help my clients develop. Has this happened in your own life, where you put an intention out to the Universe and eventually saw it come to fruition? Or do you have something you'd like to create? Can you hand it over to the Universe whilst taking appropriate action and know it will be delivered?

To help me prepare, Danielle invited me to experience CIAB in the way a client does. I enrolled in their Associate Development Programme, and she paired me up with Kenny Toh, one of their senior coaches. He was from Singapore and an absolute delight to work with. He led me through one of their standard five module programs and showed me the ropes. I was in really safe hands with Kenny, who knew that I'd been out of the corporate business scene for a while. His light and fun style resonated with me and inspired me to hone my own. When we completed our work together, I was ready to attend the next five-day familiarisation training for newly recruited coaches. It was taking place in Singapore in September. I was required to complete that prior to being given my first clients to work with.

This was a brilliant outcome. It was as if the world had adapted to fit my system of living, rather than me having to fit my life into a corporate system that I didn't advocate or desire. I'd patiently experimented and lived by my guiding principles, and it had paid off. I was living my life authentically and true to myself. I was a free person, with infinite mobility and total discretion over my time. I could do paid work without being required to sacrifice my freedom or creativity. I'd financed my life from my savings for five years, and now I'd have another source of income. That put my mind at ease and any worry I'd had about that fell away. Joining the CIAB team gave me a smooth and painless re-entry into the business world and a great experiment to run with. After a few months, I'd know exactly what integrating professional work back into my life felt like, and I'd be in a position to review what changes, if any, were needed.

Summer in Berlin
I flew to London in April 2011, went to the Thai consulate, and was granted a retirement visa as expected, which allowed me a one-year stay

in Thailand and multiple re-entries, meaning I could go in and out of the country unrestricted. It was the Rolls Royce of visas and made this one of the rare occasions when I was grateful to be the age I was.

Next, I went to Berlin. On the way, I stopped in Amsterdam for a couple of days to meet a friend and then took a seven-hour train journey to cross the border into Germany, which became country number twenty-one. Sylvia was there on the station platform at Hauptbahnhof to meet me. I saw her as I stepped out of the carriage and was in her arms about ten seconds later. It was a beautiful, tender moment as we embraced each other. She held me in a soft, warm hug for what seemed like an eternity. She was delighted I'd arrived, and I was thrilled to see her again.

My hotel was close to Sylvia's apartment. We headed there so I could drop my luggage off. I didn't want to repeat the awkward experience I'd had in Sint Maarten with Nicole, and I didn't want to be presumptuous about staying with Sylvia, even though I absolutely wanted to. Choosing a place nearby removed any pressure from her. I trusted that it would happen, if and when it felt right. We went out for the day and returned to her apartment for a nightcap. I never made it out of there. My hotel room basically became the most expensive storage locker that I'd ever had!

In some ways, life is really a classroom or laboratory for learning, experimenting, and trying out new behaviours in order to discover one's bliss. In Berlin with Sylvia, I continued practicing what I'd learned during the Hoffman process to evolve into the kind of partner I knew I could be, according to the vision I'd seen for that part of my life. It was a virtuous circle, and the more I paid attention and made the effort to show up well, the more I enjoyed being me and felt proud of who I was.

I'd intended to spend eight days in Berlin. It's one of the most interesting cities, both historically and currently, that I've visited. I'd go so far as to say it's the most attractive city in mainland Europe. Sylvia and I got on so well that I extended my stay and rented a lovely, furnished apartment about half a mile from her place for a couple of months. I'd found it through one of Sylvia's friends. I had to be in Singapore in September for my coach training and that was the only commitment I'd made. I ended up staying in Berlin for most of the summer.

Sylvia and I weren't joined at the hip, and I liked the fact we both had our own places. She was in her hometown and had to work most days. When she wasn't working, we took bicycles and went all over the city so

LIFE WITHOUT A TIE

I could discover its heartbeat and find out more about its history, which truly fascinated me.

Berlin is Germany's largest city. Most people probably know that it was divided after World War II. East Berlin became the capital of East Germany, while West Berlin became a de facto West German enclave, surrounded by the Berlin Wall (until 1989). What made it impactful for me was experiencing it through Sylvia's eyes, as she'd grown up in East Germany and had experienced how oppressive life had been during the communist era. She told me stories about the austerity they'd lived with and the bleak outlook they had as they were growing up. I realised how grateful I was to have been born and raised in a democratic country which respected the rights and privileges of its citizens.

Sylvia's apartment was in a trendy district called Prenzlauer Berg, which was formally part of East Berlin. I saw the investment and modernisation that had taken place in the twenty years since reunification, and a few bullet holes that remain in the walls of older buildings. The contrast really struck me and made it easy to imagine what it might have felt like to have been alive and present during those dark, communist times. As a tourist, the highlight was my visit to the Berlin Wall. I took a close look at the artwork that had been preserved on the one or two remaining sections. I sat quietly and wondered how it might have felt for people separated from their family and friends when it was hastily constructed in 1961. Those who ended up living in the East, including Sylvia and her parents, weren't allowed to leave. Anyone who tried to cross the so-called "death strip" from the eastern side of the wall risked being shot. The thought made me shiver.

We live in a world where you can go anywhere virtually at the click of a button. Yet, there are certain places in the physical world that can never be replicated digitally, and Berlin is most definitely one of them. Being there, I touched the brickwork, saw the bullet holes, heard people's voices, walked on the ground that had previously been a no-go area for citizens from the East and West alike, climbed the sentry towers where armed soldiers had stood guard and fired shots at their own citizens, friends, and community. It was a visceral reality that you just can't get from photos or books. Pictures don't do some things justice. When you're there, it evokes emotion and opens access to the collective wisdom of mankind, which allows for a deeper understanding of what went on. It's almost as if the earth has held that memory. As I reflected on my visit, I realised how lucky I was to have the time to experience real travelling and genuinely feel the world. I'd gone way beyond just being a tourist. It had given me a deeper connection to our humanity.

In Berlin, I also saw much to be joyful about. One example that stood out was an area called Mauerpark, which is in Prenzlauer Berg. The name means Wall Park, as it stands on what used to be called No Man's Land, which was a wide death strip between the two sides of the Berlin Wall. In 1989, the area was redesignated as a public space and grassed over to become a recreational space in the city for local residents. The park and the pop-up flea market next to it was one of the most popular places for young residents of Berlin. It was there that I experienced one of the peak moments of my entire journey.

Every Sunday afternoon, an Irish guy living there organised a hugely popular open-air karaoke festival. He used an outdoor amphitheatre which seated about five hundred people. Another five hundred people stood. He rigged up a laptop to two enormous speakers and invited people from the audience to come up and perform. Singers could choose from thousands of popular songs, and if they were halfway decent, as many of them were, the audience showered them with thunderous applause. If they were a first-timer or not so good, the audience showed their love and applauded just as much. I set my heart on singing there, but my fear initially stopped me. There was no better place to risk it, though. It had a carnival atmosphere, and you could feel the love all around.

The third time Sylvia and I were there, I couldn't resist. I asked the Irish guy if he would add me to the list of singers, which he kindly did. About two hours later, he yelled my name out and beckoned me to come and perform on stage. I chose "When You Say Nothing at All" by Ronan Keating. It's a love song, and I'd always wanted to sing it to someone special. Before my music started, I loudly and proudly announced to the one thousand people assembled that I was a visitor to their wonderful city, and my song was dedicated to my beautiful girlfriend, Sylvia, and I pointed to her sitting in the centre of the audience. Everyone could tell I was smitten, and they seemed to love being exposed to such a bold romantic act. I sang my heart out for the next four minutes and graciously accepted the love of the audience as they clapped me off the stage. Sylvia told me that no partner had ever sung to her before, in public or privately, and she loved it. I was deeply happy in that moment and thought that life couldn't get any better.

Chapter Fifteen
Coming Full Circle

IN SEPTEMBER 2011, I LEFT BERLIN AFTER A GLORIOUS SUMMER WITH SYLVIA, full of joy and optimism, and headed for Singapore. I'd been integrating myself into the Coach In A Box (CIAB) community while in Berlin, in preparation for the five-day coaches training. I'd coached one of their new associates, Pramod Gothi, who lived in Mumbai, India. He was a modest and charming man in his early sixties. He'd worked in the corporate world and had recently retired. He'd committed to use his twilight years to pass on his knowledge and experience to younger executives. He graciously allowed me to coach him and gain practice with the CIAB coaching tools. My calls with Pramod were recorded for assessment, and I received feedback at various stages from a mentor, to help me improve my capability.

Our training in Singapore was a supportive and enjoyable experience, and I was impressed with the CIAB culture. In some ways, it reminded me of my former business, so I felt at home and was surrounded by a great group of people. Working across different time zones was new; I joined a conference call at three a.m. in Berlin because I was affiliated with the Asian team, six hours ahead. I got up six hours earlier than my Asian colleagues but being able to work from anywhere, with clients everywhere as I travelled made that kind of sacrifice seem small.

It was the first chance I'd had to meet the entire team in Asia in person. There were eighteen people in our work group, and we stayed in groups of four in the Lotus Residence, near Joo Chiat in swish, modern apartments. That gave the whole event a five-star, executive summer camp feel. I felt like I'd joined a like-minded community of bright, sparkling people from all over Asia. I was happy to be part of it and realised how valuable and important community is in my life. CIAB in Asia was new and set to grow quickly, so this was a great moment to get on board, as there would be many opportunities to grow with it.

The five-day training was demanding. I felt capable but stretched at times. It'd been six years since I'd left the world of business, and I wasn't fully adjusted to my new reality. The toughest part was being asked to facilitate one of the modules on the course for the rest of the group. CIAB wanted to see who might be good at doing that, so we all got a turn. I had virtually no experience in leading training sessions, and it felt daunting, as those people in my audience were mostly experienced facilitators. I connected with my guiding principles of presence and contribution, surrendered to it, and did the best I could. I'd prepared thoroughly so that my session, which I co-facilitated with one of my colleagues, would come across well. And judging from the feedback we received afterwards, it seemed to work out.

I made a lot of new friends in Asia which made my life and world feel a whole lot bigger. There were associates from Shanghai, Dubai, Hong Kong, Thailand, India, Japan, South Korea, and Singapore. I learned a lot from the trainers and each of the participants and felt excited that I'd soon work with clients again. It had been a long time since I put my business hat on, but I was pleased to discover that it still fitted well.

Finding my voice
I returned to Chiang Mai in mid-September. There are only two seasons there: the rainy season, which runs from April until the end of September, and the rest of the year, when it's sunny and dry. The torrential rain falls daily for at least an hour or two, and sometimes longer. This was easily the wettest I'd seen it in five years. The Ping River overflowed and disrupted the daily lives of locals and travellers alike. Tourists staying by the river were evacuated as their guesthouses shipped more and more water. Small boats with outboard motors transported local residents to and from their homes. Close to the river, the business owners used sandbag barricades to defend themselves and their property.

We don't always understand the full significance of what seem like random, out of the blue events until we look back in hindsight and join the dots. Whilst I prepared to leave for India, one of those surprise events happened. At the five-day coach training in Singapore, my mentor encouraged me to practice what I'd learned to help me integrate it. She suggested I offer some free coaching to someone in Chiang Mai, which was a great idea. It was a perfect opportunity to embrace my guiding principle of contribution. Knowing I'd be away for a while in India, I hastily approached a friend called Gaston Schmitz, a Dutch guy I'd met in 2006. He worked for an NGO helping poor, underdeveloped communities tackle social problems, such as AIDS, pollution, domestic violence, and the like.

I admired the way Gaston was totally committed to his work and was delighted when he agreed to be my guinea pig. We had enough time for a one-hour session before my departure and worked through a couple of decisions he was considering related to his work. Our coaching conversation helped him clarify his thinking, and it helped me evolve my way of working. I loved how I felt when I was generous with my time and gave unconditionally. When we were done, I hadn't expected anything further to happen.

Much to my surprise, Gaston called me the next day and urgently requested my help to produce a short video about the work of his NGO, The Constellation, which was being made for their website. He wanted a native English speaker with a decent voice to narrate the video and asked me if I would donate my time. I had no previous experience, but because I love growth challenges and was open to learn something new, I said yes. I spent a few hours with Gaston and a technician to refine and record the script. I felt happy I'd given my energy to something truly worthwhile and honoured my principle of contribution once again. It was my debut in voice-over work, and it was surprisingly great fun to do. There was a lot more to the work than meets the eye, and it wasn't until much later in my journey in 2016 that I realised how fortunate I was to acquire that experience. The Universe had peeked into my future and prepared me for something I had no idea was coming.

India Beckons

Back in 2004, before my life began to follow its new path, I took part in an adventurous, week-long, fundraising event with a group called Enduro India. One hundred of us rode classic Royal Enfield motorcycles across Kerala and Tamil Nadu and covered over twelve hundred miles, in support of the World Wildlife Fund and a charity called the Rainbow Trust. That amazing experience had partly inspired my Calling All Angels Campaign and taught me a lot about how to raise money.

The journey opened my eyes and my heart to India, and I'd made a promise to myself that I'd return one day, when I had enough free time to really explore the country properly. I'd already postponed my decision once, in favour of taking on the New York marathon. Now it was time to make good on that promise, and I returned to fully experience the vibrancy, energy, colour, smells, and tastes of this incredible, challenging, and charming country. India became country number twenty-two in my epic journey.

I was excited about it for two reasons. Firstly, I had two months to travel solo and explore everything on offer, which appealed strongly to the explorer in me. The second reason was that Sylvia was there. I'd been totally loved up with her in Berlin during the summer and missed that feeling of elation. On arrival, I headed for Pahar Ganj. It's a rundown part of Delhi where most backpackers stay, and rooms can be found for a few dollars a night. It's fine as long you're not too fussy. It enabled me to get used to low expectations with regard to the type of accommodation I might end up in as I made my way around this huge and populous country. India has over 1.2 billion people, second only to China.

Sylvia was no stranger to India. She'd lived there and had been to Delhi several times. That reassured me, as I was confronted for the first time with a city that was dramatically different from what I'd been used to in England. In Pahar Ganj the streets were extremely crowded, noisy, and absolutely filthy with cows and goats—and their droppings—everywhere. It reeked of rotting garbage. In the few hours before I met Sylvia, I was badgered by numerous beggars. There was poverty everywhere, and I discovered that three quarters of the population lived on less than two dollars per day. In my budget guesthouse in Pahar Ganj, the rooms were basic and without toilet paper. Despite all of that, it was strangely wonderful to experience this timeless, chaotic, vibrant, and raw place. This was about as hardcore as budget travel could get.

Sylvia was in transit to Dharamsala in northern India to study Tibetan Buddhism at a monastic school with a group of friends. I had plenty of time to travel solo, do my own thing, and take in India at my own pace knowing that I'd see her again a few weeks later. We agreed to meet in Dharamsala so we could both attend a three-day retreat with the Dalai Lama. The small, mountainous city has been his home, along with several thousand exiled Tibetan monks, since the Chinese invaded Tibet in 1959. My horizon of certainty was now extended to about two months.

LIFE WITHOUT A TIE

The Bubble Bursts

We were both headed in different directions from Delhi, and I was grateful we could spend a couple of days together before I left for Jaipur. From my perspective, the relationship with Sylvia was evolving nicely after nearly six months of getting to know each other. Looking back, I'd unwisely set my expectations as to what our relationship should look like one or two years ahead, and I'd painted a wonderfully rosy picture. That may sound like a good thing, but it was actually a cause for concern.

One of my guiding principles for this epic journey was to be present. I'd rarely allowed myself to live fully in the present moment and simply enjoy it for what it was, without any thought for what I might gain or lose. This became crystal clear during my first Vipassana meditation retreat. For the first time, I knew that I wanted to pursue a path of mindfulness in my daily life. Up until then, my happiness had been dependent on the achievement of my goals, and I'd recognised that paradigm as a constraint.

When I arrived in Delhi, I was lost in my thoughts about the future and believed that Sylvia and I would always be together. It didn't occur to me that she might feel differently. It was a serious lapse in my practice of conscious awareness. I hadn't lived fully in the present moment in my relationship with her. I'd partially lived out a future fantasy and missed what was actually happening in the here and now. Right on cue, an unexpected event awakened me from my mental slumber. On my first day in Delhi, Sylvia told me that the fantasy I'd built of our life together wasn't the same as hers.

We were eating supper when she revealed that Graham, a close friend of hers who she'd known for a few years and studied with in Dharamsala, had declared his unrequited love for her. He now wanted to start an intimate relationship with her. I knew him because he lived in Chiang Mai, and I'd met him with Sylvia on a couple of occasions. I listened intently with a feeling of disbelief as she acknowledged that the desire was mutual. I questioned her about her feelings for him and got the sense she was pretty optimistic about their shared future. She wanted to end our fledgling relationship and accept his invitation. As if to rub salt in my wound, she asked if I'd be willing to wait a while, and perhaps restart our relationship in the event that things didn't work out with Graham. I did my best to remain calm and not react to or judge her, even though I was deeply hurt.

No matter how shocked I was to hear what Sylvia said, she'd been transparent and honest and that took some courage, especially as she knew I adored her. I respected her for that. The optimistic part of me thought this wasn't necessarily final and that it would be wise to give myself some valuable breathing space before I completely withdrew. As I recall that horrid evening, I saw it gave rise to two quite distinct responses in me. One I was conscious of and the other I wouldn't be until a few months later.

The response I was conscious of was how surprised, disappointed, and heartbroken I felt. Sylvia didn't have the same commitment to or enthusiasm for our partnership, and I wanted to sit with that for a while and reflect on it. I told Sylvia that, and we agreed we'd talk again in Dharamsala a couple of months later to see where we both were. I was fortunate I had a couple of months alone ahead of me to allow it all to sink in and take a look inside myself to gain a deeper understanding of what this event might mean. Was there a pattern that I needed to see and even dismantle? Were Sylvia and I really compatible? Was this karmic justice for the way I'd treated Annie? I had a lot of questions. Maybe you can recall a time when a surprise or disappointment caused you to reflect deeply and question yourself?

In Gandhi's Footsteps

After a sad farewell, Sylvia boarded her bus to Dharamsala. In the meantime, I continued my exploration of Delhi. When India gained independence from British rule in 1947, New Delhi was declared its capital and seat of government. It has become an enormous, multicultural, and cosmopolitan metropolis. The sprawling city has many appealing tourist attractions, but there was one place at the top of my list, and I couldn't wait to get there. It was the Gandhi Smriti, which is a museum and shrine dedicated to Mahatma Gandhi. It's where he spent the last one hundred and forty-four days of his life, before he was assassinated on January 30, 1948.

Gandhi is widely regarded as the founding father of modern India. I'm inspired by him because his existence proved that enormous changes can be achieved by one individual who speaks the truth and acts non-violently to manifest that truth. You'll remember the profound short story about him at the beginning of this book. I'd wanted to apply his timeless wisdom and integrate it into my own way of life. He was an inspirational figure for me at every stage of my adventure, and I was hungry to learn as much as I

LIFE WITHOUT A TIE

could about him.

In this atmospheric place, I learned more about Gandhi's life and his achievements, and as I stood at the exact spot where he was killed, a kind of profound energy filled me. The coloured footprints painted on the pathways marked his walk across the garden to a platform from which he had intended to address a prayer meeting. His assassin, Nathuram Godse, emerged from the small crowd gathered and fired three fatal shots into his chest at point-blank range. I was deeply moved by what I saw there, especially when I walked those last few steps that Gandhi took. I imagined how it might have felt to be in the crowd that day, witnessing such a great man being taken away forever.

Jaipur and Agra

Jaipur is about four hours away from Delhi by bus. It's in the neighbouring state of Rajasthan and going there was my first test as a solo traveller within India. It was going pretty well until we reached the outskirts of the city. About five miles away from the bus station—the place I wanted to reach—a tall guy got on the bus and told me we'd arrived. I hesitated; I didn't know the area and couldn't check where we were on the map. He saw I was confused and told me again that we were at the bus station. He insisted that I get off. I double-checked with the driver, who wasn't helpful and hardly spoke any English. He went with me to the back of the bus to offload my luggage. The tall guy got off the bus too. They asked me for the name of my guesthouse. I told them, and they said I could get there by taking a ride in their taxi at a cost of one hundred and fifty rupees, which was more than the cost of the entire bus journey from Delhi. In that moment, I realised I was being scammed. I grabbed my luggage and quickly ran back on the bus before the driver could depart. He realised I'd rumbled their devious scheme and couldn't look me in the eye after that. I worked out that these two men had arranged to rendezvous at that particular place and would have split the proceeds of their scam, had it worked. I talked to other travellers about it and soon realised this type of thing was routine in India and something I'd have to get used to. Most people are poor by Western standards and see tourists as an opportunity to prosper. They lie to you about all manner of things to get a few rupees from you. Whilst it annoyed me, I could understand it and took it as an opportunity to practice my guiding principles of presence, non-attachment,

319

and lightness.

Next, it was on to Agra. The only reason people usually go there is to visit the Taj Mahal. It's India's most famous monument and had been on my bucket list for years. It's often talked about as one of the most romantic places on earth, which appealed to my heart. With my relationship with Sylvia in the balance, I hoped for some inspiration or divine guidance. To get there, I had to take a train for the first time. The first challenge was to work out where to board. There were literally thousands of people milling around the station. Most were there to travel, while others slept on and around the platforms, and a few begged for money.

Rickshaw drivers and station porters constantly hassled me for business in their insistent, charming way. It was crowded, dusty, and hot, and my frustration rose as I failed to make any progress. Eventually, a guy directed me to the tourist information office, where I confirmed which of the twenty-five platforms my train was leaving from. The next challenge was a physical one. To get to that platform, I had to climb over scores of people sleeping in the main concourse, which made it difficult to drag my luggage without hurting anyone.

Once I'd made it to the platform, the next challenge presented itself. Where was I meant to stand? The trains carry thousands of passengers in India and have far more carriages than any train I'd been on before. Therefore, the station platforms are much longer than in England. Most of the old, rickety carriages were furnished with wooden bench seats, without any cushioning. They had completely open windows with metal bars across them like a cattle truck! If you boarded in the wrong carriage, the sheer density of people in the aisles meant it could take you literally hours to get to your seat, which would almost definitely be occupied by an impostor when you got there.

It seemed like there was no limit to the number of people allowed to board these trains. I'd booked a ticket in advance, so at least I was guaranteed a seat. A standard class ticket (seated) cost eighty-seven rupees (about two dollars). For a four-and-a-half-hour journey, that's cheap by Western standards. Yet it was still prohibitively expensive to the majority of Indians. Consequently, most people buy standing-only tickets and take up every inch of available space until the roof is the only option left. After the first two stops, the carriages were heaving. There were five people sitting on a bench designed for three, and it was literally impossible to leave the seat whilst the train was moving.

As far as I could see, I was the only foreigner in the entire carriage. I drew a lot of attention and felt hundreds of eyes on me for most of the journey. The person to my left spoke English, and we got a conversation going. The train was severely delayed, and I arrived in Agra close to midnight. My guesthouse appeared to be quite close to the Taj Mahal, which perhaps would take ten or fifteen minutes by tuk-tuk from the station. I found a driver and went through the annoying ritual of agreeing on the price. He asked for one hundred and fifty rupees and eventually agreed to accept fifty.

I don't know about you, but when my energy levels are low, my patience is stretched. I'm far less tolerant and accepting of others, especially if I judge they're behaving to my detriment. Knowing that, I paid special attention to being mindful and did my best to remain fully present without judgment, and I'm glad I did. I'd been warned by other travellers about the touts in Agra and their relentless, aggressive pursuit of extracting money from tourists. I gave my tuk-tuk driver the benefit of the doubt and chose to see him as honest and kind. When we arrived at my hotel, I noticed that he stayed outside as I went to check in, almost as if he knew that something wasn't quite right.

"Ray Martin. I have a reservation," I said wearily to the night manager.

He shook his head. "Oh, we let your room go. You never showed up when you said."

I was shocked, angry, and bewildered. Despite my mindfulness practice, I could hardly contain it. He said it in such a matter-of-fact, chirpy way. It was the match that lit the fuse, and I lost it. I desperately appealed to him to find me a room. I tried to explain that the train delay was outside of my control, but it bounced off him like water off a duck's back. To make matters worse, one of the wheels on my twenty-two-kilo holdall broke during my journey, which meant I couldn't pull it and had to carry it instead. The tuk-tuk driver, who witnessed all this, sat and smirked. I think he sensed another opportunity to make some money and help me find an alternative place. It was already past midnight, and I had no clue as to exactly where else to go, so I was actually grateful he'd stuck around. He took me to a nearby guesthouse and I was sorted. Panic over.

As I drifted off to sleep, I reminded myself that I was here to see one of the Seven Wonders of the World. From the moment I woke up the next morning, I kept my mental attention on that thought and decided to make the most of my limited time in Agra.

The Taj Mahal

The Taj Mahal has a tale of eternal love behind it that's been melting the hearts of millions for years. According to the website, Faze, in 1612, Mumtaz Mahal, a Muslim Persian princess, married Shah Jehan, who later became the Mughal emperor. Agra was the centre of the Mughal Empire back then, which was one of the most extensive and wealthy empires in the medieval world. Although Mumtaz was Shah Jehan's second wife, she was considered his ultimate love match. By all accounts, Mumtaz and the emperor were soul mates, and she was his most trusted political adviser.

She accompanied her husband on his travels and military expeditions. Unfortunately, as with any legendary love story, a tragedy occurred. In 1630, Mumtaz died while giving birth to her fourteenth child. Her death affected the emperor so deeply that his black hair and beard turned snow white in just a few months. He was overcome with grief and vowed to keep his beloved wife's memory alive forever. He decided to build her a monument. Because Mumtaz had endeared herself to the people with her kindness, the emperor's subjects were inspired to help him construct it.

After twenty-two years and the combined effort of over twenty thousand workmen and master craftsmen, the spectacular monument was finally completed in 1648, at a cost of thirty-two million rupees. (That's just over $1,000,000, which was a lot of money in the seventeenth century.) It was built with materials from all over India and central Asia, carried to the site by over a thousand elephants. An English poet, Sir Edwin Arnold, best describes it as, "Not a piece of architecture, as other buildings are, but the proud passion of an emperor's love wrought in living stones." When Shah Jehan died in 1666, his body was laid to rest beside the tomb of his beloved wife.

I entered through the main gate. It's designed like the veil on a woman's face, to be lifted delicately, gently, and without haste on her wedding night to reveal the beauty of the bride. Inside the main gate, my eyes were directed to an arch in the inner wall and a short pedestrian tunnel that visually frames the Taj. I walked towards the centre, and my eyes were treated to a teasing glimpse of the Taj Mahal rising above the surrounding red wall of the compound. Halfway through the inner gate, I was gradually able to see more and more of the entire structure. As I got my first sighting of the whole building, with its four minarets, my perspective changed. At that point, I felt like a thirsty man walking through a desert who'd spotted an oasis. I couldn't hold myself back and walked through the inner gate as fast as I could. I was fully in the presence of one of the Seven Wonders of the World.

It's a bit of a cliché to say it, but you do have to be there to appreciate the beauty and magnificence of this wonderful creation. It has a life of its own that leaps out of the white marble. Part of the thrill was the continuous suspense I felt as I walked through the outer walls of the compound, followed by a rush of awe and relief after the revelation. I literally gasped. It was about seven thirty in the morning, and the sun had just risen. Standing there left me utterly speechless, and I remained still for about twenty minutes as I took in the magnificent structure in front of me. I reflected on the power of love that Shah Jehan had for Mumtaz and how this monument to their love has touched the lives of millions of people ever since. I imagined how amazing it would feel to love and be loved that much, and at the same time, felt the pain of how far away I was from that dream in that moment with Sylvia.

The architects and craftsmen of the Taj Mahal, which is almost perfectly symmetrical, were masters of proportion and tricks of the eye. For example, when I first approached the main gate that frames the Taj, the monument appeared incredibly close and large. But as I got closer, it shrank in size—exactly the opposite of what you'd expect. And although the minarets surrounding the tomb looked perfectly upright, the towers actually lean outward, which serves both form and function. In addition to providing aesthetic balance, the pillars were designed to crumble away from the main crypt in a disaster, like an earthquake.

A central pool reflects the main building, and the gardens, an earthly representation of paradise, are divided into quadrants. The iconic white marble dome contrasts against the plains in the background across the riverbank. The view of the Taj is altered by their reflection. The colours change at different hours of the day and during different seasons; it's pinkish in the morning, milky-white in the evening, and golden when the moon shines. It's virtually impossible to convey how spectacular it really is. I hope you have the opportunity to go there yourself, if you haven't done so already. Despite all of that, I left without the inspiration I'd hoped for with regard to how I might transform my relationship with Sylvia.

Rishikesh

Anyone who has travelled through India will know the country is vast and journeys that look relatively short on a map take much longer than you might ever expect. Most people travelling to Rishikesh from Agra would head back to Delhi and take a train or bus from there. I hoped there might be a more direct route. I discovered a number of cheap, local buses went from Agra to Haridwar, which is about one hour from Rishikesh. They were cheap for a reason. The vehicles are generally about fifty years old, have terrible suspension, and slatted wooden bench seats that offer no cushioning at all. To make matters worse, there are no limits as to the number of passengers, and you could just as easily find yourself sitting next to a couple of goats as you could a human being.

These buses were extremely slow because most of the roads were nothing more than pot-holed sand traps and very few highways had tarmac surfaces. Wanting an authentic, budget travel experience, I relished the opportunity. At the Agra bus station, I was surprised to see there was a sleeper coach available, but it wasn't due to leave for six hours. I looked inside, and it was so filthy, I gave it a miss and took a regular bus instead. It took fourteen hours to get to Haridwar. I hardly slept a wink. There was a sandstorm going on inside the bus, as they have no windows, and they fill up with dust from the unsurfaced roads. You can probably understand why some people say budget travelling in India is so exhausting. However, I most certainly got the authentic experience I wanted.

Rishikesh styles itself as the yoga capital of the world, with some justification as there were masses of ashrams and all kinds of yoga and meditation classes. The spectacle of the fast-flowing Ganges River rushing through the Himalayan foothills is an awesome sight. It's about 1,360 feet above sea level, and it's believed that several yogis and sages lived and practiced penance there. The forested hills which surround it make it highly conducive to meditation and mind expansion.

According to the Lonely Planet, ever since the Beatles rocked up at the ashram of the Maharishi Mahesh Yogi, the town has been a magnet for spiritual seekers. The fab four visited in 1968 to attend an advanced Transcendental Meditation (TM) training session. Their stay was one of the band's most productive periods. For anyone old enough to remember, they composed nearly fifty songs during their time at the Maharishi's ashram, many of which appeared on *The White Album*. They adopted the maharishi as their guru, which changed attitudes in the West about Indian spirituality and encouraged the study of TM. It was on my bucket list for that reason.

It was the first place in India where I was inspired to stay for a while. It had a really great vibe, decent food and guesthouses, and most importantly, laundry services! Travellers I connected with were there for all sorts of reasons, including learning to play the sitar, doing laughter yoga, humming or gong meditation, crystal healing, no end of massage treatments, chanting mantras, and listening to spiritually uplifting music as they sipped Ayurvedic tea with their vegetarian meal. I was happy to rest and relax, take walks along the river, write my *Daily Explorer* blog, and read a book over a coffee at the rather lovely German bakery by the bridge overlooking the Ganges.

The highlight in Rishikesh was the Shiva Ghat, where pilgrims took holy dips. There was a beautiful puja ceremony each evening, which is a worship ritual performed by Hindus to offer devotional homage and prayer to their deities, to host and honour a guest, or to spiritually celebrate an event. I joined hundreds of visitors, devotees, and pilgrims each evening and gathered around the swamis, who led the ceremony. A swami is an ascetic or yogi who has been initiated into the religious monastic order founded by Adi Sankara. It was a sight to behold as the golden shadows on the river illuminated rows of devotees who sat patiently on the steps of the Ghat at dusk. Accompanied by drums, chants, and bells, we prayed to nurture our well-being as we released tiny oil lamps on flower be-decked leaf boats into the river and watched them float downstream.

The puja ceremony was a rich and colourful experience that really gave me a buzz. I became more aware of connection, one of my guiding principles. The essence of life without a tie is about letting go and trusting the Universe to guide and sustain you as you find and follow your unique path in life. Through participating in events like this, I've come to realise that the exchange of energy is a source of power and aliveness.

Amritsar

I had my first experience of travelling on a sleeper train when I headed to Amritsar. Once I'd chained and padlocked my luggage to my tiny bunk bed, which I'd been advised to do by dozens of travellers, I slept pretty comfortably and arrived in great shape. Amritsar is in the northern part of India and is close to the border with Pakistan. The Golden Temple is without doubt the most famous attraction, and I spent a couple of hours enjoying the spectacle. It's an important Sikh shrine that attracts more visitors than the Taj Mahal—over a hundred thousand people every day—and it's the number one destination for non-resident Indians in the country. The upper walls are covered in gold, which makes it visually unique, and it sits on a man-made lake which creates a beautiful, symmetrical image with its reflection in the water. Although it's a religious place, I couldn't help feeling that I'd walked into a giant James Bond movie set and kept waiting for the speedboats, soldiers with machine guns, and an evil-looking man with a white cat to appear.

Sadly, Amritsar also makes it into the history books for one of the most egregious acts of violence ever carried out by the British Army. In April 1919, a large and peaceful crowd of about five thousand Indians gathered at the Jallianwala Bagh to protest against the arrest of two pro-Indian independence leaders. In response, the British Brigadier-General R. E. H. Dyer surrounded the rectangular park with his soldiers. The Jallianwala Bagh could only be exited on one side, as the other three sides were enclosed by buildings. Dyer blocked the exit with his troops and ordered them to shoot at the crowd. They continued to fire even as the protestors tried to flee. The troops fired until their ammunition was exhausted.

At least a thousand people were killed and over twelve hundred others were injured. Some perished in stampedes at the narrow gate or by jumping into the solitary well inside the park to escape the shooting. Over one hundred bodies were later pulled out of the well, which is now a protected monument. The horrific scene was depicted in the 1982 Richard Attenborough movie, *Gandhi*. I'm an advocate of non-violent communication, and I found it hard to be there and to see and touch the bullet marks in the walls from the shells fired, aware of the mindless and utterly pointless destruction that had taken place.

Dharamsala

McLeod Ganj in Dharamsala was my rendezvous point with Sylvia. We both wanted to attend a retreat with his holiness, The Dalia Lama. The timing was fortunate, as the chaos, noise, and pollution of the cities I'd been through had depleted my energy level. Just functioning normally in those places took a huge amount of effort. Even though I was apprehensive about the coming conversation with Sylvia, I was happy to be in McLeod Ganj. It's up in the mountains, the air is clean and cool, and the ambience is entirely different from the rest of India. It actually felt more like Tibet than India, and I'd loved it when I visited there in 2008.

I'd no idea how I might prevent the breakup of my relationship with Sylvia. The inspiration I'd hoped for at the Taj Mahal hadn't materialised, and the next few days were emotionally challenging. We were still vaguely an item, but she'd signalled her intentions clearly, and nothing material had changed since our last conversation. Despite the strange atmosphere between us, Sylvia invited me to stay in the room she'd rented, which adjoined the Kirti monastery. It felt so lonely to be in such close physical proximity with her while our hearts were a million miles away from each other. In hindsight, it would have felt better if I'd found a place of my own to stay. I'd chosen not to, because I was so attached to the idea of being with her and hoped that by being around her, showing kindness and interest, that she'd change her mind and drop the idea of leaving me for Graham.

The Namgyal Monastery was a perfect space for the eight hundred people who came to the retreat, including the actor Richard Gere, who'd publicly been a vocal supporter of the Dalai Lama and a free Tibet for years. There was an audible gasp emitted by the audience as he joined the proceedings on the second day. During the retreat, the Dalai Lama talked about a number of themes including world peace, meditation, and serenity. If I'm honest, they were long days sitting on cushions on the floor, and my attention faded in and out constantly. The energy in the room was extraordinary, but I don't remember much about what was said. I was too distracted by the goings on with Sylvia and constantly thinking about what to do. I still had more inner work to do to be at peace under such conditions.

When I'd arrived in Delhi a few weeks earlier, I'd been lost in my thoughts about the future. The lapse in my practice of conscious awareness had continued, and I was on a slippery slope, spiralling downward. I was disconnected from one of my core guiding principles—to be fully present to life and accept each moment as it is, without judgment. I felt it was important to acknowledge this and let it be. We often struggle with trying to change something we don't like because of the guilt or shame we feel in that moment. I decided to practice self-acceptance, allowing myself to be in this period of mental distraction without any self-judgment and to allow it to pass. I trusted myself to recommit to my practice when I was ready.

I left Dharamsala after the retreat, whilst Sylvia stayed on for a few more weeks to continue her studies at the monastic school. Things remained stilted and awkward between us, and I questioned why the Universe had brought us together. I felt low as I left, which was not only down to the rapid disappearance of my joy and energy of being around Sylvia. The three-day retreat with the Dalai Lama had been much less impactful than the Vipassana retreat. I'd been fully present and engaged at that event and spent a number of hours in meditation. This time, there was no space for practice. We were only listening to the teachings. The experience was tiring, and my mind often wandered. I was aware as it happened and didn't address it, rather I let myself remain in my spiral of non-presence I mentioned earlier. Consequently, I wasn't touched deeply and didn't gain any insight of value. I'd been looking forward to this retreat for months, yet I'd allowed myself to be mentally hijacked by events in my personal life and failed to get the best from it. Maybe you can recall an event or situation like this.

Hampi

By the time I made it to Hampi, I'd fallen out of love with India to some extent. I'd had enough of the endless aggravation that came from being a foreign budget traveller in this chaotic, dysfunctional country. On my way there, I'd made an overnight stop in Hyderabad, which was about ten hours away by bus. For the second time, I went to the Taj Mahal. Sadly, it was not the beautiful, awe-inspiring palace that captures the imagination of millions of visitors from around the world but the name of a rather noisy, dirty, and dilapidated budget hotel! A guy who worked there offered to help with my travel logistics for the next part of my journey, and as I felt exhausted from doing it all myself, I gratefully accepted.

"To get to Hampi, you have to take this bus to a nearby town called Hospet and then change on to a different bus there."

The guy sounded like he knew what he was doing. Unusually for me, I chose to trust someone else to arrange things, something I didn't normally do. I authorised him to go and get my ticket for me. The next morning,

LIFE WITHOUT A TIE

as I left for the bus station, he showed me the ticket. It was *not* a ticket to Hospet but a town some twenty five miles away.

"I couldn't get you a ticket to Hospet directly but take this bus instead. You can change en route, all for the same price," he said.

I could smell trouble coming. It didn't sit right, but I decided to go along with the plan. I was too tired to argue with him, so I grabbed the ticket and left. At the bus station, I struggled to find the right bus from the hundreds there. Eventually, someone pointed out the bus I needed, so I jumped on and off we went. About thirty minutes into the journey, the conductor asked to see my ticket. I showed it to him, and he explained that my ticket wasn't valid, and I'd boarded the wrong bus. With frustration and anger building like a slow-boiling kettle, I mindfully and calmly asked where the bus was actually going. It was heading in the right general direction, which was a relief. I bought a new ticket and decided to stay on the bus until it reached its terminus in a small town called Gangavathi. We got there around two the next morning.

The first bus to Hospet arrived at around three-thirty in the morning. By then, I was tired, and hungry, and getting short-tempered. I hoped there might be somewhere to eat. No such luck. We arrived there around four-thirty, and everything was closed. To add insult to injury, the first bus to Hampi left at six thirty, which meant having to wait another two hours. There were a couple of tuk-tuk drivers who offered me a ride to Hampi and asked for ten times more than the bus fare. Frugality was one of the guiding principles I'd chosen to practice, so I declined their offer. I wasn't under any time pressure to get there. I reflected on the offer they'd made and noticed I'd been tempted to say yes, despite the hugely inflated price. I realised that was driven purely by the desire to avoid any further discomfort and aggravation, but there was no guarantee of that. Once I'd seen that, I relaxed and chose to take the bus instead.

This kind of hard-core, budget travel was unlike anything I'd experienced previously in my journey. It was truly character-building stuff. It was also a kind of tipping point for me. After the loneliness I felt during my few days with Sylvia in Dharamsala and my exhaustion from handling the daily challenges wherever I went, I started to think about a return to the relative cleanliness and luxury of Chiang Mai. Hampi would be my last port of call. At the same time, I also realised that life had served me with a great learning opportunity. If I could raise my conscious awareness enough to master my emotions in circumstances like these, I knew I'd be able to handle just about anything life could throw at me. I had the wherewithal to recognise the gift I was being given. I continued to work on my mindfulness practice, which had begun five years earlier.

I eventually reached Hampi just after seven in the morning, to be greeted by the usual mob of around twenty tuk-tuk drivers and guesthouse touts who waved and shouted hysterically, as each one wanted me to go with them. You can probably get a sense of how much energy it took to handle these encounters sanely. If you ever travel independently on a budget in India, no doubt you'll experience something similar for yourself. It took me a lot of getting used to.

Having said that, Hampi was a place in which I was energetically calmed and for that reason alone, I'm glad I made the effort to go there. On a par with Angkor Wat in Cambodia, you'd easily be absorbed for weeks if you were to explore every facet. It's the site of the once-magnificent capital of the Vijayanagar Empire and contains ruins spread over an area of sixteen square miles. All you could see were millions of rocks, whatever direction you looked in. After six years of travelling, one more set of ancient ruins no longer did much for me. The endless hassles I'd dealt with in the previous two months got the better of me, and to some degree I was going through the motions as a traveller, without the deep satisfaction I'd felt in earlier parts of my journey.

Hyderabad

Hyderabad is a modern city that has emerged as a major global centre for the information technology and biopharmaceutical industries. Ordinarily, it would've had no place on my itinerary until my brother Paul got in touch via email a few days earlier. You can imagine my surprise when I discovered he'd been scheduled on a flight to Hyderabad whilst I was in India. He asked me if I was or would be close by and invited me to stay at the crew hotel with him for a couple of days before they turned around and headed back to London. After two months of budget travel, it was an offer I couldn't refuse.

It couldn't have come at a more perfect time. Once again, the Universe tuned into my needs. All I had to do was endure one final ten-hour, overnight bus ride from Hampi. The thought of seeing Paul's friendly face, staying in a five-star hotel, and eating some decent Western food made me salivate. It was a perfect way to restore my energy before having to endure a night or two in Pahar Ganj on my way back Thailand.

Paul arrived at the crew hotel shortly after touchdown at around six in the morning and as luck would have it, I arrived there less than ten minutes later. It was the first time in my journey that the two of us had met outside the UK. He flies to different cities all over the world, and the chances of him being in the same place as me at the same time were pretty slim.

A little bit of luxury went a long way. I ate in the hotel restaurant, slept in the most comfortable of beds, and enjoyed the rare privilege of soft, fluffy pillows and room service, which were things I missed the most from my old life. I now appreciated those things so much more when they came my way. Paul and I did a bit of sightseeing together with a couple of crew members, as there are quite a few interesting places in the city to visit. I enjoyed the quality time I had with him. I'm not sure how it is for you when you see your siblings, but whenever Paul and I get together, it's usually not very long before we're behaving like two kids again.

When it was time to leave, I followed Paul to the airport and boarded a short flight to Delhi. From there, I travelled onwards to Chiang Mai to start work with my first coaching clients and see the year out amongst my community of friends. My two months in India had confirmed what I'd always suspected to be true. Material wealth is not the source of happiness, and you don't need material comfort to be happy. I saw literally millions of people there with very little in material terms, living in poverty, yet their spirits shone. Many of the people I saw and met were full of joy. Of course, there is a segment of Indian society that has acquired great wealth and affluence.

But I saw enough to realise that happiness is a choice. It comes from within. I felt invigorated about that after I'd had a chance to process the trip, and I continued my journey beyond India in the knowledge that my version of living true to myself was coming about. I still had work to do to be fully present and remain in a state of complete awareness, without judgment or attachment. The severity of the conditions and the culture of chaos in India had challenged me to fully embrace my ten guiding principles at times, no question. At the same time, I saw how much I'd changed since my journey began in 2005 and acknowledged my progress with joy and gratitude.

In the Coach Seat Again

I'd completed my training with Coach In A Box in Singapore and was ready to start coaching clients. Fortunately, they'd acquired quite a few while I'd been in India and were keen to hand them to me. My first three executives, who all worked for a global food company, came in November 2011. It was a gentle re-entry into the world of work, as I only needed to be available for three or four hours per month initially. I learned as much as possible from those early interactions with clients and focused on improving the quality of every conversation.

I was excited to be interacting with skilled, professional people in management roles. I loved supporting them in improving their leadership skills, and I was grateful that I was being paid to do it. It was three and a half years since I'd bombed at my first attempt as a facilitator in New Jersey. All of that was water under the bridge now. As I reflected on how I'd changed over the six years since I left England, I realised a huge shift had taken place.

When I was CEO of my own business, my authority and my value came from my technical knowledge, my ability to solve problems, the information I had access to, and the knowledge I'd acquired throughout my career. I was in a totally different role now. My value to clients no longer came from offering solutions. It came from my ability to be fully present, give my full and undivided attention, listen without judgment, and hold a space with kindness and compassion. Sylvia had a beautiful and gentle way of being that was sincere and non-confrontational. I loved that quality in her, and I'd started to emulate it in myself, to great effect. The questions I asked people were like the keys that helped them unlock their own doors. I could see and feel that shift within me, and I loved it. I had no idea that the rest of the world was also waking up and starting to realise that same shift was needed across the board in the way leadership development was being done in business. It was as if my own journey gave me a personal preview of what was to come and an opportunity to pioneer a new way to authentically and powerfully show up, without the ego in the driving seat.

Back in Chiang Mai, my guesthouse room now doubled up as my office, and I ran my coaching sessions from my laptop, using Skype. I'd effectively become a long-term resident and got to know the Thai family who owned it really well. They were kind to me and always gave me first option on my room, so that I could come and go as I pleased. I was grateful to have such flexibility with my accommodation, especially a place that was well-suited for the one-to-one coaching work that I'd started doing.

As 2011 ended, I felt at peace in practically every part of my life, except for my relationship with Sylvia. She'd also returned to Chiang Mai and was exploring her relationship with Graham. I felt somewhat estranged from her and had an unhappy and lonely Christmas and New Year. Although I didn't know it at the time, the question of how it would play out would resolve itself within a few months.

Chapter Sixteen
Metamorphosis: A New Life Begins

"A long time ago, an emperor made an unusual offer to one of his horsemen. He told him that if he were to ride away on his horse and cover as much land as he could, the emperor would give him the area of all the land he'd covered. Sure enough, the horseman quickly set off and rode as fast and as far as possible to capitalise on this offer. For days, he kept on riding and riding, whipping the horse to go as fast as possible. When he was hungry or tired, he didn't stop because he wanted to cover as much land as he could. Eventually, he came to a point when he'd covered a substantial area. He was exhausted and was dying. Then he asked himself, "Why did I push myself so hard to cover such a huge area of land? Now I am dying, and I only need a very small plot to bury myself."

Source: unknown

As 2012 GOT UNDERWAY, I COMMITTED MYSELF TO KEEP MOVING TOWARDS the vision I'd carefully crafted and to integrate part-time work into my nomadic life. My definition of success had changed from when I was in London. Back then, constant growth was the mantra. Setting bigger and bigger financial goals every year and achieving them had been the be all and end all, and you know how that turned out. I'd had six years to reflect on that and re-engineer my life. I felt compelled to construct a life that was an authentic reflection of what was important to me now. Building and living a life true to myself was at the front and centre of my attention. Slowly but surely, it was coming about.

I had a steady trickle of freelance coaching and plenty of discretion over my time, so that my needs—for personal growth, friendship, social interaction, travel, to learn, be of service to others, and personal wellness—would be met. Above all, I wanted to feel wealthy. The kind of wealth I'm talking about comes from having lots of free time, as opposed to lots of money. I'm not saying it's a bad thing to have money, but I felt time was the real source of value. To make work a priority made no sense if it meant that I was entirely committed to things which didn't lighten my heart or yield a sense of fulfilment.

I made a few short trips to Singapore, Shanghai, and Mumbai in the early part of the year to receive training and briefing about new clients. I'd done lots of that type of travelling back in the UK when I'd been a CEO, although now I was more present to the experience moment by moment, and I seemed to meet more interesting people than I used to. Six years as a nomad had taught me how to enjoy every opportunity without the stress and pressure I used to feel. Having a regular mindfulness practice had played a big part in that.

I applied myself diligently to my coaching work to feel satisfied I gave my best to it. During 2012, I slowly increased the number of clients I took on, from three to eighteen. It may sound like a lot, but I was still only working about seven hours per month on average and just over eighty hours in total for the year. My clients were managers in global companies based in Thailand, Singapore, and India. I enjoyed the work immensely and was valuable and skilful at it in equal amounts. It felt good to use my years of business experience, not in a self-aggrandising way, for the benefit of others. The fact that I'd been a CEO myself certainly helped me create solid rapport and trust with them.

It dawned on me that this amazing journey had taught me a great deal about how to live well, which complimented my existing business knowledge. I constantly looked for new ways to blend the two. People I worked with all wanted to become better versions of themselves, just like I'd been doing, and I felt a tremendous sense of kinship. I saw how valuable our conversations were, and it encouraged me to do more. It still felt like early days in my grand experiment, and I didn't want to allocate too much of my time to work. I relied on my guiding principles of presence and wisdom to ensure I maintained the balance well. When a new opportunity appeared, I connected with my intuition and only accepted those which felt absolutely right, both in my heart and to my way of thinking. I was in an economically dynamic region of the world, with plenty of opportunities to learn and grow, as long as I applied myself well.

The feeling of uncertainty around my relationship with Sylvia had

LIFE WITHOUT A TIE

intensified. She and Graham were with each other and whilst I wasn't in the picture, I hadn't completely let go of her. I doubted they would last and was inclined to believe their exploration would ultimately fizzle out. I wasn't absolutely certain though, and I struggled to take decisive action. I was in a state of paralysis. I adored Sylvia and was strongly attached to the idea of being with her. If I walked away prematurely, it would definitely be over. And if I decided to accept the status quo and wait for her to return, I'd have to swallow my pride about being rejected. It implied I wasn't as special to her as she was to me. I was caught between a rock and a hard place. In hindsight, if I knew back then what I know now regarding the nature of these things, I would have gratefully let go and carried on without the tie to her. Alas, I remained in the struggle.

Perhaps the Universe picked up on my hesitancy and uncertainty. To add a bit of spice into the mix, a woman called Ingrid turned up in Chiang Mai around the middle of March at about the same time that Sylvia departed for the summer in Berlin. Ingrid and I sat next to each other at my friend Kate's dinner party and talked all evening. She was single, from Belgium, and in the early stages of her own journey of awakening. She was engaging, light-hearted, flirtatious, and fun, and I definitely got the sense that she liked me, a sense that was discreetly confirmed by Kate the following day.

At that time, I'd committed to consciously practice radical honesty in my communication, so I laid all my cards out for Ingrid. I candidly told her about the unresolved state of limbo I was in with Sylvia. I let Ingrid know that I couldn't get emotionally involved until I'd fully resolved my situation with Sylvia. I've said elsewhere that one of my core values is integrity, especially with matters of the heart. I hate to admit it, but I'd not always lived up to that value during my journey.

Ingrid appreciated my honesty. She suggested we remain friends until such time as I may be available for something more. We didn't explicitly talk about or agree where the line was drawn regarding sex. It was a grey area, which I was happy about. The chemistry between us was powerful, and as Sylvia was miles away in Berlin, it didn't take very long before I gave in to temptation. In the name of lust, I traded my fading heart connection with Sylvia for the temporary pleasure of a physical connection with Ingrid. I gave no thought to the mess it would inevitably cause. Sylvia was with someone else, so I wasn't cheating on her. But I ignored my voice of inner wisdom, as I knew it would clearly lead to suffering. Grey areas are

337

often messy by virtue of them being grey.

Sure enough, things came to a head two weeks later after a long phone call with Sylvia. It hadn't worked out as she'd imagined with Graham, and she wanted to come back to me. She'd hurt me, and I didn't know how to forgive her fully. Regardless, I accepted her request. I agreed to resume our relationship on the same terms as before and stored my hurt away. Next, I found Ingrid and told her I wanted to bring our relatively short-lived liaison to a swift end. She took it pretty badly, which wasn't surprising and was one of the reasons why my wiser self had guided me to avoid starting something serious with her. We agreed to be friends, although we never really were after that.

My choice to reunite with Sylvia wasn't one of my most powerful decisions, and it affected my self-esteem for some time. I'd not embraced my guiding principle of non-attachment and had fallen into another cycle of craving. Not only had I failed to recognise this cycle around Sylvia, I'd suppressed my hurt and unknowingly sowed the seeds of desire for revenge, which I'll come back to later.

Second Time Around

Two and a half years had passed since I completed the marathon in New York. I'd felt satisfied on every level, with only one exception; I'd failed to finish in less than four hours. That goal was still alive in me. I'd run the Chiang Mai half-marathon on Christmas Day 2011 to see if I might mount a second attempt at the full marathon in 2012. I trained hard almost every day for five weeks to get myself ready, knowing that if I did the half-marathon in under two hours, I had a realistic chance of achieving my ultimate goal in the next marathon.

It went extremely well, and I managed to finish in 1:57:28, which was my best ever time for a half-marathon. That pace indicated a full marathon time of around four hours and five minutes. It felt like great news. If I trained well over the next four months, I was reasonably confident of breaking the four-hour barrier. Subsequently, I'd landed a place in the Phuket Marathon in June 2012.

Unfortunately, my training for the race didn't go at all well. I felt serious fatigue in my legs during many of my long runs, which undermined my confidence. The harder I pushed myself, the more problems I had. Running stopped being enjoyable and started to feel like a big, heavy task. I researched my condition and discovered I was suffering from overtraining. It's a major problem for some long-distance runners. It was a clear signal that it was time for a rethink. Running marathons is challenging, even when you love it. You have to set aside five or six days every week to train and maintain your attention and discipline around your diet.

I took a break from all training for about six weeks and let my body fully recover. The consequence was that I'd lowered my chances of success in the race, but it was the best option. Besides, Phuket is a beautiful place to visit, and I'd still have a long weekend in a great hotel near the beach, so I wasn't too unhappy about it. About five thousand people ran, which made it the largest international race in Thailand. The organisers threw a pasta party the night before, as many of us were carb-loading to make sure we'd topped up our energy reserves.

The race got underway at four thirty in the morning. I ran according to plan for the first three or four miles without any problems and thought I'd worried unnecessarily. But I started to struggle to maintain my pace after that. By the time I reached the halfway point, I'd run for just over two hours and was about ten minutes behind schedule. That may not sound like a lot, but it is. It means you have to run each mile in the second half at least one minute faster than you've trained for, when you're already feeling knackered! After fifteen miles, my legs were seriously fatigued, and I had three painful blisters on my feet. I took a small walking break, and then a couple more, which is fatal. I ended the race exhausted, in a time of five hours and twenty-two minutes. It was over an hour slower than I'd run in New York in 2009. In the context of my sub four-hour goal, I'd failed spectacularly, and I felt completely dejected. I limped back to Chiang Mai to review what happened, make changes to my training regime, and to prepare for the next attempt.

The End of the Blog

Buddhists teach us that nothing in life is permanent. By mid 2012, I'd experimented with life without a tie for six and a half years. I'd written a blog throughout, which was originally called *The Daily Lama* and later, *The Daily Explorer*. It had been one of the ways I'd honoured my guiding principle of contribution. I felt it was important to share what I'd experienced and to use my writing to enhance the lives of others. Since the first edition in 2007, I'd created new editions on a regular basis. Annie and

I, along with my fictitious team of editors and writers, published a total of sixty-eight posts, which were viewed over 126,000 times.

I loved to receive the adoration of a few die-hard readers, including my mum who was my number one fan. Yet I'd noticed that my enthusiasm and motivation for writing the blog had started to wane. Every post took masses of effort, and I had to admit that I'd got bored of the format. Something felt wrong. I didn't understand those feelings at first and criticised myself for a temporary loss of interest that I believed would pass. I also stopped taking pictures. I'd got caught in a viscous circle in which I believed I needed to capture interesting pictures, so I could write stories that would please my readers. That drove my decisions about where to go, rather than me listening to a deeper part of myself about what direction I wanted to take, whether there was a newsworthy story for my readership or not. I didn't want to continue with that cycle any longer.

In his extremely popular Psychology and the Good Life course at Yale University, Dr Laurie Santos explores the science behind decision-making and what comprises a fulfilling life. One of the questions he asks students to consider is this:

"Given what we know about the relationship between nostalgia and happiness, what's the optimal number of pictures to take on vacation?"

He posits that photographs are kind of a mixed bag. On the one hand, they help us access our fondest moments and remember things better. But they often take us out of the moment. One thing we need for the formation of new memories is to pay attention. His advice? If pictures help you stay present, if they cause you to attend to a scene and notice more things, then great. That'll give you a memento that will help you remember after the fact. But if taking pictures means that you're worried about how your hair looks or you're forcing other people out of the moment to take a picture, then that might not be such a good idea. I stopped looking for photo opportunities when I read this.

My perspective on my journey had shifted. At the start, my attention had been directed to things in the external world. Now, I was more interested in what went on with me internally. Two of the drivers of this change had been the development of my ongoing mindfulness practice and my return to part-time work as a freelance executive coach. Coincidentally, one or two of my blog readers also said they'd found my recent posts less interesting, as I'd not really gone anywhere.

LIFE WITHOUT A TIE

It was time to shake things up and make changes. I wasn't sure if there was a future for *The Daily Explorer*, but it was obvious it was time to quit doing it at the moment. I took a few months to contemplate that decision and published my final edition in June 2012, entitled *The End of The Road*. Here is an excerpt from it:

"When I began this great nomadic experiment some six and a half years ago, I wanted to prove it was possible to live in anonymity, without possessions or status, without attachment to goals, without a fixed identity or routine and be as happy (or happier) as I was when I lived a 'conventional' life in England. I thought travelling would support me to find that path, and it really has. My search for a 'new way' of living is over. The temporary has become permanent. The unknown has become knowable. I'm comfortable without having fixed goals and plans. I prefer living in each moment and being present to opportunities. My security is coming from within me and is not dependent on external events, circumstances, or relationships. There is no going back to the conventional life I knew before.

"After six and half years of modest living, with one bag of clothes and a laptop, I know deeply within myself that material wealth is not a source of true happiness. I no longer feel the desire or need to be constantly travelling and am considering what might be the best way to share the experiences I've had, and the knowledge and insight that's come from them. I no longer think of myself as a traveller per se, and my interests are taking me in a slightly different direction. I want to continue to educate myself about life and humanity. I want to know and understand my inner world, so I'll be more able to support and help others as a coach and mentor. *The Daily Explorer* was a vehicle to share my travel experiences, and it's no longer needed from my perspective.

"Exploring is not confined to geographical places. I'm just as curious about language, agriculture, history, music, the arts, my physical well-being, the financial world, the nature of power, tyranny, community, humanity, and spirituality. These are things that fascinate me. Curiosity is such a grossly underrated quality. I meet very few people who are genuinely curious about life, and it's always a wonderful, engaging experience when I find someone who is. In future, I intend to share more with you about these things as I learn more about them myself and discover information that may be of interest."

It was a huge relief to let the blog go. To some extent, it defined my identity as a traveller, and I'd begun to feel typecast as that character in *The Daily Explorer*. Yes, it was a different character from my previous life or my character, George Pigden, in *Out of Order*, but it was a character, nonetheless. He had to be killed off. His death meant there was no need for the team of fictitious writers either. They went too. Once again, I was free to be fully in the moment without any agenda and enjoy the experience. I'd re-established my commitment to my guiding principle of presence and that way of being. I didn't realise it at the time, but that decision created loads of valuable space for me to begin working on the book you're reading now. Isn't it amazing how much creativity we can unleash when we let go of something that no longer serves our growth? Can you think of a time when you've done this? What outcomes resulted from your decision? Can you think of something you could let go which would provide the space for you to do something new?

Summer in Europe

Chiang Mai felt more like home than any other place. I loved the atmosphere of that little city and had many good friends there. I enjoyed being a member of the CIAB team, with my colleagues spread all over the region. Even though my work was mainly virtual, I belonged to a family of sorts. One of my guiding principles for this journey was connection and being part of the CIAB tribe met my need for that. It allowed me to use my business knowledge and experience in Asia, and I felt extremely lucky to be part of the team. My colleagues supported me to improve my coaching and training skills too.

The great thing about working virtually was that I could be anywhere, time zones permitting. So I headed for Berlin once again to be with Sylvia and to visit family and friends in the UK, Switzerland, and Spain. Sylvia kept a demanding work schedule, and I wanted her to have a break, so I organised a week-long trip to Vienna. Austria became the twenty-third new country I'd visited since my epic journey began.

On the surface, everything in my relationship with Sylvia seemed fine. But deep down, I wasn't okay and still carried the hurt from when she'd dumped me for Graham. Despite all of the Buddhist teachings I'd received and my ongoing mindfulness practice, I was unable to let it go. Our relationship, which had seemed so perfect when it began, now felt contaminated, like food that has gone off. Without knowing how to transform it, I carried on with daily life in Berlin as it was and hoped that somehow it would right itself. The coaching work I did provided a welcome distraction from the dull ache of discontent I felt inside me.

Then something unexpected happened. During September, I visited my family in London and connected with an Italian woman. We had a one-night stand. We'd met on a dating site a few years earlier, around the time I'd started seeing Annie. I'd been abroad most of the time since then and nothing came of it, although we'd stayed in touch. She was single again, and I decided to play out an unrequited love scene of my own, as Sylvia had done to me. In my case, it definitely wasn't about love. Despite all of the personal work I'd done through being mindful and the Hoffman process, I'd relapsed into an old, harmful pattern to even the score with Sylvia.

The following day, I reflected on what I'd done. I had a chance for an immature, hurtful moment of payback, and I grabbed it with both hands. I feel ashamed to admit it, and I definitely should have known better, especially as I often explore how to get our basic human needs met in my coaching work with clients. I'd worked on myself for over a decade and lived by my ten guiding principles, yet I still did something driven solely by ego and unexamined internal conflict. I didn't like it, but I'm human, and it was a powerful reminder of that.

We all have basic human needs beyond those for food, water, and shelter. We need them to be met if we're going to function in a healthy way. In her book, *Extraordinary*, leadership coach Elke Edwards refers to these needs as our five driving forces. They are certainty, variety, belonging, recognition, and service.

We may get a job so that we have *certainty* around having food to eat and a roof over our heads. We try different things at the weekend to experience *variety* in our lives. We build families and friendships to give us a sense of *belonging*. We strive to improve ourselves to gain *recognition* from others. We commit to acts of *service*, in which we give unconditionally with no expectation of reward to people in our community, so that we can feel part of something bigger than ourselves. You may recall a time when one of these driving forces was at the forefront, while the rest were perhaps less important, as they change with time. If we are aware and skilful, we get our needs met in a positive way and set ourselves up for success. If we're not aware, we tend to resort to negative strategies and behaviours and hope these will bring the result we want.

With Sylvia, my need for recognition hadn't been met. I wasn't consciously aware of that at the time and fell into the trap of behaving unskilfully, which ultimately contributed to my downfall a few months later. As George Pransky says in *The Relationship Handbook: A Simple Guide to Satisfying Relationships*, "Self-inflicted emotional pain, resentments, and grudges are just bad habits that make things worse by adding more insecurity to a situation. Forgiving and forgetting are the answer." I know that now and looking back, I wished I'd known it then. Obviously, Sylvia had no knowledge of my one-night stand, but it didn't matter. I became more distanced, and it solidified my position as her suffering victim.

In my ignorance, I repeated this pattern and had three further encounters with different women in the months that followed. My actions lit the fuse that inevitably brought about an explosive end to our relationship. One of the women I hooked up with knew Sylvia. I'd given her the false impression that my relationship with Sylvia had ended. When she found out I'd lied to her, she told Sylvia what had happened. The end for Sylvia and me came in February 2013, when we both returned to Chiang Mai after a difficult and unhappy week in Bali. Once again, I'd created a situation where I couldn't have been further from the person I'd been trying to be. I loved her, yet I'd set that aside, held a grudge, and taken momentary pleasure in exacting revenge, when she'd actually been forthright and honest with me about her conflicting feelings for me and Graham.

I wasn't fully living according to my guiding principles, and it was a massive step backwards. On one hand, I'd created a vision of the man I wanted to be at my very best in a loving relationship. On the other hand, I showed up and behaved in a way that ultimately contradicted and undermined that vision. It felt horrid to be a cause of pain for Sylvia, and I was racked with guilt and shame. With that insight, I renewed my commitment to align with my vision of becoming the best version of myself I could imagine. I say this not because I'm proud of it, but as an example of how hard it can be to stay on the path you've set yourself. Life has a way of humbling you sometimes and even after years of working on myself, I'd reverted to a destructive pattern. Perhaps you can remember a time when you were in a scenario with complex emotional dynamics, and you knew you weren't being true to the person you wanted to be.

Earlier, I talked about people coming into your life for a reason, a season, or a lifetime. When I reflect on the season that Sylvia was in my life, I particularly remember her soft and gentle way of being with me and everyone I saw her with. She was always present, and calm, and listened deeply when we talked. I observed how she showed up, and I was in awe of the effect it had on me. I'm thankful the Universe brought us together for that season. I've emulated and incorporated her kind, gentle, and present way of being into my coaching work. I can only hope that I left her with something positive in her life as well, even after the pain I caused her and the way I treated her. We still connect regularly and have healed from these past events, like I'd managed to do in my relationship with my ex-wife, Charlotte.

The Suited Monk

During my first trip to Shanghai, I attended a four-day advanced coaching masterclass with a company called Progress U in my search for freelance coaching work. I met and became friends with a cheerful and inspiring young Belgian guy called Raf Adams. He was writing a book about spirituality called *The Suited Monk*, and I'd had a strong hunch that our paths would cross again. The draft of his book was now complete, and I'd read it. I thought it was outstanding, and his ideas resonated strongly with me.

According to Raf, we live in a society in which a multiplicity of external experiences, pressures, stresses, choices, and distractions constantly pull us away from our inner wisdom, our intuition. Our persona, built from our limited notion of time and resources is the suit we wear as we try to negotiate the fast-paced world around us. We fail to realise that this notion has hijacked our ability to listen to our inner self, our monk, and thus can't find lasting peace and happiness. Raf had brought together these two worlds. The inner world of happiness, love, purpose, and meaning and the external world of success and achievement. *The Suited Monk* was a perfect mirror for the journey I'd been on and was still creating with every step.

Raf spoke English perfectly well, yet some parts of his book were laboured and unclear, which was inevitable as it wasn't written in his native language. I know from personal experience how difficult it is to write a book, even when it *is* in your native language! It was way more challenging to attempt it in a second or third. Raf had done exactly that, and the power of his ideas still leapt off the page. When he asked me for feedback, I kindly shared my observations about his language construction and how I thought it could be improved.

I often wondered if the Universe was behind the two of us meeting. He needed help from someone who had to be a native English speaker. They also had to have business leadership experience, understand the process by which individuals learn, grow, and transform, and be able to identify with and appreciate the models which were the foundation of his teaching. I was probably the only person alive in his vicinity who ticked all those boxes. Working with him to rewrite some of the chapters also gave me a great opportunity to practice and improve my own writing skills.

In that sense, it was absolute synchronicity. A perfect opportunity for both of us to collaborate and support each other. Two total strangers, from different parts of the world, twenty-five years apart in age, and both with stories to share had magically found and recognised each other without any effort or understanding as to why. As I reflected on the miraculous nature of that, it struck me that meeting Raf was the *real* reason I'd gone to the masterclass with Progress U in Shanghai and not the coaching work, which never materialised.

Raf came to Chiang Mai, and I blocked out two weeks in my calendar. We planned a writing schedule and got down to it. Each day, we had breakfast together and started writing. We'd review what we'd done and then move on to the next chapter, stopping for breaks here and there. Most evenings, we'd relax and go out to meet people in my community of friends, as they were the kind of people who'd benefit most from Raf's book. In two weeks, we'd rewritten the sections we'd identified and the manuscript linguistically did justice to his teaching. It was an exciting, energising, and fun process and was the first time I'd collaborated with someone in the creation of a book. It confirmed that if and when I sat down to start my own, I had the basic skills and ability to produce a well-written, enjoyable, and informative read. The seeds I'd planted on my fiftieth birthday on the beach in Cherating with Christine were definitely being watered.

The Blog Returns

Raf left Chiang Mai just before Christmas with his freshly rewritten manuscript in hand. With him and Sylvia gone, the Christmas and New Year period felt pretty flat, and I was miserable for most of it. To top it all, Mo Tejani, one of the writers at the five-day workshop with me in January the previous year, had died from an unexpected heart attack on New Year's Eve. Mo was a published author and a popular figure in the Chiang Mai community. His light had shone brightly, and he had been the life and soul of the party. His sudden passing was a huge shock, and I reflected deeply on the fact that none of us know when our time is up. It was a signal from the Universe that I should make a start on my book as soon as possible.

Collaborating with Raf on *The Suited Monk* had injected excitement into my work with people in the business world. Through his book, I saw a way to integrate the spiritual experiences I'd had in my journey with my business leadership knowledge. The vision for that inspired me. I hired a couple of people in Chiang Mai to design a new website, which described my journey so far and the kind of coaching support I could offer. That also gave me a reason, and a home for the relaunch of *The Daily Explorer* blog.

This time around, the blog would be centred around the exploration of our inner world, rather than the external world, as its previous incarnation had been. To bring more truth and authenticity to my writing, I decided to write in the first person and dropped the irreverent style of the original blog. This enabled me to talk about topics related to my newly emerging coaching work, as well as my ongoing personal journey of learning. It was a major reconfiguration of my thinking and identity and felt like the different parts of me were being re-assembled in a new way.

In Shanghai, Raf's book was published, and people were buying it. The Chinese economy was growing rapidly and interest in effective leadership methods was at an all-time high too. This was reflected in the fact that in 2012, the number of wealthy Chinese entrepreneurs (3.3 million) had overtaken those in Europe (3.1 million) for the first time. The foreword of Raf's book was written by Mike Thompson of the China Europe

International Business School (CEIBS), who was a huge advocate of Raf's work. Mike was a visionary who ran the MBA programme at CEIBS and wanted all of his students to gain exposure to these ideas, so they would know early on in their careers that financial success alone would not guarantee their happiness.

In April 2013, I returned to Shanghai to join Raf, Mike, and two other potential facilitators who'd flown in from Taiwan and Australia to learn Raf's approach to using the life-changing concepts within the book. It was a pleasure to work with Raf and be part of the team he was building. He asked us if we were interested in, and capable of delivering Suited Monk workshops in Asia. I definitely was and saw a strong alignment between my own path and Raf's vision for the world. I also had plenty of spare capacity as my coaching workload with CIAB was relatively small. I felt excited and inspired about the potential impact that the Suited Monk workshops could have, assuming the marketing activities in hand would generate opportunities to work with groups of people in China and the rest of Asia.

A Lucky Escape

Working virtually, there was no need to rush back to Chiang Mai after Raf's meeting. He kindly offered me the use of his spare room, and I decided to stay a few more weeks in Shanghai. Raf knew I was single and wanted to introduce me to someone he thought I'd like and get on well with. He arranged for the three of us to meet one afternoon at her apartment. Little did I know that it was going to be the start of a nightmare that I'd be relieved and happy to walk away from about two months later. Her name was Nancy, and she was French-Canadian.

She'd lived in Shanghai for about six years and was settled there. Home was a twenty-second floor apartment in the middle of the city, and the views were spectacular. She spoke fluent Mandarin, had fully embraced the life there, and had become integrated into the culture. She had the presence of a confident, successful person. She was a highly accomplished athlete, having competed internationally in kayaking for over ten years, and had won medals in some of the toughest races in the world. That was of particular interest to me. She knew about peak performance, and I hoped she'd be able to help me achieve my dream of running a marathon in under four hours. She was also an artist and drew on her creativity, as well as her winner's mindset, to coach people in the corporate world. It seemed like we had a lot in common.

During our first conversation, Nancy asked me a few deeply penetrating questions about my life and listened attentively to the answers I gave her. She heard, understood, and admired the nature of the life without a tie journey I'd been on. When she talked to me, I felt like the most important person in the room and was captivated. I know what it's like to create that space for clients, yet I'd rarely experienced it being created for me. This was different. Nancy was present, charming, smart, attractive, fit, engaging, and single. What's not to like?

After our introduction, Nancy offered me a free creative coaching session to help me map out the contents and theme for this book. She knew that I'd made a commitment to myself around it and had struggled to get started. One of the reasons was that I hadn't worked out the key messages, the arc of the storyline, or what should be in each chapter of the book. I was amazed how good she was at helping me clarify these. After three hours, I'd covered two sheets of flip chart paper with loads of dates, events, boxes, and lines. It was all I needed to see my story emerge for the first time in written form. It was a huge revelation. It released me from my inertia and gave me the energy to push forward and start getting words on paper.

That session was so powerful, it got me hooked on her. She met most of the criteria on my list for a partner, and I couldn't see any downside if we got together. She had tons of energy, enough to work in the corporate world, serve on several committees, run creative painting workshops, *and* raise a child. In her late thirties, she'd desperately wanted a child for some time. With no partner in sight, she'd decided to adopt. I'm not entirely sure how adoption works in China but to cut a long story short, she was temporarily fostering a two-and-a-half-year-old Chinese girl called Huan, while at the same time applying to the authorities to adopt her permanently.

Over the next month, we met several times and got to know each other. We went walking, and Nancy would bring Huan in the pushchair. I'd sometimes take over from her when she nipped into a shop to get something, and I'd practice two of my guiding principles, by being fully present to Huan and connecting with her. She was adorable and although I found it challenging, I loved being in the presence of her young, unconditional energy. Nancy saw that I enjoyed being with Huan. One evening, we were having dinner in her apartment when she gave me an invitation I wasn't expecting.

"I know we've not known each other very long, and we seem to get on pretty well. We've got a lot in common and I'm wondering how you'd feel about staying here, moving in with me, and raising Huan together?"

I was shocked and surprised by what Nancy said, whilst at the same time honoured to be asked and relieved to hear it. After nearly eight years of being a nomad, my mind was plagued with thoughts about finding a life partner and creating a home. I was tired of moving around so much. My vision for these things had become clear when I'd done the Hoffman process, yet I'd made relatively little progress in some areas. Was Nancy the person I'd been waiting for? It was impossible to know, and I left her apartment that evening with a lot to think about. If I accepted her invitation, my life was going to change irrevocably and look totally different from the one I was living. Raising a child meant taking joint financial responsibility and that probably required a return to the world of full-time business for a while.

When I weighed it up, it seemed like a high price to pay for my potential happiness. Yet there was something compelling about the spontaneity of her offer. I wanted to believe that the Universe had sent Nancy to me, with the guidance that I follow the path being signposted. Of course, it was a highly risky choice after only four or five weeks of knowing her. We hadn't even had sex or slept together.

As strange as it may sound, I accepted her invitation. She was happy, and we talked through what we needed to do next for it to become a reality. China isn't an easy country to reside in for foreigners, as they have strict rules about who is allowed to be in the country at any given moment. I needed a long-stay visa and the only way to get one was to leave the country and apply in person at a Chinese consulate. The nearest one was in Sydney.

I hastily booked a flight. My friends Matt and Elizabeth agreed to let me to stay with them whilst I went through the process of obtaining my visa. They were as surprised as I was about Nancy and thrilled that I finally had an opportunity to build a life that would move me closer to my vision of happiness. Looking back, I remember a disturbing Skype call with Nancy in Sydney after just five days away from her. I noticed what seemed like a huge shift in her mood towards me and not in a good way. One of the things she said to me was (with the risk of sharing too much information), "Don't come back here without shaving the hair off your balls."

She meant it. It struck me as odd, given that we weren't in a physical relationship yet. To keep the peace, I agreed and added it to my list of new experiences to be undertaken. That conversation raised serious doubts as to whether I was doing the right thing. But I dismissed those thoughts. I'd made a commitment and for some reason, I let it pass. Perhaps I'd failed to embrace my guiding principle of non-attachment once again. One thing was certain, I didn't listen to my intuitive wisdom. I blamed that on the pressure that came from being consumed with the need to generate work in Shanghai. The cost of living there was sky high compared to what I'd been used to in Chiang Mai. To pay rent and raise a child, I needed the equivalent of a full-time income. It was time to get creative.

I reached out to Progress U. They knew enough about me to know I could add value to their clients. I asked if they could find me some immediate work opportunities, and they responded brilliantly. Within a couple of weeks, I had a contract to work on a project for several months with one of their biggest clients. I took the ease and speed with which this happened as a confirmation signal from the Universe that I was doing the right thing.

After a couple of weeks in Sydney, my visa was ready and I departed for Shanghai with my passport, work contract, and newly shaved balls, as well as some cash for Nancy. I was ready to start a new life with her and Huan. I couldn't wait to return, knowing that Nancy would be thrilled about the shared future we were about to walk into.

I couldn't have been more wrong about that. When I reached the twenty-second floor of Nancy's apartment building and knocked on the door, there was no warm welcome, no words of elation, no smiley greeting, no hugs and kisses, nothing.

"I'm in the middle of my work. Drop your things over there. We'll talk later," she said before she turned around and went back to her office.

The cold abruptness of her tone, as well as the emotionless expression on her face, startled me. For a moment, I wondered if I was in the right apartment. Perhaps this was a dream, and I'd wake up. It wasn't; I felt anxious and uncomfortable, just like I had during that Skype call with Nancy when I was in Sydney.

"Did you bring the money with you?" she asked when we finally sat down to talk a few hours later.

It was strange there was no acknowledgement of what had happened earlier when I arrived. "Yes, I did. Let me get it for you." I took the £2,000 from my bag and offered it to Nancy. I swear I've never seen anyone in my entire life grab something out of my hand as fast as she did.

"Thanks," she said and immediately went into her office and closed the door.

My anxiety ratcheted up significantly, and I began to cry, wondering what on Earth was going on. It was as if she'd had her brain exchanged while I was away. The shift in her personality was like comparing chalk with cheese. Gone was the smiling, engaging, charming, and attractive woman I'd hung out with for a month. She'd been replaced by her evil twin sister, who was harsh, unkind, and self-centred. To cap it all off, she came out and told me I had to sleep on the couch, making me wonder why I'd shaved and was currently enduring an inordinate amount of uncomfortable itching.

This pattern of behaviour carried on for another five days. Whenever I attempted to start a conversation about how I felt in her presence and ask for her help with it, she dismissed me. I started to think I was imagining it all and that everything was normal. Being around her was intense and deeply disturbing. I lost my capacity for giving energy and attention to Huan. It was all I could do to survive what felt like slow torture. Occasionally, for a few minutes, Nancy's lovely former self appeared, and I'd think that things between us could improve. But those moments came and went quickly and most of the time, she appeared to have zero empathy or ability to hear what I thought or felt. I pulled out everything I'd learned about people to find a way through this nightmare but to no avail. I was slowly sliding down a greasy slope towards unhappiness.

After a week, I felt like I was heading towards some kind of mental breakdown. I forgot to apply my guiding principle of self-acceptance and constantly berated myself for having been dumb enough to accept living with someone I hardly knew. I wasn't smart enough to change my predicament, despite my knowledge and experience. I discreetly reached out to people I trusted, like Charlotte, and asked for advice and guidance. That helped me to see things more objectively and created a bit of space to think about what I could do.

Kenny Toh, who was one of my colleagues from CIAB, was working in Shanghai while this was going on. I'd worked with Kenny and confided in him about the Jekyll and Hyde nature of Nancy's behaviour. I invited him around to the apartment at a time when I knew she'd be home, so he could see for himself what I'd been dealing with and assure me I wasn't imagining things. No such luck. Throughout Kenny's visit, Nancy behaved like a snake charmer. She was erudite, soft, gentle, engaging, and curious, as she had been when Raf introduced me. He failed to see that my story had any truth in it. That sent me into a spiral of self-doubt in which I chastised myself further.

To add petrol to the flames, it was one of the busiest work periods I'd had so far, with three online coaching sessions per day at home. With the tense atmosphere, it was incredibly hard to show up in those calls as my best self. I'm amazed that I somehow managed to compartmentalise what I felt and be fully present to each person during those conversations. It's incredible how resilient we can be at times like these. Maybe you can recall such a time when you experienced feeling anxious or chaotic in one part of your life but you managed to stay present and calm in other necessary situations like work. What toll did it take on your energy and well-being?

After Kenny's visit, every single minute in that apartment felt like a bad dream, and I decided to leave. Despite numerous attempts to collaborate with Nancy and find a way through this, I failed to achieve a satisfactory outcome. It was time to go, for my own mental health. I let Nancy know what I was doing, and she shrugged her shoulders in a gesture of indifference, whilst she attempted to squeeze more money from me. After everything I'd seen, it was hardly a surprise. During my final evening, I let Nancy know the impact of her behaviour on me, to no avail.

"I can honestly say, and it breaks my heart to do it, that you are the only person I've ever met who I wouldn't want to give a single penny to or reach out to if you were in trouble."

"Whatever," she said coldly.

This was a huge contrast with the honour, kindness, and generosity I'd experienced when I got divorced from Charlotte, and we'd settled our affairs in harmony. Next, I faced the embarrassment of updating my colleagues at Progress U about this torrid situation and admitted to them I'd made one of the biggest mistakes of my entire journey, possibly even my life.

Since I'd given my word that I'd be available to work on a contract for the next six months with them, I'd made a contingency plan to stay in a hotel for the entire period at my own expense to fulfil my obligation, which they appreciated. They showed a huge amount of compassion and understanding towards me around what had happened. Luckily, it wasn't a problem for them to replace me with someone else on their team, which came as a huge relief.

Twelve days after my arrival from Sydney, I left the apartment, jumped in a taxi, and headed for the airport and a return to Chiang Mai. Can you believe that Nancy came down to the lobby with Huan to walk me to the taxi?

"It's been lovely having you here," she said. "Know that you are welcome to stay here anytime you're in town."

It was baffling and it underlined the surreal and unbelievable experience I'd been existing in. Once I was back in Chiang Mai, I caught up with my friend Peter, who listened to the story I've just shared with you.

"She's a narcissist," he said. "It's an open and shut case. Both my parents were narcissists, and I'd be able to spot one a mile away. You've done the right thing by walking away."

In the eight years since my life without a tie journey began, in fact, in my entire life, this was my first direct encounter with a person who had diagnosable narcissism. It was the first time I'd heard the term, and his comments brought some much-needed relief. I had no idea that such people existed. He gave me a book to read, which explained narcissism in more depth and contained a checklist of around twenty behaviours that narcissists exhibit. Nancy matched virtually every single one on the list. The penny dropped, and I suddenly felt the weight of anxiety lift off my shoulders. I hadn't imagined the things I'd experienced. It all made sense in light of the new data Peter had given me. It was a tough lesson to learn but at the same time, I was grateful for the learning that life presented to me during that bizarre time.

Coming back to the notion that we meet people in life for a reason, season, or lifetime, it was crystal clear that I'd met Nancy for one specific reason. She'd enabled me to glimpse what my unwritten book might look like, and it had sparked me into action. I now had the architectural blueprint for the construction of *Life Without a Tie*. It was a small step in the process and a huge leap forward in making it happen. Yes, it was one of the most unpleasant experiences I'd ever had, but sometimes the best gifts come wrapped in shitty paper.

I thought a lot about what happened over the next few weeks. I'd been looking for love and complete acceptance for a long time. Finding it had become an addiction, which drove me to enter into, and subsequently leave, many relationships. I was exhausted from the cycle. Somehow, I'd managed to attract some women who had either been badly treated or who were incapable of participating in an honest, open, and trustworthy way. Yes, I'd made my share of mistakes too, but I was firmly committed to learning and growing and had sufficient awareness to see where and when I lost my way. I'd still questioned my self-worth, until now. That episode with Nancy inspired me to make a change, and I decided to consciously value myself way more highly going forward. Instead of waiting for the love, acceptance, and recognition from someone else and then valuing myself, I reversed it to break the pattern. It served me better to believe that my self-worth isn't up for grabs and that I deserve a partner whose behaviour honours my values.

Teaming up with Nancy had offered the potential to create a home, which was definitely a part of my vision. Afterwards, I realised I hadn't defined my terms around it specifically enough. In my hasty attempt to put that tie back in place, I gave up too much independence and power, and too quickly. It had actually been a great deal for Nancy and a pretty crappy deal for me. Such big decisions are high risk, and identifying and testing my assumptions was something I wasn't doing well. Even though I'm a romantic at heart, snap decisions like that one didn't serve me in the long run and were out of alignment with my values.

I added it to my list of ongoing improvements to be worked on. It's good to remind ourselves sometimes that we never stop growing, and it serves us well to reflect on who we are in any given moment. I've come to think of it as a constant state of motion, which requires careful, considered action rather than passivity. Perhaps you've hit or are approaching a point in your life where you can see a need to reflect on areas where you have the potential to grow.

In Chiang Mai, life returned to simple, uncomplicated normality for a while. I continued to look after my small and growing portfolio of coaching clients. In 2012, I'd worked an average of seven hours per month. In 2013, that had increased to around seventeen hours per month. I also doubled down on my commitment to break the sub four-hour barrier and applied for a place in the 2014 London Marathon. My application was successful, which gave me a solid platform from which to attempt my goal for the third time in a unique and unforgettable setting. I started disciplined training in October 2013. That Christmas, I set a new personal best time in the Chiang Mai half-marathon, indicating that I had an excellent chance of breaking the four-hour barrier in London. I'll let you know what happened in chapter seventeen.

The Power of Hugs

In some ways, 2013 had been an awful year. The ending of my relationship with Sylvia and the realisation that I hadn't lived by my guiding principles fully had tainted it. The tortuous time in Shanghai added to my negative assessment. I wanted to bring the year to a close in a way that felt wholesome and fulfilling. I'd seen a video of a girl in Paris who'd stood in the street and offered strangers a free hug, and it was incredible the joy it brought the many people who'd accepted.

The original idea is attributed to a guy called Juan Mann in Sydney, who started the movement in 2006. That French girl's video had been viewed millions of times, which suggested many people resonated with the spirit of it. I had a conversation with Caroline and Johan, a couple of running friends, and the three of us agreed to stage the first-ever free hugs event in Chiang Mai on Christmas Day. We chose that day as there were tons of travellers there, away from family and friends back home. It gave me a golden opportunity to practice my guiding principle of contribution and offer some loving kindness to all of them.

Caroline, Johan, and I had the willing support of a few friends in our Chiang Mai community. We stood in the plaza at Tha Pae Gate in the city centre, held up our photocopied "Free Hugs" sign, and waited eagerly to see what would happen. I felt slightly nervous about getting into several intimate clinches with complete strangers, so I took a few deep breaths to calm myself down. After a few minutes, my initial apprehension about getting up close and personal with people I didn't know had gone. They were happy about it and enjoyed receiving their hug, despite them not knowing anything about me. Most people are basically open and trusting of others. Of course, there were one or two cynics who asked, "What's this in aid of?" or "Which organisation is behind this?" Once I'd reassured them the event was totally makeshift and spontaneous with absolutely no agenda at all, some were happy to be a recipient. One or two joined our group and started dispensing hugs to others.

What I experienced surprised me and reminded me of a few valuable truths. First, we all want to connect with people. There's no substitute for it. If you want to feel a powerful sense of aliveness, unconditional love, belonging to the human race, and a multitude of positive thoughts, then all you have to do is hug someone unfamiliar and really mean it. During that afternoon, we must have collectively hugged in excess of a thousand people. However, there was one particular person who really touched my heart, and that was Luciano Pozzi.

In Modena, Italy, he'd hit hard times and now he lived rough in Chiang Mai. He couldn't walk properly and rode a tricycle for better mobility. When I showed up, he asked me what I was doing. It was difficult to explain as his English wasn't so good, so I stopped talking, reached out my arms, and gave him the biggest, most loving hug I could. For me, it was an early opportunity to practice as we set up. For him, it was literally life-changing. He hadn't been hugged by anyone for about ten years, which brought tears to my eyes. I saw the power of unconditional love in action, right there. His physiology completely altered before my eyes. He became alive, energised, and beamed with a huge childlike smile.

For the rest of the day, there was no stopping Luciano, who hugged everyone in sight—even the Thai traffic policemen. He discarded his tricycle for a while so he could fully engage with people. That day, he became a man with a purpose and a new connection to life. I was curious about why a simple hug is so enriching to our soul. According to scientists, the average human hug lasts three seconds. Dr Emese Nagy, who led a study at Dundee University's School of Psychology, stated, "It's obviously difficult to measure because hugging is such an intimate experience, and different for each person. However, what we have is very broad research showing that we experience the world in these three-second time frames."

Just imagine; in three seconds you could literally change someone's life! Did you know that when a hug lasts twenty seconds or more, there's a tangible therapeutic effect on the body and mind, not to mention the energetic effect on our spirits? That's because a sincere hug produces a hormone called oxytocin, which is also known as the love hormone. This substance benefits our physical and mental health. It helps us to relax, feel safe, and calm our fear and anxiety. This wonderful calming is offered free of charge every time we hold a person in our arms, cradle a child, cherish a dog or cat, dance with our partner, or just hold the shoulders of a friend. According to Marcus Julian Felicetti, a contributor to the website *Mind Body Green*, hugs are as beneficial as meditation and laughter. They teach us to let go and be present in the moment. They encourage us to flow with the energy of life. Hugs get you out of your circular thinking patterns and connect you with your heart, your feelings, and your breath. They encourage empathy and understanding. Respected family therapist Virginia Satir, says, "We need four hugs a day for survival, eight hugs a day for maintenance, and twelve hugs a day for growth."

Eight or more might seem quite high to you. When Satir was doing her research, she asked her child how many hugs a day do you like? She said, "It's way more than eight." You can do some research of your own. Ask the people you care about how many hugs they'd like and let people know what your needs are. And, if you feel like it on the odd occasion, simply offer a hug to a stranger and notice what happens.

Ordinarily, I'd leave the story there and move on. However, there was another chapter that unfolded in Luciano's amazing tale that illustrated the enormous ripple effect of what we collectively did that day. At best, we'd hoped that our free hugs experiment might bring some Christmas cheer to people for a few minutes or even a few hours. Luciano allowed the experience to alter the course of his life. In the days and weeks after that event, he made his own signs and stood outside Tha Pae Gate every day, dispensing hugs to strangers. Some days, he'd be there for sixteen hours, from nine a.m. to one a.m. A year later, December's issue of Chiang Mai Citylife Magazine carried a special feature about him, written by Marcus Villagran, called *A Year of Free Hugs*. Here is an excerpt from his article:

"Luciano Pozzi, 54, has given free hugs to weary tourists and locals in Chiang Mai every day since last Christmas. In just one year, he's become part of the Tha Pae Gate experience; for many, he's considered a worthy reason to visit Chiang Mai. "You are famous in China!" shouts an excited young tourist. At his usual spot the girl inches towards him for a hug. "Can I take a picture?" she asks. "Of course." They pose together and she continues on her way. That's how it usually goes.

LIFE WITHOUT A TIE

Luciano has lived most of his life as a recluse. "My family is a little bit destroyed," he explains. "My father died at a very early age. My sister died two years ago. My family and friends screwed me over many times, and abandoned me, so I preferred to be alone." In his mid-thirties, he sold his home in Italy, moved to India and lived by himself for 20 years. "I didn't like people, I didn't want to talk to them," he says. "I needed to be free for myself, so I left."

Whilst there, a bad motorcycle accident left him paralysed. He went back to Italy for medical care but they told him he wasn't going to be able to walk again. Determined to find a way to move again, he went to Chiang Mai to checkout a Chinese medicine clinic he heard about and began to receive acupuncture treatment. "I improved slowly. Before I walked with two sticks, after I walked with one stick. Now with the bicycle I've gotten better."

His foray into free hugs didn't begin until last December when he stumbled upon an Englishman at Tha Pae Gate. The man was at the plaza with friends giving out free hugs for the holiday season. He spotted Luciano alone and asked him to join them. "He opened the door for me. It's very nice to hug people. You talk, you exchange experiences."

When I read the article, I got goosebumps and an intense feeling of joy flooded my body. The connection we'd made with him went beyond anything we could have dreamed of. It astonished me that a small man with a wiry body, who found it difficult to walk and move his arms, found a way to cope with the physical demand of giving free hugs for a whole year. In his interview, he said, "I walk out of my dormitory and immediately there are four or five people I need to hug. In the evening I'm tired, sure, but I enjoy it."

The story of Luciano spread like a bush fire. Following the article, he was the subject of a short documentary about his life by a Chinese filmmaker. They spent the entire day at Tha Pae Gate capturing hugs with nearly two hundred people on camera. Some of the friends Luciano made have come back to Chiang Mai with gifts for him. A Japanese guy massaged his hands with oil, and another girl brought him cheese and crackers from Italy. Clearly, we can underestimate the impact that an action born out of kindness can have on a fellow human being. Luciano took the practice much further than we'd ever envisaged and committed to extending the same kindness to Chiang Mai residents and visitors alike for years to come.

When I started my journey, I was aware how important connection was. I'd made it one of my guiding principles and committed to seeking it wherever I went, in any way I could. What better way is there than through the power of the physical connection you create by hugging another human being? It's so easy at times to feel small and alone in this world, like you can't really change anything or that nothing you do has an impact. And yet, we're always rippling out, touching other people. I've come to understand that miracles can happen when we do it consciously. I believe I was put on Luciano's path for a reason. Can you think of anything that would create that kind of ripple effect in your life? Maybe just bringing in donuts for people at the office can sometimes be enough to show you care. It doesn't have to be something big.

The free hugs day turned out to be a beautiful and fulfilling end to a challenging year. I had no idea that the events which were about to unfold would result in me spending the following Christmas in Warsaw, Poland.

Chapter Seventeen
The Long and Winding Road Home

"We shall not cease from exploration
And the end of all our exploring
Will be to arrive where we started
And know the place for the first time"

T.S. Eliot, *The Four Quartets* (1943)

AS 2014 BEGAN, I PREPARED FOR THE LONDON MARATHON, WHICH WAS TAKING place in April. I'd started training a couple of months earlier, and everything had gone according to plan. One Wednesday morning at the track, the muscles in the calf of my left leg were a bit tight. It got progressively worse as I continued, and I stopped after fifteen minutes. It was exactly the same injury I'd experienced whilst training for my first marathon in 2009, only back then I tore the calf muscle in my right leg. This time, the injury happened at the beginning of my fourteen-week endurance building phase of training, before I'd conditioned my body to run for two to three hours or longer.

Without completing that phase, it's virtually impossible to work on pace. If I could recover from the injury rapidly and resume training, I hoped I'd be able to make up for lost time. To increase my chances of doing that, I enrolled the help of Dr Jia Gottlieb, who is a great friend of mine. Jia is a medical doctor from Boulder, Colorado, and experienced in giving acupuncture treatments. He was in his mid-sixties and lived in Chiang Mai. Half Austrian and half Chinese, he looked like a Native American with long white hair, which he wore in a plaited ponytail that almost touched his waist. Jia came to my room three times per week and carefully placed needles in a number of key positions around my body and legs and sat quietly with me for twenty minutes or so while the healing effects took place.

Sometimes, I'd drift into a sleep and wake to see Jia sitting peacefully meditating or reading in a chair close to my bed. Other times, we'd talk about life, the Universe, and everything. He was a worldly man and a brilliant listener, and I loved the way he engaged me with his deep, reflective questions. We were pretty close, and he was aware of the emotional pain I'd suffered at Nancy's hands. His own experience of relationships had been a great teacher for him, and he was generous and helpful with his wisdom. During one of our conversations, he asked me to describe the kind of woman I hoped to meet.

"I'm not sure. I don't mind what she looks like or where she's from. What's most important is a powerful sense of equitability. By that, I mean that both of us want to be in and co-create the relationship with each other to exactly the same extent as the other. If I want it more than her, it won't work. And if she wants it more than me, that will also fail. It has to be *exactly* the same amount of desire from both of us."

Looking back, these conversations were powerful. I've often referred to them as reality-creating conversations. When I reflect on my journey, there were times when the Universe picked up the signal I transmitted without me knowing. As I was about to discover, this was one of those times. It's valuable to have friends with whom we can have honest, open, and vulnerable conversations in order to shift realities and create possibility, especially at times when it feels like there isn't any. I was extremely grateful to Jia for the way he looked after me and for those amazing chats.

Unfortunately, the acupuncture treatments didn't work as well as I'd hoped and after a couple of weeks, I was a long way away from being able to run again. The clock was ticking down to the London marathon, and I fell further and further behind. Seven weeks passed before I could train again. By then, I'd missed around half of my training runs, and I seriously considered dropping out. I didn't think I'd reach the level of fitness required to run a sub four-hour time. On the other hand, getting a place in the London marathon is like winning the lottery, and I didn't want to let go of it until it was absolutely necessary.

Jia knew I'd set my heart on breaking my sub four-hour goal in my home city and saw that my inability to train was a source of despair and depression. To aid my recovery, he suggested I visualise an animal which represented speed, power, and agility and instructed me to find an image of the animal to place on my bedside table, so it would be in the forefront of my mind. I conjured up a cheetah, which I visualised running at full tilt.

LIFE WITHOUT A TIE

I promised Jia I'd go out and find something suitable.

In the meantime, Jia hatched a plan B. In Boulder, there was a Kiwi woman by the name of Lorraine, who was an accomplished long-distance runner and had coached athletes to reach peak performance. They were friends.

"If you like, I could reach out to Lorraine and ask if she'd be willing to help you. I know it may be tough, but maybe with all her experience, she could help you put together a recovery training plan that might still put you in with a chance of reaching your goal. I think it's worth a shot."

It was kind of him to offer. I was sceptical that she'd be able to help me but remembered to adhere to my guiding principle of non-attachment and went with the flow. I was pretty desperate and agreed to his suggestion. I had no expectation that she'd actually respond, as I was a total stranger, and there was nothing in it for her to help me. Happily, she reached out and offered to have a phone call. In that conversation, she asked me lots of questions about my running experience, how I'd been training, my age, health, and available time, and she clearly understood that I'd wanted to run a sub four-hour time for the last five years.

"I think I can help you," Lorraine said. "Assuming Jia can get you moving again within a couple of weeks, I'll put together a recovery training program that will give you the best chance of finishing in London in under four hours. I'll draw it up in the next couple of days. How does that sound?"

I was moved by her generosity, and her confidence was contagious. Perhaps there was some hope after all. I was still slightly sceptical about what she'd proposed and waited to see her suggested plan before deciding to follow her guidance. A couple of days later, she emailed it to me. "Are you sure about this, Lorraine? There are no runs over fifteen miles in this plan, and you've split the training into two separate sections, with hills and speed intervals towards the end. I've never trained like this before, and it's very different from what I'm used to."

Jia had told me nothing about her background or who she was. Had I known at the time who I was speaking to, I might not have not been so opinionated and forthright. This was Lorraine Möller. I had no idea that Jia had connected me with a former Olympian marathon runner, who won a bronze medal at the 1992 Olympics in Barcelona at the age of thirty-seven. She was also a three-time winner of the Osaka International

Women's Marathon (1986, 1987, and 1989). She's considered to be one of the greatest female marathon runners of her era, and I was immensely lucky to receive her guidance. I served myself a large portion of humble pie as I became aware of Lorraine's history and achievements.

After that conversation, I saw my calf muscle injury as a massive piece of serendipity. Just a few short weeks earlier, it had seemed like the end of the world. Without the injury, I wouldn't have enrolled Jia for the acupuncture treatments, or had the personal conversations with him, or connected with Lorraine, who became my coach going forward. I couldn't believe how fortunate I'd been to find her and that she agreed to coach me to improve my performance.

I'd inadvertently found the exact thing I needed to take my running to the next level and recondition myself to achieve my goal. We often don't know the meaning of events as they unfold and can choose to interpret them in a myriad of different ways. It was another confirmation signal from the Universe to let me know it had my back. I really didn't like being injured, but I trusted it was happening for a good reason. That reason revealed itself a few weeks later in London.

A Chance Encounter
As my healing continued, I scoured the shops and the local markets in Chiang Mai to find a statue or image of a cheetah. I found plenty of pictures and statues of elephants, tigers, and lions, but no cheetahs. One afternoon, I dropped in at Blue Diamond for a serving of Pad Thai. As I chose a table in the garden, I saw a young woman nearby with thick, dark curly hair, writing postcards. She was obviously a traveller, and I couldn't help but smile as I was astonished that people still sent postcards in the digital era. "Excuse me for being nosy and asking, but who are those postcards for?" I asked after she'd caught me staring. "I didn't realise that people still sent them."

"They're for my parents," she said in a Slavic accent. "They are not really able to travel, and they love it when I send them postcards from the countries I visit. They stick them on the fridge and shelves at home."

"And where is home?"

"Warsaw, in Poland."

"Oh, wow. Tell me more about Warsaw. I've never been to Poland."

What followed was a wonderful, flowing conversation between two complete strangers. Her name was Dorota, and she was on holiday in Thailand for one month, including a week in Chiang Mai. She'd only just arrived which meant she'd be around for a few more days. She loved to travel and worked as a tour guide, escorting retired American and Australian couples on coach holidays in Eastern Europe. I told her about my passion for running marathons, and my calf injury, and shared my frustration about being unable to find a cheetah. She kindly offered to keep her eyes open during the next few days as she explored the shops and markets and said she'd drop me a message if she found one.

Dorota was a breath of fresh air. We had a love of travel in common, as well as our interest in personal growth. "It was lovely to meet you, Dorota. I've got to go now. I'd invite you to join me, but I suspect that meditation isn't your thing."

"Oh no, I'd love to come," she said. "It's top of my list of things I want to try, along with learning Thai massage and finding a good art class."

She jumped on the back of my motorbike and off we went. We met almost every day that week and got to know each other. One thing I noticed about her was that she always did what she said, and whenever we made an arrangement to meet, she was either early or on time. I didn't know many people who did that. It was obvious we had a good connection, and Dorota clearly signalled her interest in me, but the significant difference in our age worried me. I was fifty-four and she was thirty-two.

"I can't believe you're interested in a relationship with a guy my age. We're at such different places in our lives and most likely want quite different things. I doubt it would work out well. You'd be much better off finding someone your own age."

"Age isn't important to me," she said. "What are these differences you see?"

"Well, for starters, I don't think I want to have kids. I'm not saying one hundred percent no, but at this point, I think it's unlikely." With that cat out of the bag, I expected the conversation to end.

"Well, I don't want to have kids either."

I smiled. "You might change your mind. You're only thirty-two. You could want them sooner or later." Obviously, she had no way of knowing if my assertion was true. Neither did I. There was no way to resolve the different perspectives we both held, and it didn't really matter because in those moments we shared in Chiang Mai, we were happy in each other's company and simply enjoyed being present with each other. One evening, we arranged to meet at the Tea Tree café for their film night. I'd made it clear to her in advance that I'd leave there at nine on the dot, as I had to be up at five a.m. for a training run. At nine, I left and Dorota returned to her guesthouse. The following day, we met after breakfast, and she had a perplexed expression on her face. "What's up? I sense that you're not comfortable about something. Is that true?"

"Well, actually, yes, it's true. When you told me you'd have to leave at nine last night, I was really surprised you actually went. Most of the guys I've met would've changed their minds and spent the night with me. I think you're probably the only person who has turned me down. Not that I mind, but I'm impressed with your dedication."

She smiled, and I took her words as a compliment. Dorota stopped by my guesthouse on the day she left Chiang Mai with an unexpected gift.

"I've come to say goodbye. I've made something for you which I'd like to give you. Close your eyes."

I stood beside my bed with my eyes firmly closed.

"Okay, you can open them now," said Dorota.

On the bed was a beautiful watercolour painting, about the size of a hand towel, of a cheetah running at full tilt. I was speechless and moved to tears. I was gobsmacked that she remembered I'd mentioned it on the day we met at Blue Diamond. Not only that, she'd used all of the sessions at her art class to create the painting. If she was looking for a key to unlock the door to my heart, she'd found it. It was a touching moment of intimacy and kindness. Perhaps she was the woman I'd described to Jia in our conversation a couple of weeks earlier. She left Chiang Mai, and I didn't know if we'd see each other again, although there was an open invitation to call her if I was ever in Warsaw.

Dorota's presence, as well as her amazing gift, lifted my spirits, and they had a big impact on my marathon training. There were only a few weeks left to reach the highest level of fitness and strength I could to give the London marathon my best shot. With my injury now fully recovered, and with Lorraine's backing and encouragement, I threw myself into training desperate to salvage my dream of a sub four-hour finish.

Fail Forward, Fail Fast
A few weeks later, I went to London and ran my third marathon in a

personal best time of four hours and seven minutes. A part of me was disappointed but at the same time, I felt a sense of elation. I saw the huge impact the shift in my training methods had brought about in just seven weeks. In my work as a coach, I encourage people to adopt a fail forward, fail fast habit to cultivate the willingness to persist with challenging goals. There's nothing wrong with failing, because it can yield useful data which you can use to improve your next attempt. The more attempts you have, the sooner you're likely to reach your goal.

In the New York Marathon, I'd been too slow by sixteen minutes. In London, I wasn't even at full fitness, but I'd reduced that deficit by nine minutes. That left just seven minutes to be taken care of in the next race. If I could train for the next marathon without getting injured and follow Lorraine's plan from start to finish, I'd definitely break the barrier I'd set myself. Despite being so agonisingly short of my goal in London, I was definitely on the right track (no pun intended!), and I'd formed an empowering self-belief which took my confidence to a new level.

Lorraine had given me a gift in the form of vital information about how to train effectively without getting injured. There was one further gift that came out of my failure to reach my sub four-hour goal in London, and it didn't become clear until a couple of months later. If I had finished in less than four hours, I wouldn't have run another marathon. But now, it was a certainty that I'd be in another race in 2015, and that gave me a huge and unexpected opportunity to raise more money for my Calling All Angels Foundation.

The Camino El Santiago

It was April 2014. As I rested in London after the marathon, I realised I'd been living my life without a tie journey for nine years. During that time, if there was one experience I'd heard fellow travellers talk about more than any other, it was walking the Camino El Santiago. People from all over the world were drawn to the religious pilgrimage. For centuries, they've walked from the base of the Pyrenees in France to Santiago in Northern Spain. If you walk it in one go, it takes between thirty and forty days, depending on how fast or how slow you go.

I was in Europe with plenty of time on my hands. With virtually no coaching work booked for the summer, I'd enrolled for the three-week summer retreat with Thích Nhất Hạnh, a Zen Buddhist monk at the Plum

Village Monastery. He was a profound teacher and was at the monastery near Bordeaux, France. It was due to start on the first of June, so I stayed in Europe, as it made no sense to return to Thailand only to come all the way back again two months later.

That meant I'd enough time to walk the Camino, so I committed to start at the end of April. I got in touch with Dorota in Warsaw and offered to visit her before heading to France. She was delighted and invited me to stay with her for the week. Poland became the twenty-fourth country in my journey. Warsaw was way better than I'd imagined or expected. It's amazing how our minds are conditioned by what we see in the media. My view of Poland was almost entirely based on news footage I'd seen in the early eighties about the Solidarity movement under the leadership of shipyard worker Lech Wałęsa. Instead of the grey, drab, dull and austere vista I remembered from those days, I encountered a modern, thriving, energised, and colourful city with beautiful parks, a wide river, and loads of creative and enterprising people who enjoyed a relatively high standard of living at substantially lower cost than London. It was comparable to Berlin, where I'd spent a lot of time a couple of years earlier.

Dorota's apartment was a plain, simple, modern refurbishment inside a beautiful old building on Aleja Szucha in a well-heeled part of town close to Plac Uni. Inside, it was plain white, with minimal furnishings and splashes of colour here and there, much like I'd imagined when I'd visualised my future home during the Hoffman Process. I couldn't help wondering if this was going to be my home or whether it was purely a coincidence. It was hard to know, but that week in Warsaw opened my eyes and my heart to the possibility of living there at some stage, if Dorota and I got involved. We'd certainly got off to a great start.

I packed up my stuff and set off for Saint-Jean-Pied-de-Port in southern France, country number twenty-five. As I arrived, I began a two-month period of mindful contemplation. I'd evolved my mindfulness practice since doing my first Vipassana back in 2006, and it was a firmly integrated part of my life. Walking the Camino was a personal challenge that had the potential to provide new insight and wisdom. It was also an excellent way to prepare myself for the three-week meditation retreat in Plum Village afterwards.

You may have seen a movie called *The Way*, about a bereaved American father called Tom (played by Martin Sheen). He heads to France to recover the body of his estranged adult son who dies mid-way along the Camino. Tom decides to take the pilgrimage himself, to honour his son and finish the journey for him. The entire walk is around five hundred miles. Most of it is along winding gravel paths across fields and over hills, with parts of the route taking you through a couple of amazing cathedral cities and a few smaller towns and villages. If you don't know what the Camino is or cannot imagine why anyone would want to walk it, that film may give you a valuable introduction and understanding. Hollywood doesn't necessarily portray things the way they really are, but that film does give a fair representation of what to expect if you were to undertake it yourself.

If you walk the Camino alone, as I did, you'll quickly discover there are hundreds of other pilgrims from around the world, each with their own issues and challenges, who come to find greater meaning in their lives, and they walk alongside you every day. In the thirty-five days it took me to reach Santiago, I talked to men, women, and teenagers who came for many different reasons. Some wanted to undertake a religious pilgrimage. Some wanted to know themselves better. Some came to grieve the loss of loved ones. Some came to unburden themselves from a particular form of suffering. Some came because they were nearing the end of a personal transition and wanted to perform a ritual that would give them a sense of completion. Others came for the exercise and to simply enjoy the physical challenge that a five hundred mile walk across northern Spain provides. We all embraced the spirit of community and camaraderie that made walking the Camino a unique and unforgettable experience that touched my soul.

A pilgrimage is often considered a transformational journey during which significant changes takes place in one's life. To help prepare my journey, I bought the extremely popular book, *Pilgrims Guide to the Camino de Santiago* by John Brierley. I can confidently say that it's the only book you need. Obviously, you'll find a lot in there about practicalities like routes, distances, where to stay, etcetera, but what really fascinated me was his guidance about preparing for the inner journey. He provided an excellent self-assessment questionnaire to reflect on that journey before it started. Doing this helped me to think about what changes would be most desirable.

His suggestions encouraged me to articulate my intention for the walk. This is what I committed to:

* Reconnect with my true, spiritual self, strengthening my ability to make decisions more intuitively
* Establish a strong dialogue with my inner guides
* Feel a sense of renewal around my creativity
* Know deeply that miracles happen and prepare for these to be regular and normal events in my life
* Enjoy the power of the present moment

As you know by now, I'm a big believer in the power of setting an intention. By doing this, I created a context to notice and pay attention to tiny events which I might normally miss in my daily life. The Camino became a five-week walking meditation. I observed conversations and events with awareness as they happened and recorded my observations in my journal at the end of each day. I reflected on these periodically and waited for insights to arise. By the end of my trek, I'd confirmed or reinforced these ten empowering beliefs:

1. People Are Kind
When I'm busy or in a hurry, it's easy to judge other people as being unhelpful, lazy, or worse. On the Camino, I experienced the unconditional generosity of fellow travellers every day, and it restored my faith in humanity. On day one, a marvellous Kiwi lady called Maria saw I was a bit lost and made sure I boarded the right bus for Saint-Jean. She helped me get my bearings for what was about to follow. In Pamplona, a tall, wiry guy from Switzerland called Micha saw I didn't have a sleeping bag (to keep the weight of my rucksack down to six kilos, I didn't take one). The hostel blankets were rough and uncomfortable, so he offered me his own silk liner to sleep in, so I'd be more comfortable.

In Logrono, I struggled with a couple of huge blisters. A Spanish guy saw me, insisted on giving me his own foot cream, and helped me bandage them up, despite obviously being in pain himself. I also sprained my ankle, and a young girl from San Francisco called Lauren came to my aid. She told me to sit on my bunk and rest, then she walked into town to get me a compression bandage (which she refused to let me pay for). She sent her friend to get me some food. The following day, in Hornillos, the manager of the Albergue (a municipal pilgrim hostel) saw my swollen ankle as I soaked it in a bowl of cold water and invited me to stay a couple of days. Pilgrims are only allowed one night in each hostel as there are so many people walking, but he made an exception for me. He found me a local doctor, who wrapped a bandage around it so I could continue my journey. He didn't ask me for a penny. All along the Camino, locals set up makeshift stalls, voluntarily make coffee, and offer fruit to all pilgrims, free of charge, to make our journey easier. I could go on. Suffice to say that the kindness I encountered blew me away.

2. Space is Healing
When I worked out what to take in my small backpack, my laptop would have been the largest and heaviest single item. With the cable and adapter, it weighed two kilos. Nervously, I decided to leave it behind and felt slightly anxious at the prospect of being offline every day. To my surprise, it turned out to be a great decision. My attention and energy were directed towards the experiences right in front of me, enabling me to fully embrace my guiding principle of presence. I enjoyed having the space to see the sunrise each morning, listen to the sound of long grass as it blew in the wind, hear birds sing, and feel the warm sun on my face. I felt uplifted as I walked mile after mile with a total absence of noisy traffic, music blaring from shops, and thousands of other people rushing in all directions. I felt my body calm down and a sense of well-being infiltrated me. I'd been so used to living in cities that I no longer noticed the continuous distraction of all the noise and chaos going on around me. After a few days in nature, I felt like a different person. While I walked, I mindfully contemplated times in my past when I hadn't treated people well and forgave myself. The tenth anniversary of my divorce from Charlotte occurred during my Camino. It provided a wonderful moment to fully appreciate the many gifts that life had brought since then.

3. Go At Your Own Pace
I'd hooked up with a great bunch of younger people at the start who were energetic, fun, and excellent company. They were fast walkers and on a tighter schedule than me. They had to reach Santiago at least ten days before I did, due to work and other commitments. Walking with them meant I covered more miles each day than I really needed to, which was painful and left me feeling exhausted when I arrived at my hostel for the night. I didn't want to let them go as they were such good fun to be

around. But trying to keep up with them wasn't good for me either. I felt caught between a rock and hard place. Ultimately, I developed a serious ankle injury, and the choice was made for me before I took ownership. Maybe the Universe had stepped in to help. I couldn't know for sure but letting go of them was a great opportunity to practice my principle of non-attachment.

On reflection, I observed a tendency in me to keep doing something that doesn't work in order to be accepted socially and not feel alone or left out. I'd made that more important than my own health. Once I'd had a couple of days to rest and recover my badly swollen ankle, I proceeded at my own pace. Each day, I travelled around half the distance that I'd been doing with my now-absent friends. I noticed how much more I enjoyed the experience of walking without any pain. It made me wonder how much joy we miss in our lives because we are living too fast.

4. Listen to Your Body

I'd pushed myself to my limit to keep up with a great group of people, covering no less than twenty-five miles per day, as opposed to a gentler average of fifteen miles. The pain in my ankles and legs was intense. I'm embarrassed to admit I took painkillers to numb the sensations just so I could keep up. This was truly silly behaviour, and I was astonished to catch myself doing it. As a marathon runner, I really should have known better. I'd ignored the messages my body was constantly sending me to slow down and rest.

In the end, my body quit on me. One of my ankles was the size of a baseball, and it forced me to stop. As I wanted to continue running long distances for some years to come, I surrendered to it. Once my body and I were back in harmony, I continued. In everyday life, it's easy to miss some of the cues our bodies give us, because we are busy, tired, or overwhelmed. Perhaps you've done that yourself. There are plenty of stimulants we can purchase to keep ourselves going when slowing down or even a complete stop would be a much better option.

5. Happiness Is Right Here, Right Now

On the Camino, there was no need to think about anything in the past or worry about anything in the future. I just walked, one step after the other, and enjoyed each moment. It was a great feeling to know that all I had to do was walk, and of course, eat and drink too. Surprisingly, some days were quite challenging. One started when I received an unpleasant email from Dorota (I had my smartphone with me), and it played on my mind. My attention moved away from the beautiful landscapes that were right in front of me and the people I was walking with. Instead, I got lost in my thoughts as I continuously played out an imaginary conversation with her. When that went on, I stopped noticing things outside. I'd catch myself doing it and bring my attention back to the present moment. Once again, I'd appreciate what was right in front of me and feel the joy of walking and being alive. I've noticed over the years that the more I pay attention in the present moment, the greater my sense of joy and appreciation is for life. I find less things to complain about.

In Calzada, I stopped after several hours of walking to enjoy a beer and a sandwich at a heavenly little bar. The owner radiated a beautiful energy. It was a remote place, miles from anywhere. I sat there and enjoyed it so much that I stayed for thirty minutes longer than I'd intended. That delightful and refreshing stop enabled me to continue another four miles that day with ease. In Leon, I sat in the park at the end of the day to enjoy the last hour of sunshine. In those sixty glorious minutes, I fell in love with life all over again. In the hills at Foncebadón, I sat with a group of lively French pilgrims and shared great food and conversation. And in Ponferrada, I bathed my tired feet in the whirlpool at the albergue.

6. *The Journey Is More Important Than the Destination*
When I'd walked with my young, energetic friends at the start, I'd felt like stopping early, while they wanted to push on. On one particular day, I was aware of thinking I should go with them, but my instinct spoke to me from a different place. To put it into words, it said something like, "It's much better for you to stop early today and maybe catch them up tomorrow." So I followed my instinct and stayed in a different albergue. In the dormitory, I met and started talking to a girl who was from the same tiny town I was born and grew up in, a place that most people have never heard of. That felt like a blessing, and I was stunned by the power and effect of following one's instinct.

It happened again in Hornillos. I chose to honour the needs of my body and rest for a couple of days. I met a guy called Christian from Cologne, Germany, who was in deep contemplation about how to construct his life after the Camino. We talked for a couple of hours, and it became obvious that the nomadic experiment I was conducting was relevant to him. I had a sense that the Universe had made our paths collide so he could receive this information from me. In that moment, I experienced the power of going with the flow and the heartfelt joy and happiness it brought to both of us. We sometimes fixate on reaching our destination at the time we've planned and miss out on spontaneous opportunities that could really help us grow. Alternatively, if we hold our vision lightly, follow our instincts, and change our original plan, our destination may also change.

7. *Hold Your Vision Lightly*
One morning, my friends and I agreed on a plan to walk to Burgos and find beds in the municipal albergue. We set off much later than intended and took more rest stops along the way, mainly due to the great people we met who engaged us in some brilliant conversations. Consequently, we arrived in Burgos later than we expected and it was full. Disappointed, tired, and a bit annoyed, we let go of our original plan and looked for an alternative place. Eventually, we found two suitable rooms in a backstreet hotel. We checked in, dumped our stuff in the room, and went out to get some food.

Upon my return, I couldn't believe my eyes! In the hotel, in the room next door was a girl I knew from Chiang Mai. I'd heard on the grapevine that she was on the Camino, but I didn't know when or what her itinerary was. I would have bet a thousand pounds there'd be no way we would bump into each other. It occurred to me that if we'd stuck to our original plan and arrived at the time we'd originally set, there would have been no way I would've found her. It was precisely those unexpected developments that brought us together. I'm no mathematician, and I guess the probability of such an event materialising is slim. We both rejoiced at the wonder of life and continued with our separate journeys. I didn't see her again. Nonetheless, our encounter was truly miraculous. It's worth noting that witnessing and acknowledging miracles was one of the intentions I'd set when I'd started the Camino.

8. *Whatever You Truly Need Shows Up (If You Stay Calm)*
When it comes to domestic chores, I can be a bit lazy. Living in Thailand, I was spoilt, as there are many places which do laundry for next to nothing. I was slightly dreading having to wash my own clothes each night at the

hostels. My first day was long and tiring. When I arrived at the albergue in Roncesvalles, a huge, converted monastery with four hundred beds, I was amazed to discover a group of volunteers doing laundry for pilgrims for a small charge. My gratitude knew no bounds.

On the way to Los Arcos, after an early start with no breakfast, I started to feel hungry and according to my guidebook, there was nowhere to eat for some time. Five minutes later, I clapped my eyes on one of those portable burger vans. The owner had temporarily set up shop right beside the pilgrim's path. I was overjoyed. That same evening, my feet ached from the day's walk, and I craved a relieving Thai foot massage, which were abundant in Chiang Mai. Half an hour later, I saw a couple of women from France who were massaging each other's feet, and they kindly invited me to join them. Last but not least, I secured one of the last remaining beds at the municipal albergue in Najera on a day when my ankle had flared up again. Had I not done so, I'd have needed to walk six more miles, which I was in no fit state to do.

9. We Carry More Than We Need
You don't need much stuff for the Camino. I walked for thirty-three days and carried a small backpack weighing six kilos, washing and wearing clothes as I went along. I'd lived out of a twenty-two-kilo holdall for the last nine years, so was well-adjusted to travelling light. Having said that, I managed to pack one or two items that I didn't need or use. I saw many people along the way who'd packed far more than they needed, for reasons I'm sure they could justify if they were asked to. I guess that some overpacking is inevitable as it can be hard to anticipate what your exact needs are going to be. It made me wonder if we all tend to carry much more than we need in our lives. You can see this in the incredible numbers of people who rent additional storage space for stuff that won't fit in their homes, not to mention the emotional baggage that some of us carry.

One of the few rituals awaiting pilgrims is at Cruz de Ferro, just past Foncebadón. Traditionally, you carry a stone in your pack which you've brought from home. The stone represents a burden you're carrying that you wish to let go of. At Cruz de Ferro, there's a simple iron cross atop a weathered pole that has become one of the abiding symbols for all pilgrims. I stopped for a while to reconnect with the purpose of my journey and placed my stone at the foot of the pole. When I did that, I felt a release and a flood of emotion. Other pilgrims told me they'd had a similar feeling. It was moving to witness our collective journey through this life, and that ritual was the spiritual highlight of my Camino.

10. Leave It As It Was Or Better

I hope you've now got a sense that walking the Camino is a pretty incredible and rewarding thing to do. Understandably, as more and more people make the choice to go, it raises the possibility that those who walk this path with no awareness or care could spoil it for others who follow. I witnessed a pilgrim in one hostel drawing graffiti on his bed. I felt sad, as it appeared he'd no idea he might be spoiling the experience for those who would follow him the next day, or month, and in years to come. We all face the same issue with our entire planet, so in that sense, the Camino is no different. One of my aims is to tread lightly whilst I go about my life. If you decide to walk to Santiago, you can safeguard the beauty of this amazing journey for everyone.

For all sorts of reasons, not everyone who walks the Camino does the entire thing in one go. Some can't get five weeks off work. Many pilgrims complete one section each year, or whenever they can, and eventually complete the Camino after several years. Some never finish, yet still enjoy each of the sections as a standalone experience. Over a quarter million people walk the Camino every year, with at least half of those doing it during July and August. If you don't like crowds, it may be worth going when the route is less busy, and the temperatures are lower.

Whenever you complete it, you will eventually reach Santiago. I witnessed the traditional ritual in the cathedral, when the priests swing a giant incense burner suspended from the roof backwards and forwards. Originally the smoke from the burning incense was intended to cleanse pilgrims, who were so filthy and smelly after their long walk. These days, it's purely a visual spectacle and well worth seeing if you're there.

For most pilgrims, the Camino formally ends with the collection of your compostela from the Pilgrim's Reception Office in Santiago. Throughout the entire walk, I'd carried my pilgrim passport with me, which had been issued at Saint-Jean at the beginning and had been stamped at every albergue I'd stopped at en route, as proof that I'd completed the walk. My certificate was signed and validated at the completion of my Camino de

LIFE WITHOUT A TIE

Santiago. It's a treasured memento.

Plum Village: the Summer Retreat
Before I reached Santiago, I received a heartwarming message from Dorota. Knowing I had a few days to spare before entering the Plum Village monastery, she offered to meet me in Bordeaux. It was a welcome invitation, and I said yes without hesitation. We enjoyed four wonderful days in the city, walking, sightseeing, eating, and larking around. I'd met a French woman called Olivia on the Camino. She lived in Bordeaux and invited both of us to a party at her house. I enjoyed Dorota's presence and made a commitment to return to Warsaw for another month during the summer, so we could continue getting to know each other.

First, I went to Plum Village. It was my first visit there, and I was thrilled to finally arrive for the three-week retreat on the nature of death and dying with Thích Nhất Hạnh. His presence was *truly* awesome. He was the most conscious, gentle, kind, compassionate, and loving man I've ever sat with. He didn't need to speak to have an effect on me. Just being around him in silence felt inspiring. Together, we examined and practiced ways of being that bring nourishment and healing to ourselves. I loved the accessibility and down to earth nature of his teachings. He helped me become aware that in any given moment, I really do have all the conditions in place that are required to be truly happy.

Every day when I wake up, I immediately feel myself breathing normally. I'm aware that I can see and hear, I'm able to walk and move freely, I have somewhere safe, warm, and dry to live, and I have food and water to sustain myself. Nothing else is needed for me to be in a state of pure joy and gratitude. This way of seeing life has become my new normal and is an enormous shift in mindset from my former life. Of course, there are many things that can bring pleasure for a while, and I welcome those whenever they materialise, although I see them for what they actually are. I think that one of the most difficult concepts to come to terms with is the nature of not wanting, which I first learned about during my Vipassana retreat. Culturally, it's all we know, so to be told that it's not a mentally healthy way to live can be hard to accept. It's something that I have found requires a lot of experimentation.

Above all, Thích Nhất Hạnh inspired me to grasp the most important thing when it comes to being mindful. That is, how to *apply* our knowledge in the way we relate to and communicate with others. He talked about how you can help other people grow through practicing loving kindness towards them. He used such a beautiful, down to earth way of describing it. To him, it's like watering flowers. Every time you're with one of your loved ones, always look for things to appreciate in them and tell them what it is about their presence that you're grateful for. When you do this, you're watering a seed inside them, and they'll bloom like a flower. Applying this powerful, simple imagery enables me to live a happier, more peaceful life in which I'm being true to myself.

Plum Village is a beautiful, mindful environment to be in. The monks and nuns are friendly and engaging, and I felt like a part of their community. They are well-practiced in being non-judgmental, and you can really feel it energetically when you're around them. I loved the daily opportunity to break into small groups of about fifteen to twenty people, which they call family groups, to discuss the content of the dharma talk each day and ask questions of each other. Whatever I chose to share in my group, I felt totally accepted for the way I am, and was gently encouraged to apply the same loving kindness to myself. I always left those sessions feeling incredibly light, happy, and enriched.

In hindsight, I was extremely lucky to attend that retreat, because about three months later, Thích Nhất Hạnh suffered a stroke and wasn't able to teach again. Sadly, he died in January 2022, aged 95. The highlight of the retreat for me was my decision to undertake the Five Mindfulness Trainings. These are essentially five vows that would enable me to evolve my mindfulness practice and take it to a deeper level. They are actually commitments you make to yourself regarding your own personal conduct. By honouring these commitments, you constantly train your mind to deeper levels of awareness, resulting in an ability to consistently generate mindful energy for yourself and others around you.

You may ask why someone might want to do that? To answer that, I'll share a wonderful story I heard from the American spiritual teacher Radhanath Swami, during a 2013 talk entitled "Consciousness: The Missing Link."

"I sat quietly beside the river. A hawk flew overhead. It was hovering lower and lower, till he was just a few metres above me. I looked up at him. He had brown, white, and

LIFE WITHOUT A TIE

gold feathers with his wings expanded, and extremely sharp claws. His beak was curved down and pointed very sharp, and his yellow eyes seemed to unblinkingly gaze at me as he came lower and lower and lower. Naturally, I was thinking, maybe he's hungry? Maybe I'm his food? Suddenly, he dived into the water and went under a little. There was a skirmish. About thirty seconds later, he emerged from the water with a flapping fish in his claws. That fish was about a foot long. And it was really bewildered.

"It was just a few yards in front of me. I looked into the eyes of that fish. He looked so disoriented and bewildered. And I was thinking, he was probably just going about his day like every other day, swimming upstream, swimming downstream, maybe with family, friends, looking for food, playing. He couldn't have known that at the least expected moment, he'd be ripped out of his complacency by the hawk of destiny.

"And I was thinking how many people I know, how many people I hear about who are much like that fish, just going about their days. And all of a sudden they're diagnosed with a terminal disease, or they're betrayed by a loved one, or they get in an accident, or there's an earthquake that devastates everything around them. It happens every day. No one expects it. That hawk of destiny is kind of flying over everyone's head and could come down to get us.

"And I was thinking how we shouldn't be complacent. We can make priorities in our life of what really is sacred, what really is important. Moments pass, and we're so preoccupied with superficialities. How much time do we really invest in trying to discover what's meaningful and important in life? And then I reflected how, if that fish was swimming deeper, the hawk couldn't reach it. And similarly, if our fulfilment, if our pleasure and meaning in life is deep, then whatever happens in this ever-changing world cannot really disturb what we have achieved within

379

ourselves and cannot alter the integrity and the character in which we live."

Wanting to cultivate the kind of clarity and inner strength he talked about, like the fish swimming in deeper water, was my inspiration for taking the Five Mindfulness Trainings. There was no pressure placed on us by the monastics to do so. It was purely a choice. Being on the path of waking up and raising my awareness, I felt open to anything that would intensify my own learning. This was one of the most concrete ways I could practice mindfulness and truly live according to my own values. Their nature is universal. They are practices of compassion and understanding. When we are mindful, we can see that if we refrain from doing one thing, we can prevent another thing from happening. We arrive at our own unique insight. It isn't something imposed on us by an outside authority. We aren't lost in confusion about our life in the present or in our fears about the future.

1. *Reverence For Life*. I'm committed to protect life, to decrease violence in myself, in my family, and in society, and to prevent the suffering caused by the destruction of life. It applies to people, animals, plants, and minerals too. Harmful actions can arise when I feel anger, fear, greed, and intolerance. I know that it's my own judgmental thinking that inflames these feelings, not someone else making me feel that way. I practice this to cultivate openness, non-discrimination, and non-attachment to views in order to transform violence, fanaticism, and dogmatism in myself and in the world.

2. *True Happiness* is about the practice of social justice, generosity, not stealing and not exploiting other living beings. This has created great expansion for me. A lovely example is at my local coffee shop when I nip in for a takeaway. They are always changing staff and sometimes, one of the new girls has undercharged me. I gently let her know she's made a mistake and ask her to check the price. The same applies when I'm given too much change by mistake. I'm aware that my gain is their loss, and I don't want them to suffer in that way. I see in my heart that the happiness and suffering of others is not separate from my own happiness and suffering. I know my happiness depends on my mental attitude and not

on external conditions and that I can live happily in the present moment simply by remembering I already have more than enough.

3. *True Love* is the practice of responsible sexual behaviour in order to protect individuals, couples, families, and children. This one was the hardest for me to accept. After my divorce and life as a traveller, I was quite used to transient relationships and didn't think it was wrong or dishonourable when I had sex with partners soon after meeting them, which was inevitably before true love had developed. I'd thought that as long as we were upfront with each other and acknowledge we don't want to make a commitment, it was okay. It's a bit like a legal disclaimer tagged on the end of a radio or TV commercial. It's an apt comparison, as they're said so quickly that you don't really hear or reflect on the terms properly. As my mindfulness practice evolved, I started to experience it differently. I saw that sexual activity motivated by craving was harming myself as well as others. I decided not to engage in sexual relationships without true love and a deep, long-term commitment made known to my family and friends. I committed myself to learning appropriate ways to take care of my sexual energy and cultivate loving kindness, compassion, joy, and inclusiveness—which are the four basic elements of true love—for my greater happiness and the greater happiness of others.

4. *Loving Speech and Deep Listening*. Our words can create happiness or suffering. I'm committed to speaking truthfully using words that inspire confidence, joy, and hope. When I was married, I was sometimes full of anger. My language became violent and abusive. It was highly destructive. I committed myself to not speak in such a tense situation but practice mindful breathing and walking so that I could look deeply into my anger and be curious about it. I know that anger arises out of my own beliefs and perceptions and is not caused by another person. I'll speak and listen in a way that can help myself and others see the way out of difficult situations. I'm determined not to spread news that I don't know to be certain and not to utter words that cause division or discord. I'll nourish my capacity for understanding, love, joy, and inclusiveness and gradually transform any feelings of anger, violence, and fear that lie deep in my consciousness.

5. *Nourishment and Healing* is about mindful consumption. The intention

is to avoid putting toxins and poisons into our bodies or minds. This wasn't a huge stretch for me, as I'd already cultivated good physical and mental health through running marathons. In Buddhist texts, there are four kinds of nutriments: edible foods, sense impressions, volition, and consciousness. What we eat, what we see and hear, what our actions are motivated by, and how the quality of our thoughts collectively affects our ability to maintain skilful states of mind. The Buddha's advice on this was amazingly simple. Identify the kinds of nutriments that feed our pain and stop ingesting them. It includes things like gambling, using alcohol, drugs, or any other products which contain toxins. Looking at pornography, electronic games, and TV programs and films depicting mindless violence can harm us at a deeper level. Residing in the present moment, it's easier to connect with the refreshing, healing, and nourishing elements in me and around me. I try my best to not let regrets and sorrow drag me back into the past or let anxieties or fear or craving pull me out of the present moment. Last but not least, I'm determined not to cover up loneliness, anxiety, or other suffering by losing myself in consumption.

There's something powerful about rituals that accompany key moments in our lives. When I made these commitments, I sat in the meditation hall with the other retreat participants, Thích Nhất Hạnh, and hundreds of the monks and nuns in the Plum Village community. They all witnessed me as I took that step, and I felt a tidal wave of unconditional love and support as they surrounded me. As if that wasn't special enough, three of my dear friends from the Green Papaya Sangha in Chiang Mai came all the way from Thailand to attend the retreat with me, which made it feel even more alive, joyful, and meaningful. One of these was Gaston Schmitz, and I'll come back to him shortly.

I don't want to create a false impression. Although I undertook these commitments in 2014, there are times when I don't honour all of them. I forget sometimes or lose my awareness. I'm far from perfect. Making the commitments has elevated my practice, and as I continue to work on myself, pushing towards the edges of my discomfort, I feel as if I'm always growing in clarity and strength. That inspires me to keep making the effort and pay attention to how I'm being in all areas of my life.

My practice of mindfulness has expanded my awareness in a number of ways and that has led to a happier and more harmonious way of life.

LIFE WITHOUT A TIE

For example, by paying attention to how I speak to others, I see my own non-acceptance, blame, and judgment. If I pay even closer attention, I see my righteousness and the desire for vengeance or punishment. My story about Sylvia is a perfect example. When I pay more attention to how I feel and what I think, I notice that I'm often living in the past or the future and rarely in the present moment.

You may see that your thinking patterns don't always reflect reality. A great example is when we tell ourselves, "I'll be happy when..." (I get a new boyfriend/girlfriend, job, car, new shoes, etcetera). We tend to believe our happiness is dependent on something external to us and often use the absence of that thing to postpone being happy. It's a part of the cycle I talked about earlier.

Without mindfulness, we spend a great deal of our lives on autopilot. Scientific research indicates that about eighty percent of our behaviour is directed by our subconscious mind. It's based on well-formed emotional and behavioural patterns, belief systems, filtering, and biases, to name just a few of the influencing factors. The field of neuroscience has advanced significantly since I began my great nomadic journey, and we now know that the brain isn't hardwired, as was commonly believed for many years. Once we become aware of our patterns and consciously practice new and better behaviours, our brains have the plasticity to rewire themselves and create new neural pathways, so that we can change the habits of a lifetime. There really is no need to maintain the illusion of who we think we are. This idea can initially be scary for some people. I feel it's worth experimenting with, but to always remember that it's an ongoing process.

As I continue to practice, I experience a growing sense of equanimity inside me. I no longer confuse real happiness with temporary pleasure. This hasn't only changed my own life. In most of my coaching work these days, I spend time with clients to help them understand why awareness of our emotions is so important. When people escape pain through the use of alcohol, drugs, sex, or whatever their numbing agent of choice is, a path of mindfulness can enable them to find their way back home to their true selves. My encouragement to you is to learn and practice mindfulness for yourself. I know from personal experience that it's not easy, and you will most probably need support. It would be my honour to support you if you choose to start the journey.

I've also observed an increase in access to my own wisdom when faced with dilemmas and less of a need to search for answers outside of myself, although I sometimes like to approach trusted, wise friends, or teachers for a second opinion. Mindfulness as a daily ritual is the ultimate challenge and practice. It's a way of living, of being, of seeing, of tapping into the full power of your humanity. It will allow you to:

* Access your intuition and higher-level brain functions
* Gain deeper insights
* Use your imagination and creativity more
* Improve your peripheral vision
* Reveal opportunities
* Align with your purpose in life

Which of these six would you most like to focus on right now?

The Asian Leadership Institute
I was thrilled that Gaston Schmitz came to the retreat at Plum Village and witnessed the commitments I made. I'd met him eight years earlier when I'd first arrived in Chiang Mai and was searching for a sangha (community) to join. He's twenty-five years younger than me, and I'd always admired his mindful way of being and living. He totally embodied the spirit of Plum Village, and he'd become one of my role models. He always gently encouraged me to keep developing my own practice. People like Gaston help us move towards being the greatest version of ourselves. They are real gems. I'm sure you can probably think of people like that in your own life.

In 2012, Gaston joined forces with Brian Bauerle, the founder of the Asian Leadership Institute (ALI), based in Chiang Mai. Together, they devised a way of coaching people using the wisdom and knowledge from the kind of teachings I've shared with you. I'd experienced the benefits through my own mindfulness practice. Gaston's vision was to create an easily accessible, modular online programme for leadership and personal development. There are many people in the world who don't have time to study at monastic retreats or dedicate large parts of their lives to a mindfulness practice.

Gaston and Brian came up with a programme of self-study and applied practices that people could take online in groups of three called a Triad course. Each group is guided by an experienced, mindful facilitator. The group dynamic is important because, like the family groups at Plum Village, it provides the support and encouragement that each of the participants needs on the learning journey. Back then, the interest in mindful leadership in organisations was growing steadily, and the Triad course started to rise in popularity. That generated a demand for a global team of skilled facilitators to lead these online groups. These people can be hard to find because they must have a dedicated mindfulness practice of their own, as well as extensive leadership, coaching, and/or training expertise. Fortunately, I had these *and* a huge desire to lead others to acquire greater consciousness.

In the final week of our retreat, Gaston invited me to join the ALI team and become a certified facilitator. Without hesitation, I accepted. That kind of work put me in my element, where your passions and what you're really excellent at doing overlap. Through learning how to become a great facilitator, I could continue to develop my own practice and improve my ability to help others on a growth path. And it could be an additional source of freelance coaching work. The following year, I completed my facilitator training in Chiang Mai. Since then, I've run many online Triad courses with groups of business leaders from all over the world.

I had no idea that I'd be leaving Asia about a year later. The power of love is one of the greatest forces in the world, and it was quietly preparing the ground for a major shift in orbit and a taste of life in Warsaw.

Chapter Eighteen
Goodbye Asia, Hello Warsaw

WHEN I RETURNED TO WARSAW IN JULY 2014, DOROTA WAS IN THE BUSY SEASON with her own work, but we still found a way to go on a health retreat in Gołubie for a week, where we'd committed to a strict regime of juices and vegetables. It's run by a clinic way out in the Polish countryside, about twenty-five miles from Gdańsk, and surrounded by totally unspoilt nature. The clinic sits close to an enormous freshwater lake, and it's the kind of place where you can still camp literally anywhere without anyone to disturb you. That week did wonders for our health and well-being, and it brought us closer together.

That summer, I finally got to tick another experience on my bucket list after I'd visited what remains of the former Nazi concentration camp at Auschwitz near Krakow. As you can imagine, it was spine-chilling to see the gas chambers and railway lines that brought carriage loads of Jewish people into these death camps. Coming from a Jewish family, I've been familiar with the holocaust for most of my life. Being there brought it home in a visceral way and made me realise just how valuable being free to be one's self truly is. It's one of many examples in which physically being at the place can never be replaced by watching videos or reading about it. I'd had a similar experience when I'd visited Berlin.

When I eventually arrived back in Chiang Mai and reflected on my summer in Warsaw, I realised that being there and spending time with Dorota had grown on me, and I wanted to go back. I'd pushed aside my initial concerns about our age difference and focused on taking one day at a time. We were in a long-distance relationship of sorts, with Skype being our main medium of communication. Because of the difference in time zones, it meant that Dorota could never chat with me in the evenings. For her, calls had to be the morning or early afternoon, when it doesn't feel so natural to be talking intimately with someone on the other side of the world. That was a challenge, but we seemed to navigate it okay. Despite the difficulty, I felt happy about our relationship and how it was slowly evolving.

To ensure I'd have to return to Warsaw, I committed to run my next marathon there and signed up for a place in the 2015 race, which was taking place the following April. I started training for it in October, following the new methodology that I'd successfully tried out earlier that year in London. Lorraine made some slight tweaks to my programme based on our review of that race, and I was good to go. About one month into my training, I was in a meeting with Gaston Schmitz and Brian Bauerle at ALI, and I let them know I was getting ready for my fourth marathon.

Because of his work with ALI clients over many years, Brian had a huge personal network of people all over the world. Many were supporters of a charitable venture he was involved in called Schools of Hope. It was in Nong Ook Village near Chiang Dao in northern Thailand, about two and a half miles from the border with Myanmar. This opened up the possibility for me to raise a decent sum of money to support their work, whilst finally breaking my sub four-hour target. After a visit to the school, I agreed to dedicate my run in Warsaw to raise money for them. I'll tell you more about how that turned out later.

Christmas in Warsaw
Choosing to spend my first winter in Poland after nearly a decade in Asia was a great decision in some ways and not so good in others. What made it a good decision was that I spent more time with Dorota and experienced a full-on Polish Christmas at home with her massive, extended family. They made me feel welcomed, and I loved being surrounded by the laughter, the fun and joyful energy of the young kids, who were the offspring of Dorota's numerous cousins.

The delicious Polish food seemed to flow in a never-ending stream of new dishes throughout the day and evening. Some of Dorota's family could speak English, which meant I didn't have to be a spectator. Unfortunately, her parents didn't, so Dorota had to translate our rather short conversations, which felt slightly awkward, but they helped break the ice.

Speaking of ice, the temperature in Warsaw in December was around minus eleven degrees. That was the reason that coming for the winter wasn't such a good decision. There was snow and ice everywhere. To stay on track for a sub four-hour finish next April, I needed to maintain my training routine and I had to force myself out in the mornings. I was well-protected with several layers of running gear, including long trousers, thermal gloves, a woolly hat, and face buff.

I ran four times per week in the huge and picturesque Royal Łazienki Park, which is spectacular, and it became one of my favourite places to go in the city in later visits. Thankfully, I'd get warm after twenty minutes but tumbling out of the centrally heated apartment into the freezing temperature outside was always a shock to my system. For that reason alone, I was happy to return to Thailand at the start of 2015 and complete the next three months of my training in Chiang Mai, where it was much warmer, and I had all of the support and resources I needed to make it work.

Training and Fundraising in Thailand

Once again, I launched a global fundraising effort with the aim of raising over $10,000 for Schools of Hope, under the aptly named Hope is in Your Hands campaign. Think about it for a moment; a lot of things you and I are able to do like work, travel, study, and enjoyable recreational activities are possible because we grew up in a country where you automatically receive a good basic education, have access to good food and clean water, and enjoy a reasonably good standard of living.

After nine years of globetrotting, I was acutely aware how that privilege had opened doors and opportunities for me that were simply not available to people born in less developed parts of the world. I'm deeply grateful for the good fortune and privileges that life has brought me. At the same time, I felt desperately sad there were so many people in Asia who struggled to make ends meet and who didn't have access to the basic amenities of life.

Myanmar (formerly Burma) is one country that caught my attention, as the citizens there try to reform the way the country is governed and attempt to modernise their way of life. Over the last few years, tens of thousands of people from the Burmese Shan State have fled persecution and entered neighbouring Thailand as immigrants. For them, life in Thailand often means they are subject to exploitation and constant anxiety about their legal status, yet it's still a far better life than what is now possible in their native Shan state.

Schools of Hope is a Thai non-profit organization, which was established in 2008 with an inspiring mission. Their aim was to set up schools along the Thai/Burmese border to ensure the availability of free basic education and proper assistance to disadvantaged children of displaced and migrant families from Shan State and other ethnic minorities. The Venerable Phra Virote, the abbot who founded the first school said, "We welcome support from anyone willing to help educate these children whose parents have fled from Myanmar. I want the children to have access to a good education. We built this school for the orphans and the children from poor families. I'd like to see these children have the chance to follow their dreams and to build a future."

I knew that any money raised would help provide Schools of Hope with basic amenities and facilities that many of us take for granted, such as learning materials, clothes, three healthy meals per day, healthcare, and shelter. I met and spoke to a number of them during my initial visit and understood how critical this was to their future.

"I want to study to become a surgeon and help people who are sick and injured," said one young girl.

Everyone who spoke to me touched my heart and inspired me to step up. One of the things the Schools of Hope badly needed was a new building closer to Chiang Mai. The new site for the kids who were ready for secondary school had to be located in Chiang Mai because it gave the older children a better chance to find a paid job when they'd finished. There was no secondary school anywhere within miles of Nong Ook. The estimated cost of construction for the new building was around $120,000. With ten percent of that, Brian and his team could authorise the start of construction in the knowledge that the rest of the funding could be raised through their network of donors and some government sources.

Even though raising money was time consuming and extremely hard work, I loved doing it for three reasons. First, it gave me a strong sense of meaning and purpose, and I felt that I was using my life energy well. Second, it aligned well with my guiding principle of contribution and allowed me to be of service to the greater good. Third, the campaign encouraged me to be creative in coming up with ideas for the personal and social media communications that were needed. My good friend Reuben Lowe produced an incredible four-minute video so that I could show people what my campaign was all about and inspire them to get involved. Setting a financial target gave me the opportunity to connect and catch up with hundreds of friends and colleagues all around the world as I pleaded with them to make the biggest donations they could.

LIFE WITHOUT A TIE

Noom Hkurh, the manager of the school in Nong Ook told me, "We have thirty-one boys here between five and sixteen years old, and ten girls, as well as a further five boys who have already started at high school in Chiang Mai. They are aged between seventeen and nineteen. A charity in Singapore pays for their accommodation costs. It's fantastic that we will get some help from the Calling All Angels Foundation as I have dedicated my life to making sure they get a better chance in life than I had when I was younger."

Calling All Angels Comes to Warsaw

By the time I returned to Warsaw in March, my fundraising campaign was well underway, with nearly $9,000 secured. With three weeks to go to the race, I wondered how much support a complete stranger in a new city might be able to generate. Luckily for me, Dorota had a few contacts who worked in the media and one of them had access to the producers of two national radio stations. I hastily wrote a press release and got one of Dorota's friends to translate it into Polish, then emailed it to the various contacts we'd identified. We set up the means for people in Poland to make donations, as we hoped that many would, if I could get an interview on one of the breakfast drivetime shows.

To cut a long story short, I was interviewed on two shows, one at breakfast time and one at the weekend. Dorota agreed to translate on one of them as the host was speaking and broadcasting in Polish. Going into those studios was an adventure of sorts, and quite different to some of the physical adventures I'd encountered earlier in my journey. To start with, I was nervous, but once I started talking, my nerves gave way to my passion for the Schools of Hope, and I think I managed to inspire a few of the listeners. A week later, a local girl saw me in a restaurant and heard my voice and asked me if I was the guy that had spoken on the radio about running the marathon. When I said it was me, she told me how uplifted she'd felt by my story. It was one of my most memorable moments in Warsaw, and I saw the power and reach the media has to influence people's thinking. It was also a confirmation signal from the Universe that following my guiding principles was affecting people's lives there and further afield.

The race was on April 26, 2015. By then, I'd received over two hundred donations from people in thirty countries around the world, raising a staggering $13,225. It was enough to ensure that construction of the new building in Chiang Mai would start in early 2016, although more money would be needed to complete it. My failure to run a sub four-hour marathon in New York and the dogged pursuit to lose those sixteen minutes for six more years had been a blessing in disguise. Life works in mysterious ways sometimes, and it led to a scenario that would change the lives of hundreds of Burmese refugee kids, who will attend the school in years to come. There was a strange and beautiful perfection to the chain of events that had unfolded.

Following Lorraine's training guidance, I reached Warsaw in the best condition I'd ever been as a long-distance runner. I'd made steady and solid progress through the twenty weeks of winter and spring, running an average of forty miles per week. I ran in the Warsaw half-marathon on March 29 in a blistering one hour and forty-eight minutes, which was a personal best. It was a solid confirmation that I was on track. I knew I was fast enough for another attempt.

The final choice was my strategy for the race. For those of you that know about running long distances, I chose a negative split strategy. In a big race, with ten thousand runners or more, everyone's inclined to go out too fast at the start. It takes a lot of self-restraint to allow others to run ahead of you and not be pulled along with them. With a negative split strategy, you intentionally complete the first half of the marathon slower and run the second half faster. It's counterintuitive. If you're fuelled properly, it works well because your body gets more comfortable as the race progresses and starts to speed up naturally. I'd never used this strategy before. Lorraine convinced me this was the right way to go.

Experienced runners will confirm that the marathon really starts when you reach twenty miles, and I can verify this. When I reached that point, it was well beyond any distance I'd run in training. I felt fairly fresh, as Lorraine predicted I would. With an hour still to go, I'd dropped my pace a little but I had plenty of time in hand. With two miles to go, a feeling of elation started to ripple through my body, as I knew I was going to achieve my goal. Even though my legs were getting heavier by the minute, and every stride felt like I was dragging a shopping bag full of bricks, the voice of my self-coach was jubilantly yelling, "Keep going, Ray, you've got this. You've waited six years for this. It's yours for the taking. This is your moment."

LIFE WITHOUT A TIE

Crossing the Świętokrzyski bridge in the final mile, I saw the Polish National Stadium in the distance, where the race had begun and where it now was about to end. Summoning one final burst of energy, I smiled inside and out as I jubilantly crossed the finish line, with a final time of 3:56:39. It had taken me six years to finally achieve my sub four-hour marathon. When I considered how many people in the world had been touched by my Calling All Angels Foundation, as well as the personal growth and satisfaction I'd experienced by committing to this goal, it had been worth every single minute of training.

Farewell Asia

I spent the rest of the summer in Warsaw. It's a wonderful city when the sun is shining. A huge river runs through the centre, and it had plenty of green spaces, cafés, and places of interest to visit or hang out in. I enjoyed being at home with Dorota and waking up in the same bed every day, as well as being able to unpack my bag and put my clothes in proper cupboards and drawers. I had a daily routine that I'd missed during many of my travelling years, and I'd slowly started to make friends and connections in the neighbourhood. I even had a favourite local coffee shop where I could work or sit and read.

My freelance work for Coach In A Box was virtually at a standstill, and I ultimately stopped taking on work from them later that year. It had been a fantastic re-entry into the business world, and I'd learned a lot. Looking back, I believe the Universe was secretly at work, helping me to grow towards my greatest potential. The reason for that relationship existing had been fulfilled, and I sensed that I wasn't quite aligned with the vision and values their leader in Asia espoused. It was best to let it go, and I'm happy I did, despite my fear about the loss of income.

Letting go gave me the space to take on my first coaching Triad for the Asian Leadership Institute, with three women from Australia, Portugal, and Romania. I loved that work because it enabled me to draw on my business leadership experience, my mindfulness practices, and everything else I'd been learning from my journey. It drew out the best in me as it was so aligned with everything I valued about life itself. I was totally in my element.

At the end of September, I returned to Thailand for the winter and Dorota came a couple of months later to join me after she'd wrapped up her tour guide work in Europe. Our relationship was by no means perfect, but it felt solid, and we'd really got to know each other well in the eighteen months since we'd met. I was pleased she was with me in Thailand. We'd had a great summer together, and I was thrilled that she'd be able to see the massive impact the Calling All Angels fundraising campaign had on the kids at the Schools of Hope. She'd heard me talking about it constantly in hundreds of phone calls to friends and colleagues when I was soliciting their support and asking for donations.

One of the most joyful moments of my life was handing over the money raised from the Warsaw campaign to Noom Hkuhr. Just as I'd done with Lek Chailert at the Elephant Nature Park, I had a huge ceremonial bank cheque printed, payable to Schools of Hope, for the sum of $13,225. We organised a gathering at the headquarters of the Asian Leadership Institute, which is in the forest on the outskirts of Chiang Mai. We invited twelve of the older boys, who were dressed in their white karate gis for a weekly class, to be photographed during the handover. They were thrilled to bits as they knew they'd soon have a proper home in Chiang Mai as they entered secondary education. A few short weeks after the handover ceremony, I visited the site for the boys' new home, which had been fenced off and had electricity and water supplies installed. I returned about a year later to see the finished building.

If you were one of the amazing people who contributed to this campaign, please give yourself a huge acknowledgement. I am deeply grateful to each and every one of you. Without your help, there is simply no way my Calling All Angels Foundation would function in any meaningful sense.

With the conclusion of the campaign, there was space for me to simply be for a while, which gave me time to reflect on my relationship with Dorota. Despite the challenges of a long-distance relationship over Skype, we'd managed to make it work. I'd effectively been commuting between the two cities since we met. I'd stayed two or three months each time I'd been in Warsaw, but the gaps in between were difficult for both of us to get through. I saw the potential for a great life with Dorota, and we talked a lot over Christmas and the New Year in Chiang Mai about setting up a home together in Warsaw. It meant I'd become tied again for the first time in ten years. It excited both of us and we agreed on a plan to make it happen.

Dorota returned to Warsaw in January 2016 to look for a suitable apartment to rent. By the middle of February, she'd signed a lease on a place in Mokotow, close to the centre of the city. Everything fell into place perfectly, which I took as a confirmation signal from the Universe that it was the right decision. It was a wrench to leave Chiang Mai, as I'd truly loved living there and been deeply changed by the community I'd been part of.

On March 24, 2016, I packed my twenty-two-kilo holdall for the last time in Chiang Mai. I said an emotional farewell to Noi and her brother Dang, who'd been kind hosts during the nine years that I'd been in and out of the city and headed for the airport. I returned to Europe for a new life with Dorota, one that would place me within a couple of hours of London. I had no idea of the surprises that were in store as I made my way to my new home in Warsaw.

A New Tie

I'd settled in at our new apartment when Dorota suggested we hold a party to bless our home. That sounded like a great idea, though I didn't have any friends in Warsaw, with the exception of three people. One was a Polish chap called Jan, whom I'd met when I trekked the Annapurna Circuit in 2008. We'd got to know each other quite well as we walked side by side for a couple of days during our ascent. When he told me he lived in Warsaw, I'd said, "Warsaw! Well, I doubt very much that I'll be in Poland any time soon—if ever—but give me your contact details and if I come to your city, I'll definitely let you know. That's a promise."

And with that, we had hugged and said goodbye. Can you imagine how surprised he was when I called him after I arrived in Warsaw six years later? He was delighted I was there but wasn't able to come to the party. We eventually met up some weeks later.

The second person I had a connection with was a lady called Eileen Gricuk. She was Canadian and married to a Polish guy. She'd lived in Warsaw many years and spoke the language fluently. She was also a freelance coach and worked for Coach in a Box in Europe. We'd met once before at a training day in the UK.

The third guy was a friend I'd met at one of the popular meet-up groups that were going in Warsaw the previous summer. Martin Budny was also from Canada and of Polish descent. Like Eileen, he spoke Polish fluently. He was an open minded, artistic man and worked as a professional actor. We'd hung out together a few times, had a solid connection, were on the same wavelength regarding our everyday lives and challenges, and shared an interest in personal growth. At the party, he asked me if I was free the following Monday. I asked him why.

"I'm going to a casting for a TV commercial that's being shot in a couple of weeks and thought you might like to come along. It'll be fun."

Whilst he knew that wasn't my line of work, he remembered I'd played the lead role in a comedy play in Australia and loved the world of acting. The timing couldn't have been better. I'd been thinking about ways to increase my income as I'd been packing up my life in Thailand. The cost of living in Europe was substantially higher than in Asia. The amount of freelance coaching work I was doing was growing slowly but wouldn't be enough to sustain my costs in the long run. It wasn't an immediate problem but something I'd need to address if I wanted to remain in Poland for the next couple of years. I'd chosen the city as home because of my relationship with Dorota, so it was a choice made out of love rather than fear. For that reason alone, I embraced my guiding principles of presence and non-attachment and held the empowering belief that things would work out and all my needs would be met. Eleven years on the road had given me all the evidence I needed to know I could trust the Universe with that.

Taxi!
At the casting for the TV commercial, I milled around and talked to people in the studio. The casting director heard me call out to Martin in English and immediately came towards me. I was half expecting her to challenge me on why I was there but something quite different happened.

"Are you a native English speaker?" she asked. "Where are you from?"

"Yes, I am. I'm from London. Why do you want to know?"

"The ad we're shooting is for an electrical retailer in Turkey called Arçelik, and the story in the ad takes place in London. We've been looking for an English actor, preferably a Londoner, who can play the part of a London taxi driver. Would you be interested in auditioning for it?"

"Sure, what do you need me to do?"

The casting director's assistant took me aside and gave me a brief description of the character, whilst someone else set up four chairs in the shape of a car in two rows of two. The assistant handed me a round clock that had been hanging on the wall and told me to pretend it was a

LIFE WITHOUT A TIE

steering wheel. The actor playing the part of the passenger, a marketing executive for this electrical retail brand, sat in one of the two rear seats. We were asked to make small talk, which meant I had to consciously look in my rear-view mirror from time to time as I would if it were a real conversation between a cabbie and a passenger. After a couple of minutes, the casting director told us we could stop and thanked us both. She went off into another room to talk with her colleague and a couple of people who worked for the client company. She emerged about ten minutes later and to my delight and surprise, offered me the part. I was totally chuffed and couldn't believe how easily it had all happened. Ironically, my friend Martin wasn't chosen to be in the commercial.

It felt like the Universe had once again stepped in and made something happen for me. I was probably the only English-speaking Londoner in the right age range in the whole of Warsaw on the day of that casting, which randomly came about due to the timing of our housewarming party and Martin's invitation. Had the party been the following weekend, this would never have happened. As a result of landing the part, albeit tiny, the production company insisted that I appointed an agent to manage my arrangements with them, mainly for legal and administrative reasons. Martin introduced me to his agency, Skene, and I signed a contract with them the following day.

A couple of days later, I went back to the studio to be fitted for a costume, which basically involved trying on loads of clothes until the director made a final decision. That gave me a chance to meet some of the other actors cast in the ad although some were in different scenes to my own, as the story in the ad was spread across the three cities of London, Istanbul, and New York. It was all pretty exciting.

The day of the shoot was a real adventure. Everything was taken care of for the actors, and I felt like the ultimate VIP. When I arrived, I was shown to the dining room. The production team had set up a huge caravan with two chefs, who made food all day long for the cast and crew. After a cooked breakfast, I was ushered into another caravan for make-up and costume fitting. The production crew spoke to each other via walkie talkies, and it wasn't long before I got my call to go on set, which was a street in the centre of Warsaw that closely resembled the look and feel of London.

To make it appear totally realistic, the production company had shipped in a double decker London bus and several black cabs. They'd also changed the road signs to English ones and gave the shops English names and signage. This was the only part of the shoot in which I genuinely had to drive the taxi. On the call of action from the director, I had to turn a corner into the street in which the passenger was waiting, stop, and ask him, "Where can I take you?" as he climbed in and sat in the back. It was filmed from several different angles to allow for the editing process, so we ended up retaking that part about ten times over a couple of hours.

The rest of my scene involved me driving, while in conversation with my passenger, just as I'd done at the audition. They lifted the taxi up on to a trailer, secured it, and mounted cameras and spotlights to the sides of it so they could film us talking as I pretended to drive it. The director and production crew followed us in another truck that had all the recording equipment. The director gave instructions to us through a speaker they'd set up in the car.

I can see why acting is such an attractive profession. It was like playing a game of pretend and being paid well for it. My fee for that day of shooting was around £1,000. I remember thinking that it was so much fun, and I wanted to do more of it. I wasn't aware how fortunate I'd been to have landed the part in the first place. My bubble of euphoria burst a couple of weeks later when I saw the final cut of the ad. Despite having filmed for a total of about six hours, my appearance amounted to about two seconds in the televised version of the ad.

Two seconds isn't even enough to use for a showreel, which you need to have in order to secure more casting opportunities. My agent started sending me to auditions for similar work and whenever I attended them, there were literally hundreds of people waiting in line to get a thirty second chance to convince the casting director they were the right person. It was as hopeful as entering the lottery. I went to enough auditions to realise I probably wouldn't generate enough income from acting to sustain myself, especially as I didn't speak Polish. Most films were ultimately going to be broadcast on Polish TV and although commercials usually don't have any dialogue, I wasn't asked to do any more of them.

It wasn't quite the end of my performing career. Word had got around that I was in Warsaw and spoke English. I received a few invitations for voice-over work, particularly from post-production studios that dubbed corporate videos in multiple languages. It turned out to be a godsend that

LIFE WITHOUT A TIE

I'd recorded my first voice-over in Chiang Mai in 2011. It proved I'd had some experience in that area and gave video producers confidence in my ability. It wasn't long before I'd added a couple more completed voice-overs to my portfolio of finished work, which included a promotional video on YouTube for a new musical instrument for kids and a marketing video for a massive retail property development on the Vistula river.

Through one of Martin's connections, I was cast in two corporate films designed to help companies with their data security. Martin was also cast as the IT Director in one of them, and we shot a scene together, which both of us enjoyed immensely. I loved doing those films because I had a character to assimilate and plenty of dialogue to master. When Dorota wasn't away on a tour of Eastern Europe, she'd often help me rehearse my lines.

In both films, I played the part of a powerful corporate executive in a stressful, dramatic situation. The irony of that wasn't lost on me, as I was playing a character who was the same as the real-life businessman I'd been in London for years before my life without a tie began. It was much more fun to *play at* being the character and to drop it again as soon as shooting was over.

For the first time since I left the UK in 2005, I was close enough to England for my mum to come and visit me. Dorota helped me organise a mini tour of Warsaw and Krakow for her, and it was wonderful to have four uninterrupted days to spend together, especially as it was around the same time as my birthday.

In My Element

In September 2016, I travelled to Berlin to take part in my fifth marathon. It's just over four hours by train from Warsaw. I'd trained as diligently as in previous marathons but found it hard to really push myself because I'd already broken the sub four-hour barrier and had nothing to achieve apart from improving on my time. I actually finished the race some thirty minutes slower than in Warsaw. I didn't mind though. Running through the Brandenburg Gate, the symbolic dividing line between East and West Berlin before the collapse of communism, in the final mile made me aware how much I value my freedom, and I had a fabulous week in one of my favourite cities. In my relatively short marathon career, I'd completed the courses in New York, London, and Berlin, which are three of the top six marathon races in the world. The other three are Tokyo, Chicago, and Boston, which I have yet to do.

My life had slowly shifted into a more conventional pattern in Warsaw. I genuinely enjoyed having domestic routines, being at home, and making new friends. Living in a new city felt novel and fresh, and there were no end of places to explore. I continued to do my coaching work and develop new skills. I was happy to be learning and growing. From time to time, I did bits and pieces of acting and voice-over work to keep one foot in that world.

A major milestone occurred in June 2017, when I made my final return trip to Thailand. I took part in a facilitator training with the Asian Leadership Institute (ALI), which allowed me to reconnect with my colleagues and friends and enjoy the laidback lifestyle that Chiang Mai offers. I knew intuitively that it would be the last time for a long while before I'd be back again. I loved the facilitation and coaching work I was doing, and I was getting better and better at it, especially as I was fortunate enough to be part of the global ALI community, with some of the best practitioners I'd ever come across. When we came together, it felt like we all collectively stretched the boundaries of our comfort zones, and I always left those events feeling empowered.

The vision I'd created for my professional work during the Hoffman Process six years earlier was fully materialising. I was helping people feel great about themselves. I was helping them find their strength and courage. I could travel frequently around the world, and there was the potential for more. I was constantly learning and growing, yet I'd freed myself from the desire to be perfect and the struggle to be great. Instead, I measured my feeling of success by the sheer love of my work and the beautiful feeling of being fully engaged by it. I had also accessed my inner wisdom and experiences in service of others regularly, which I'd dreamed of doing for years.

Of course, there's always plenty of room for improvement. I'd imagined speaking to groups, and I hadn't made any progress with that. That started to change when I returned from Chiang Mai and was invited to address a group of changemakers at one of the first well-being conferences in Warsaw towards the end of 2017. To prepare for that, I reflected deeply on everything I'd learned during my journey and selected some of the best practices and habits I'd adopted to cultivate and maintain my own well-

LIFE WITHOUT A TIE

being to share at the conference. I watched the video of my talk afterwards and noticed how happy I was about the person I'd become. It was obvious that I was living a life in which my core values of freedom, integrity, love, and exploration were being honoured most of the time.

One of the big advantages of living in Europe was that it gave me easy and convenient access to the UK business marketplace. It's one I know well and being so close meant I could open the door to more opportunities to do the kind of work I was passionate about. If only I could find people who I really resonated with in terms of our vision, purpose, and values. I'd been away a long time, and I admit I had one or two limiting beliefs about the likelihood of finding such a group or tribe. I'd been able to in Asia, so why not in England? Just like I'd done before, I gave my request to the Universe and asked for help to find the right people. In the meantime, I carried on with my life in the knowledge that something would show up sooner or later. I didn't have to wait long.

Chapter Nineteen
The Explorer Returns

"I trust that everything happens for a reason, even if we are not wise enough to see it."

Oprah Winfrey

IN APRIL 2017, DOROTA DECIDED TO TRY HER HAND AS A VIRTUAL PERSONAL assistant, and I offered to let people in my personal network know in case they might have a need for her services. I emailed a few coaches and friends in the business world. A friend and former colleague called Clare Mitchell responded. She'd worked alongside me at First Place. We arranged to have a long overdue personal catch-up on the phone. After all, it had been thirteen years since we worked together.

I don't think we'd spoken for about a decade. In that time, Clare had got married and become a mum of two kids. She'd blossomed into an accomplished, wise, and successful businesswoman, and it was a joy to hear about her journey. I discovered that Clare, together with another woman called Elke Edwards, intended to launch a brand-new, cutting-edge leadership development business called Ivy House. What really appealed to me was that it was aimed exclusively at younger people who were at the start of their leadership journey, which meant they would receive the kind of support that was normally only given to senior executives. By bringing their development forward, the intention was to equip them to become extraordinary leaders much sooner. As I listened, I instinctively knew I'd found the tribe I was looking for. Once again, the Universe had stepped in.

I'd learned so much from being a successful business leader and from my twelve-year nomadic journey in which I'd transitioned into becoming a coach. I knew in my bones that being part of the team with Elke and Clare would put me squarely in my element. Their vision, principles, and knowledge, which would be a core part of their programme, were so closely aligned with my own to the extent that I felt at home immediately and was excited about being involved. Their plans were still on the drawing board, so I let Clare know straight away that I wanted to support their new venture. They eventually launched the company at the end of 2017 and the rest, as they say, is history. I came to London and took part in my first programme as a performance coach in May 2018 and I've proudly continued to be a part of the constantly evolving Ivy House community ever since.

As a brief aside, there is a sublime perfection to the way life unfolds sometimes which we can never see in the moment. Take my relationship with Clare Mitchell as an example. When I saw the end was coming for First Place back in 2004, I set an intention to honour my value of integrity with regards to all my team members. I recognised that every single one of them had helped to build our success, and I was determined that those who wanted to continue learning and growing found new, and ideally better, work opportunities to move on to. To that end, I'd discreetly approached Elke Edwards and her brother, Marc, who ran a rival training and consulting business, to let them know that Clare had done an amazing job for us and been an outstanding member of our team. They met her and subsequently invited her to join their organisation.

I hadn't stood to gain anything by doing it except the personal satisfaction and inner peace I felt once I knew that Clare was taken care of. I had no idea at the time that Clare and Elke would work together for several years and lay the foundations for the creation of Ivy House. Fast forward about thirteen years, and I'd returned to Europe in search of a tribe to align with. Only then did I unwittingly discover this new venture, and there was a place for me on their team. It seems almost impossible to believe that this kind of random event can steer one's life in this way. Yet it confirmed that when you live according to your values and act honourably, the Universe does its best work on your behalf. Can you recall a time in your life when a random, unexpected connection or conversation led you to find exactly what you had been looking or hoping for? Or at the least, changed your trajectory to put you on the path to where you are now?

Itchy Feet
The novelty of living in Warsaw was something I valued and appreciated daily, but it wasn't the same for Dorota. She'd had a couple of brief stints when she lived in the USA and Italy whilst studying but apart from those, she'd never lived outside of Poland as an ex-pat. The desire for a

LIFE WITHOUT A TIE

Mediterranean climate and lifestyle and a nagging feeling of restlessness pushed Dorota to declare halfway through 2017 that she wanted us to move to a different country, at least for a while. At first, I was reluctant, because I was enjoying the way in which life was unfolding where I was. I saw and felt how unhappy she was with the status quo, so I eventually got on board with the plan to relocate. We decided to go and check out Lisbon in December 2017. As lovely as it was, it didn't feel quite right, and we quickly ruled it out.

At the start of 2018, we were offered a month-long house-sit in Malta for two friends of mine, Pete and Marianne Gable. Malta was on our list of possibilities for a move, and it became the twenty-eighth country in my journey. We jumped at the opportunity. It was enough time to get a good sense of what it would be like on a long-term basis. We weighed it up and came to the conclusion it didn't fit the bill either.

Soon after, I discovered that another couple I knew, who'd been living in Florida for the last few years, had upped sticks and moved to Spain. They resided in a small, pretty mountain village called Jimena de la Frontera in the southern part of the country, about half an hour's drive inland from Estepona. The houses, in the classic, whitewashed Spanish style, were stacked on the hillsides, with an old castle at the top of a hill overlooking the dwellings and the surrounding countryside. It looked like an idyllic place and was a chance to experience a more remote lifestyle.

I saw Joel and Helen's home via video and heard how happy they were as they described their life in the village. We went for a three-day trip to have a look around and sense if it felt good being there. Helen worked part-time at one of the two estate agents in the town and showed us some homes that were available to rent. Jimena was remote, picturesque, had charm and character and was only about a thirty-minute drive from Gibraltar. I could easily fly in and out of London when I had workshops to attend there, and they were becoming a regular part of my routine. We decided to move to Jimena as soon as we could find a house to rent and buy a car. The latter was necessary as everything we needed to take could just about fit in the back of a large estate car (station wagon for US readers), and I'd definitely need the car to get to Gibraltar, not to mention the beaches, which were about forty minutes away.

We found a house pretty quickly and took out a lease for six months. It was furnished and spacious, with two guest bedrooms. If things worked out well, my intention was to invite clients to come and stay for three or four days for their own personal coaching and well-being retreat. We were surrounded by beautiful countryside, and there were plenty of great hikes and walks around Jimena. It was incredibly peaceful, which made it very conducive for the kind of work I was intent on doing. I also had the space to invite additional practitioners to team up with me. They could stay at the house if and when they were needed.

We packed up our stuff and left Warsaw at the end of September 2018. The drive to Jimena took us about seven days, and we dropped in on one or two people on the way. The first was Charlotte in Switzerland, so I could introduce Dorota to her. We stayed overnight at Charlotte's house. It was over seven years since we'd shared our photographs there, and I was grateful we'd both come so far since our divorce, and our friendship was as strong as ever.

We made a stop for two days in Milan, making Italy the twenty-ninth, and final, country that I entered during my epic fourteen-year journey. The rest of our drive took us through Nice, Cannes, and Montpellier in France and our last stop was in Valencia, Spain. There we stayed with a lovely lady called Caroline Leon, who'd become a close friend of mine whilst I lived in Chiang Mai. We'd run together at the track a few times. She works in the coaching field and was now married, with two boys.

The irony of staying with her wasn't lost on me. I met Dorota for the first time when she'd been writing postcards in Blue Diamond. The night before, she'd attempted to enter a popular café bar in the old city called the Tea Tree, only to be turned away at the door because the place had been booked for a private party. I was at that party, which had been organised to celebrate Caroline's birthday. In fact, my gift for her was performing a song I'd written based on the seventies Neil Diamond hit, "Sweet Caroline." I penned my own words, which reflected stories about her, and it was exceptionally well-received. Had Dorota managed to blag her way in, things may have turned out differently. Who knows?

We eventually made it to Jimena and were delighted to move into our new home. It took a few weeks to get used to the extremely slow pace of life in the sleepy town, which I quite liked. There were a few ex-pats around, mostly retirees. Dorota and I signed up to the free, twice-weekly Spanish classes at the Town Hall, where we met most of them. One thing that really bugged me about our house was that it was really cold inside.

LIFE WITHOUT A TIE

Built in the traditional old Spanish style, it had three-feet-thick concrete walls and no central heating. That was great when it was baking hot in the summer as it made the inside of the house refreshingly cool.

But we'd chosen to move there at the beginning of winter, and the only way to heat the house was a wood-burning stove in the lounge, which basically meant all the other rooms were like fridges, especially our bedroom. The owners had an electric blanket we put on the bed, which helped make it a bit more comfortable. Despite that, it was so cold that I could see my breath when I was in bed. I resorted to wearing my dressing gown and socks, as well as the woollen hat I'd been using during my winter training in Warsaw, where the temperature was usually around minus fifteen degrees. I hate to admit it, but I rapidly lost interest in getting naked in bed.

During the day, my fingers were so cold, I ran my hands under the hot water tap to get my blood circulating properly. Bizarrely, one of the best ways to warm up was to go outside, because the sun shined more or less daily, and the temperature was pleasant enough. Inside, when I had an online coaching session with one of my clients, I'd sometimes become short of breath because I was that cold, my body was tensing up. I wished I'd thought about all of this more before we left Warsaw. It was bloody freezing back there in the winter, but at least they were prepared for it. Our apartment building had a wonderful, always-on central heating system that worked superbly.

It constantly niggled me to be in that predicament, and I blamed Dorota for it. I was resentful about it, which took its toll on our relationship. I know I'd agreed to move and had made my own choice freely yet somehow, I'd conveniently forgotten that. Deep down, I knew it wasn't her fault, and she couldn't do anything about it. Ironically, this type of situation is one I sometimes challenge my clients to reflect on in coaching sessions, when I get a sense that they may not be taking ownership for their circumstances or can't see a way out. We all have the propensity to ignore our truth and go into victim mode when it suits us. Perhaps you can recall an occasion where you've blamed someone or something for a crappy circumstance you've been in simply because you haven't fully owned the choice you'd made.

The Rescuer Makes a Comeback

My portfolio of clients grew steadily as Ivy House started to fill the places in their ground-breaking leadership programme in the UK. I attended several two-day workshops in London to coach participants in small groups and returned to Spain to coach some of them individually in between. As word spread, more clients came, and the number of workshops increased. I enjoyed the work immensely and loved being part of the Ivy House team. It really energised me. Consequently, I spent more of my time working than either Dorota or I had envisaged when we planned our move.

That didn't sit well with her. The way she'd envisioned it, we were supposed to do a lot more shared activities. She'd imagined that we'd regularly walk or hike forest trails, travel to other parts of Spain or neighbouring countries, hang out at the beach or explore the local area where we lived. I was happy to do those things, but occasionally, and not at the expense of missing out on a growth opportunity. As time passed, I started to judge her vision to be a fantasy, even though I'd seen our potential life in a remote Spanish village in much the same way before we moved. That didn't go down very well, and the stresses between us built up as we both became more entrenched in our different perceptions.

Deep down, I hadn't admitted the raw fact that my relationship with Dorota felt like it didn't really work for me any longer. And so I came back to the idea that people will come into your life for a *reason*, a *season,* or a *lifetime*. When I look back and reflect with complete honesty on my relationship with her, I'd felt a couple of times that I'd reached the end and the purpose for which we'd come together had been served. It was even confirmed in an astonishing session I'd had with a family constellation facilitator.

The first time I'd had this sense was only a few months after I'd moved to Warsaw in 2016. Dorota struggled to author a vision for her life and sometimes spiralled downward into a dark place. She seemed unable to take a solid step forward towards a new future, especially related to her work. She wanted to work as a coach but lacked confidence and didn't take decisive action. Instead, she'd chosen the path of a virtual PA, which she lost interest in after a few weeks. Someone in my professional network was advertising a job in a support role with a company in which she could use her skills working remotely. I helped her to apply, and she landed the role. She seemed to enjoy that at first, but the shine soon wore off.

LIFE WITHOUT A TIE

None of this was a problem per se, but Dorota's inability to move forward activated the rescuer in me. Anyone who understands basic psychology will know that this isn't a healthy role to play for any length of time. It was a behavioural pattern I'd dropped into a lot when I was married, and I thought I'd jettisoned it after my divorce from Charlotte years before. But it seemed I hadn't quite eradicated it. I did everything I could to fix things for Dorota, including reluctantly moving to Spain. Once again, I'd forgotten to pay close attention to my own needs as time had elapsed and was now paying the price. Somehow, I couldn't summon the courage to let go and face life on my own, so I resisted admitting the truth about it. The delusion of being a happy couple seemed better than the fear of breaking up and being alone again.

I realised that I hadn't embraced my guiding principle of presence during that time. Throughout my entire journey, I'd been committed to being fully present to each experience in the moment, accepting each one, and being grateful. I hadn't been distracted by worries concerning the past or the future. But with Dorota, I'd put expectations on how it ought or should be and was quietly suffering internally with the frustration and disappointment that resulted.

During what was a difficult period emotionally for both of us, there were short periods of sunshine amongst the dark, stormy rainclouds. We took a five-day trip to Valencia to join a few of my colleagues from the Asian Leadership Institute who were based in Europe. Although it was a working trip for me, Dorota and I managed to carve out some time together in between and after meetings which generated a sense of connection and closeness between us that we'd missed. Tarifa and Cádiz were also lovely places that were easy to reach by car, and we made the most of the fact that we were living so close. We'd go there at the drop of a hat whenever we could.

The Brighton Run

In November 2018, I'd started training for a half-marathon in Brighton, England. I'd made the decision to take part to support an amazing man called Stephen Kakouris, who I'd met through the Ivy House programme. He was a participant, and I'd been assigned to him as his coach for six months. During that time, I'd witnessed him grow enormously. He diligently applied himself to learning and improving his professional life. He was fantastic to coach because he was willing to experiment, and he took on feedback well. As a result, I liked and respected Stephen enormously, and we became friends.

One thing you should know about Stephen is that he was born with mild motor disabilities. As a result, he has a speech impediment. This is what he said about it:

"I'd adapted my life so it didn't affect me in any way, but I still felt quite uncomfortable talking about it publicly. On the Ivy House Programme, I challenged myself to get up in front of a group of people I'd never met before and openly discuss it. Talking about my speech impediment with them, I experienced a greater acceptance of myself. It was very powerful for me."

He'd shown great courage in doing that, not to mention how much it had inspired others, including me. He'd pushed himself beyond the edges of his comfort zone, which is something I often encourage people to consider from a growth perspective. But he wasn't content to leave it there. His motor disabilities also impede his walking, so he wanted to conquer a physical challenge that would induce the same radical sense of breakthrough he'd experienced when he took on the mental challenge of the Ivy House programme. He'd accomplished that with flying colours.

"I want to run a half-marathon," he said when I asked him what he had in mind. "I recognise I'm holding a limiting belief that I'll never be able to do it, and I want to smash that. I've always hated running. But as I've learned more about stepping out of my comfort zone in the work we've done, I'm ready to challenge myself."

Not sure if he was serious, and also knowing what that would demand from him based on my own personal experience, I asked him when he wanted to run and which event. He said he'd look into it and let me know in a couple of days.

"I think it's a brilliant idea to take this on," I said. "If you decide to commit, I'd like to run it with you. These are tough events, and I believe you'll need the support of others running alongside. Maybe we could open up the invitation to the other people in your cohort? The more, the merrier."

I wondered if Stephen had said he wanted to run as an act of bravado and if he would actually commit to doing it. A tiny part of me even hoped he wouldn't, so I wouldn't have to go back into training. In this case, commitment would be confirmed when he registered online for the half-marathon race event of his choice and got an acceptance. If he did that, I'd know he was committed. When I lived in Chiang Mai and people heard I trained at the track most mornings, they often asked if they could come running with me. "Of course," I always said. "Meet me outside my place at six a.m., and we'll go together." In the six years I lived there, I'd say that the no show rate was around ninety-nine percent, so I had a low level of expectation that Stephen would follow through.

I'm happy to admit I was mistaken.

"I've registered for a place in the Brighton Half-Marathon in February 2019," he said a week later. "I'll send you the link so you can do the same, if you're still up for it."

I promptly registered and quickly put together a training plan for myself. Whilst I was no stranger to running this distance, I wasn't exactly in shape and needed to make a concerted effort to get myself ready. I was there in support of Stephen and needed to be sure I'd finish the race. We both individually got on with our training—Stephen in London and me in Jimena—and had conversations over the phone to check in with each other every few days. He was running between three and four times per week, building up his endurance to be sure he could handle the distance.

When word spread amongst the Ivy House community that Stephen was doing this, others in the alumni jumped in to support him, which reflected his popularity as well as the Ivy House spirit of radical support. On the day of the race, Stephen's posse was seven strong. We were behind him all the way, and some had pushed themselves outside their comfort zone too. The feeling of love was palpable. I acted as his pacemaker, to ensure he ran an even pace for his ability. I didn't want him to run too fast in the early stages, which can crush the hopes of highly competent, experienced runners. I'd decided that Stephen was going to finish, no matter what and was prepared to carry him over the line with a couple of our fellow runners if necessary. It wasn't. Stephen finished the race in a totally respectable two hours and fifteen minutes. He didn't even take a single rest break and had energy to spare.

"I can't think of a more committed coach than Ray," Stephen said to one of my Ivy House colleagues. "During the race, he set the pace the entire way and helped me to accomplish something I never thought I'd be able to do. At the end of the race, I put my medal around my neck and didn't want to take it off! I never gave up, even though it hurt. One or two of the pictures show the pain I was in. I'm so happy that I finished the race, I even wore my medal the next day at work. I thought people would think that I was walking funny because of the half-marathon ordeal I'd been through. Then I realised that I walk funny anyway and felt proud of what I'd done."

What Stephen did in that race is a shining example of someone who was prepared to step right out of his comfort zone. When anyone does that, it lifts and inspires everybody else. He smashed the boxes he'd been put in all his life because of what other people perceived his limitations to be. For him, the race was a metaphor. He was running towards a goal and put in the hours to achieve something great. He no longer tells himself there's something he can't do due to his limitations. To quote the man himself a few days afterwards; "If you put in the time and effort, if you show up, I believe you can achieve great things. When I crossed the finish line, the pride I felt made me reflect on other opportunities in my life. Those who showed up this weekend, raised money, and proved something to themselves. They did it for their own reasons. The fact that I committed to do this started the ball rolling for them too. The mindset of possibility is contagious. I wore my medal into work today and showed it to someone who'd thought I couldn't do it. He'd been genuinely worried for me and had tried to talk me out of it. Seeing the medal, he felt inspired. It made my morning. I hope that people will say, "If Stephen can do it, why can't I?"

In many ways, finishing that race hand in hand with Stephen was more satisfying than running the Warsaw marathon in under four hours. It gave me a great opportunity to embrace two of my guiding principles of connection and contribution. I already knew Stephen at a fairly deep level from the coaching work we'd done together but running this race with him took our relationship to an even deeper level. He completely put his trust in me to be there for him, which enabled me to feel the joy of a selfless act, something that I don't often do. It was one of the greatest honours of my life. We've become close personal friends, and I'm so happy to see him flying in his career and his life. And seeing Stephen collect his runner's medal afterwards gave me a deep sense of contentment. I'd felt the same way when I took care of my friend Elizabeth in Australia when she had cancer and when I handed over the money from my Calling All Angels campaign to Lek at the Elephant Nature Park and the Schools of Hope. I'd set a specific intention around this in my vision work during the Hoffman Process and made the following statement, "I love the outward expression of the love I feel inside and get great pleasure from loving people." Seven years later, it felt blissful to acknowledge that my life without a tie was taking shape, bit by bit and week by week, exactly as I'd imagined it would.

It's worth mentioning that doing the half-marathon with Stephen also opened my eyes to Brighton. It was a sunny weekend in the coastal city, and there were thousands of people from all walks of life. It had a carnival-like atmosphere. A few people I'd met on my travels had spoken highly about it and described it as a great city to live in. I made a mental note that if I ever returned to the UK, it would be at the top of my list.

A Volcano Erupts in Jimena

At the beginning of my story, I wrote about the time when the cracks first started to appear in my marriage to Charlotte, which I likened to seismic tremors that people who study earthquakes and volcanoes constantly observe. We know these tremors happen weeks or even months before an explosive event, and their purpose is to indicate in advance that a big shift or movement is going to happen. That's precisely what was happening at home with Dorota. We argued more frequently without resolution, and we'd slowly drifted apart. I valued my free time at home to write, study, and read, whilst Dorota advocated day trips and other outdoor activities. She hoped I would join her for most of these, and I didn't want to. The tension had ratcheted up, and the tremors were more exaggerated.

On the day I'd left Jimena to get to Brighton and the race with Stephen, the tension had boiled over. Dorota had exploded with rage like a volcano, and hot lava spewed everywhere. And just to stretch the analogy a little further, I got burned in the process. That event was quite a shock. I can't recall what caused it, but I sensed it'd been coming for a while. In that moment, she appeared to have had enough of me, the status quo between us, and our life in remote, rural Spain. As she vented, she went to our bedroom, collected all of her things, and moved them to one of the guest bedrooms downstairs.

"I'm going to stay in here from now on," she said and closed the door behind her.

Obviously, I was distressed by her behaviour and wanted to engage her in a conversation and do whatever I could to turn this ghastly situation around. But there was no permission or time to do it in that moment. With a plane to catch in Gibraltar, I had to leave. I hoped that when I returned a few days later, I might get a receptive audience. When I came back, nothing had changed. Dorota wouldn't speak to me about it and despite my best efforts to create a useful conversation, I couldn't find a way forward. The volcano continued to smoulder for days.

It was the end of February 2019, and the lease on the house we'd rented was due to expire at the end of March. Dorota broke out of her silence and told me she no longer wanted to stay in Jimena. She'd decided to return to Poland. There was an absence of collaboration that didn't sit well with me. She might have said, "I'm thinking about returning," or "I don't feel I can stay here any longer. Would you like to talk about what's next for both of us?" Sadly, that didn't happen. She'd made up her mind.

I'm embarrassed to admit it, but despite all my life experience, knowledge, coaching skills, and dedication to a mindful way of living, I felt helpless and unable to shift the dynamics between us. I couldn't quite accept it was happening, and I judged myself harshly because I couldn't figure out how to change it or let it go. I had no idea what to do to remedy this awful situation and felt anxious about the future. In my work as a coach, I sometimes have to say that you can't change other people. The focus of any change must always be on yourself and what you can do differently to come to a place of acceptance around a challenging situation. I was now in self-coach mode, desperately trying to embrace this guidance for myself.

It didn't make sense. On the one hand, I wanted to change the situation and keep things in harmony between us. But on the other hand, I'd known for a long time that I wasn't really happy and neither was Dorota. We all have the propensity to stay in a situation we know isn't right for us for fear of losing an undefinable something. And yet, when it's over, it's usually better for both parties involved to let go. I didn't fully trust my guiding principles and was being held hostage to my fears about the future. Can you recall a situation where you hung on out of fear or worry about what the future would be like, even though you knew you needed to let go?

I informed the owner of our house that we'd decided to leave and organised the seven-day drive back to Warsaw. With the heavy atmosphere between us, packing up our stuff and loading the car was painful, and I did my best to bring some lightness to the situation. Over the next week, we had hours and hours to talk as we made our way back to Poland. Dorota seemed more open than she'd been during our last days in Spain, and at least we had a conversation about what the future might look like.

Whatever that future turned out to be, we were definitely not going to live together. Dorota made an arrangement to move in with a friend of hers. In less than a week, I was going to be homeless, which created a sense of panic. I didn't know Warsaw especially well and hadn't had to find a place there before, as Dorota took care of that for us in the past. I couldn't speak or read Polish well enough to search online, and Dorota refused to help, which added to the pressure. Whilst I understood her decision to do that, it felt unnecessarily harsh. I felt abandoned and spiralled into a paralysing sense of self-pity, when I least needed it. It was like trying to walk a tightrope wearing a rucksack full of bricks.

I should have remembered that the Universe never lets me down. At the eleventh hour, after I'd emailed and called the handful of people I knew in Warsaw, one kindly offered me a room to use for a few days until I could get myself sorted out properly. I'd met Agnieszka at a conference in Wrocław, Poland over a year earlier, when I'd given a talk about mindfulness. She'd been in the audience and given me her business card. I was amazed and deeply grateful to her for coming to my rescue in my moment of need. Even though the Universe had my back, I hated it being so last minute!

Back in Warsaw again, Dorota suggested one potential remedy for our failing relationship and that was to have a child. A few of her friends had started families during the two years that we'd lived together. I knew some of these women and saw how strongly the birth of their kids had impacted her. Her desire and interest had definitely been sparked and validated the concern I'd had when we first met in Chiang Mai, that this day would eventually come. It had finally surfaced. Given the perilous state of our relationship, I struggled to see how or why having a child would fundamentally change the dynamic between us.

Had I felt that Dorota was the love of my life—I felt a long way from that place—it would still have been a huge decision for me to become a father at fifty-eight. I was caught in an impossible dilemma and out of ideas about how to change it. These emotional matters are complex and riddled with subtleties that are hard to remember, let alone convey to you. Despite my intuition telling me otherwise, I clung to the hope it might be possible to keep our relationship going.

Dorota sent me articles which implied the root of our problems as a couple laid firmly with me. When I read them, I spiralled into self-doubt and questioned myself. Was there something wrong with me? Had my entire fourteen-year journey been a complete waste of time in terms of my awareness and development as a man? Maybe she was right, and I was incapable of opening my heart? There were moments when I was besieged with thoughts like these and the low feelings that accompanied them.

I suggested to Dorota that we seek help from a qualified relationship counsellor or therapist in Warsaw to help us navigate this. I'd thought that if I could genuinely find a way to fall in love with Dorota once again, then it might be feasible to consider starting a family together. I found a therapist called Gustav, who had great credentials and spoke fluent English. Dorota and I had been distant since we returned to the city and hadn't had much contact. That made me nervous about what was to come, but I let that go and focused on making the best use of the session that I could.

I met Dorota outside his office, and the three of us sat down for our first conversation. What happened did not bode well for the future. In my coaching work, I sometimes draw a single horizontal line on a piece of paper and ask people to consider how much of the time they spend living above or below the line. Naturally, they ask what the line is and what being above or below it means. I explain that when you're above it, you are open, curious, and committed to learning. And when you're below it, you are closed, defensive and committed to being right. It's a simple and effective way of seeing your state of mind in any given moment, and your state of mind will almost certainly affect your behaviour.

During the three-way conversation, I observed Dorota was below the line for most of our conversation. She spoke in a way that sounded closed and defensive and seemed intent on blaming me entirely for the state of our relationship. There was no doubt I was partly responsible and acknowledged that openly. But Dorota wasn't able to take ownership for her part in it. There was nothing I could do to change that. I was hugely disappointed and left that session feeling despondent and uncertain as to what to do next. Several conversations between us followed. Any hope I'd had that therapy was going to help was short-lived.

To make things worse, Dorota stated that for her to continue with further therapy sessions, she needed me to commit to have a child with her from the outset, or she wasn't willing to make the effort. It was the first time in my entire life that I'd faced such an ultimatum. Given the magnitude, I asked for time to reflect on what she was asking. I'd envisaged these sessions would help me explore what would make it possible for me to go down that road with her, and then I could make an informed choice. Similarly, the therapy sessions were meant to help her work out if that was a desirable direction to go with me. Dorota had put the cart before the horse, and I found myself in an impossibly difficult place. To be fair to her, she said what mattered most to her was me being honest about what I wanted and that if I wanted out, she'd accept it.

I wish I could tell you there was a happy ending to this tale, that I was able to find some way of transcending this challenge and came through triumphant. I'm afraid that's not the case. Facing into the fear of letting go, which felt desperately uncomfortable, I took refuge in the things that had worked best for me in such difficult times throughout my nomadic journey. Firstly, I made time to be still and meditated. Secondly, I decided to tune in to my guiding principle of wisdom and listen to my deepest intuition. *What is the right way to go here?* I asked myself that a few times and observed what came to my awareness. Third, I spoke to two trusted friends, although that step probably wasn't necessary as my intuition did the heavy lifting.

It was time to bring our relationship to an end. It was one of the hardest decisions I've ever had to make in my life, as it came with a couple of serious implications. The first was that I'd probably never have children, at least biologically. I'd looked deeply into that during my contemplations and decided I could live with that. The second consequence was that I'd face a completely unknown future. The fear of that is what had held me back from ending the relationship sooner. I knew it was highly unlikely I'd remain in Poland, as it was the relationship with Dorota which had taken me there in the first place. Without that, I no longer had a compelling reason to stay there.

In the difficult conversation that followed with Dorota, I let her know I couldn't have a child with her in the absence of a deep, loving connection between us. Neither could I give her the guarantee she wanted in order to continue with the therapy sessions I'd proposed. Despite her assurance that me being honest was okay and that she wouldn't judge me for it, she was unable to accept the reality that I conveyed to her. A couple of days later, she emailed me to let me know that she no longer wished to have any contact with me.

I was shocked and gutted. The voice of my self-judge kicked in immediately, and I became overwhelmed with feelings of guilt, shame, and not being good enough to love someone well. Of course, none of these things are true. There was only so much I could take ownership for, and I was okay with that. I'd done the best I could, and I'd seen that, when compared with my most significant previous relationships, I'd made progress. This was the first time that I'd taken full responsibility for what was true for me and stated it cleanly and clearly without an agenda. Realising that made it easier to accept the consequences, even though her way of relating to me now felt harsh.

Dorota and I had been together for five years. I'd hoped that we could have at least acknowledged the gifts our relationship had brought to each other and the people around us and connect with some gratitude. Sadly, that didn't happen, and it's something I regret. It was so different to the ending of my marriage to Charlotte, which showed me that it's possible to show up with kindness and compassion towards another person in the most difficult of times and circumstances.

To this day, Dorota and I have never spoken again. Sometimes, but not often, I wonder what I'd say if she did open the door for a conversation. Even though she'd specifically stated that she didn't want me to contact her, I felt compelled to do so from a place of compassion.

Dear Dorota,
A week from now, I'll be leaving Warsaw, most likely for the last time.
I wanted to send you a short note to say goodbye and let you know that despite our relationship ending, my heart is open to you, and I care about you. My heartfelt wish is that you will have a life in which you can be happy, healthy, whole and feel deeply satisfied.
From the messages you shared with me some weeks ago, I'm aware this has been a difficult period for you. I sincerely hope you have found ways to heal yourself and be peaceful after this experience.
You've made it clear that you have no desire to hear from

me and I have no wish to disregard this. I fully respect your wishes and understand your feeling this way.

At the same time, I want to acknowledge that a significant chapter of my life is coming to an end in a few days. You have been a big part of that chapter and I wanted to thank you for the numerous happy memories I'll be taking with me from the majority of my time here. I do hope that one day, we'll be able to connect again.

I have no expectation of, or need for, a reply to this message. I wish you well for the future.

Love to you,

Ray

She didn't reply.

The End of the Journey

Without my tie to Dorota, I felt like a fish out of water, lost and alone in a foreign land with no place to go. I knew it was time to leave. The question was where next? This moment had a strange déjà vu feeling about it. When I got divorced from Charlotte in 2004 and when I first broke up with Annie in 2007, it had felt just like this. As uncomfortable as it was, I recognised that once again I was entering a new transition. My awareness of that made it easier to accept. Not only that, I knew I could handle it, especially as I'd been around this cycle before and now had a deeper understanding about how to navigate it well. I applied my guiding principles of self-acceptance and wisdom. We often repeatedly go through the same type of experience, but it can be hard to trust in our ability to traverse that ground, even when we've done it before. Fear of the unknown is still scary, even if you're familiar with it. Can you recall a time when you were frightened of something you'd already encountered before?

Thanks to Sean Palmer, an actor friend who lived in Warsaw, I found a small, furnished, one-bedroom apartment in Warsaw to rent. He'd reached out to a friend of his called Paulina on my behalf when he heard that I desperately needed to find a place to live. He'd gone out of his way to help me, and I was blown away by his kindness, especially as we'd only met once on a movie set.

Paulina was looking for someone trustworthy to rent her apartment.

Ideally, someone who only wanted to stay between three and six months and who wouldn't mind if she left all her stuff there. She wanted to stay at her boyfriend's home for a while and didn't want the hassle of taking on a formal tenant. For these reasons, she only asked for half the normal rent. Come on! It was as if the Universe had compiled the specific criteria for me and come up with the perfect place, fully furnished and equipped, including Netflix and high-speed internet so that I could work from home. On top of all that, it was in one of the best neighbourhoods in town. There was a bus stop right outside the apartment, so I could get directly to the airport, which I regularly needed to do. It was absolutely perfect and tailor-made to fit my needs.

Having said that, I felt anxious and lonely for much of the time I stayed there. Dorota didn't live far away but she was completely out of bounds, which was painful to accept. On my birthday, there was no one I could celebrate with. I spent the entire day alone at home and spent the evening by myself at the cinema in the local shopping mall, watching *Yesterday* (a charming comedy about a guy who gets knocked unconscious, and when he wakes up, is the only person who knows all the songs by The Beatles). Ironically, the lyrics of that song are about a man suffering from the effects of loneliness.

I watched hours of YouTube videos uploaded by people living in different cities or countries, hoping to find some inspiration about how to maintain my well-being and to see where I might go next. No matter how much I thought about it, it was hard to visualise or imagine what I wanted, which made it virtually impossible to search for it. It was like being trapped inside a box with the instructions about how to get out stuck on the outside of the lid. I remained in the discomfort of that dilemma for weeks, whilst I tried to get on with life. I did notice how good it felt each time I went to London to work with my colleagues and clients. I came back rejuvenated and energised from those trips.

I was stressed by my inability to resolve the issue of where to base myself. In desperation, I reached out to an old and dear friend called Elizabeth Lovius, who agreed to meet me at the Charlotte Street Hotel in London during my next visit. She's one of the wisest women I know, with a huge capacity for deep listening and a nurturing soul. She'd known me and Charlotte for years and had been at our wedding. Even though we hadn't spoken for ages, we had a heart connection and I hoped she'd give me some guidance. As soon as I sat down and started to talk, I poured my heart out and burst into tears. It was so good to be with someone who understood what I was experiencing without any judgment. She held a space for me to think out loud.

"Why don't you come back to the UK for six to twelve months?" she asked. "You could easily find a room to rent on Spareroom.com. I've done it myself a couple of times, and it's worked perfectly well."

I let the idea sink in. It was a good suggestion. Elizabeth also said she'd spent a lot of time in Brighton and really liked the vibe there. As I'd been there recently to run with Stephen in the half-marathon, I'd had some exposure and agreed with her. There was definitely an appeal to life by the sea, whilst still being only an hour away from central London by train. Brighton had a great community of vibrant, colourful individuals. It would be a safe place for me to stay for a while until a clear, longer-term vision emerged. I wasn't exactly excited about coming back to the UK. I felt completely lost, untethered, and disappointed that the end of my relationship with Dorota had catalysed the need to change things. I gave myself a hard time about that and hoped that a few months in the UK would at least be a useful stepping stone.

In July 2019, a lifelong friend called Andy Loveless turned sixty and threw a wonderful party in his garden to celebrate. I flew over from Warsaw for the weekend. I was thrilled to be invited as we go back a long way, and I reconnected with a lot of friends that Andy and I used to work with. I hadn't seen or spoken to many of them for over twenty years. It felt good to connect with people who knew me, and my energy levels went up as we chatted about our lives. On my way back to Warsaw, my inner voice whispered, "You need to head back to the UK, at least for a while."

Brighton was at the top of my list. All I needed from the Universe was a confirmation signal, which came shortly after my return to Warsaw. I called Jane Duncan Rogers, a friend of mine in Scotland, and she asked what was next for me. I told her I was thinking about moving to Brighton. I knew she had a good personal network, so I asked if she happened to know of anyone who might have a spare room in a house or flat there.

"Funny you should ask, Ray. A friend called Sally moved there a year ago and she has her own house. I'm pretty sure she's got a spare room, and I think the two of you would get on really well. Let me connect you."

You probably won't be surprised to hear that I met Sally during my next trip to the UK and we clicked, just as Jane had predicted. She offered me a room in her house for six months. The Universe answered my call, and it was effortless. It felt like what was happening was exactly as it was meant to be. I flew out of Warsaw for the last time at the beginning of October 2019. I was ready to start reimagining life once again and document the incredible journey that you've now read about. Within a few short weeks of being in England, the COVID-19 pandemic started, and in March 2020, the lockdowns began. That was an event that few of us could ever have envisaged, let alone anticipate the impact it would have on our lives. But that's another story.

Chapter Twenty
Looking Back

"Your time is limited, so don't waste it living someone else's life. Don't be trapped by dogma — which is living with the results of other people's thinking. Don't let the noise of others' opinions drown out your own inner voice. And most important, have the courage to follow your heart and intuition. They somehow already know what you truly want to become. Everything else is secondary."

Steve Jobs

You've REACHED THE END OF MY STORY. I SINCERELY HOPE YOU'VE TAKEN something of value from the experiences I've shared with you in *Life Without a Tie*. My journey took me to some wonderful places, both inwardly and in the outside world. I'm curious to know which parts of it most resonated with you. I'd be delighted if you got in touch and shared your thoughts with me.

In reality, there is no end as such to any of our individual stories. We are all works in progress. I left the UK back in November 2005 during a major life transition and returned in 2019 to begin another one. In that sense, I'd come right back to where I'd started. Only the 'I' to whom I'm referring is clearly not the same man as the one who left. There are debates as to whether or not our physical death is even the end point of our journey.

As far as I can make out, life is simply a relentless, continuous flow of events that invite us to respond to each one in the most conscious and skilful way we can in any given moment. With experience, we get better and better at responding skilfully and authentically, if we can be present and pay close attention to what's happening inside us. I believe we are all trying to navigate our journey in such a way that we feel a sense of meaning, fulfilment, inner peace, and genuine happiness.

Before I embarked on this epic experiment, I'd estimated that just over 12,600 days of my life remained. I'd calculated that after the funeral of my father, and it was one of the pieces of data that influenced my decision to commit to my life without a tie. Upon my return to England, around seven and a half thousand days remained. I've consumed about a thousand more days writing this book, which leaves me with around nine hundred and fifty-eight weeks. I'm always aware of the time I have left.

How about you? What's most important for you in the time you have remaining? What if you only had half as much time? Or half of that? As Robert D. Smith points out in his book *20,000 Days and Counting: The Crash Course For Mastering Your Life Right Now*, you don't need a complicated system to get on your way. He says, "It's simple, and by now you may have guessed. The best preparation for living well is to be prepared to die at any time."

Now I'm back in England. Ironically, I'm excited about putting some ties in place that have been absent from my life for a long time, especially regarding relationships and home, or at least a base of sorts. One of the questions I get asked a lot is, "What did you learn from your fourteen-year journey?"

The answer to that question largely depends on who is asking and more importantly, where they are in their life journey. And my answers can be split into two categories—what I've learned about myself and what I've learned about life. Let me start with what I've realised or become more aware of with regards to myself.

First and foremost, I'm human, which means being vulnerable, fallible, and imperfect, and I'm okay with that. I've realised I'm not someone who likes to be alone; my fulfilment comes from being among and connected with other people. Relationships are hard, complicated, and often messy, and they're wonderful and totally worth it. Living by my guiding principles is fundamental to my growth and happiness. Perhaps the greatest gift for me is that I trust the Universe always provides whatever I truly need.

Regarding the second category, it's virtually impossible to capture all of the wisdom I've gained in these pages, although I've done my best to point to that throughout each stage of my story. Having said that, I believe that to navigate life well, I have six suggestions that are worthy of your close attention, and I've set them out for you below. Collectively, these form an empowering belief system. They point towards practices and habits that are worth your time and effort to apply if you want to gain self-mastery. My perspective on this comes not just from my life as a nomadic traveller, but also incorporates the experience I gained from all my years as a participant in society as a career builder, business leader, and more recently as a coach to hundreds of different people in a wide range of careers and occupations, as well as different ages and stages of life.

Hand on heart, I echo Gandhi's way of seeing things. My journey has qualified me to step fully into the role of a coach and mentor. I have answered the question I set out to answer when I left the UK in November 2005, "What does living life true to myself mean in reality?" Now I know the answer deep in my bones. To show up in relationships with love, compassion, and kindness. To act honourably and with integrity at all times. To relentlessly explore new frontiers. To continuously learn and grow. To do work I absolutely love, every day of my life. These underpin the deep happiness and gratitude I feel most of the time. I wonder what your answer would be if you were asked what life has taught you? What might your own journey look, sound, or feel like?

No matter what, I suggest that these six rules apply to all of us to a greater or lesser extent and you'll certainly see some great results from paying attention to them.

Six rules for Happiness

1. Build a Solid Foundation

When I trained to run marathons, I learned that I needed to first develop my core strength. Most runners work hard to strengthen their abdominal muscles, hips, and joints in the pelvic area to ensure their posture is optimised throughout their endurance and speed training. Without that foundation, serious injuries can occur, and there's a risk your performance will plateau.

It's the same with the game of life. In that context, core strength means paying attention to your values and beliefs. What needs to be in your life for it to be fulfilling for you? What do you really appreciate and respect in others? What empowering beliefs do you hold? Can you learn how to let go of your limiting beliefs? What needs are driving your decisions? These are often subconscious and include things like variety, security, belonging, recognition, and being of service.

In her book *Extraordinary*, Elke Edwards refers to core mental strength as your personal blueprint. It includes knowing your purpose, the reason you are here on this planet, which will potentially change everything and release masses of energy for you. Mine is to be a torchbearer for greater human consciousness. Clarifying your vision will enable you to steer your life in the right direction. What does an amazing life look like for you? How would it feel? What would you like to leave behind you when you go? Knowing what kind of activities put you in your element, where your strengths and passions overlap, will nurture your soul.

2. Fully Own Everything That Happens

As a child, I remember listening when grown-ups had conversations. All of the woes in their lives, and of the world in general, seemed to happen to them because of someone or something else. The same was true during most of my career. There was a collective mindset which was mostly in denial when things didn't go according to plan. Everything that happened was someone else's fault and someone else's responsibility to sort out. It didn't occur to me until I was in my early twenties that there may be a radically different way of thinking, which led to different choices of response that were a much better alternative than to blame, make excuses, or wait and hope things would change.

I had to take ownership of my life when it fell apart, and you've seen how it changed when I did. Miracles happened, literally. I can't guarantee they will for you, although the probabilities are good. I've heard from many people I've coached that miracles occurred when they completely let go of the belief that their success was down to someone else. They took positive action and made something happen that they'd only dreamed was possible until then. What would you like to be known for? What would you like to achieve through your work? What things would you like to own? Cultivate a "can do" belief system. The most liberating lesson you'll ever learn is that nobody else can make you happy. And you are not responsible for anybody else's happiness either.

In her book *The Gifts of Imperfection: Let Go of Who You Think You're Supposed to Be and Embrace Who You Are*, Brené Brown puts it like this:

"I now see how owning our story and loving ourselves through that process is the bravest thing that we will ever do. I now see that cultivating a Wholehearted [sic] life is not like trying to reach a destination. It's like walking toward a star in the sky. We never really arrive, but we certainly know that we're heading in the right direction. I now see how gifts like courage, compassion, and connection only work when they are exercised. Every day."

3. Become Your Own Observer

I learned about this in my first Vipassana retreat in 2006 and have practiced it ever since. If we watch ourselves as we go about our daily business and reflect on what we think, feel, and do, we can identify sources of discomfort and distress and learn to be okay with pain in our life. Having some form of regular meditation practice is really beneficial. We spend so much of our daily lives on autopilot that we rarely examine, let alone change, the way we react to certain people and situations.

We're often distracted. Our minds and our bodies are rarely in the same place at the same time. In meetings and conversations, you may notice yourself drift away and get lost in thoughts about the past or the future. Thoughts come in and out of your head constantly, but it's your choice what you do with them. You can hold on to them and let them overpower you or let them go so they don't affect you. Much of the time, you're probably not even aware that you're thinking, and you fail to notice that your thoughts influence your emotions, which in turn drives the behaviour you respond with. The net result is that you may be disappointed or frustrated with the outcomes that follow.

Become aware that you are a living being with conscious awareness, and you can proactively pause when you react to circumstances and notice that you're having particular thoughts that give rise to familiar emotions. When you observe yourself with curiosity and without judgment, you create a separation between you and your thoughts. You step outside the conditioned confines of your programmed personality, free from biases, distortions, and labels. You start to become aware of the negative patterns of behaviour you habitually turn to. You find new and better alternative responses. You understand yourself and others better and foster a deeper connection with your colleagues, clients, family, and friends. You transform limiting beliefs and drop habits that no longer serve you. As a result, you make better decisions which align more closely with your values, vision, and purpose. I've found that over time, being my own observer has also given me greater access to my inner wisdom, and I trust my intuition more than most other sources.

What would your life be like if you paid more attention to what you're thinking? How often do you slow down enough to observe what is happening in the moment? What habitual patterns of behaviour and automatic reactions continually cause problems for you? How would your life be different if you consciously chose to let these go and replace them with behaviours that were more useful?

Sendhil Mullainathan, Professor of Computation and Behavioural Science at the University of Chicago Booth School of Business wrote, "**Metacognition is the capacity or skill** to become aware of one's own mental process. So on the one hand it seems kind of obvious, but if you say, today I'm going to try to simply just notice a part of my mental process I had not yet been aware of. Now that's interesting because that's not just an observational thing. You'll notice it opens doors to things you never thought of."

4. Create Powerful, Purposeful, and Sustainable Relationships
I shared a story about a former colleague and friend called Clare Mitchell, and how we reconnected in 2018 after thirteen years to start working together again. That might appear to be a random stroke of luck at the surface level, but it wasn't. If you read the story again, you'll realise that when you show up to others in each moment with an intention to behave according to your values and act honourably, the Universe does its best work on your behalf. You experience the kind of luck and serendipity that others may only dream of.

Throughout my life, and my life without a tie journey, I listened to people I met with intense curiosity. I paid close attention and became consciously aware of the emotional dynamics on a subtle level, so I could connect with them in a way that felt significant. Over time, this cultivated more depth and richness in our relationship because I was attuned to them on a feeling level. I sometimes call this vibrational communication. If you understand beyond mere words what others are trying to communicate and provide your undivided attention to truly see, hear, and feel the other person, your relationships with others can last a lifetime. You may find your collaborations with them produce remarkable outcomes, as well as a sense of well-being. Be curious. Take an interest in their life. Find out about their vision for life and what's important to them and support them to achieve that. When it feels right to do so, openly and consciously create a shared vision for your relationship. It will carry you both a long way. It's a two-way thing. Trust comes from honesty, openness, and transparency and when you bring these qualities to your relationships, you set yourself up for a life full of potential.

What relationships do you have that truly empower and sustain you? What relationships might have served you once but are now holding you back? How open, transparent, and willing to be vulnerable are you in your communication with others? How often do you let people know what your dreams are and ask about theirs? How much radical support and challenge do you offer others around you?

5. *Pay Attention to Your Health (Spiritual, Physical, Mental, and Emotional)*

In my work with the Asian Leadership Institute, I often invite clients to become still for a minute and quietly examine their inner state, which I sometimes refer to as their internal weather report. I ask them to feel it and pay attention to whether they have an overall sense of expansion or contraction. See if you can do it now. If you feel contracted, you may sense frustration, a loss of energy, a lack of inspiration and motivation, feeling blocked from your creativity, unable to access your imagination, and a feeling of hopelessness or pointlessness. You may even find yourself judging others or comparing yourself with people who seem to have a better life than you.

If you feel expanded, you'll most likely act with equanimity and feel psychologically stable and undisturbed, despite experiencing highs and lows of emotions, pain, or other phenomena. You'll probably have a sense of resilience and avoid creating unnecessary frustrations that stem from the ebb and flow of life's emotional extremes. You'll see the potential and possibilities that are available—to have a bigger picture view—and use this energy source to shift you into action.

All of this is possible if you're looking after your health and well-being on every level. You can practice feeling expanded consciously. I've adopted habits such as behaving in a mindful way, regular meditation, and proactively connecting with feelings of gratefulness, love, joy, and appreciation at least once a day. I continue to work on my ability to connect with colleagues, clients, friends, and family members, especially in challenging situations when the temptation to be right, as opposed to be curious and open to learn, is strongest. I've also found that regular exercise, a healthy diet, good rest, being in nature, and minimising time spent online all support me to be at my best. Last but not least, learn how to let things go. There is little to be gained from holding on to ideas, beliefs, possessions, or relationships that no longer serve you. I've found that less is more and letting go generally leads to a profound sense of well-being.

What do you do daily and/or weekly to look after your body? How much attention do you pay to your emotions, and how do you resolve difficult issues in your relationships? What brings you mental relaxation and rejuvenation when your energy levels have dropped? How many times per day do you look at your smartphone or endlessly scroll online? How often do you create time and opportunities to do absolutely nothing? What activities nurture your soul?

6. *Empower and Support Others*

I've rediscovered the power of this many times. Examples include setting up my own leadership development business twenty-five years ago and launching my Calling All Angels Foundation in 2009. Today, I'm fortunate to work as a coach and mentor, as it means that I recycle virtually everything I've learned. Writing this book is a great example. I find supporting others to become the best version of themselves helps me to appreciate and integrate my own learning. I create value and meaning from our interactions, and I feel wiser and happier with every conversation I have with collaborators. You must find ways to take what you learn and empower others to do the same. As Gandhi said, "You must be the change you wish to see in the world."

Most people want to be inspired and are looking for others who lead their lives well, so they can model what they see, hear, and feel. If you build a solid foundation within yourself, fully own everything that happens, become your own observer, create powerful relationships, pay attention to your health, and have the courage that allows you to go beyond the edges of your comfort zone, you'll learn, and grow, and accomplish whatever you set out to do. When you need others to help you achieve your goals, they will willingly climb on board and take the journey with you. And you will know exactly how to lead them to reach their full potential.

The Great Awakening

In her book, *Your Money or Your Life: 9 Steps to Transforming Your*

LIFE WITHOUT A TIE

Relationship With Money and Achieving Financial Independence, Vicki Robin says,

> "The new road map says that there is something called 'enough' ... Your 'enough point' is having everything you want and need, to have a life you love and full self-expression, with nothing in excess. It's not minimalism. It's not less is more (because sometimes more is more), but it's that sweet spot or Goldilocks point... Once people start to pay attention to the flow of money and stuff in their lives in this way, their consumption drops by about twenty-five percent naturally because that's the amount of unconsciousness that you have in your spending. So, when you become conscious, that falls away and many people say they don't even know what they used to spend their money on."

I was in my mid-forties when I left England at the start my journey, and I know what she says to be true. I've returned to my former life and am in my early sixties, applying the knowledge and wisdom I've gained. As the world rapidly changes, it feels like the goalposts continually shift. Mastering the art of living consciously requires ongoing reflection and re-evaluation. In these times, when more and more of us are working from home or via technology, it's more important than ever that we cultivate our humanity and boldly bring that to all our relationships. Going forward, I'm optimistic that we're part of a great awakening, and I'm thrilled to be alive to witness history in the making.

My mission is to guide myself and others towards a life that is uniquely truthful, authentic, joyful, and meaningful. To be a trusted companion on the path for people who want to live their life true to themselves. My heart's desire is to show up with humble curiosity. My dream is to see miracles become a part of everyday life, for you and the rest of our society. But enough about me.

How about you? Where are you headed next? To help you reflect on that, I've pulled out the questions I invited you to reflect on in each chapter and listed them in the appendix, with a note in some cases to remind you of the context. You may find it revealing to set aside time and reflect on these questions and notice what occurs to you. Take your time and don't censor. In all likelihood, only you will see what you write down, which means you want to be as open and honest with yourself as possible. That's what our journey is all about.

Going Forward and Connecting With Me

If you've enjoyed reading this book and it resonates with you, I'm happy about that. Many of the questions I've included come up in coaching conversations frequently. Have you considered what differences you might want to make in your own life to help you grow and become the person you want to be? If you're interested in asking that question of yourself and you'd like some support, let me know. If you feel it would be beneficial for you to have a chat with me directly about your life journey, your leadership, career, or any aspect of your journey, please get in touch. I'd be delighted to connect with you and get to know you.

I'm happy to talk about my journey in public forums, in podcasts, at conferences, company gatherings, and in small family group settings. If you want to organise an event and would like to invite me to take part, please get in touch to let me know what you need.

> "I don't care if you live your 'best' life. I hope you live your freest life. Your most *unburdened* life. Your *lightest* life. I hope your life is a patchwork of lessons and trials and joys and mistakes and growth and evolution and expansion. I hope you understand that rejection, failure, disappointment means you care, you're trying, you're out there in life, alive to it. I hope your life feels beautiful to you more than it looks beautiful to everyone else. I hope you're free. And that you keep freeing yourself. From who you thought you should be. From who society told you to be. From heavy expectations and weighty ambition. I hope you know when you're in a moment you'll remember forever. I hope you know how good you have it when it's good. And I hope your life is an ongoing evolution, a constant becoming. I hope you shrug off old selves with ease. I hope you leave empty space in your life for the unknown, the magic, the surprises, the unexpected. I hope you don't just aim

LIFE WITHOUT A TIE

for 'best' and instead aim for full, whole, ever-evolving, unconfined, and unrestrained. Mostly, I hope you take the path that is *meant* for you, not the one *expected* of you."

Jamie Varon,
Capital T Truth: Little Hits from the Universe

Appendix
Questions For You to Consider

From **Introduction**, *The Journey Ahead*
What do you first need to master in yourself, in order to lead, guide, and support the development of others?

From **Chapter One**, *Making the Most of the Time You Have Left*
The average life expectancy in the UK is 79.9 years, or 29,200 days. It may be different if you were born elsewhere. Assuming that is true for you, how many active days do you believe you have left in this lifetime? What are the questions you feel you must answer before you go?

From **Chapter Two**, *Living life With Happiness and No Regrets*
The five big regrets of life. People wished they had:
1. Lived their life true to themselves
2. Not worked so hard
3. Stayed in touch with close friends (who drifted out of their lives)
4. Expressed their feelings more
5. Allowed themselves to be happier

Which of these are most important to you?

The four main ties which keep our lives held in place:
1. Partner or Spouse
2. Career
3. House/home
4. Community (family and friends)

How does each one influence or affect your life choices? Who do you see yourself as? Who is the character that you commonly refer to as "me?" What story have you been sold as the "ideal" life? What are the ties that bind you to your life and character? What are you putting off because it would not be consistent with the story you have written so far? Which of these could you let go of or change? Which of these could you not?

What beliefs did you hold as a child that you have long since forgotten? How did you imagine the life of an adult would feel way back when you were a child, long before it actually materialised?

We all have the tendency to acquire way more stuff than we need. Minimalist living, as a concept, is in perfect harmony with and an antidote to excessive consumption and global warming. Can you imagine who is likely to have to deal with the stuff that will be left by you when your time is up?

From **Chapter Three**, *Guiding Principles*
Presence
In your life, how often are you fully present in the moment you are in, without getting lost in thoughts about the past or the future?
Self-acceptance
Can you recall a time when you felt there was a gap between how you should be and how you actually were? Did you judge yourself as not good enough? How did it make you feel?
Non-attachment
Do you recognize the delusional cycle of craving, desire, pleasure, cessation, and more craving? How often do you fixate on something specific—an object, person, outcome, or role, rather than go with the flow and accept whatever comes?
Wisdom
Is there an area in your life right now where you could trust your own inner wisdom more than you do?
Lightness
Can you recall times in your life where you felt and/or chose to bring more lightness to your way of being? Can you think of an area right now where you could apply it?
Modesty/Frugality
Maybe you can review a couple of your expenses related to consumer spending and ask yourself what would happen if you were to reduce, or even eliminate them? What do you truly need to spend money on, and what is taking more of your resources than necessary?
Minimalism

LIFE WITHOUT A TIE

What are you addicted to when it comes to buying stuff? What items in your life would you consider truly essential?

Connection

Who are the important people in your life? How are you staying connected, or are you letting them drift away? How strong are your friendships? How could you deepen your connection with people you work with?

Contribution

What part does making a contribution play in your life? In what other ways would you like to contribute more? To your loved ones, friends, family, colleagues, community and society?

Health

What steps could you take right now to take better care of your own health?

Your guiding principles

If you had to write your own principles for life, what might they be?

From **Chapter Four**, *Living Mindfully*

What delusions do you currently have about your life and the world around you? In what way are you deceiving yourself in the way you choose to look at events and relate to others? What beliefs and attitudes are helping you and which ones are holding you back?

How many moments each day do you spend in total silence? Can you imagine being in a place where it's nothing but you and your thoughts? How would you feel about that? When was the last time you willingly went into something knowing it was going to be uncomfortable? Have you ever taken part in something where you felt the people around you were on the same path as you?

How often do you get to sit with a bunch of people in total silence while you eat? How often do you eat alone without any distractions, like watching TV, or looking at your smartphone? How often do you just enjoy the sensation of eating food and bringing your full attention to the texture, smell, and flavours in your mouth as you chew? How much do you appreciate all the people and effort that brought the food you're eating from the place it was grown, like the local farmer who grew your lettuce and tomatoes or the person who prepared the salad? Do you truly experience gratitude for it being there? And when was the last time you slowly enjoyed eating your food with no urge to finish quickly and move on to the next thing?

Appendix

Cultivating Inner Peace

My meditation practice has shown me the value of remaining calm and maintaining inner peace, no matter what the external circumstances around me are. The Buddhists call this state equanimity. Cultivating this ability has allowed me to:

1 Access my intuition and higher-level brain functions
2 Gain deeper insights
3 Use my imagination and creativity more
4 Improve my peripheral vision
5 Reveal hidden opportunities
6 Align with my purpose in life

Which of these six would you most like to develop right now?

From **Chapter Five**, *Creating Community*

How often in our tethered lives, in our comfortable and safe bubble of reality, do we fail to notice suffering going on? Not just on an epic scale but with our neighbours or members of our own family? Even if we become aware, how often do we look the other way, or take effective action to change it?

How often do you consciously find time to socialize with people in your community around your busy work schedule? How could doing more of that foster more joy and lightness in your daily life?

From **Chapter Six**, *The Universal Intelligence Behind All Things*

The Universe provided me with exactly what was needed, as I had intuitively known it would. How often does this happen in your life?

From **Chapter Seven**, *Being Selfish, Moving Beyond Fear, and Connecting with Nature*

Can you recall a time when you let go of your fear and leapt? Are there situations in your life where you would like to do that more often? In what ways do you currently sacrifice your own needs unnecessarily, for the sake of others?

How often do you get back to nature? How does it affect you? When and how often is solitude valuable to you?

LIFE WITHOUT A TIE

Some years ago, a friend shared some pertinent wisdom with me; he said people will come into your life for a *reason*, a *season,* or a *lifetime*. When you know which one it is, you'll know what to do for that person. Can you think of at least one significant person in each of these groups? What did you learn from them? Why did they show up?

If independent travel is something that calls you, what might keep you from doing it? And is there some way you could work around that?

From **Chapter Eight**, *Expectations, Habits, and Compassion*

Can you imagine how different your life would be if you suddenly decided to question even one or two of the routines and habitual commitments you've made? Is there something happening in your life that prevents you from being at peace in yourself? And how does that affect the way you relate to the people you care about?

Perhaps you can recall a time when you made plans or set some expectations, which didn't turn out quite how you envisaged, and used hindsight to see where you went wrong? What was the lesson you received from it?

It can be liberating to awaken your heart and learn how to be more compassionate towards people you meet, especially those you do not easily get along with or those who have judged you in a way that has hurt you. Can you think of people like that in your life at this moment?

How difficult do you find it to stay up to date with close friends? How often do you avoid awkward or challenging conversations with them? Do you leave your assumptions, judgments, fears and concerns unacknowledged, and unexamined? How might you feel if something terrible happened to you, like a freak, fatal accident, and you died knowing you'd been unable to clear the air with people you had unresolved issues with?

Perhaps you can recall a time when hearing someone else's story of overcoming a challenge empowered you in a similar way?

Trying things out is often one of the best ways of testing a desire or interest. Are there any opportunities like that in your life which you could investigate in a safe, bite-sized trial? Something you may be passionate about? What could unleash your energy or set your creativity free? What would you do if you gave yourself permission to have a go? Who might you be if you weren't trapped by your current identity?

Appendix

From **Chapter Nine**, *Letting Go and Trusting the Universe*
Have you experienced a time in your life when you felt that something you'd done for a long time was no longer working for you and called you to make a change? Was it difficult to do? Could you do it now?

Have you ever experienced a time in your life where the Universe helped guide your thinking and decisions? How long was it before you were able to join some of the dots you might have found? If you look back now, can you see how things were linked?

From **Chapter Ten**, *Renewal*
Can you think of a time or event in your life when you realised that a period of change had reached completion and you had shifted from an old you to a new you?

Being open to new experiences played a big part in my traveller's mindset, because it's a great way to immerse yourself in the culture. In the Himalayas, Yak meat was extremely popular, and I'd never had the opportunity to try it. Tired and hungry after a long day's climb, I went for it. When was the last time you tried something new from another culture?

Undefended Love was a gift from Annie and reading it had a profound effect on me and how I wanted to be in our relationship. Have you ever come across a book that affected you so deeply, it enabled you to look at yourself and life differently?

Being alone is different from feeling lonely. Maybe you can remember a time when you were on your own for a longer than normal period, without the accompanying loneliness or anxiety that you can sometimes feel?

From **Chapter Eleven**, *Setbacks and Finding Purpose*
Can you think of a time when you've taken on a commitment impulsively out of fear, and soon realised you may have been better to sit and wait a while? If it set you back, what did you learn from it? How did you move forward? If you're still stuck, how can you embrace the changes you need to make?

Can you recall a time when you've shared something that you're passionate about? How did it feel for you? Did it bring more people in? What happened as a result?

Have you ever found yourself in a situation where you're not living true to your authentic self when it comes to someone you care about? What did you do? If that's happening now, what do you need to do in order to live by your guiding principles and create a better space for yourself, and potentially, them?

From **Chapter Twelve**, *Trust in Yourself and in the Journey*

Someone once said to me, "No matter where you go, you always take yourself with you," (a quote from Neil Gaiman), and it's hard to fully enjoy life when you're suffering under the weight of knowing you have something fundamental to change about yourself. Maybe you can recall a time when you knew you needed to change something big, but weren't sure how to approach it?

Can you recall a time when you had the feeling that something was meant to be? What was the meaning of that event for you?

Have you ever had a powerful insight or made a vital discovery about yourself that you weren't aware of?

What was the catalyst that brought it to your awareness?

From **Chapter Thirteen**, *Defining Moments and Peak Moments*

Like my divorce at the beginning, the end of my relationship with Annie felt like a defining moment in my journey. It's sometimes easier to recognise our defining moments when we take the time to look back. Perhaps you can recall one of your own, that may have been pretty rough at the time, but felt like a gift later on? Can you create a list of your defining moments? How have they led you to where you are now?

My peak moments were usually accompanied by feelings of deep satisfaction, happiness, contentment, and peace. Can you recall a peak moment and how you felt? Or perhaps imagine an experience that you believe would result in it becoming a peak moment for you?

How often are you fully present in the moment you are in, without getting lost in thoughts about the past or the future?

If you are in transition, especially the neutral zone, do any of my ten suggestions resonate with you?

From **Chapter Fourteen**, *The Power of Setting Intentions*

Can you recall something that you've imagined doing and set an intention around, then perhaps seen it come to a full realisation later? Or is there something bubbling under the surface you might want to undertake at some point?

Manifestation often means examining why it's important to you and how it will look and feel when it happens. Has this happened in your own life, where you put an intention out to the Universe and eventually saw it come to fruition? Or do you have something you'd like to create? Can you hand it over to the Universe while taking appropriate action and know it will be delivered?

From **Chapter Sixteen**, *Letting Go of What Doesn't Serve You*
Can you think of a time when you've been able to let go of something that no longer served you? What were the outcomes that resulted from your decision?

Can you remember a time when you were in a scenario with complex emotional dynamics, and you knew you were not being true to the person you wanted to be? If that's happening now, what changes in your behaviour would enable you to be the person you want to be? How can you bring your own guiding principles into play?

From **Chapter Nineteen**, *Finding Your Tribe, Taking Ownership*
Can you recall events in your life when you found exactly the right people to be with for that moment in time? Or at the least, changed your trajectory to put you on the path to where you are now? Do you have a tribe now that supports and encourages you to be the person you want to be? What might you need to do in order to help the Universe bring more of those people into your life?

Can you recall an occasion where you've blamed someone or something for a crappy circumstance you've been in, simply because you haven't fully owned the choice you'd made?

Can you recall a situation where you hung on to someone or a situation, even though you knew you needed to let go, out of fear or worry about what the future would be like?

Fear of the unknown is still scary, even if you're familiar with it. Can you recall a time when you were frightened of something you'd already encountered before?

From **Chapter Twenty,** *Looking Forwards*
What's most important for you in the time you have remaining? What if you only had half as much time? Or half of that?

What does living life true to yourself mean in reality?

Calling All Angels

IN 2004, BEFORE MY LIFE WITHOUT A TIE JOURNEY BEGAN, I TOOK PART IN A major fundraising event called Enduro India. With the support of my community of friends, we raised a substantial sum of money, which was deeply satisfying. Afterwards, I realised I wanted to dedicate a part of my life to volunteering and fundraising wherever help was most needed. As a busy CEO, that remained a fantasy until I sold my company in 2008. Being free of it liberated me to honour the commitment.

During the early years of my journey, I came across several inspiring people and organisations who were doing great work to improve the lives of individuals, communities, animals, and the environment. I wondered how I could financially support what they were doing, and I talked to friends about them. Many said they'd be willing to donate money if I made sure that all of it ended up directly in these people's hands.

In July 2009, I officially launched my Calling All Angels Foundation. I ran my first marathon in New York and raised $15,275. Since then, I've ran four more, and over $50,000 has been donated from people all over the world. It has been used to support:

- The World Wildlife Fund
- The Rainbow Trust, UK
- The Namaste Children's Home in Pokhara, Nepal
- The Elephant Nature Park in Chiang Dao, Thailand
- The World Cancer Research Fund
- Schools of Hope, Nong Ook, Thailand/Myanmar border
- The Bring Will Welch Home Appeal

When I find people who are doing something extraordinary to improve the world around them, I love being able to help them financially. It fuels my desire to create new fundraising events and ask for support.

If you want further information about any aspect of my foundation, please contact me, and I will be very happy to talk to you. And if you feel inspired, please make a donation! It will help create badly needed resources for some less fortunate people around the world who will be truly grateful for your generosity.

You can donate here: https://www.thedailyexplorer.com/foundation/

References, Books, and Helpful Websites

Introduction
Wallman, J., (2013), *Stuffocation: Living More with Less*, Penguin Life, London

Chapter One
Brown, B., PhD, (2010) *The Gifts of Imperfection*, Hazelden Information & Educational Services, Minnesota
Kübler-Ross, E., M.D., (1969), *On Death & Dying: What the Dying Have to Teach Doctors, Nurses, Clergy & Their Own Families*, Macmillan Company, New York

Chapter Two
Altucher, J., (2013), *Choose Yourself!*, Lioncrest Publishing, USA

Chapter Three
Ware, B., (2012), *The Top Five Regrets of the Dying: A life Transformed by the Dearly Departing*, Hay House UK, London

Chapter Four
Carolyn Gregoire (2016), *Why Silence Is So Good For Your Brain*, *Huffington Post*, May 3, 2016 (http://www.huffingtonpost.com/entry/silence-brain-benefits_us_56d83967e4b0000de4037004)
Questionnaire adapted from the Freiberg Mindfulness Inventory & material from The Asian Leadership Institute
http://www.suanmokkh-idh.org

Chapter Seven
https://www.elvismuseum.co.nz/
https://edition.cnn.com/travel/article/worlds-15-best-bungee-jumping-sites/

References, Books, and Helpful Websites

Chapter Eight
https://www.astro.com/astro-databank/Welch, Walden

Chapter Nine
https://www.elephantnaturepark.org
https://lovesho.com/blog-1/tea-ceremony
https://www.aussietowns.com.au/town/coober-pedy-sa
http://earthchakras.org/Locations.php

Chapter Ten
https://www.ncf-nepal.org/program/namaste-childrens-house-lakeside/
https://en.wikipedia.org/wiki/Kodari
https://en.wikipedia.org/wiki/Lumbini
Psaris, J., PhD & Lyons, M.S., PhD, (2000), *Undefended Love: The Way That You Felt about Yourself When You Fell in Love is the Way You Can Feel All the Time*, New Harbinger, California

Chapter Eleven
http://www.undefendedlove.com/
https://thedailyexplorer.wordpress.com/calling-all-angels-the-2009-new-york-marathon-fundraising-campaign/
Scott, S., (2013), *Fierce Conversations: Achieving Success at Work and in Life, One Conversation at a Time*, Piatkus, London

Chapter Twelve
Opening tale: oral folklore, some say from China, others, from India
https://www.hoffmaninstitute.co.uk/

Chapter Thirteen
https://en.wikipedia.org/wiki/Machapuchare

Chapter Fifteen
https://faze.ca/taj-mahal-monumental-love-story/

Chapter Sixteen
https://thedailyexplorer.wordpress.com/previous-issues/
https://www.mindbodygreen.com/
https://main.citylifeadmin.com/citylife-articles/a-year-of-free-hugs/

LIFE WITHOUT A TIE

Adams, R., (2013), *The Suited Monk*, WOW! Books, London
Edwards, E., (2020), *Extraordinary: How to Lead a Bigger, Braver, More Meaningful Life*, Rethink Press, London

Chapter Seventeen
https://santiago-compostela.net/
https://harekrishnabooks.com/product/consciousness-the-missing-link-english/

Chapter Twenty
Robins, V., (2008), *Your Money or Your Life: 9 Steps to Transforming Your Relationship With Money and Achieving Financial Independence,* Penguin Books, USA
Smith, R.D., (2013), *20,000 Days and Counting: The Crash Course For Mastering Your Life Right Now*, Thomas Nelson Publishers, Scotland

Lightning Source UK Ltd.
Milton Keynes UK
UKHW010128161022
410526UK00002B/148